I Came This Day to the Spring

I Came This Day to the Spring

Va-avo ha-Yom el ha-'Ayin; a Treatise of Sabbatian Kabbalah, Attributed to Rabbi Jonathan Eibeschuetz

TRANSLATED AND ANNOTATED,
AND WITH AN INTRODUCTION BY

David J. Halperin

CASCADE Books • Eugene, Oregon

I CAME THIS DAY TO THE SPRING
Va-avo ha-Yom el ha-'Ayin; a Treatise of Sabbatian Kabbalah,
Attributed to Rabbi Jonathan Eibeschuetz

Copyright © 2025 David J. Halperin. All rights reserved. Except for brief quotations in critical publications or reviews, no part of this book may be reproduced in any manner without prior written permission from the publisher. Write: Permissions, Wipf and Stock Publishers, 199 W. 8th Ave., Suite 3, Eugene, OR 97401.

Cascade Books
An Imprint of Wipf and Stock Publishers
199 W. 8th Ave., Suite 3
Eugene, OR 97401

www.wipfandstock.com

PAPERBACK ISBN: 978-1-5326-1343-2
HARDCOVER ISBN: 978-1-5326-1345-6
EBOOK ISBN: 978-1-5326-1344-9

Cataloguing-in-Publication data:

Names: Halperin, David J., translator and annotator.

Title: I came this day to the spring : *va-avo ha-yom el ha-'ayin*; a treatise of Sabbatian Kabbalah, attributed to rabbi Jonathan Eibeschuetz / Translated and annotated by David J. Halperin.

Description: Eugene, OR: Cascade Books, 2025. | Includes bibliographical references.

Identifiers: ISBN 978-1-5326-1343-2 (paperback). | ISBN 978-1-5326-1345-6 (hardcover). | ISBN 978-1-5326-1344-9 (ebook).

Subjects: LCSH: Sabathaians—Controversial literature. | Eybeschuetz, Jonathan, –1764. | Mysticism—Judaism. | Judaism—Mysticism. | Cabala—History.

Classification: BM755 H355 2025 (print). | BM755 (ebook).

VERSION NUMBER 11/04/25

Nearly all Scripture translations are my own. Those marked RSV are from the Revised Standard Version of the Bible, copyright © 1946, 1952, the Division of Christian Education of the National Council of the Churches of Christ in the United States of America. Used by permission. All rights reserved: *Oxford Annotated Bible: The Holy Bible, Revised Standard Version Containing the Old and New Testaments*, New York: Oxford University Press, 1962.

Translations from the Zohar and from the Talmud and other rabbinic works are mine unless otherwise noted.

For Rose

*My companion on this
and every journey*

Contents

Introduction | 1
Prologue | 18

1 The Creation of God | 19
2 The Anatomy of God | 41
3 The Gestation of God | 59
4 The Shattering of God | 96
5 The Restoration of God | 132
6 The Symbolisms of God | 180
7 The Geography of God | 216
8 The Virgin of God | 224
9 The Salvation of God | 292

Appendix: Zoharic Passages Quoted and Interpreted in *Va-avo ha-Yom* | 311
Bibliography | 313

Introduction

> By this time it is quite obvious that Shloimele was a secret disciple of Sabbatai Zevi. For even though the False Messiah was long dead, secret cults of his followers remained in many lands...
>
> —Isaac Bashevis Singer, "The Destruction of Kreshev"[1]

Of course the master fantasist of modern Yiddish literature exaggerated when he depicted eighteenth-century Judaism as riddled with depraved cults, each bent on corrupting the faith's sacred mysteries in "homage to the forces of evil." Of course he overdramatized. His "Destruction of Kreshev" was fiction, a tale of sex and piety gone horribly wrong, and not a historical essay. Yet in Isaac Bashevis Singer's gripping portrait of a religious civilization haunted by its own repressed shadow, there was much historical truth.

True—that in 1665 and 1666 a Jew from Izmir named Sabbatai Zevi had set the Jewish world agog with his claim to be the long-awaited Messiah, his promise of imminent Redemption. Before the year 1666 was out, he shattered his believers' dreams by committing the ultimate transgression, a disgrace for any Jew and for a Messiah unimaginable. He abandoned Judaism for an alien faith, taking on the Muslim turban and a Muslim identity in the presence of the Turkish sultan, who otherwise would have had him executed. True also—that a stubborn minority among his followers kept on believing in him even after his apostasy, even after his death in 1676. As the seventeenth century passed into the eighteenth they learned to keep their faith a secret in the face of the

---

1. Singer, *Spinoza of Market Street*, 188.

harassment, bordering on persecution, of Jewish religious authorities who wanted only to put the messianic madness behind them.

These sectarians paid no "homage to the forces of evil"; on that point, Singer was echoing their enemies' caricature. Yet, with their apostate Messiah, they could never again believe in Judaism as they once had known it, as most Jews still did. Out of the riches of their heritage—the sacred Scriptures, the rabbinic Talmud and midrash, the arcane medieval theosophy of the Kabbalah—they created their own unheard-of visions of the true, the good, the holy. These visions might be pathetic or grotesque. They could also be brilliant, inspiring, even prophetic.

The text that lies before us falls into this second category. It surely ranks among the most extraordinary creations of early modern Judaism. Among the most abstruse and difficult to grasp, as well; and in the pages that follow I will set out for the reader my understanding of what this supremely strange book is, and what message it was intended to convey.

2.

It first came to light in the spring of 1725. The Jewish authorities in Frankfurt had detained a Jewish traveler from Prague and points east, on suspicion of being a Sabbatian emissary. They ordered his luggage searched. There they discovered a number of Hebrew manuscripts, including one that bore the title *Va-avo ha-Yom el ha-'Ayin*, "I Came This Day to the Spring," the words taken from Gen 24:42. There was no indication of who had written it. Contemporary testimonies, however, identified the author as Rabbi Jonathan Eibeschuetz, then a young man of about thirty, the rising star of the Prague yeshiva. Eibeschuetz never acknowledged authorship, and the following September he would implicitly deny it by signing his name to a rabbinical ban denouncing and excommunicating the Sabbatians, which if he had written *Va-avo ha-Yom* would have to include himself. The consensus of modern scholarship is that the denial was insincere, or at least misleading, and that this text was indeed Eibeschuetz's work.[2]

---

2. The case for Eibeschuetz's authorship was set forth in 1947 by Moshe Arie Perlmuter, *Rabbi Jonathan Eibeschuetz*, and has been accepted by nearly all scholars. I will presuppose it in this introduction, while in my notes to the translation I will take a more neutral stance, and speak only of "the author" or "our author." On the circumstances of the text's discovery and the controversy it stirred up, see Carlebach, *Pursuit of Heresy*, 177–94; Maciejko, *R. Jonathan Eibeschütz*, i–xx.

INTRODUCTION

Soon enough, the learned folk had their chance to examine *Va-avo ha-Yom*, which no one had ever seen or heard of before. They came away horrified. "After reading two or three paragraphs the hair of my head stood up," one rabbi testified, "for it contained many curses and blasphemies against the word of the Living God and it turned Kabbalistic mysteries upside down. Nothing like this was ever seen or known from any heretic or disbeliever of this world . . . and it certainly deserves to be burned."[3]

Horrified—and baffled. No one knew quite what to make of a book like this. It was obviously Sabbatian. Yet it was no run-of-the-mill work of Sabbatian propaganda, finding prophecies of Sabbatai Zevi in Bible or midrash or Zohar, piling honorifics upon him, rationalizing his apostasy. The false Messiah was represented in it only by a few cryptic allusions, never by name. It seemed, some thought, more like a throwback to ancient paganism, and indeed the divine manifestations described in the book disport themselves like the gods and goddesses of some pagan mythology. Its sexual passages were raw enough to make anyone's hair stand on end, one of them so obscenely blasphemous that sometime during the years that followed an outraged reader hacked it out of its manuscript with a knife. (The book circulated only in manuscript, and would not be printed for another three hundred years.) Its more careful readers may have noticed that it was deeply engaged with Christianity, represented as in some respects superior to Judaism.

But *Va-avo ha-Yom* was more radical than any of its early readers guessed. As I read it, it was intended as *a charter for the world religion of the future*, rooted in Kabbalistic Judaism but unlike any religion ever known. The tenets of this religion included *universal brotherhood*, without distinction between Jew and Gentile; *gender equality*, the woman treated as man's equal and with equal right to erotic gratification; and what we would today call *marriage equality*, homosexual and heterosexual eros recognized as having equal value, meriting equal respect.

That such notions should be propounded in the early and mid-eighteenth century is, perhaps, not by itself extraordinary. It was an age of spiritual ferment, of an international, interconfessional "sexual-spiritual underworld" (as Marsha Keith Schuchard has called it), which produced, amid much else, a poet and artist of the fantastic named William Blake.[4]

---

3. Maciejko, *R. Jonathan Eibeschütz*, ix, quoting Rabbi Jacob Emden.
4. Schuchard, *William Blake*.

But that they should be set forth in the traditional language of rabbinic and Kabbalistic discourse, buttressed by repeated invocations of Jewish Scripture and the ancient Jewish sages of blessed memory—by Jonathan Eibeschuetz, the man who would become the foremost rabbinic scholar and preacher of Central and Eastern Europe?[5] This is something wild and amazing, bound to intrigue and perplex all who wander amid the tangled thickets of *Va-avo ha-Yom*'s argument.

3.

How shall we begin our wanderings? Perhaps by posing the question: Can a book like this, with its plurality of divine beings, possibly have been written by a believing monotheist?

The answer is yes, but not in the familiar Biblical sense of exclusive monotheism, which affirms the One by denying or demonizing the Many. Rather, in something more akin to the inclusive monotheism of the ancient Greek thinkers, which affirms the Many as multiple aspects of the One. To call the entities that teem throughout *Va-avo ha-Yom* "divine potentialities" pays homage to the author's essential monotheism. To call them "deities" recognizes the mythological garb—indeed pagan-sounding; the book's early critics were right about that—in which this monotheism is expressed.

The story begins, as must any Kabbalistic theogony or cosmogony—the two words amount in Kabbalah to much the same thing—with Ein Sof, "Endlessness," the infinite and eternal substrate of all being. Coeternal with Ein Sof was a consciousness, a Will to create worlds at some point in the future. (Why at that point? Why not earlier? We do not and cannot know.)[6] There was thus a duality within Ein Sof,

---

5. And who, twenty-six years later, would come to grief over his hidden or perhaps only half hidden Sabbatianism, when Jacob Emden—the same rabbi whose hair stood on end at the reading of *Va-avo ha-Yom*—would denounce amulets written by Eibeschuetz as containing allusions to Sabbatai Zevi. This ferocious "amulet controversy," unleashed by Emden in 1751, would drag on even past Eibeschuetz's death in 1764, darkening the great rabbi's final years. Before it was finished, Jewish communities all over Europe and even some of the Gentile authorities would be drawn into it, taking sides for or against Eibeschuetz, for or against his accuser. The definitive history of the controversy has not been written; in the meantime, see, e.g., Maciejko, "Jews' Entry"; Leiman, "When a Rabbi Is Accused."

6. *Va-avo ha-Yom*, chapter 1, section 2. As noted below, the chapter and section divisions are my own; the text itself is one unbroken stream of discourse.

between its Will and its dark and silent substrate, which comes to be female to the Will's maleness. For gender distinctions are primordial, go back to the timeless beginning of all differentiation.

When we speak of creating "worlds," we do not refer to anything like this terrestrial globe. The creation of physical reality is a hardly significant hiccup at the end of the creation process, so minor that *Va-avo ha-Yom* never even gets around to talking about it. Rather, we speak of the divine worlds of Kabbalah, particularly the loftiest of them, the World of Emanation, of the divine entities that are not precisely "created" but emitted from their source in Endlessless, like sunbeams from the sun—a process called Emanation, which like much of its technical language *Va-avo ha-Yom* shares with the earlier Kabbalah. And as this happens, the Will undergoes a shift, not of its essence but of the perspective from which it is viewed. What from above, from the vantage point of Ein Sof, was the Will, now is perceived from below—we cannot escape these spatial terms, misleading and distorting though they are—as the Root.[7] Of all that is about to emerge.

It is at this point that *Va-avo ha-Yom* becomes more complex and confusing, and at the same time more accessible, for we are no longer dealing with abstract processes but with beings possessing personality and quasi-physical shape, which must not be taken literally but have a real truth, which we can use as handles for our imagination to grasp them. We can extrapolate from our bodies to learn of these beings; "from my flesh I can visualize God" (Job 19:26),[8] for was it not in God's image that we were created? And Scripture, which now begins to be invoked more profusely in *Va-avo ha-Yom*, provides a multitude of characters that serve as symbolic representations for the divinities that are Scripture's true subject.

Of the shoots that branch forth from the Root, the central one is he whom *Va-avo ha-Yom* calls "the God of Israel." This is the male God of the Hebrew Bible, he whom the ancient rabbis of the Talmud call the "Blessed Holy One," by whom the physical universe was created and who continues to guide and sustain it with his balanced attributes of Mercy and Justice. He has, as in the older Kabbalah, a female counterpart—a goddess-consort, if you will—the Shechinah. (*Va-avo ha-Yom*

---

7. Chapter 2, section 2.

8. First invoked near the end of chapter 1, section 1, and several more times throughout the treatise.

complicates matters by introducing three Shechinahs, one Higher and two Lower; but this need not concern us yet.)

The symbolic representations of the God of Israel are multiplex, confusing, and often contradictory, and give this deity a human appeal beyond anything the Bible, read literally, can provide. He is Adam, disobedient but also repentant;[9] he is the suffering Job.[10] In a fantastic inversion of Biblical values, he is the cruel Pharaoh who decrees the death of the infant Moses.[11] But he is also Moses, rescued from the roiling waters by the Higher Shechinah, who is Pharaoh's daughter and therefore the God of Israel's daughter as well as his sister and his lover—throughout the Song of Songs he calls her "my sister, my bride." "I am the singing rose," she says in Song 2:1, meaning that whenever she wants sex she must serenade the God of Israel. This, like so much else in their relationship, is to be reversed in the ideal messianic future, when he will do the serenading, as hinted in Exod 15:1, "Moses shall sing."[12]

The God of Israel, as indicated, balances justice with mercy in his dealing with his creatures. But there is another divine being, loftier and more mysterious than he, who knows no such balance, but is pure Mercy and Grace. This is *'Attiqa Qaddisha*, as the traditional Kabbalists called him, a designation that properly means "Holy Ancient One" but which Jonathan Eibeschuetz—at least the youthful Jonathan Eibeschuetz, author of *Va-avo ha-Yom*—understood as meaning "the Distant One."[13] This Distant One "consists of pure Mercy, without any bit of Judgment even for those who violate the Torah"—for the Torah and commandments, the shalts and shalt-nots of the Jewish religion, imposed on the God of Israel by the Root and imposed by him on those covenanted to him, are of no relevance to the Distant One.[14] He therefore " 'loves the peoples' [Deut 33:3], even the Gentiles, inasmuch as he is without any Judgment." On the Purim festival, when the Distant One holds sway, one is bidden to drink until all moral distinctions, even that between the noble Jew Mordecai and the ferocious anti-Semite Haman, have disappeared, bathed in the indiscriminate sunlight of the Distant One's smiling Grace.[15]

9. Chapter 6, sections 6-7.
10. Chapter 6, section 8.
11. Chapter 6, section 3.
12. Chapter 9, section 6.
13. Chapter 2, section 1.
14. Chapter 5, section 2.
15. Chapter 9, section 5.

INTRODUCTION

This last sentence hints at a downside. In Kabbalistic theory, the universe of divinity is sustained by what is called "effluence" (Hebrew *shefa'*), a sort of liquid light that flows from the higher beings to the lower. Like so much in Kabbalah, this is envisioned in sexual terms: a spermatic emission from male into female. ("From my flesh I can visualize God," and seldom is human flesh closer to divine transcendence than in the arousals and transports of sex.) This will work well for the God of Israel, who has a Shechinah-female to receive and contain his ejaculate, filtering it so it will be suitable for the lower entities. The Distant One, however, has no female. As we have seen, he is "without any bit of Judgment" that might dam up and hold back the free generosity of his Grace. And, like any liquid, the "effluence" of Grace can be deadly when it comes in excess.

> When [the effluence] takes the form of uncontained ejaculate, then it is that *flooding of mighty waters* [Ps 32:6] . . . All this is the evident lesson of the Shattering of the Vessels: they received their effluence in the form of uncontained ejaculate, and therefore were shattered . . . we [therefore] must not pray to the Distant One or even to the God of Israel when he is not coupling with the Shechinah. For the consequence will be uncontained ejaculate, laying waste to the worlds.[16]

In the Kabbalistic myth that Eibeschuetz inherited, the "Shattering of the Vessels" was a primordial catastrophe long antedating the physical universe (although the Bible alludes to it in symbolic terms in the story of Noah's Flood). The "vessels," divine entities generated to contain and define the flow of light poured into them from above, proved too weak for the purpose. Under the unbearable pressure of that "effluence" they shattered, exploded; their fragments tumbled down into the darkness of the abyss, bits of light clinging to them.[17] Eibeschuetz takes this myth and gives it a central place in *Va-avo ha-Yom* (chapter 4). It was after this event, we are told, that the God of Israel took charge, rebuilding the divine "worlds" with the aid of his Shechinah, installing safeguards to ensure the disaster would not be repeated (chapter 5).

These measures had the effect of making the God of Israel the only real, functioning deity. The Distant One was confined to exalted irrelevance, the "worlds" sheltered from the deadliness of his Grace. And so

---

16. Chapter 9, section 4.
17. Scholem, *Major Trends*, 265–68.

he will remain—until somehow he can be provided with a Shechinah equivalent, a female or quasi-female to receive and contain his spermatic emissions. And this is where the Messiah will come in.

4.

> You must not loathe an Edomite, for he is your brother.
>
> —Deut 23:8

By now, the reader may have begun to suspect: the God of Israel and the Distant One are the Gods of Judaism and Christianity respectively. The suspicion is correct.[18] The dualism of a divinity acting in accordance with justice and mercy, and a higher divinity of mercy alone, is found in the traditional Kabbalah; the *Idra Rabbah*, a self-contained section of the thirteenth-century Kabbalistic classic called the Zohar, is mostly devoted to it.[19] But Jonathan Eibeschuetz takes a further step no earlier Kabbalist would have dared. He explicitly identifies the Distant One with "Edom"[20]—which, as any educated Jewish reader of the eighteenth century would have known, means Christianity.

The name "Edom" has a long history in Hebrew literature. Originally it was a small kingdom bordering Biblical Israel, to which it was normally hostile, in what is now southwestern Jordan. The Israelites, who reciprocated the enmity—Deuteronomy's command not to "loathe an Edomite" was seldom followed—regarded the Edomites as the descendants of Jacob's evil twin Esau.[21] Later the name became code for the Jewish people's great enemy, Rome and the Roman Empire, the oppressive regime that had destroyed their Temple and crushed their hopes for independence. The Christian church, inheritor of the Empire, inherited also (in Jewish eyes) the name "Edom" and the resentment attached to it. Seldom if ever was it used with affection or respect.[22]

---

18. Similarly Maciejko, *R. Jonathan Eibeschütz*, xxxvi–xli; Maciejko, "Rabbi and the Jesuit," 176–79.

19. Hellner-Eshed, *Seekers of the Face*.

20. Chapter 2, section 5; chapter 3, section 9.

21. Modern readers of the book of Genesis are apt to find Esau a fairly sympathetic figure. Not so the traditional Jewish expositors, who could see in his character only a snarl of brutality and malice, with a dash of hypocrisy (as in his pretended reconciliation with Jacob, Gen 33:1–16) mixed in.

22. Hacohen, *Jacob & Esau*.

INTRODUCTION

The Kabbalah knows a supernatural "Edom," a pocket of divinity given over to severe, unmixed Judgment. Its defining color is blood-red—the Bible had already etymologized "Edom" as derived from *adom*, "red" (Gen 25:25, 30)—its hunger for retribution so intense and concentrated as to be literally demonic.[23] In *Va-avo ha-Yom*, Eibeschuetz reverses all this. For him, Edom takes its name not from "red" but from the root meaning "to be silent," since this is so lofty and august a realm that it is hardly permitted to be spoken of.[24] Far from being unmitigated Judgment, it is the opposite, undiluted Grace.

All his life, Eibeschuetz was on terms of respect and affection with Christian scholars.[25] His contacts with Christianity may go back to his teen years. In places like Ivančice in Moravia (where his father died in 1707 when Eibeschuetz was about twelve, and from whose German name Eibenschütz he took his own) or Mladá Boleslav in Bohemia (where at age fifteen he was head of the yeshiva),[26] he could have encountered not only Catholics but also cells of the crypto-Protestants from whose long-banned faith the Moravian church was soon to blossom.[27] He would have learned that Christianity was not a monolithic oppressor but had its own repressed and persecuted, with whom a sensitive Jewish adolescent—perhaps already attracted to the Sabbatians, that despised minority within a minority—could empathize. On this basis we can understand how it is that *Va-avo ha-Yom* shows the influence of Moravian Christianity's distinctive features, notably the lurid yet compelling adoration of the sacred wounds of a divine being (Jesus on the cross).[28] And how it was that the author might appreciate Christianity to the extent of elevating it above Judaism, as the Distant One is elevated above the God of Israel.

Yet we have seen the cruel paradox: the very abundance of the Distant One's Grace turns that Grace deadly, so ill-suited to the needs

23. Tishby, *Wisdom*, 1:332–33 (Zohar, III, 135a–b, *Idra Rabbah*).
24. Chapter 3, section 9.
25. Maciejko, "Controverse"; "Rabbi and the Jesuit."
26. Zinz, *Gedullat Yehonatan*, 4–8.
27. Ever since the Catholic victory at the White Mountain in 1620, dissident forms of Christianity had been harshly repressed in the Hapsburg lands: Louthan, *Converting Bohemia*. Ivančice and Mladá Boleslav had previously been important centers of Czech Protestantism (Evans, *Making*, 12; Atwood, *Theology*, 172, 317). It is hardly farfetched to suppose that remnants of the old faith hung on there in secret, taking new forms, ready for discovery by a curious and sympathetic Jewish boy.
28. See the introduction to chapter 6, section 8, below; and cf. chapter 8, notes 195, 237.

of those it is supposed to nourish that it can only destroy them. In theory, Christianity is the embodiment of love and kindness. In practice, it spawns malignant phenomena like the religious wars that devastated Europe in the sixteenth and seventeenth centuries—the last and most vicious of which, the Thirty Years' War (1618–1648) had its beginnings in Eibeschuetz's city of Prague and left its lasting mark on Jewish society's group consciousness.[29] And the centuries of anti-Jewish persecution . . . Commenting on Deut 23:8, *Va-avo ha-Yom* remarks that it is only the archetypal Edom, the Edom-root within divinity, that can be called "your brother."[30] In these lower realms, Jews and Christians have hardly been "brotherly" at all.

The paradox has a solution. Christianity, the faith of the Redeemer, itself requires a Redeemer—and he is not Jesus of Nazareth. Eibeschuetz hints at his identity when he observes that the name Esau has the same numerical value in Hebrew as *nahash hai*, "the Serpent lives."[31] What can this possibly mean?

The initiate will understand. The Serpent is Sabbatai Zevi, who was known even in his lifetime as the "Holy Serpent," for (as Eibeschuetz notes in another place) "serpent" has the same numerical value as "Messiah."[32] *The Messiah Sabbatai Zevi has his enduring life within the domain of Christianity*. At first sight, this seems strange. Does Eibeschuetz not know that it was to Islam, not Christianity, that Sabbatai Zevi converted? Surely he does. But for him this is an antiquarian detail, of no essential significance. The essential reality is that in an act of messianic self-sacrifice *Sabbatai passed into the domain of the Other*, thereby erasing the boundaries not only between Self and Other and between Jew and Gentile, but between what the Christian God historically has been and what he is capable of becoming.

In the brilliance of that messianic act—so blinding, that hardly anyone but the author of *Va-avo ha-Yom* has been able to see it for what

---

29. Greenblatt, *To Tell Their Children*, 117–59.

30. Chapter 2, section 5.

31. Chapter 3, section 9. Each letter of the Hebrew alphabet can serve as a number—*aleph* as 1, *bet* as 2, and so forth—and so every Hebrew word or phrase has a numerical value that is the sum of the value of its letters. The name "Esau," spelled *'ayin, shin, vav*, thus has the numerical value 376 (*'ayin* = 70, *shin* = 300, *vav* = 6), which happens to be the same value as *nahash hai*. The Kabbalists, for whom the Hebrew language was in its very structure the repository of divine mysteries, found that equivalences of this sort were not fortuitous but profoundly meaningful.

32. Chapter 6, section 6.

it was—differentiations within the "Other" vanish, lose all importance. Silently, *Va-avo ha-Yom* expands the scope of Deuteronomy's injunction, universalizes "the Edomite": *You must not loathe any Gentile. For they are your brothers and sisters.*[33]

5.

Sabbatai Zevi's transition from Self to Other, which for Eibeschuetz was a turning point not only of human but of cosmic history, is described twice in *Va-avo ha-Yom*—first in purely mythic terms, the second time as a historical event, albeit so heavily disguised that only the initiated could have obeyed his summons to "understand."

> Know this: the true Messiah copulates with the Distant One in the Shechinah's role, such that with him as well [as with the Shechinah] the ejaculate is not uncontained; and he prays in [the Distant One's] presence. This is the *prayer of Poor-Man ... when he enwraps himself* [Ps 102:1], which is to say, he enwraps himself in prayers unto the very highest heights ... he being in the role of the Shechinah. Thereupon does he *pour out his speech before YHVH*, praying to the Distant One who is called *before-YHVH*.[34]

That from a page or so before the end of the book. And at the very end, tacked on as though an afterthought:

> This is why David, when *he came to the Head* which is the Distant One, *where he was to prostrate himself for God* [2 Sam 15:32]—the language of copulation—*David sought to engage in alien worship* [Talmud, b. Sanh. 107a], in accord with, *Af* [=the Distant One] *loves the peoples* [Deut 33:3]. Understand.[35]

"David" in this passage is code for King David's most illustrious descendant, Sabbatai Zevi. "David's" intent to engage in "alien worship" alludes to Sabbatai's apostasy. The Bible had spoken of how David, in flight from his rebellious son Absalom, had "come to the head," which

---

33. Eibeschuetz's student Carl Anton, who became a convert to Christianity, would later testify that "Rabbi Jonathan did not agree with those who claimed that the doctrine of love of one's neighbor should be restricted only to the Jews, who should care only about other Jews, but claimed that this love is universal in character and that it is as great a sin to cause detriment to people of another religion as to harm members of one's own family" (Maciejko, "Rabbi and the Jesuit," 179).

34. Chapter 9, section 5.

35. Chapter 9, section 7.

in the Biblical context means, the summit of the Mount of Olives. The Talmud, ignoring this context, understood "the head" as equivalent to the head of the Babylonian image in Dan 2:32. David would worship idols, so as to keep people from speaking ill of God's justice: he must commit a crime so monstrous as to deserve the punishment that his son is trying to kill him.

Eibeschuetz takes this a giant step farther. In the Talmud, David was dissuaded from his "alien worship." As Sabbatai Zevi, "David" carries it out—*and precisely through that monstrous crime, that supreme betrayal of his Judaism*, he ascends "unto the very highest heights," the realm of the Distant One (who throughout *Va-avo ha-Yom* has been known by the code term "Head"). There he "prostrates himself for God," offering his buttocks for the divinity's anal penetration.

It is impossible to avoid comparison with the Crucifixion. Like the Crucifixion, the Apostasy is an event both historical and mythic. Thousands were crucified in the Roman Empire; thousands abandoned their Judaism for Christianity or Islam in the centuries that followed. Only one Crucifixion is a salvific act; just so, only one Apostasy. Both provide mending for a primordial rupture: the disobedience in Eden in the one case, the catastrophe of the "Shattering of the Vessels" in the other. By the one, God and sinners are reconciled. By the other, with a feminized Sabbatai Zevi to serve as his Shechinah substitute, the Distant One can intervene in the life of these lower worlds without destroying them. For the first time since the Shattering, the fullness of this higher God's love and grace is made accessible, with all the world's "peoples" sharers in it.

6.

The sacred history of the cosmos, then, divides into four stages:

1. Christianity was tried and found wanting.
2. Judaism stepped in, successfully, to remedy Christianity's deficiency.
3. Sabbatai Zevi, through his redemptive apostasy, makes Christianity once more viable, and indeed preferable.
4. But Christianity, as enabled by Sabbatai Zevi as Messiah, *is no longer Christianity but a new religion, unlike anything ever seen on this earth.*

7.

Divine sexuality, as we have begun to see, is at least in some measure transformed in this new dispensation. Can human sexuality stay unchanged?

Va-avo ha-Yom's attitude toward sex is confusing and ambivalent. At first reading, at least, it seems to share in the puritanism of traditional Judaism. Nor does it lack the overtones of divinity and demonism which the Kabbalah attached to this puritanism, intensifying it into a near-pathological dread of sexuality and its power. "One must take care," says Eibeschuetz, "not to touch even a woman's little finger, for at the higher level . . . that is a complete sex act."[36] The devastating power he attributes to "uncontained ejaculate" echoes the rabbinic and Kabbalistic horror of masturbation and its deadly dangers.

Even lawful marital sex is too potent to be allowed in its full intensity. Eibeschuetz quotes, as though it were a Talmudic enactment, the requirement that "one makes a hole in the sheet and through it he copulates."[37] This is the infamous "hole in the sheet" of the ultra-Orthodox Jews, customarily dismissed as an urban legend;[38] in the eighteenth century, at least, it was plainly something real. The Lower Shechinah, patrolling nightly with her purifying fire amid the chaos-waters that surround and menace the divine structures, must remain ever virgin lest those waters find a point of entry into her.[39] (Her virginity seems only technical, though. She manages to enjoy a fairly active sex life in spite of it.[40])

But there is another side. The numinous power of sex, so central to the Kabbalistic understanding of divinity, can work for good as well as for ill. Eibeschuetz allows his divine entities a range of erotic activities, homosexual as well as heterosexual, that goes far beyond the traditional repertoire. He describes them with an explicitness that gives some color to Yehuda Liebes's judgment that "the Sabbatian Kabbalah has the quality of pornography," and Paweł Maciejko's that *Va-avo ha-Yom* is "possibly the only truly pornographic text ever written in the rabbinic idiom."[41] The God of Israel, he tells us, will at times attend to the "virgin"

---

36. Chapter 2, section 2, following the Talmud, b. Shabb. 13b, 64b, Ber. 24a.
37. Chapter 6, section 8.
38. E.g., Mikkelson, "Orthodox Jews."
39. Chapter 4, section 3; chapter 8, section 1.
40. Chapter 8, section 16.
41. Liebes, "Ketavim Hadashim," 196; Maciejko, *R. Jonathan Eibeschütz*, xix.

Shechinah by masturbating her with his finger.[42] At other times this God is "the recipient of anal sex, as implied in the words, *I made love to Israel boy-fashion*." (Hos 11:1, more normally understood as "when Israel was a child, I loved him." If there had been nothing else objectionable in *Va-avo ha-Yom*, this by itself would have been enough to get it banned.) The active partner in these encounters, the superior entity called the Root, periodically subjects the God of Israel to sadomasochistic rapes, leaving him wounded and presumably bleeding.[43]

On earth as it is in heaven? If not today, the author says, someday it will be. In the messianic future, once the chaos-waters have disappeared, "the Shechinah will engage in anal sex in the lower realms." To inaugurate this new dispensation, it would seem, someone—Sabbatai Zevi, apparently—is represented as having "carried the Torah scroll into the latrine" as an act of theurgy, a Kabbalistic "mending" designed to set this lower world aright.[44] The sexual symbolism is too blatant to be mistaken. This thought, of bringing Judaism's most venerated religious object[45] as a penis representation into a place of excrement, was so outrageous to the copyists' sensibilities that some altered "the latrine" to the meaningless "the synagogue." One reader, as noted earlier, simply hacked out the offending passage. In this context, Sabbatai's offering his buttocks to the Distant One seems something akin to a normal courtesy, from one divine or quasi-divine being to another.

The traditions of one eighteenth-century Sabbatian community preserved a story of an oracular ritual allegedly performed under Sabbatai Zevi's direction. In the course of the ritual, the Bible's sexual prohibitions were revealed anew—transformed, however, from "thou shalt nots" into "thou shalts."[46] It is doubtful whether Eibeschuetz, whose personal conduct throughout his life was blameless as far as we can tell from the viewpoint of conventional Jewish morality, would have

---

42. Chapter 8, section 16.

43. Chapter 6, section 8. On the connection with Moravian wounds theology, see the introduction to that section.

44. Chapter 6, section 8.

45. Just to accidentally drop a Torah scroll would have been in Eibeschuetz's time the occasion for a fast, while a familiar story from the rabbinic literature tells how the Roman conqueror Titus showed his supreme contempt for the Jewish God by spreading out a Torah scroll on the Temple altar and having sex on it with two prostitutes (*Midrash Leviticus Rabbah* 22:3, b. Git. 56b).

46. Molho and Shatz, "Sabbatian Commentary," 440–42; Shatz-Uffenheimer, "Portrait," 408–11.

gone this far. Yet the passages we have just considered could hardly have been written by someone who regarded homosexual activity as the "abomination" that Lev 18:22 says it is. The regime of Torah and commandments, imposed *on* the God of Israel and then *by* him for the best of reasons, is passing away. Something freer, more accepting of human sexuality in all its variants, is emerging.

The precise role to be played by the God of Israel, in this new dispensation of the Distant One no longer distant, is not very clear. One thing is certain: he is in no way dismissed or diminished. On the contrary: *Va-avo ha-Yom* climaxes with a glowing description of the new era of conjugal rapture into which he and his Shechinah will enter.[47] A rapture, moreover, that overturns the centuries-old Jewish tradition of female subordination.

Once the Shechinah was forced into virginity, as a defense against the chaos that surrounded her. Now she will be fearlessly opened, bidden to "spread wide" the place of her "tent" (Isa 54:2), "dug" by the "rod" of the God of Israel.[48] He will "linger" always with her: their sex, currently intermittent, will in the messianic age be unending. Not only that: "In future time the Higher Shechinah will be above the God of Israel ... *the moon's light shall be like the light of the sun*" [Isa 30:26], conveying that the Shechinah will be in a lofty rank like the God of Israel, who is represented by the sun. [In contrast to the present, when the Kabbalists see the "moon's" inferiority as indicated by her having no light of her own, but only that which the sun gives her.] The sun's light will take the place of the moon ... not meaning, of course, that his light will be diminished; rather, that the Shechinah's rank will be elevated until the God of Israel is in comparison to her as the Shechinah is now in comparison to him." If she is on top for a change, this will not do him one bit of harm.

Did Eibeschuetz and his wife, Elkele, whom he dearly loved and lost too soon,[49] practice for themselves what he preached for his God? We can only imagine—and hope.

8.

Some notes on the text and translation:

47. Chapter 9, section 9.
48. Isa 24:23, interpreted in accord with Num 21:18.
49. Leiman, "Epitaph."

I CAME THIS DAY TO THE SPRING

Va-avo ha-Yom was first published in 2014, in a critical edition by Paweł Maciejko.[50] Five manuscripts of it, not all of them complete, survive from the eighteenth century:

- Oxford Bodl. 955 (Mich. 157)
- Jerusalem, Jewish National and University Library Heb 80 2491
- Jerusalem, Jewish National and University Library Heb 80 3100
- Oxford Bodl. 976 (Mich. 170): incomplete
- Cincinnati, Hebrew Union College Library ms. 85: incomplete

Maciejko took the manuscript Jerusalem 2491 as the base text for his edition, recording variants from the other manuscripts—except for the Hebrew Union College manuscript, which he did not use—in his apparatus. No one of the manuscripts, however, consistently offers the best readings. In doing the translation, I have found it best to work directly from the manuscripts in an eclectic fashion, choosing at each point whichever reading seems the most lucid. On those infrequent occasions where the manuscript variations have a significant impact on what the author is trying to say, I have noted that in my footnotes.

To aid readers in consulting the original Hebrew, I have inserted (in brackets) the page numbers of Maciejko's edition, as well as the folio numbers of ms. Oxford 955, which much of the literature on *Va-avo ha-Yom* uses as the standard for citations.

The Hebrew text is one unbroken, continuous flow of discourse. For the sake of intelligibility as well as for convenient reference, I have divided the treatise into nine chapters and subdivided these into sections, and provided each chapter and section with a title. It must be emphasized that these divisions and their titles are entirely my own, and reflect my own understanding of the text. At the beginning of each section I insert, in brackets, a summary of the direction the argument takes in that section, and how it fits in with the argument of the book overall. This argument is extremely subtle, extremely complex; and I hope thereby to have provided readers with a road map to help them make their way through its intricate twists and turns.

A literal, word-for-word translation of this text would have been of very small use. Instead, I have tried to maintain fidelity to the author's intent and the ways he chose to convey that intent, while allowing myself

---

50. Maciejko, *R. Jonathan Eibeschütz*.

the freedom to render these into naturally flowing English discourse. To give one example: the word *be-sod*, literally meaning "in the secret" or "in the mystery," is used over and over in this text, close to a thousand times. One often feels there is hardly a sentence without it. I translate it, at each occurrence, according to its use within the specific context, normally to convey that one thing is *symbolic of* or *a representation of* another, or simply that the two are in some way equivalent. To translate *be-sod* literally would almost invariably have obscured rather than conveyed the understanding of the passage where it appears. Such literalism would be the very opposite of fidelity.

I have only sparingly translated the word *ki-ve-yakhol*, "as though it were possible," invoked as an apology for some anthropomorphism or sexualization of the deity that is bound, if taken literally, to shock orthodox sensibilities. Since the flow of the argument requires that the offensive image or assertion *should* be taken literally, I take *ki-ve-yakhol* in most instances as a conventional effort to soften the shock, not intended seriously, and have normally preferred to avoid cluttering the translation with it.

The author's quotations from Biblical or rabbinic sources (Mishnah, Talmud, midrash) are given *in italics* in the translation; his quotations from the Zohar, which are sometimes very extensive and subjected to the most minute textual analyses, IN SMALL CAPITALS. I have found this to be the most effective way of intelligibly rendering the author's Zohar exegesis, upon which so much of his argument depends.

The diagrams found in two clusters in chapters 3 and 7 occur in all the manuscripts, with only small variations among them. There seems no doubt that they, no less than the surrounding text, are the author's work. In reproducing them, I have replaced the Hebrew letters of the original with their equivalents in the Latin alphabet (ABCD for אבגד, in chapter 3, section 3), and transliterated the names of the *sefirot* (in chapter 7, section 2).

Prologue

[Fol. 1a] [p. 11] For the sake of the unification of the Blessed Holy One and his Shechinah:

I came this day to the spring[1] of wisdom; and to begin: It is written in the Zohar to the Torah portion *Shemot*, fol. 9a: HE ALSO AROSE AND SAID: YHVH OUR GOD, LORDS OTHER THAN YOU HAVE MASTERED US; BUT ONLY IN YOU SHALL WE MAKE MENTION OF YOUR NAME[2] up to the words AND NOW IN EXILE THE OTHER SIDE RULES OVER THEM, and so forth; consult the text.

To understand what is meant by MYSTERY OF FAITH and BEGINNING OF MYSTERIES and so forth,[3] one must first consider a passage in the Zohar to the Torah portion *Va-yehi*, fol. 245a: COME AND SEE: THERE ARE THREE SOULS as far as the words LIKE THE BODY, WHICH IS AN INSTRUMENT BY WHICH THE SOUL PERFORMS ITS WORKING, and so forth.[4] Consult that text at length.

[p. 12] And now I shall enlighten you with words of understanding.

---

1. Gen 24:42.
2. Isa 26:13, quoted in Zohar II, 9a. See Appendix for the full translation (by Daniel C. Matt) of the Zoharic passage abridged here.
3. From the portion of the Zoharic passage omitted by the author; see Appendix.
4. Zohar I, 245a; see Appendix.

1

The Creation of God

1. In the Beginning Was the Will

[We begin with the first stage of existence: the primordial Endlessness (*Ein Sof*) and its Will, which has neither beginning nor end and is absolutely without internal differentiation in both time and space. The Will to create "worlds"—meaning not just or even primarily the physical universe, but the Kabbalistic "worlds" that include the entity we know as "God"—is primordial like Ein Sof itself; there never was a time when this was not its intent. The Graces and Judgments by which the "worlds" are governed were already present in the Will, in potential, from all eternity; it was their distinction as "gracious" or "harsh" that was to emerge later, with respect to the worthiness or unworthiness of their objects.

Two problems are raised. First, why is Endlessness designated as *Ein Sof*, "without end," when it might just as well have been called *Ein Reshit*, "without beginning"? Second, given that the Will is eternal and unchangeable, why does the Kabbalistic master Isaac Luria (1534–1572) speak as though the idea of creating "worlds" was somehow innovated within it? The first question is answered—*Ein Sof* is "endless" rather than "beginningless" from the perspective of us lower entities—although a deeper resolution will be provided in section 5. The second is left hanging until section 5.]

Know that before any existence, before the Emanation, there was only *him*: the solitary Infinite, Ein Sof, without any end or beginning whatsoever. He existed before any existent thing, and had no inception or end whatever.

But why is he called *Ein Sof*, "the one without end," and not *Ein Reshit*, "the one without beginning"?—for whatever has no end will obviously have no beginning. The reason is that we stand in this lowly world and lift up our eyes to grasp and understand the abilities of the Lord our God from our vantage point here in the World of *'Asiyah*,[1] going as far as the end of all the rungs, this being the Measure of the [Divine] Stature. (So it is written: *Lift up your eyes to the heights*, and so forth.[2]) We start out the project of comprehending, of discoursing, from the World of *'Asiyah*, which from our perspective is the first rung although in terms of its quality it is the last of them all. Then the World of *Yetzirah*, then *Beriyyah*, then to the World of Emanation, and thus we proceed from level to level until we reach Ein Sof, at which point we find ourselves incapable of comprehending him to his end, for he has none. That is why he is called Ein Sof.[3] We shall presently have more to say on this subject.[4]

Now, when Rabbi Isaac Luria began to discourse on the thought of Ein Sof, he chose to start with the words: "When it arose in his undifferentiated Will to create the worlds," and so forth. (See the holy book

---

1. The Kabbalists envisioned a sequence of four "worlds," descending from the highest "World of Emanation" (*atzilut*) through the worlds of "Creation" (*beriyyah*), "Fashioning" (*yetzirah*), and "Making" (*'asiyah*). The last of these is sometimes, as here, equated with our physical world, sometimes treated as a realm above it.

2. Isa 40:26. The verse continues: "... and see who created these." The author alludes to the exposition of this passage in the Zohar, I, 1b–2b, which he will revisit near the end of chapter 1 (section 5).

3. The same question is raised Eibeschuetz's *Shem 'Olam*, in passages written a few years after *Va-avo ha-Yom*, but there it is given a very different answer: Ein Sof is not called *ein reshit*, because in fact he does have a beginning, namely the "First Cause" (*sibbah rishonah*) out of which he has emerged (*Shem 'Olam*, 132). In *Shem 'Olam*, the ultimate primordial entity is the First Cause, not Ein Sof as here. (The First Cause is not even mentioned in *Va-avo ha-Yom*, although it is perhaps implied by the remark in section 2 that Ein Sof is "the Cause of all effects," *'illah le-khol ha-'alulim*.) Ein Sof in *Shem 'Olam* is the first "effect" (*'alul*) of that First Cause, equated furthermore with the "God of Israel," the "Blessed Holy One," and the "image of the ten *sefirot*." It would appear that the First Cause in *Shem 'Olam* corresponds more or less to Ein Sof in *Va-avo ha-Yom*, while Ein Sof in *Shem 'Olam* corresponds in part to the Will in *Va-avo ha-Yom*, in part to the entity that will come to be known as "Emanation-Human." It is very curious that these two texts ask the same question about two distinct entities, and accordingly give two different answers.

4. In section 5 of this chapter, where a more profound explanation will be offered for Ein Sof's name.

Tree of Life.⁵) The expression "undifferentiated Will" [*retzono ha-pashut*] conveys two aspects: first, that this Will extended itself [*nitpashet*] to the highest degree of extension through the whole space of Ein Sof, whose will, unlike a human being's, cannot be located in any single one of his intellectual organs. Rather, just as Ein Sof is inconceivably extended, so also his Will extends itself into every place, and he and his Will are one.⁶ Second, he experiences no alteration of will, such that we might speak of something arising in his Will that had not previously been inscribed in his thought. Rather, it had already been in his undifferentiated Will, without any alteration. Thus is his Will most supremely undifferentiated.⁷

[Fol. 1b] [p. 13] On the surface, [Luria's] words seem to contradict themselves. He says, "When it arose," implying an alteration of will, for otherwise how could it have "arisen"? How would it be possible, for instance, to say that any given object or person "arose" to a certain place unless it had earlier been in a lower place? This is quite impossible. Rather, when we say that "he arose to a certain place," our intent is that he had not previously been there but rather in a lower position, and now has "arisen." The same applies to the Will. When we say "it arose," we must intend an alteration of will. And then [Luria] goes on to speak of "his undifferentiated Will," indicating the highest degree of unalterability!

But understand: inasmuch as it is true that [Ein Sof's] Will is undifferentiated in the same way as [Ein Sof] himself, it follows that just as he has neither end nor beginning, so this Will has neither end nor beginning; and this Will to create worlds was always present with him. For one cannot possibly say of the Primordial Ein Sof, which serves as vehicle to nothing else,⁸ that his thought, his will was not from the beginning to create worlds in this place, but only afterwards did he make the decision to create. Even apart from Luria's word choice—"his

---

5. *'Etz Hayyim*, the compendium of Lurianic teaching written by Luria's disciple Hayyim Vital. The passage quoted is from Vital, *Sefer 'Etz Hayyim*, 1:27 (I.i.2).

6. Perlmuter, *Rabbi Jonathan Eibeschuetz*, 283–84, calls this interpretation of *pashut* "strange," and finds a parallel to it in *Shem 'Olam*, 60.

7. That is, it is absolutely uniform both spatially—the first "aspect" of the word *pashut*, "undifferentiated"—and temporally.

8. As the lower entities, subsequently brought into existence, will serve as vehicles for the higher. The language is taken from the late Zoharic strata *Tiqqunei Zohar* (*tiqqun* 70, p. 135b) and *Ra'ya Mehemna* (Zohar III, 230b). The point, as the next paragraph makes clear, is that one's intentions can change only under the influence of some superior entity.

undifferentiated Will," which indicates the highest degree of unalterability—such a notion cannot even be entertained.

Such a thing may indeed be said of a human being, who has a cause superior to himself that grants him knowledge. But who is there to give Ein Sof a thought he did not have before? Are not he and his Will one and the same? He is not like a human being, whose will is distinct from himself; he and his Will, rather, are one. So how can one say such a thing? *God is not a man*, says the Bible—specifically designating him as *El*, "God," which is Ein Sof as I shall explain below[9]—*that he should change his mind*,[10] i.e., turn from one thought to another. Rather, his thought at any given time is identical to what it was before, as long as he has existed.

[p. 14] Now, the world is governed through ten *sefirot*, five Graces and five Judgments, which constitute the image [*tziyyur*] of Ein Sof's Will.[11] By means of them is the divine governance complete, lacking nothing; everything great or small happens just as it should, as the Kabbalists have expounded at length. This being so, it is a necessary postulate that his Will is unalterable and all was known to him from the beginning. For this governance through attributes and *sefirot*—five Graces, five Judgments—was part of the Primordial Will, and all of them were included in this Will.[12]

Say, for example, that an individual intends to do something, whatever it may be. This is generally called "thought" or "will." Yet the content of the thought may be to do good to one person, ill to another, and consequently this "will" or "thought" contains within itself two aspects, the good and the bad. *From my flesh I can visualize God*;[13] and thus in the

---

9. The author never quite keeps this promise; but cf. chapter 5, section 1, and chapter 8, section 10, where the divine name *El* is applied to the superior divine entities.

10. Free quotation of Num 23:19.

11. Perlmuter, *Rabbi Jonathan Eibeschuetz*, 280–81, compares the usage in *Shem 'Olam*, where the first "effect" of the First Cause is called, among other names, *tziyyur 'eser ha-sefirot*, "the image of the ten *sefirot*," i.e., the archetype after which they were patterned. Here the usage is reversed: the *sefirot* are the "image" of their archetype in the Will.

12. Cf. Perlmuter, *Rabbi Jonathan Eibeschuetz*, 280–81, 302–3. I am not as sure as Perlmuter that the "Primordial Will" (*ha-ratzon ha-qadmon*) and the "Will" containing Graces and Judgments are distinct entities. This seems to me an artificial attempt on Perlmuter's part to harmonize the cognate but conflicting Kabbalistic systems of *Va-avo ha-Yom* and *Shem 'Olam*.

13. Job 19:26. The Kabbalists regularly used this verse to argue that, since humans are made in God's image, the processes within divinity can be inferred from those of the human body and psyche. Here, the "good" implications of a human thought are

same way the overall aim of the undifferentiated Will is to create worlds, yet it incorporates the ten aspects, five Graces and five Judgments. These are primordial as Ein Sof himself, extending themselves to the fullest throughout Ein Sof, as has already been said of the Will.

This is what Luria said in *Entering the Gates*, and in the interpretation of Luria in the book *Moses Assembled*:[14] the ten *sefirot* existed in potential within Ein Sof. After what we have said, the sense of this is perfectly clear. They always existed with him as aspects, and were the potential for all the worlds.

This also: inasmuch as his Will is not susceptible to alteration, [fol. 2a] it follows that the worlds stood in their present place even before their creation.[15]

2. Next: The Spot

> [The second stage: within Ein Sof, a finite Spot is designated inside which the "worlds" are to come into being. As a receptor, the Spot is female: it/she is to receive from Ein Sof the archetypal Graces and Judgments ("aspects"), which it/she will actualize. It/she is likened to "a stone within an abyss" and a gathering of waters, as Biblical and Talmudic images begin to be applied to the processes within divinity.]

Prior to the Contraction,[16] the light of Ein Sof was everything. Yet, inasmuch as all was known to him from the beginning, he set aside a certain place within his being where presently, when it should be his Will, the worlds would all be created. It was toward this place that his thought, and

---

comparable to the five Graces, the "bad" implications of that same thought to the five Judgments.

14. *Va-yaqhel Mosheh*, a Kabbalistic work first published in 1699 by Moses ben Menahem Graf. Eibeschuetz alludes frequently to this book in *Shem 'Olam*, e.g., 113, 129, 197. I do not know what specific passages from *Va-yaqhel Mosheh* or from Vital's *Mevo She'arim* ("Entering the Gates") the author has in mind.

15. The apparent self-contradiction of Luria's language is left unresolved. It will remain so until near the end of this chapter (section 5), when the author will take it up again.

16. *Tzimtzum*, a term in the Lurianic Kabbalah for Ein Sof's self-"contraction" of his light so as to provide a free space in which to create things other than himself. Uses of the term in *Shem 'Olam* suggest that Eibeschuetz may have envisioned the *tzimtzum* as the cosmic equivalent of an orgasmic contraction, and something of the sort may underlie the account of the *tzimtzum* in the next section. Cf. the thorough discussion in Wolfson, "*Malkhut Ein Sof*."

his undifferentiated Will in its ten aspects, were directed. He prepared this place as an integral part of himself,[17] for the worlds to exist.

In this place were gathered the totality of the Will and its infinitely extended aspects. All their longing and desire was directed toward it,[18] for there the light of the thought was to dwell. As if one were to point a finger to indicate the object of one's will and all its aspects, just so—even though all remained an integral part of [Ein Sof], and no action could be said to have occurred—still we may think of this spot [p. 15] as having been singled out over against Ein Sof's extension, more than any other place.

You may easily see that when a person bearing some poison looks into a mirror, he makes a mark on it with his gaze. This is common knowledge with regard to a menstruating woman's staining a mirror,[19] and the natural philosophers[20] have provided many other examples. Thought will similarly carve its mark, which is why we are forbidden to entertain any thought of sin or the like. It goes without saying, then, that the exalted Ein Sof—of whom we are forbidden to use any descriptive term, even in his praise, on account of the sheer magnitude of his greatness—will by his gaze and his thought make an instantaneous mark.

Within Ein Sof, though all of him was his essence,[21] there was nevertheless a certain Spot [*nequdah*] within that essence. This Spot originated from him, yet was eternally coexistent with him in time, sharing his undifferentiated quality. Yet inasmuch as it was his unaltered[22] Will that all the worlds be created at that very time in which they were created—

---

17. *Mineh u-veh*. Later in the text the phrase seems to have autoerotic undertones (cf. Wolfson, "*Malkhut Ein Sof*," 35–63), but these are not yet present.

18. Using the language of Gen 3:16, 4:7.

19. This notion, that "if a woman looks into a highly polished mirror during the menstrual period, the surface of the mirror becomes clouded with a blood-red color" goes back to a passage in Aristotle's *On Dreams*. It entered the mainstream of Jewish thought via Nachmanides's Torah commentary (on Lev 18:19); see Koren, "Kabbalistic Physiology." It occurs in *Shem 'Olam*, 114. There Eibeschuetz declares, with a hauteur worthy of *Peanuts* character Lucy Van Pelt, that if his correspondent and occasional critic Shimon Buchhalter had any knowledge of "the science of optics" (חכמת אפאטיקי), he would know that "when a menstruating woman looks at a mirror she leaves a stain on it . . . and if the eye's gaze has no substance, how could that stain on the mirror have been formed?"

20. *Hakhmei mehqar ve-teva'*.

21. *Atzmut*, later normally to be translated "substrate."

22. *Pashut*, here stressing the temporal aspect of the Will's uniformity.

(And one cannot ask why they happened to be created at that time and not earlier. This is no question at all. In order that all his creations know and recognize that it was he who emanated the worlds and brought them into existence, and that he is the Cause of all effects, he intentionally did not allow other beings to exist in time with him from the beginning, but rather to come into existence after some long interval. And since his existence is entirely timeless, it is not a problem why these came into existence at the time they did and not earlier. The question would be endless, [p. 16] for if creation had indeed taken place earlier, one could then ask why it had not taken place before *that*, given the timelessness of his existence.)[23]

—inasmuch as that was his unaltered Will for that [appointed] time, that designated place or Spot grew more intensely charged each moment with the action that was to transpire there. You may observe that, when a person conceives the intention to perform a certain deed one month from now, with each passing day [fol. 2b] his intention grows stronger within him in intensity and power until the day fixed for its execution arrives, at which point the intention is at its maximum strength. So it was with this Spot. Indeed, it was engraved within him from the beginning. Yet, as the time of the intention's fulfillment grew progressively nearer, the intended action grew ever stronger and more distinct. At last it was at the height of its power vis-à-vis the Spot, and in it were contained in potential all the worlds from the first to the last, the ten Graces and Judgments.

True enough: the Graces and Judgments were extended to the fullest, as has been indicated. Yet their longing was directed toward that Spot; thither they were to go and that Spot to gather up within itself all the encampments of the Holy; and because it was more highly actualized than those aspects, it was called "Female." It was not a distinct entity, for all remained integral [to Ein Sof]. Yet by extension it might be called "his Female," for it is common knowledge that potentiality is

---

23. This side remark is an old chestnut in the Sabbatian literature. Cardozo quotes Nathan of Gaza as having heard from Sabbatai Zevi "a most excellent reply" to the question of why the world was not created earlier than it was, namely, "that this question has no end. Had the world been created one thousand or two thousand years earlier than it was, the same question could still be asked, inasmuch as the world has to have had some beginning. But the Creator has it within His power to create it at whatever time is appropriate for its creation" (translated in Halperin, *Abraham Miguel Cardozo*, 295); cf. Yosha, "Ha-beri'ah ve-ha-zeman."

male in its quality, actuality female.[24] Most particularly, since everything set its course into that Spot and there would arrive, it became, qua female, a receiver of effluence.

This is why [that Spot] is symbolically represented by the "Foundation Stone" and "Zion Spot," female in quality, from which the world was founded.[25] It refers to that Spot, which is truly a part of Ein Sof's essence, and yet by comparison with the above-mentioned aspects is a female; and from it the world was founded. This was what Luria had in mind when he said that all the worlds were built within the *Malkhut* of Ein Sof, as suggested by the verse *Your Malkhut is the Malkhut of all the worlds*, referring to the above-mentioned [Spot] and its female quality.[26] This is why the Bible specifies *Your Malkhut*: [p. 17] though it is male vis-à-vis the construction of the worlds, in relation to the above-mentioned aspects it is a *Malkhut*.[27]

So the spot has a female quality in relation to the aspects, these having the quality of a male. It is known, moreover, that the male is called *hu*, "he," for the letters *hei-vav-aleph*[28] represent all the sefirotic ranks,

---

24. *Ha-koah hu be-sod dukhra ve-ha-po'al be-sod nuqba*, literally, "potentiality is in the mystery [*sod*] of the male and actuality in the mystery of the female." This is the first occurrence of *sod*, "secret" or "mystery," which will later appear in nearly every sentence of the text. I find it unhelpful to translate the word literally, but render it in accordance with its context, usually as conveying some idea of "quality" (as here) or "symbol" (as in the first sentence of the next paragraph), or the "inner meaning" of a Biblical passage.

25. The "Foundation Stone," *even shetiyyah*, appears in rabbinic tradition as the rock that took the place of the Ark in the Holy of Holies of the Temple, given its name because "from it the world was founded": Mishnah, m. Yoma 5:2; Tosefta Kippurim 2:12; Talmud, b. Yoma 54b. (This is presumably the *sakhrah* around which the Muslims built the Dome of the Rock.) The phrase "Zion Spot," *nequdat tziyyon*, though perhaps hinted at in the Talmudic reference to the Foundation Stone, is drawn from the Zohar, I, 186a, 226a, cf. III, 296a (*Idra Zuta*). The author's point is that the Foundation Stone/Zion Spot is a hint, embedded within the physical world as depicted by Jewish tradition, at the super-sensible realities after which that world is patterned. This passage is a turning point in the treatise, in that it is here that the abstract processes so far described first become concretized.

26. Ps 145:13. *Malkhut* is the tenth, lowest *sefirah*, female in its character. The "*Malkhut* of Ein Sof" would thus be Ein Sof's female aspect; the author has explained in the preceding paragraph how the undifferentiated, genderless Ein Sof could have such a thing as a female aspect. Liebes, *On Sabbateaism and Its Kabbalah*, 308–9, confesses himself unable to identify the Lurianic passage referred to here, and I can do no better. Cf. Wolfson, "*Malkhut Ein Sof*," 20.

27. And therefore female. *Your Malkhut* is understood as "that which is female in respect to you," the Ein Sof, but not to anything else.

28. Spelling the Hebrew masculine singular pronoun *hu*.

moving from lowest to highest. *Hei* is the Female, who is part of [the male] in her capacity as "corona";[29] *vav* is *Tif'eret*;[30] while *aleph* is *Keter-Hokhmah-Binah*.[31] This much is common knowledge, and it is the reason why the male is called *hu* and the female called *shem*, "name," as is well known. Thus, BEFORE THE WORLD WAS CREATED, HE EXISTED—i.e., the aspects—WITH HIS NAME, the Spot, CONCEALED WITHIN HIM—within the Ein Sof, as part of his essence.[32]

This Spot is like a stone within an abyss, the location to which all the waters are gathered, *the place to which they go and return*,[33] alluding to this Spot. Scripture says of it that *I was made in secret; I was given my features in the depths of the earth*[34]—alluding to this Spot and therefore using the verb *'usseti*, "I was made." This language indicates the Female, who, as is well known, has the quality of "making" and is the potentiality for the whole earth.[35] This is the meaning of, *I was given my features in the depths of the earth*. Cf. below.

3. The Contraction and the Shape

> [The third stage: the potentialities diffused through Ein Sof are actualized in that single Spot, through a process that the author compares to the "un-dissolving" of a quantity of wine from the vastly larger quantity of water in which it has been diffused. This process is called "Contraction" (*tzimtzum*), a term taken from the Lurianic Kabbalah but here given an orgasmic connotation. (Recall that the Spot is female, while the potentialities actualized in her are male.) The potentialities remain within Ein Sof as they were before. But now, actualized in the Spot, they have taken on something new: a human Shape (*partzuf*).]

---

29. That is, the female element of the sefirotic system, represented by *Malkhut*. In the ideal fusion of the male and female elements of the system, the Female is incorporated into the Male as the corona of his penis (*'atarah*), as indicated in the Biblical verse *A worthy woman is the crown* [*'ateret*, corona] *of her husband* (Prov 12:4).

30. The primary masculine *sefirah*. *Tif'eret* is the Male of the sefirotic system, while the entire system is collectively the super-sefirotic "male" within Ein Sof.

31. The three highest *sefirot*.

32. Zohar, I, 29a, the opening words paraphrased.

33. Eccl 1:7.

34. Ps 139:15.

35. This seems to contradict what has been said above, that potentiality is male and actualization female.

The Will comprising ten aspects (to resume our discussion) was extended through the full extension of Ein Sof. *From my flesh I can visualize God;*[36] and we see that when a person intends to do a certain thing and thinks about it day after day, the power of his intention growing ever stronger within him, then all his senses [fol. 3a]—that is, the perceptual senses of the human psyche, parts of one's human faculty—cease to function, all of them subordinated to this intention. When one's mind is on that intention one hears nothing, does not even feel a needle pricking his living flesh, so intensely absorbed is he in the intention. All his senses abandon him, subsumed under that intention, without awareness of anything else. [p. 18] That intention and the bringing of it to fruition are the sole focus of his faculties.

Thus a natural philosopher has said that "there is no power like that of an ingrained love, all one's senses marshalled toward its fulfillment."[37] When a man loves something and can achieve it, even through great effort, you will find that he perceives it as done with ease. (So Scripture says, *He thought them but a few days, such was his love for her.*[38]) We find, too, that a single man can perform an action that in terms of physical strength could hardly be done by ten; yet all that man's strength is like raw material given shape by his intention, and the act is easily accomplished. So says the Gemara: *He lifted the ladder and ran . . . "Fire in Amram's house!"* and so forth, as you may see for yourself.[39] The reverse is also true: when a person does not act with his ingrained thought, his strength is enfeebled. The Bible says this explicitly: *I am sick with love*, and, *my strength has faded away in calamity.*[40]

It follows that all a man's senses, all his human faculties, are subordinated and in thrall to thought. Great is the power of thought, which draws everything after it—so great, that it can be perceived only potentially

---

36. Job 19:26; see above, note 13.

37. I do not know the source of this.

38. Gen 29:20.

39. Alluding to the Talmudic story in b. Qidd. 81a: When Rav Amram the Pious caught a glimpse of a woman lodged in his upper chamber, he was so energized by lust that he "lifted a ladder that ten men could not carry, carried it by himself [and set it in place], and began to climb it. Halfway up he got hold of himself and cried out, 'Fire in Amram's house!'"—his aim being to bring out a crowd whose presence would restrain him from going any further.

40. Song 2:5, Ps 31:11.

and not in actuality. For whatever is hardly perceptible has great force, whereas the perceptible is subject to negations of all sorts.[41]

Thus it was with Ein Sof. His Will was in a state of extension, comprised of the ten aspects mentioned earlier. It grew ever stronger and more powerful up to the time of the worlds' creation. Accordingly, all Ein Sof's power was contained within that Will (or intention), in a state of preparedness for carrying out its plan. I shall say no more on this topic out of respect for its august greatness. From our simile, however, you may infer on your own all the aspects and details of the reality toward which it points.

To sum up, the power of Ein Sof is contained in his overall Will, composed of the ten aspects that are five Graces and five Judgments. [p. 19] You must also recognize the well-known fact that a man's facial appearance changes with his thoughts. *A man's wisdom brightens his face*, says the Bible; and *edema is a marker of sin*,[42] and there are many other examples. In consequence, those aspects of which the Will is comprised brought it about that the Ein Sof, though undifferentiated to the highest degree and entirely without color, took on through his own internal processes colors corresponding to the ten aspects, in the place of the Will and the aspects. These are the root of the four colors spoken of in the Zohar.[43]

Imagine wine spilled into water, distributing itself throughout the water so that neither its color nor its taste is at all detectable. Yet the individual wine droplets do not cease to be wine, and they maintain their essential "wine" quality.[44] So it was with the Will and the aspects.[45] When the time arrived for actualizing Ein Sof's intention, the day targeted through his undifferentiated Will for the creating of worlds, he planned

---

41. This is evidently a philosophical principle of some kind. But I do not know its source or what it means.

42. Eccl 8:1; Talmud, b. Shabb. 33a and Yebam. 60b, referring to the *hydrops* ("dropsy") of the Greek physicians, presumably understood as facial edema. See Preuss, *Biblisch-talmudische Medizin*, 190–91.

43. E.g., Zohar, I, 15a, where the colors are enumerated as white, black, red and green, symbolizing the *sefirot Hesed, Malkhut, Gevurah* and *Tif'eret* respectively. The "colors" (*sefirot*) do not yet exist at this stage, but only their prototypical "root" (*shoresh*) within Ein Sof.

44. Even though they are microscopic, perceptible to neither eye nor tongue. The author imagines the "Contraction" to be a reversal of the natural chemical process, wine becoming "un-dissolved" from the water that contains it.

45. The "colorless" Ein Sof is equivalent to the water, the aspects ("colors"), to the wine.

for a process of Contraction to take place[46]—namely, that [fol. 3b] all those extended aspects should concentrate themselves in one place, the place of that Spot, which would be a kind of root and a location for the event to take place, like a sponge soaking up water into itself.

Such was the power of that Spot in the generation of worlds. As long as all remained thoroughly extended, that very extension precluded the creation of worlds. The quality of Judgment, delimiting and granting regularity, was required. The infinite extension of the Graces left no place for the design necessary to all worlds; design is through measurement and rule, all of which belongs to the quality of Judgment.[47]

So the extended lights had to be contracted into a single place, the essence of Contraction being Judgment as we well know. Only thus could a place be prepared for the event of world-building. [p. 20] Returning to our image, the wine has no color or recognizable feature when distributed throughout the water. But now suppose the water were possessed of a will, that all the wine droplets be concentrated in a single place, recognizable there as wine by its quality and color, intact and ready for any use to which it might be put. That was the essence of the Contraction: the concentration of all the aspects that had stretched out every which way into the place of the Spot, a complete and well balanced concentration enacted through the Contraction, through that quality of Judgment that can grant rule and regularity to all the worlds. *Thus far shall they come*, and *he says to his world, Enough*.[48]

A key principle: *whatever is done to build worlds, is done only through male and female*. This applies particularly to the Contraction, which essentially derives from coupling with the female in a state of

---

46. In Lurianic Kabbalah, "contraction" (*tzimtzum*) is the process by which the infinite Ein Sof withdraws a portion of himself so as to create a space in which worlds external to him can emerge. Our author, by contrast, treats it as the concentration of the imperceptible potentialities within Ein Sof into a single Spot where those potentialities can take on concrete reality, like wine "un-dissolving" from water.

47. The antistructural character of Grace is a fundamental principle of this treatise, drawn from the earlier Kabbalah. Herbert Weiner offers a striking image to illustrate it: "I thought of those ice-cream machines which poured their contents on to the cone below, the shape being only able to form when the machine stopped. What would happen if there were no stopping? Why, there would be no shaped ice-cream cone, only an ever-changing blob" (*9½ Mystics*, 33–34). Judgment is the quality that does the "stopping," as indicated in the Biblical and Talmudic quotations at the end of the next paragraph.

48. Free quotations of Job 38:11 and Talmud, b. Hag. 12a. Both passages illustrate the restrictive, defining function of Judgment.

arousal, happening through the force of Judgment and "love squeezing the flesh";⁴⁹ understand. Here also, inasmuch as [Ein Sof] was comprised of ten aspects, some male and some female, inherent within his Will, this took place in the quality of an autoerotic male-female coupling.

For intelligibility's sake we may allow ourselves to go into the details, inappropriate as they may be to this lofty and fearful place. Rabbi Shimon ben Yohai has warned us that *cursed is the man who makes a graven or molten image*,⁵⁰ and we are prohibited from entertaining thoughts of sex between man and wife because such thinking begets arousal. Yet the very things prohibited in these lower regions, where we are engaged in constant combat and the demonic holds sway, are [allowed] in the upper regions where the demonic has no power, where all is unified and constructed solidly.

From this you may grasp that, having willed this, he underwent an autoerotic act of coupling and arousal, and the Contraction was done, as though ejaculating his seed and expelling drop after drop. All the aspects that once had been diffused came together in one place, the place of that Spot which received the aspects and they were made into a single place: the aspects of a complete Shape, as is well known; for any set of ten aspects has the quality of a Shape.⁵¹

[p. 21] Yet all was still inherent within [Ein Sof], and so these had the quality just of aspects and not *sefirot*, yet now in the quality of a human being. All this was in the place marked out for the worlds, where the aspects were joined and made into a Shape incorporating the Will and power of Ein Sof. This was the "place of the world."⁵²

---

49. Talmud, b. B. Mesi'a 84a, offers "love squeezes the flesh" (i.e., compresses, contracts it) as a retort to a noblewoman's gibe that two obese rabbis cannot be the fathers of the children attributed to them, since their genitals could not connect with their wives.'

50. Deut. 27:15, quoted by Shimon ben Yohai at the beginning of the Zohar's *Idra Rabbah* as a warning against taking the stunningly anthropomorphic images that follow as literal descriptors of the Deity.

51. *Partzuf*, often translated "configuration" or "person," one of the five humanoid shapes (Long-face, Father, Mother, Little-face and His Female) into which the Lurianic system, following the Zohar's *Idra Rabbah* and *Idra Zuta*, organizes the ten *sefirot*.

52. In rabbinic usage, God is regularly called "the Place," *ha-maqom*. The midrash, *Genesis Rabbah* 68:9, explains this idiom as conveying that God "is the place of the world, not the world his place."

4. The Mother of God

[The potentialities that have become actualized in the Spot, though male vis-à-vis that Spot, among themselves include both male and female. The male and the female together are God, a.k.a. "esoteric Human"; they are "born" of the female Spot, which now is given the title "Shechinah." (This title will later be applied to other, lower female entities.)

This relationship is hinted at in Gen 3:20, where Adam gives his female the name "Eve," "mother of all living." Historically this is false: Eve was never Adam's mother, and therefore cannot be called the mother of *all* living. But on the theosophic plane conveyed symbolically by the Bible story, and on which the Bible story has its deepest truth, Eve (= the Spot) is indeed the mother of Adam (= the Shape or "esoteric Human" who is God). Hence: "Mother of all living."]

In their pre-Contraction state, extended and mingled together, these aspects bore the name *karmela*, akin to the rabbinic term *karmelit* for the mingling of private and public domains.[53] It is a composite word, *kar* + *mal*, [the *sefirah*] *Malkhut* being a *kar*, "pillow," for her husband, and *kar* also being an anagram for *rakh*, which refers to *Malkhut*, "kingship."[54] (Thus one speaks of "*rekha* son of *rekha*," and our ancient sages demonstrate that *rekha* is a term for kingship.)[55] *Mal* is masculine: the mark of circumcision.[56] Hence the place where the aspects are intermingled is called *karmela*, as hinted in the verse *Your head is like karmel*[57]—above, in the place [fol. 4a] of that "head" to be discussed presently, Graces and Judgments cannot in practice be distinguished. Graces and Judgments, male and female elements,[58] are mingled; and this is *karmel*, the intermingling of the aspects.

---

53. The Talmudic theory of "domains," important for the laws governing the carrying of objects on Sabbath, recognizes beside public and private domains a category called *karmelit*, "neutral ground, localities which show characteristics both of public and of private territory, for which reason intercourse between them and those territories is forbidden" (Strack, *Introduction*, 34).

54. The male *sefirah Tif'eret* is "husband" to the female *Malkhut*, whose name literally means "kingship."

55. Talmud, b. B. Bat. 4a, from which Rashi reasonably deduces that *rekha bar rekha* means "a king, son of a king."

56. The verb *mal* means "circumcise"; this is the second syllable of *karmel*, while the first syllable has just been shown, through its association with *Malkhut*, to be feminine.

57. Song 7:6.

58. Somewhat counterintuitively, the Kabbalah perceives the "gracious" aspects of

In accordance with what we have said so far, the essence of the Contraction—by which was constructed the esoteric Human[59] who is "Cause of All Causes," for he is truly the essence of Ein Sof and all Ein Sof's power is contained within him—was enacted by means of the female aspects. This is why the Blessed Holy One, who in essence is that Human, calls the Shechinah "my Mother," for when the limbs of his body came together he was born through her and from her aspect.[60]

So you are to understand the Biblical verse *He called her name Havvah* ["Eve"], *for she was the mother of all living* [*em kol hai*].[61] The passage is problematic; what sort of explanation is this? By this logic she should have been called *Hayyah*.[62] Furthermore, how was she the *mother of all living*? Was the Human[63] a child of death, and not the inception of all life? [p. 22] The reply, that her name *Havvah* encapsulates the whole [sefirotic] structure contained within [the Human]—the letter *het* indicating [the *sefirah*] *Hokhmah*, *vav* indicating *Tif'eret*, *hei* indicating the Female[64]—raises the fresh problem of why she should be named for *Hokhmah* and *Tif'eret*. Is she not the Female[65] and no more? This is why the Bible tells us that *she was the mother of all living*, meaning that the Human was himself her offspring (as has been said), and she was therefore named *Havvah* after the totality of [his] structure.

From this you may understand how it was that David and Bathsheba, both symbolic of the Shechinah,[66] gave birth to Solomon, who

---

divinity as male, its "judgmental" aspects as female.

59. *Raza de-adam*, literally "mystery of a human being," the "Shape" spoken of earlier. *Adam* can mean both "human being" and "Adam"; hence the ambiguity of the next paragraph.

60. The female "Spot" yields the "Shape," which brings to actuality the potential within the undifferentiated "aspects" of Ein Sof. "Blessed Holy One," the standard rabbinic designation for God (Hebrew *ha-qadosh barukh hu*, Aramaic *qudsha berikh hu*), functions in Kabbalah as the male aspect of deity, "Shechinah" as the female aspect. Here "Shechinah" is the primordial Spot; we will presently see the term used also for inferior and derivative female entities. I do not know the source of the Blessed Holy One's calling the Shechinah "my Mother."

61. Gen 3:20, with Adam as the subject.

62. The name that would naturally be formed from *hai*, "living."

63. Or, "Adam."

64. The letters *het-vav-hei* spell the name *Havvah*.

65. *Malkhut*, the Shechinah, whom our author regularly understands to be symbolized by the Biblical Eve. We will hear a great deal more of this below.

66. It seems paradoxical that the hypermasculine King David is understood, no less than his paramour Bathsheba (2 Sam 11–12), as a symbolic representation of the

symbolizes the God of Israel as we will later see.[67] For in accord with what I have said, it makes perfect sense that she was *the mother of all living*, being the instrument by which the Contraction took place, without whom those aspects of which the worlds are constructed would have remained infinitely extended.[68] She it was who granted them limitation, and the Shechinah is thus the "*Shaddai*" who said to the world, "*Dai!* Enough!"[69] Understand.

5. The Unlimited Versus the Limited; "Mindless" Versus "Mindful" Light; "Colors" Versus "Substrate"

[In what was once a uniform, undifferentiated Endlessness, therefore, dualities have begun to appear. First, there is the duality of the finite and bounded God over against the infinite extension from which, through the "Contraction," God has emerged. Even within that infinite extension, however, there is a duality, always present but until now of no consequence: on the one hand, the "colored" aspects of the infinite Will that brought into existence the Spot and then the Spot-begotten Shape; on the other hand, the "colorless" substrate of Ein Sof.

The author now gives the "colored" Will a new name, drawn from Sabbatian tradition: "the Mindful Light." The substrate is "the Mindless Light"—not "mindless" in any absolute sense, but unmindful of such petty matters as bringing God and the universe into being and afterward maintaining their existence. As human beings, our concern is with the Mindful Light, which, with the "Contraction," leapt the abyss separating potentiality from actuality. This leap is what (answering the question posed in section 1) Luria had in mind when he spoke of the idea of creation "arising in his Will."

---

female Shechinah. Yet this equation has deep roots in the Kabbalah, is taken for granted by Sabbatian writers, and has important implications for the feminization of the Davidic Messiah Sabbatai Zevi. More on it below, chapter 8, section 12.

67. This use of "the God of Israel" as equivalent to the "Shape" emerging from the "Spot" is in accord with the Kabbalistic doctrine of Eibeschuetz's *Shem 'Olam*, where the "God of Israel" (a.k.a. "Blessed Holy One") is the first "effect" of the First Cause. (See above, note 3.) Later in this text, however, the "God of Israel" is redefined as a more limited, less exalted entity with a more distinct personality, of whose specific existence *Shem 'Olam* gives no hint.

68. And therefore useless for world-building.

69. Drawing on the Talmud, b. Hag. 12a, where the Biblical divine name *Shaddai*—usually but dubiously translated "the Almighty"—is explained through God's having said to his chaotically expanding creation, "*Dai!* Enough!"

The Mindful and Mindless Lights are called "Father" and "Mother," respectively. They are also indicated by the two words of the term *Ein Sof*, "Endlessness" (taking up another question posed, and provisionally answered, in section 1). *Ein*, "Nothingness," is the Mindless Light. *Sof*, "End," is the Mindful.]

And so, through the process of Contraction, that Spot was made into a complete Shape. Know that the Will of Ein Sof had been extended to the ultimate, comprised of ten aspects, whose whole yearning, goal, intentionality and thought were concentrated on that Spot. The nature of the Contraction, therefore, was such that it would partake of the quality of Judgment, the place of that Spot becoming distinguishable in actuality, as though a boundary defined it and turned it into a Shape. Without the Contraction, there would have been only extension, without any sort of design or form of a Shape that could be recognized. Thanks to Contraction and Judgment, however, this Spot and the Shape's design became recognizable in actuality over against the infinite extension. By contrast, the ten aspects of the Will in its extension, though possessing colors,[70] were prevented by their inconceivable extension from taking on human form.

They remained in this state even after the Contraction. It was only the ultimate fruit of their essence that came to the place of the Spot and was transformed through the Contraction into something like a Shape, while the Will in its aspects remained as it had been, inconceivably extended. [p. 23] You surely know the saying that *the Shechinah does not budge from its place without leaving a mark*,[71] and it applies all the more strongly to this case, in which their extension remained precisely where it had always been.[72]

70. See above, note 47. The opposition of the "colored" aspects of the Ein Sof's Will to its colorless "substrate" will be developed later in this section.

71. I do not know the source of this "saying," which will be quoted repeatedly in the course of the treatise. The opening words, "the Shechinah does not budge" (from the Temple, or from the Western Wall) are taken from the midrash, *Exodus Rabbah* 2:2, but the "leaving of the mark" does not seem to appear in any rabbinic source. Maciejko cites a parallel from Menachem Azariah of Fano, *Yonat Elem* (Amsterdam, 1648), chapter 1, p. 2a, which quotes only the opening words but seems to imply the rest. "Shechinah" is used as in the rabbinic literature to indicate the divine presence, without the Kabbalistic refinement of applying it specifically to God's female aspect.

72. Perlmuter, *Rabbi Jonathan Eibeschuetz*, 284–85, compares the doctrine of *Shem 'Olam* that the "image of the ten *sefirot*" (which *Shem 'Olam* seems to equate with the "God of Israel") remained as it had been even after the *sefirot* themselves came into being, just as the blueprint for a house does not cease to exist after the house has been built. The Kabbalistic systems of the two texts are not quite consistent, but plainly related.

You may think of the rock and the fire-producing flint.[73] The fire-potential is in each and every part of the rock; yet crumble that rock to the finest dust and you find in it no [fol. 4b] fire whatever. For throughout its parts the fire exists only in potential, and it is when you strike it to the point of heat that its parts draw near one another and the fire emerges from the potential into the actual.[74] If it were possible to fasten onto the flint the spark leaping from it, then it would be one with the flint and especially with its roots, the components of fire within the rock. And though it would cling to the rock, one with it and dwelling inside it, three dimensions[75] would seem to be involved—

1. the dimension of the spark, as it exists in actuality;
2. the dimension of the fire-components mingled within the rock, permanent and limitless (for no matter how long you were to strike it, they would never be lacking);
3. and the rock itself a third element—

even though it is one,[76] unified in the highest degree.

Such is the case with Ein Sof. It contains [3] the Mindless Light, analogous to the rock's essence; [2] the Mindful Light, analogous to the fire-components distributed everywhere throughout the rock;[77] and

73. Here the "rock" and the "flint" appear to be two distinct objects, struck against each other. Later they seem to be two names for the same thing. In *Shem 'Olam*, 106–7, Eibeschuetz quotes this same spark-from-the-rock simile from Moses Cordovero's *Pardes Rimmonim*, part 5 (*Seder ha-Atzilut*), chapter 4 (via Isaiah Horowitz's *Shenei Luhot ha-Berit*): "We may aptly compare this to a flint rock from which fire is produced by the striking of iron . . . that fire is latent within the rock, united with it so truly and powerfully that there is no distinction at all between the rock and the fire inside it. Similarly . . . the *sefirot* were united with the [divine] essence, bound to it so powerfully that one could hardly speak of the *sefirot* existing at all, but only of true unity."

74. Two manuscripts (Oxford 976, Cincinnati) add here: "So it is in the present case. Through the process of Contraction and autoerotic arousal, its parts draw near one another until it emerges from the potential to the actual." The same word, *himmum*, is used for heat and for sexual arousal.

75. *Gevulim*, the word whose singular is translated "boundary" in the first paragraph of this section. On the philosophical use of *gevulim* for the three dimensions of the physical world, see the entry in Klatzkin, *Thesaurus Philosophicus*, 1:98.

76. The spark, the fire-components, and the rock's essence (or "substrate"; see below) are all one.

77. This is the first occurrence of the terms "Mindless Light" (*or she-ein bo mahshavah*) and "Mindful Light" (*or she-yesh bo mahshavah*). The author's employment of them is a mark of his Sabbatian pedigree, for the antithesis between these two species of light—the Mindful Light that "seeks after building," the Mindless Light that "seeks

[1] the God of Israel, like the spark, clinging perpetually to [Ein Sof] and sharing its essence,[78] yet in actuality more perceptible, as though marked off [from it] by a boundary.

Know also that the two kinds of light may be compared to a king. Would we say of him, wishing to praise him to the utmost, that all day and all night he gives his thought to the care of his fields, how they may be cultivated and preserved? Would it not rather be to his discredit, indeed contempt, that so great and mighty a king should squander his valuable time on the rustic concerns of the field? [p. 24] But if we were to go so far as to say that "so tremendous and exalted are his thought processes that, amid his great and weighty concerns, he manages to think *even of peasants' labor*"—is this not much to his credit? And should some peasant wish to discuss his work with [the king], he must pick a time when [the king's] thoughts are on this work and not other, loftier matters.

Similarly, if we were to say of a man that he possessed none of the senses other than smell, this would be to his discredit. Yet if we were to say that he possessed all the senses, it would certainly be to his disadvantage if he did not have this one as well. If he were brought something to smell, one would not be told to bring it to the sense of speech that this might smell it, or to the sense of voice or the like, but to the sense of smell only. Thus it is with Ein Sof, exalted above all praise. How might it be conceived that all his thought is devoted to the creation of worlds so lowly by comparison with him? One must rather say that he encompasses many thoughts, deep and lofty, that have nothing to do with creating worlds, and that "Light" that is "Mindful" of the creation of worlds is but one among them.

Of the Mindless Light, surpassingly lofty though it is, we have no way to speak. From our perspective it is "darkness," *hoshekh*, from the verb *hasakh*, "to withhold," meaning that it is beyond our comprehension.[79] It is the Light "Mindful" of the creation of worlds that is crucial for us, and toward which our attention is directed.

---

after destruction"—was a creation of Nathan of Gaza, pivotal to his Kabbalistic system (Wirszubski, "Te'ologiyah"). The suggestion that follows, however, that the Mindless Light is not really "mindless" but occupied with higher things than the paltry business of creation, is an innovation of our author's.

78. Combining the readings of the different manuscripts, which diverge considerably at this point. The God of Israel is mentioned only in ms. Oxford 955, yet seems essential for the point the author is making.

79. As Perlmuter points out (*Rabbi Jonathan Eibeschuetz*, 289–90), this is a drastic reversal of Nathan's disparagement of the Mindless Light as "utter darkness." It only

[p. 25] So if you are troubled by Luria's having indeed used the language of "arising in his Will," implying alteration of will, do not allow yourself to say that his godlike words were in error.[80] His point was that when a person plans to accomplish something on a given day and on that day his intent is fulfilled, one says that he planned to do such-and-such and it "arose in his hand."[81] So here: the intent to create the worlds at a given time was part of his very existence, [fol. 5a] and when that time arrived and this construction was completed, this was called "arising"—"it arose in his Will," meaning that the Will was achieved and became something real.

Thus it happened in the process of Contraction and autoerotic arousal. His parts[82] drew near to each other until [his intent] emerged from potentiality into actuality. Everything—all Ein Sof's power—was contained in the parts of the undifferentiated Will; and the intentionality of all those parts, the ultimate fruit of their essence, was in the place of the Spot. When a man continually thinks about something, when he never turns his musings or his attention to anything else, all his strength and all his thought are in that one thing. Just so, the undifferentiated Will comprised of ten aspects had its eyes and mind, as it were, continually fixed on this one place, where the ultimate fruit of their intention became actualized. With each passing day they etched themselves deeper, in actuality, upon that Spot; and the Spot, like a sponge, drew into itself the power and fruit of all their essence.

Know and understand from this: *the place of that Spot contained all the will and power of Ein Sof*.[83] In it the purpose of the action was accomplished; and to the extent that a man's will is enacted in a given place, to that extent his power will be contained within that place. Thus it was with that Spot. Inasmuch as there the aspects became actualized, more of Ein Sof's power was contained there than where the aspects were extended. Outside this spot, the Ein Sof was—I beg his forgiveness! but

---

seems dark to us, the author says, because it is entirely beyond our ability to grasp.

80. The author now resolves the problem he raised near the beginning of the treatise (above, section 1).

81. 'Aletah be-yado, idiomatic for "he succeeded." Perlmuter, *Rabbi Jonathan Eibeschuetz*, 296–97, points out that precisely the same (highly eccentric) interpretation of "arising in his Will" occurs in *Shem 'Olam*, 60, and there is no way this parallel can be a coincidence.

82. Corresponding to the fire-components in the rock.

83. And thus the "God of Israel," as described in the next chapter, has come into being.

this is Torah and I need to learn[84]—in the quality of "place of colors," namely the extension of the aspects throughout his essence. What was not the "place of colors" is called "substrate[85] of Ein Sof."

Now the "place of colors," [p. 26] inasmuch as that Spot was the goal and fruit of their actions, has the quality of *Abba*, "Father" and is therefore called *Mi*, "Who."[86] The remaining substrate of Ein Sof has the quality of Female, inasmuch as that Spot was an integral part of it as if conceived in its womb. It is called *Elleh*, "These"; it is symbolized by Leah;[87] it is implied by the phrase *she is grown weak as a female*,[88] for all strength resides in the aspects and the colors. For this reason the Will does not adhere to it,[89] yet it also is called Ein Sof. *Ein*, "Nothingness": Ein Sof's substrate, without colors, it is called "Nothingness" because it is beyond all ability to grasp. *Sof*, "End": represented by *Mi*, END OF ALL RUNGS,[90] the extension of the colors. Remember this: the colors are represented by *Mi*, the uncolored by *Elleh*.

84. The two Jerusalem manuscripts omit this exclamation.

85. *'Atzmut*, the word translated "essence" in the previous sentence. I shift to "substrate" here and in what follows, better to bring out the contrast between the active "colors" and the passive "substrate," developed in the next paragraph.

86. The subtext for what follows is a passage near the beginning of the Zohar (I, 1b–2b), where the words of Isa 40:26, *who created these*, are taken hyperliterally as "'Who' created 'These'": the *sefirah Binah*, the supernal Mother, for whom *Mi* ("Who") is a standard code term, created "These" (*Elleh*, the lower *sefirot*). From the combining of *Mi* and *Elleh*, *Elohim* ("God") was formed, both graphically (מי+אלה=אלהים) and in actuality. The author reworks his source with his usual bold creativity. *Mi* is no longer the Mother (*Imma*) but the male potency of "Father" (*Abba*), who impregnates the Spot within the passive womb of the strengthless *Elleh*; the action is shifted from the sefirotic to the super-sefirotic realm; and the Zohar's assertion that *Mi* created *Elleh* is left problematic, since "colors" and "substrate" are coeval elements of Ein Sof.

87. Whose name, in Hebrew, is an anagram for *elleh*. The Zohar understands the Biblical Leah as a representation of the *sefirah Binah*. I know of no other source that connects her with Ein Sof or any of its elements.

88. Talmud, b. Ber. 32a, which represents this as a taunt of the Gentiles against the Jewish God. The author quotes it with a significant alteration, from "he is grown weak" to "she is grown weak."

89. Language drawn from Zohar, I, 99b, but with a fresh significance which does not square very well with the author's stress on the unity of the Ein Sof and his Will.

90. *Sofa de-khol dargin*, commonly used in the Zohar for the *sefirah Malkhut*, so called because she is the lowest of the *sefirot* (e.g., I, 106a, 163a, following Matt's translation). But the "end of rungs" can be the highest of entities rather than the lowest, depending on one's perspective, as the author observes at the beginning of section 1; and the Zohar's exposition of Isa 40:26, which has plainly inspired that passage, seems so to understand it. ("Once a human being questions and searches, contemplating and knowing rung after rung to the very last rung . . . "; I, 1b, trans. Matt, *Zohar*) This is a

And so the totality of Ein Sof is called "God," *Elohim* = *Elleh* + *Mi*. That *Elleh* is also called "darkness," *hoshekh*, from the verb *hasakh*, "to withhold," meaning that it is by its nature incomprehensible.[91] Its quality is that of the female, of the moon that has nothing of its own,[92] of THE BEAUTIFUL GIRL WHO HAS NO EYES.[93]

---

new explanation of the name *Ein Sof*, deeper than the one proposed at the beginning of the treatise: it is formed from *Ein* + *Sof*, the names of its two components, just as it is called God, *Elohim*, from *Mi* + *Elleh* (below).

91. Said earlier of the Mindless Light, which the author identifies with the *Elleh* component ("substrate") of Ein Sof.

92. *Malkhut*, the Shechinah, is regularly symbolized in the Zohar by the moon, which has nothing (i.e., no light) of its own, other than that poured into it by the sun (= *Tif'eret*).

93. The subject of the last of the three cryptic riddles posed by the *Sava de-Mishpatim*, the mysterious "old man" who dominates the Zohar to the Torah portion *Mishpatim*. "Who is a serpent that flies in the air, moving in separation, while an ant lies comfortably between its teeth? . . . Who is an eagle that nests in a tree that never was—its young plundered, though not by created creatures? . . . Who is a beautiful maiden without eyes, her body hidden and revealed? She emerges in the morning and is concealed by day, adorning herself with adornments that are not" (Zohar, II, 95a; Matt, trans., *Zohar*).

2

The Anatomy of God

1. The Tripartite Shape

> [The Shape, into which the Spot has been transformed in the process of Contraction, has like all organisms a beginning, middle, and end—the head, the heart, and the sex organ respectively. The Shape's "head" is the superior entity called ʿAttiqa, traditionally understood as "Ancient One" but here treated as meaning "Distant One." The "heart," actualizing what is present only in potential in the Distant One, is the entity called "God of Israel." The sex organ is the *sefirah Yesod*, which at this primordial stage still incorporates the Female.]

Turning our attention back to that Spot, we may say that it consists of an end, a middle, and a beginning.[1] The "beginning" corresponds to the organism's[2] head, its characteristics wholly unknowable in spite of its being the soul's abode. The "middle" corresponds to the heart, the organ that clarifies and reveals those characteristics, purifying the entirety, apportioning life to every living being and giving measure and tempo and nurturance to the whole organism, as those conversant with natural philosophy well know. So it is here: the "middle," functioning as heart, actualizes all characteristics, clarifies them, regulates their comings and

---

1. *Sof tokh rosh*, the initial letters of which spell out *seter*, "secret."
2. *Partzuf*, the word that I normally translate "Shape." But here the author seems to be talking about living organisms in general, to which the Shape is then compared.

goings, and apportions life to the entire living being.³ The "end" corresponds to *Yesod*, the sex organ.⁴

[p. 27] So it is with this Spot [fol. 5b]. Through the process of Contraction it was made into the image of a human Shape, with all its characteristics. The head, on account of its proximity to its root,⁵ had as yet no perceptible Graces and Judgments, all having the quality of an extension of Mercies. It is called "Distant One, holiest of all the holy, most concealed of all the concealed,"⁶ the reason for which appellation will be elucidated below. The heart is designated "God of Israel,"⁷ and it is this that distributes and actualizes Graces and Judgments, combining them and imposing orderly measure upon them. This appellation, too, will be elucidated.

The "end" corresponds to *Yesod*, the sex organ, with *Malkhut*, the Female, still incorporated within him.

This is the inner meaning of the name YHVH.⁸ The Distant One, as is well known, contains the name *Yah* (YH),⁹ which is [the sefirotic triad] *Keter-Hokhmah-Binah*. The God of Israel, corresponding to the heart, is the V, *vav* formed out of *yod* by extending it.¹⁰ The Female incorporated within him, eventually to be made into a Shape unto herself, is the final H.

---

3. *Kol hai*, perhaps alluding back to the Biblical description of Eve (= the Spot) as *em kol hai*, "mother of all living," i.e., the "living" Shape (above, chapter 1, section 4).

4. The *sefirah* Yesod, the divine phallus, sometimes referred to in the Zohar as *siyyuma de-gufa*, "the end of the body."

5. That is, the Will that pervades the entirety of Ein Sof, its distinctive "colors" as yet present only in potential. Later the author will shift into speaking of this as "the Root" and giving it anthropomorphic features.

6. *'Attiqa qaddisha de-khol qaddishin setima de-khol setimin*, usually abbreviated *'attiqa qaddisha*—normally translated as "Holy Ancient One," but taken by our author to mean "Holy Distant One." See below, note 15.

7. Earlier, the entire Shape had been called "God of Israel," a usage more or less in accord with Eibeschuetz's in *Shem 'Olam*. This narrower usage, for a segment of the Shape that will presently take on its own distinctive human-like characteristics, is to predominate in this treatise.

8. The Tetragrammaton, *yod-hei-vav-hei*, used throughout the Hebrew Bible as God's name.

9. As in *hallelu-Yah*, "praise Yah."

10. The lower appendage of the letter *yod* (י), extended downward, makes it into a *vav* (ו). For the author, this graphic feature symbolizes the divinity's becoming increasingly manifest in its devolution from its lofty origins.

A key principle: at the higher level, before the line[11] had been extended down to the God of Israel, the *vav* was as yet unknown and therefore in a state of concealment in all words. *Qadosh*, "holy," for example, applies to the God of Israel, whereas above him the word is *qodesh*, "holiness."[12] So with all words; which is why, at the higher level that has the quality of "head," the Father is called *Mi*, "Who,"[13] while the God of Israel receives an added *vav* and is called *Yom*, "Day."[14] It is why the head is called *'Attiqa*, from *'Attiq Yomin*, meaning that he is superior to and "removed," *ne'etaq*, from the "Days," *yomin*.[15] (On the term *ne'etaq*, see below.)

2. Androgyny Divine

[The Spot is female, and so therefore is the Shape into which it has been transformed. When the Shape copulates with the Will that is its Root—a new term making its way into the author's discourse—it takes the female role, being then in a state of "entrancement" or "dream." This happens when the Root comes to encounter the Shape in the latter's place. But the Spot/Shape is also male vis-à-vis the substrate of Ein Sof, to whose dark realms it sometimes rises. When this happens, the Shape experiences a deathlike state in which sexual activity (such as between the Root and the Shape *qua* female) cannot occur.]

We have already said that the Spot had the quality of female vis-à-vis the extension of the ten [aspects],[16] inasmuch as it was a receiver of

---

11. Of the *yod*; see the preceding note.

12. One may speak of the God of Israel as "holy" (*qadosh*, written with a *vav*, קדוש), whereas at higher levels of divinity one speaks only of "holiness" (קדש, without the *vav*). Like so much in this treatise, and in Kabbalah in general, this passage conceives linguistic and cosmological realities as interlocking and reflecting one another.

13. Above, chapter 1, note 86.

14. If one reverses the order of the two Hebrew letters of *Mi* (מי) and adds a *vav* between them, one gets *Yom* (יום).

15. Eschewing the obvious explanation of *'Attiqa* as "Ancient One," from the "Ancient of Days" (*'attiq yomin*) of Dan 7:9, for an extremely strained etymology based on another meaning of the same root, which underscores the Distant One's lofty superiority over the God of Israel. This superiority will take on a new dimension when we come to realize that, for our author, the Distant One is specifically associated with Christianity.

16. Of Ein Sof's Will.

effluence and was, moreover, more highly actualized than they.[17] At the highest level, therefore, the Spot couples with the Will-Root,[18] that is, when the Will and the aspects increase and intensify their concentration upon it. This qualifies as copulation because the measure of effluence is increased, and it takes place wherever the aspects' extension comes with full force to encounter the Spot. It is no less copulation for not being in the area of the womb, for every place where the Spot is encountered is equivalent to any other.

This implied by the verse *What* [p. 28] *are these wounds between your hands? . . . which my lover did to me.*[19] It is why one must take care not to touch even a woman's little finger,[20] for at the higher level, in this august realm, that is a complete sex act; understand. It is the reason for Eve's addition when she said, *Nor shall you touch it, lest you die.*[21] The command,[22] as we know and as I shall discuss below, essentially concerned the sex act, and Eve assumed that the norms of this august realm were applicable. She therefore said that touching was forbidden here as well, for it is the sex act as we know. Understand.

Keep this principle in mind: that *this Shape is female vis-à-vis the Root.*[23] This is the inner meaning of *YHVH is Elohim,*[24] meaning that he is

17. Since potentiality is male, actuality female.

18. "Will" and "Root" are two names for the same entity. The distinction is one of perspective: what from the Ein Sof's viewpoint is its "Will," is for the lower realms emerging from it their "Root." This will explain why, as our perspective shifts downward, the use of "Will" is eclipsed by that of "Root," which takes on a strongly anthropomorphic quality.

19. Free quotation of Zech 13:6: "When one says to him, 'What are these wounds between your hands?' he will reply, 'Where I was struck in the house of my lovers.'" The point is that sex can take place, not only at the genitalia, but at other parts of the body such as "between the hands." We will hear more of these erotic "wounds" in chapter 6, section 8.

20. Combining Talmud, b. Shabb. 13b with Ber. 24a and Shabb. 64b, where a woman's little finger is put on par with her genital. The hypersexuality of divinity, mirrored in the human body, calls for hypervigilant avoidance.

21. Gen 3:3. Eve, speaking to the serpent, quotes God inaccurately as having prohibited, not only eating from the Tree of Knowledge, but also touching it; cf. *Midrash Genesis Rabbah* 19:3.

22. Not to eat of the Tree of Knowledge.

23. What has been said of the Spot is now applied to the Shape ("God of Israel") that emerged from it.

24. E.g., 1 Kgs 18:39, "the Lord he is God." The four-letter name YHVH denotes the Shape (above, section 1), while *Elohim* ("God") is understood, following the Kabbalistic tendency to apply the name specifically to the Shechinah (= *sefirah Malkhut*), as a marker of the female. See below, note 27.

female vis-à-vis the Root. Know also that when their coupling takes place the Shape is in a state of "Deep Sleep" or "entrancement,"[25] a dream-state. It is just as when the spirit of prophecy comes upon a man; he loses his senses and becomes as though sleeping, dreaming; thus it is when the Shape experiences coupling and excess effluence from the Root. He is then a dreamer also through his female status, as we know, for everything female is in a state of sleep. Because the coupling has at times the quality of "touching yet not touching," "sleeping yet not sleeping," and "racing back and forth," it remains unstable.[26]

Know that, when we call [the Shape] *Elohim*,[27] we do so vis-à-vis the Will that is called *Mi*.[28] Yet vis-à-vis the substrate of Ein Sof, called *Elleh*, he is perpetually male, this *Elleh* being female with respect to him. This is the inner meaning of the verse *Ein* (that is, the *Elleh*) *is Elohim with me*,[29] i.e., female with respect to me.

Now you must grasp an important distinction. Male lust is directed toward the female; so says the Zohar to the Torah portion *Va-yehi*, quoted [fol. 6a] above. COME AND SEE: EVERYWHERE MALE PURSUES FEMALE AND AROUSES LOVE TOWARD HER.[30] Therefore, when the Root (called *Mi*) arouses love toward [the Shape], he descends and encounters him in a state of Deep Sleep, "entrancement," dreaming. This is

---

25. "Deep sleep" (*tardemah*) is the Biblical term for the mysterious condition that Adam entered when Eve was created out of him (Gen 2:21); while *dormita*, apparently from Latin *dormitio*, is a Zoharic term that glosses *tardemah* (III, 142b, *Idra Rabbah*) and, in I, 207b, is linked to death. (Matt's translation: "From there below are sixty other breaths, all from the side of death, the rung of death above them; they are called *dormita*, wakeless sleep, all tasting of death." See his note *ad loc*.) My translation "entrancement" is based on the use of the term in *Va-avo ha-Yom*.

26. "Touching yet not touching" is the language of the Zohar, e.g., I, 16b. "Sleeping yet not sleeping" is from the Talmudic definition of a "doze," e.g., b. Pesah. 120b. "Racing back and forth" is from Ezek 1:14, describing the "living creatures" of the *merkavah*. I am not sure of the precise point the author is making in this sentence.

27. That is, female; see above, note 24. The copyist of ms. Jerusalem 2491 wrote *Elohim* in the text, along with the other manuscripts, but crossed it out and wrote *nuqba*, "female."

28. Above, chapter 1, section 5.

29. Deut 32:39, usually translated "there is no other God with me." *Ein*, "Nothingness," was defined in chapter 1, section 5 as the substrate of *Ein Sof*, the *Ein* as opposed to the *Sof*.

30. Zohar, I, 245a, slightly adapting Matt's translation. This is not actually part of the second Zohar passage quoted in the Prologue, but occurs just a few lines before it.

a sexual act, [p. 29] for the Spot remains in her place and he reveals himself to her by coupling with her.[31]

But sometimes [the Root] does not come to him. Rather the Spot, the Shape, bestirs itself to rise to the Root, to the place of extension, as the Scripture says, *I will go to my place.*[32] He is then in a state of burial—and the discerning reader must understand on his own, for this cannot be put in writing.

For that extension is concealed within its substrate, which is called "darkness";[33] and the spirit of the God of Israel (the Holy Distant One included)[34] rises from him, up to the place of extension where it must extend itself through the darkness. This is called "burial," as in the verse *Man knows not his burial,*[35] for it is in a place of concealment,[36] and also the words *knows not* negate sexual coupling (*know* used as in *the man knew*).[37] Similarly, *Love is strong like death:*[38] when the Shechinah arouses love and pursues her husband until her spirit beats for him and she yearns to leave her place and pursue him, this is indeed *like death*.[39] By contrast, when the Root pursues the God of Israel,[40] lusting for him, this is an act of coupling, since [the Shape] remains in his place.

This is the inner meaning of *Every berekh shall bend to you.*[41] *Berekh* is the Root, for whereas in the God of Israel everything involves the letter

31. The Spot and the Shape that emerged from her are treated as equivalent. See the next sentence.

32. Free quotation of Hos 5:15.

33. Above, chapter 1, section 5.

34. That is, "God of Israel" is used in its broad sense to indicate the entire Shape, and not just the Shape's middle section or "heart" (above, section 1).

35. Deut 34:6, referring to Moses.

36. *Itkasya*; allusion to Sabbatai Zevi, who was said by his believers to be "concealed" after his death?

37. Gen 4:1, referring to Adam's having sex with Eve.

38. Song 8:6.

39. I.e., she/he enters into a deathlike, sexless state. "Shechinah" has earlier been used for the Spot (chapter 1, section 4), which can be equated with the Shape, and that is apparently the intention here. ("Her husband" = the Root.) Still, the sexualized language is surprising, given we are told in the same breath that there is no sex. I suspect the influence of the prior context in Zohar, I, 245a, where Song 8:6 is quoted and expounded.

40. The author anticipates what he will say in chapter 6, section 8, where the androgynous Shape becomes the male God of Israel, and its sexual connection with the Root explicitly homoerotic.

41. Isa 45:23, as paraphrased in the Jewish liturgy. *Berekh* is normally translated "knee."

vav and he is therefore *barukh*, "blessed," at the higher level the proper term is *berekh*;[42] while "bending" is known to be the male's copulating with the female (as in the 31st chapter of Job, *Let others bend upon her*).[43] Thus *every berekh*—i.e., the Root, named for the supernal pool[44]—*shall bend to you*, have sex with you, "bend" with you, come to you.[45]

This is implied by the verse *The Elohim seeks out the pursued*.[46] Consider well the Zoharic dictum that EVERYWHERE MALE PURSUES FEMALE, suggesting that the one who lusts is a "pursuer," chasing after another in his love, and the beloved is consequently the "pursued." So when the Root lusts for [the Shape], he meets him in [the latter's] place, and hence *the Elohim*, namely the Ein Sof,[47] *seeks out the pursued*, namely the God of Israel, "pursued" by him in his love.

[p. 30] You might object that this implies alteration in the Will, in that it sometimes arouses love and at other times hatred. You need not concern yourself. It was all part of Ein Sof's undifferentiated Will to respond thus to humans' actions at any given time, always in accordance with their conduct. When they comport themselves rightly they stir up desire, and also conversely. This was all the undifferentiated Will, to alter itself in accordance with human action so that all might recognize it as a righteous judge and adjudicator, untainted by corruption, acting not with indulgence but only strict justice. So it is written, *None can rescue from my hand*,[48] and anyone who speaks of God's "laxity," may

---

42. See above, section 1, for the idea that the letter *vav* is a distinctive property of the God of Israel. When this letter is subtracted from *barukh* ברוך, "blessed" (a habitual designation for the God of Israel), the word becomes *berekh* ברך, understood now to designate a higher level of divinity where the *vav* is not yet operative.

43. Job 31:10, where the sexual meaning is very clear.

44. *Berekhah*, from the same Hebrew root as *berekh*.

45. Perlmuter, *Rabbi Jonathan Eibeschuetz*, 301, cites a parallel from *Shem ʿOlam* (240–41) that expresses basically the same thought but without the heavily sexual imagery. In that passage, Eibeschuetz notes that what the Kabbalists call "complete unification and coupling" is called by the philosophers "contemplative awareness [by the lower entity] of its cause and occasion [the higher entity]"—that is, the same process of fusion, expressed in either sexual or intellectual language.

46. Eccl 3:15.

47. Strictly speaking, only the active "Will" component of Ein Sof. At the end of chapter 1, however, the entirety of Ein Sof is called *Elohim* (combined of *Elleh* + *Mi*), and the author follows that usage here. After his earlier use of *Elohim* for the distinctively female (above, notes 24 and 27) this feels inconsistent and confusing.

48. Isa 43:13.

*his guts turn lax!*⁴⁹ For in attributing laxity to him one wreaks havoc, leaving the problem⁵⁰ without resolution. This will be elucidated, God willing, more fully in what follows.

3. The Female Emerges

[So far, the Female in the stricter sense of the word has existed only as a potential within the Shape. For the construction of "worlds," it is necessary that the Female emerge as a discrete form, which the Root accomplishes through a second act of "coupling." (The first "coupling" was the Contraction that brought the Shape into existence.) The Root couples with the Shape and begets from it the Female, an event represented symbolically in the Bible story of the creation of Eve from Adam (Gen 2:21–23). The title "Higher Shechinah," originally applied to the Spot (above, chapter 1, section 4), now passes to this Female.

The author reflects on the consequent completion of the sacred name YHVH, the four letters of which point to different aspects of the Shape, among which the Female has now taken her place. He makes an observation which will have implications for his subsequent argument: if ʿAttiqa, "the Distant One," is represented by the "head" of the Shape, the Shape's hidden Root is represented by the "hairs," from which the Shape grows downward like an inverted tree.]

Up to this point—resuming our exposition—that Spot or Shape still had its Female incorporated within it. Now, the building of worlds can in no way be properly effected other than through the Female; without the Female it has the quality of uncontained ejaculate,⁵¹ requiring her for its full shaping and for its regularity and measure. (Thus she is called "measuring line" [fol. 6b], as we shall see presently.) Therefore the Root, i.e. the Will in its ten aspects, said that *it is not good for Adam to be alone.*⁵²

---

49. *Genesis Rabbah* 67:4; cf. Talmud, b. B. Qam. 50a.
50. Of capricious alteration of the Will.
51. *Zeraʿ le-vattalah*, literally "wasted seed," a rabbinic expression for semen ejaculated other than into its appropriate receptacle inside a woman. The author's concern throughout this treatise, however, is not with the "waste" of the semen but with its chaotic and dangerous potency, which it is the female's function to contain, restrain, keep within appropriate bounds.
52. Gen 2:18. Adam ("human") is understood as symbolizing the Shape, while the "God" of the Genesis story is the Will/Root. The author will develop this symbolism

What did [the Root] do? He came to him and coupled with him in a state of "Deep Sleep," casting "Deep Sleep" upon the human[53] at the start of his copulation. He had sex with him in a condition of "Deep Sleep" on account of the intense illumination that flowed into him, as we have said.[54] This is the meaning of *the Lord God cast deep sleep upon the human*[55] and performed a full sex act with him. The sex completed, [the Shape] gave birth, sprouting and producing and bringing forth fruit. [p. 31] The Female, once concealed within his power and contained inside him, emerged to actual discrete existence and became his Female. So the Bible says, *He took one of his ribs*, and so forth; and the female aspect became a distinct entity, a female shape unto itself, with whom a male king might engage in sex.[56]

This is the process by which the Shechinah emerged from the God of Israel, through sex with the Root which is *Mi*, the Father.[57] It is the meaning of what the Zohar says in several places, that THE FATHER ESTABLISHED THE DAUGHTER;[58] the discerning reader must understand on his own. It is the meaning of the verse *Indeed she is my sister, daughter of my Father yet not of my mother*.[59] Understand.

Thus it is that all the kings of the Davidic line, who symbolize the Shechinah, have their origin from Moab, whose name hints at *me-av*, "from a Father":[60] she was in fact born of her Father.[61] This is why a Moabite woman is permitted in marriage in accordance with the supernal structure, the Shechinah having been born from him; while the Male

---

below, chapter 6, sections 6–7.

53. That is, the Shape.
54. Above, section 2.
55. Gen 2:21.
56. Possibly alluding to Zohar III, 66a, which speaks of sexual pleasure between the "king" and the "noble lady," the male and female aspects of divinity.
57. Above, chapter 1, section 5.
58. Zohar III, 258a (*Ra'ya Mehemna*), *Tiqqunei Zohar* 21 (61b), 69 (106b), expounding Prov 3:19.
59. Gen 20:12, spoken by Abraham of Sarah. The author takes it to mean that "Father" (the Root) has begotten the Female, not of any "mother" but of the very same Shape who is the Female's consort. See below, chapter 6, section 3.
60. Gen 19:37 traces the Moabite people to incestuous sex between Lot and his daughter; King David was descended from Ruth the Moabitess (Ruth 4:17–22).
61. Some mss. have "his Father," presumably referring to the Shape. The language is a bit confusing but the thought is clear: the Shechinah was born of a sex act between the "Father" and the Shape, which was itself the Father's offspring. The act of incest, discreditable in Gen 19, turns out to be a symbolic representation of divine necessity.

was not thus begotten and [Moabite] males are therefore forbidden, as contrary to the supernal structure.[62]

This [newly emerged] Shape constitutes the Higher Shechinah, for she is superior to all, all worlds being constructed from her; she is the *mother of all living*, sometimes designated "Leah."[63] Since she emerged from the second coupling,[64] which was through a process of Contraction—for all coupling occurs through Contraction and arousal—the Shechinah is actualized to a degree beyond that of the God of Israel. She is therefore called "tool" and ascribed the quality of "dream," meaning strength (as the Bible says, *Strengthen and vivify me*).[65]

The Name [YHVH] was now complete. The "head," Holy Distant One, is represented by YH, *yod-hei*. The hook of the *yod* indicates the Ein Sof, the Root and its extension,[66] imperceptible except through that hook. At times it is designated "Supernal Crown,"[67] and this is what the Zohar means when it says that *Keter* is essentially Ein Sof.

If that "head" comprises *yod-hei*, then the "heart" aspect, constituting the God of Israel, is represented by the *vav*, which is the extension of the "Straight Line."[68] The final *hei* [of YHVH] represents the Female.

[p. 32] When we visualize the Shape in this manner, with the "head" indicating the Distant One, then the Root with its extension is indicated by the hairs on that head, dividing and extending themselves

---

62. Deut 23:4, forbidding intermarriage with Moabites, is interpreted in rabbinic sources as referring only to Moabite males, Moabite women (like Ruth) being entirely acceptable upon conversion to Judaism. See Mishnah, m. Yebam. 8:3; Talmud, b. Yebam. 76b–77a.

63. The author redefines his symbolism: "mother of all living" (Gen 3:20) was earlier applied to the primordial Spot, which had been called "Shechinah" (above, chapter 1, section 4), while "Leah" was the passive substrate of Ein Sof (chapter 1, section 5).

64. Of the Root with the Shape. The first "coupling" was the Contraction that made the Spot into an androgynous Shape, which was thereby brought into existence.

65. Isa 38:16, which suggests that *tahalimeni*, from the same root as *halom* ("dream"), is to be understood as "strengthen me." Hence "dream," already associated with the female (above, section 2), can be understood as "strength," i.e., the solidity of her superior actualization.

66. That is, the Will that extends itself throughout the Ein Sof.

67. *Keter 'elyon*, usually called just *Keter*, the highest of the *sefirot*. In the traditional Kabbalah, the hook at the top of the *yod* indicates *Keter*, while the *yod* itself is the second *sefirah*, *Hokhmah*. The Sabbatians never tired of pointing out that the phrase *koah keter 'elyon*, "power of the Supernal Crown," has the same numerical value (814) as "Sabbatai Zevi."

68. *Qav ha-yosher*; see below, chapter 5, note 8. The Hebrew letter *vav* (ו) has the shape of a vertical line.

in all directions and serving as its roots. You may see in a tree when it is cut that its roots are like hair; and so it is with a human being, that his roots are above and he grows downward. That is why "hair" is its designation; and why the Bible says that *the Lord's path is to the End is through the hair*,[69] meaning that his path takes him to the "end of the ranks," which the Bible calls "End," and that these [ranks] are represented as "hair." It is also the sense of *the Ancients grasped the hair*.[70] For these "Ancients" are the Distant One and the God of Israel, and they "grasp" and are grasped within this hair, the "hairs" that are not revealed even to the smallest extent, *hidden among the ranks*.[71]

4. An Alternative Anatomy: If Ein Sof Could Be Part...

> [The author now suggests, parenthetically, an alternative anatomy that might be possible, if the premise were granted that Ein Sof might have bodily shape. The Root would then be the "head" of that shape, the Distant One its "trunk," and the God of Israel its sex organ. However, the Shechinah's status as perpetual sex partner for the God of Israel and his genital would, in this arrangement, remain unchanged.]

But suppose we were to speak of Ein Sof as though (*per impossibile*)[72] it had bodily form, starting out by treating this Root as a shape. The Root would then function as "head," the "Head That Is Unknown,"[73] consisting of *Keter-Hokhmah-Binah*[74] and represented as YH, *yod-hei*. The Bible hints at this when it says that *the Lord shaped the worlds through yod-hei*:[75] there all the worlds were given shape, for [the Root] is the Will's

---

69. Nah 1:3, the words *sufah* and *se'arah*—in their Biblical context certainly referring to the "storm-wind"—taken as *sof*, "end," and *se'ar*, "hair." On *sof* as "end of the ranks" (or "rungs"), see above, chapter 1, note 90.

70. Job 18:20.

71. Song 2:14.

72. *Ki-ve-yakhol*, literally "as though it were possible," a rabbinic phrase sprinkled throughout this treatise to soften the blow of particularly shocking ideas. Normally I understand it as homage to conventional piety and leave it untranslated. But here the author seems really to mean it. Ein Sof *cannot* be thought of as partaking of bodily form; yet suppose we imagine that it *might*; what would the consequences be?

73. *Resha de-la ityeda'*, used in the Zohar's *Idra Zuta* (III, 289a–b) to designate the head of 'Attiqa.

74. The triad of highest *sefirot*.

75. Isa 26:4, following the midrashic tradition of reading *tzur* ("rock") as though it were *tzar* ("he shaped"); *Genesis Rabbah* 12:10.

extension in its ten aspects, containing all the worlds in potential. The Holy Distant One functions as *Tif'eret*[76] in relation to it, while the God of Israel serves as Ein Sof's *Yesod*, its genital organ. This is why all the effluence comes forth from him.

The Shechinah receives from him. All worlds are nourished by him, for he is the one who "allots grain"[77] to them all. There is no need to expand on this, for the power of *Yesod*, the genital, is familiar throughout the Zohar. It gives life to everything; it is called "vitality of the worlds."[78] It purifies Graces and Judgments by means of the two apertures [fol. 7a] of the penis, for urine and semen. [p. 33] This is why [the God of Israel] is called *bara*:[79]—apart from his being revealed (as in *go out and teach bara, outdoors*),[80] *bara* is also an anagram for *ever*, "membrum," alluding to *Yesod*.

This is why the Zohar says several times, WE TREAT THE BODY AND THE SEX ORGAN AS ONE,[81] inasmuch as within the bodily form of Ein Sof, [the God of Israel] is the body for the sexual organ and also, as the letter *vav*, the organ itself.[82] Hence the majority of *Tif'eret*'s appellations are applied also to *Yesod*, for, if Ein Sof is granted a bodily form, he will be that form's *Yesod*. Thus the Bible says, *The Lord is Righteous*,[83] giving "the Lord," which designates the God of Israel, the title *Tzaddiq*, "Righteous," whereas *Tzaddiq is the world's Yesod*.[84]

---

76. The *sefirah* marking the trunk of the divine body, which would normally be connected with the God of Israel.

77. Alluding to Gen 42:6, which speaks of Joseph, the Biblical representation of the *sefirah Yesod*.

78. I am indebted to Daniel Matt for this translation of *hei ha-'olamim*.

79. *Bara* ("Son") and *bara qaddisha* ("Holy Son") are Zoharic appellations for *Tif'eret*. The author gives the word *bara* two entirely different etymologies, connecting it not with *Tif'eret* but *Yesod*.

80. A Talmudic phrase (e.g., b. Shabb. 106a) which our author uses as lexical support for connecting *bara* with the "revealed," exoteric character of the God of Israel, as opposed to the "concealed" Holy Distant One.

81. E.g., III, 283a (*Raya Mehemna*).

82. If the Ancient One is the "head," as above, the God of Israel is the "body." If the Root is the "head," as here, the God of Israel is the sexual organ. The author emphasizes the phallic shape of the letter *vav* (ו), with which the God of Israel is associated.

83. Ps 11:7.

84. Prov 10:25, normally understood as "the righteous is an everlasting foundation." This is a standard Kabbalistic proof-text for the use of *Tzaddiq*, "Righteous," as an epithet for the *sefirah Yesod*. The author's point is that the God of Israel = *Tzaddiq* = *Yesod*; therefore the God of Israel can, as in this "alternative anatomy," function as *Yesod*.

But the Shechinah remains in the position of *Malkhut*, the final *hei* [of YHVH].[85] *I am the Lord; I do not change*, says the Bible,[86] meaning that she is ever the Female, her rank immutable, perpetual sex partner for the God of Israel and his *Yesod*. These are the two "Righteous Ones": the God of Israel, the higher "Righteous," vis-à-vis the bodily form of Ein Sof; and *Yesod*, the lower "Righteous," vis-à-vis the bodily form of the God of Israel.[87] When the Bible says, *The Righteous Ones shall inherit the Land*, and the Zohar explains this to mean TWO RIGHTEOUS ONES, THE HIGHER "RIGHTEOUS" AND THE LOWER "RIGHTEOUS,"[88] the intention is as I have said. Understand.

5. Grace, Judgment, and the secret of Esau

[Existence as we know it requires differentiation and boundedness, which are properties of Judgment. It follows that, as the cosmic evolution (or devolution) progresses, Judgment tends to predominate over Grace. This contrast, between the primordial Grace-fulness of the Root and the "worlds" devolved from it, is mirrored in the human body in the contrast between the body hairs (predominantly Judgment) and those of the head (Grace and Judgment mingled).

This will explain what the Bible says about Jacob's brother Esau, and by implication about the Christianity for which Esau is the symbolic representation. Esau's head is holy, his equally hairy body unholy. His body hairs—representing historical Christianity, as opposed to the ideal Christianity of the head—are bent on "destruction and shattering." But in that concealed "head," which connects Esau to the Distant One—and thus, as will emerge, marks Christianity in its ideal form as superior to Judaism—Esau is the "brother" whom the Jews are forbidden to "loathe" (Deut 23:9).]

---

85. Although in this "alternative anatomy" the Distant One has become *Tif'eret* and the God of Israel demoted from *Tif'eret* to *Yesod*, the Shechinah remains exactly as she was in section 3.

86. Mal 3:6. *Ani*, "I," is understood in the Zohar to refer specifically to the Shechinah, and the author draws the inspiration for his exegesis from Zohar, III, 281a (*Ra'ya Mehemna*).

87. "God of Israel" used in its more inclusive sense to designate the Shape.

88. Ps 37:29; Zohar, I, 153b. "Land" is a common Kabbalistic designation for the Shechinah.

Once the shape and "tool" that is the Female had emerged, [the Shape] could be called a complete Human. He is known to represent the Name of Forty-five,[89] being "of-the-Path-of-Emanation" as we shall presently see.[90] Therefore he is called "Human," a name with the numerical value of 45: "YHVH" is 26; the Shechinah is symbolized by "Eve," who is 19, adding up to 45, "Human."[91]

[p. 34] He[92] occupies the entire place of the Spot, "the place of the world." This was the intent of the undifferentiated Will, since a world could not have been constructed in that place[93] on account of the intensity of its light and the unlimited extension of its Graces. In relation to the Root it [the Spot] was Judgment and Contraction, yet in relation to the worlds it was still an extension of the Mercies, without any space suitable for world-building or any design. This was particularly so, in that within the form of that Spot the Graces and Judgments were not yet recognizable, persisting in a state of admixture.

Know that when Graces and Judgments are mixed, upon extending themselves downward the Judgments are bound to gain the upper hand. The reason is that as they descend, they emerge increasingly from potentiality into actuality, and by its nature actuality partakes of Judgment when set against potentiality. So all through that process of descent the Judgments grow ever stronger and more powerful, while Mercies steadily diminish. The Judgments were thus bound to triumph over the Graces, had the Balance not been fashioned to keep Judgment

---

89. One of the four *millu'im* of the name YHVH, a *millui* being a numerical computation based on the full spelling of all the letters of the word in question. The letters of YHVH are *yod-hei-vav-hei*, which can be spelled in such a way (יוד הא ואו הא) that the grand total of the values of the letter-names comes to 45. (Computed without *millu'im*, the numerical value of YHVH is 26, as the author will soon note.) In the Lurianic Kabbalah the "Name of Forty-five" is associated with the divine aspect called Little-face (*Ze'ir Anpin*), more or less equivalent to the *sefirah Tif'eret* of the older Kabbalah and the "God of Israel" of our author's system. *Adam*, "human," also has the numerical value of 45.

90. "Human of the Path of Emanation," more concisely referred to as "Emanation-Human," will become an important figure later in the treatise. Here he is identified as the Shape.

91. The female (19, the numerical value of the name "Eve") now stands side by side with YHVH (26), now understood specifically as the male component of the Shape. The two together are the "Human" (45).

92. The Shape, now differentiated like the once-androgynous Adam into male and female.

93. The Spot as it was originally, prior to the operations described in this chapter.

by itself and Grace by itself, each in its own vessel, with a "center-bar" and a single channel effecting their mixture.[94]

This is the significance of *the Noble cannot be recognized in the presence of the Poor*.[95] *Shoa'*, "the Noble," is Mercy (as in *the base shall not be called noble*,[96] for "noble" means "generous," which is a quality of Abraham and of pure Mercy, as our sages interpret *generous man's daughter* as "daughter of Father Abraham"[97]). *Dal*, "the Poor," is Judgment (as in "those poor [*dallat*] in silver"[98]).

So in that Root comprising ten aspects, where no solid structure[99] or balance has been enacted, Graces and Judgments are commingled. This is hinted at in the words, *the dallat of your head*—*dallat* meaning the tips of the hairs, with overtones of *dal*, Judgment—*is like purple*,[100] combining the qualities of Judgment and Mercy; for *purple* represents *Tif'eret*, composed of Judgment and Grace.[101] [p. 35] While they were in the higher realm, the place of the Root, they were still Mercy. But as they stretch downward and become manifest, Judgments predominate.

94. The "Balance" (*matqela*) appears in the Zohar's cryptic (and appropriately titled) *Book of Concealment*: "... until there was a balance, they did not gaze face-to-face, and the primordial kings died... This balance hangs in a place that is not; weighed upon it were those who did not exist. The balance stands on its own, ungrasped and unseen. Upon it rose and upon it rise those who were not, and who were, and who will be" (Zohar, II, 176b, trans. Matt, *Zohar*; we shall presently hear much more about the death of the "primordial kings"). In the Zohar the "balancing" seems to be of male and female; our author understands it as Judgment and Grace. "Center-bar," from Exod 26:28, 36:33, is used in the Zohar of the *sefirah Tif'eret*, which mediates between and synthesizes the opposing attributes of Grace (the *sefirah Hesed*) and Judgment (the *sefirah Gevurah*); e.g., I, 148b (*Sitrei Torah*).

95. Job 34:19.

96. Isa 32:5.

97. Song 7:2, so interpreted in the Talmud, b. Sukkah 49b. In the Kabbalah, Abraham is the embodiment of the *sefirah Hesed*, the divine Grace. So "noble" = "generous" = Abraham = the divine attribute of Mercy.

98. The phrase *dallat ha-kesef* occurs nowhere in the Bible; perhaps the author is thinking of *dallat ('am) ha-aretz*, "the poor of (the people of) the land," 2 Kgs 24:14, 25:12. He presumably intends the Kabbalistic symbolism of silver = Grace; "those poor in silver" are the Judgments, lacking in Grace.

99. *Tiqqun*, a pivotal and multivalent term whose basic meaning is "mending" or "repair." I translate each occurrence according to context.

100. Song 7:6, the preceding words of which ("your head is like *karmel*") were interpreted in chapter 1, section 4, to speak of the mingling of Graces and Judgments. Now the author expands his understanding of the verse in accordance with his new insight into the meaning of *dal(lat)*.

101. Cf. above, chapter 2, note 94. The "purple" = *Tif'eret* equation comes from the Zohar.

For this reason the Zohar warns that hair must be concealed and not exposed, and in this is a profound mystery. The "head" is still part of the "concealed," as stated above and in accordance with the *Idra* in the Zohar, where one uses the pronoun "he" in the place of concealment to designate the Distant One,[102] who is still part of Ein Sof. His hairs are still in a state of admixture; yet they grant proper warmth to that "head," essential for the Shape's maintenance, as the natural philosophers are well aware.

The hairs of the body, by contrast, are exposed. Therefore the Judgments are bound to dominate and cause destruction and shattering—as happened during the Shattering of the Vessels,[103] when there was no Balance as we shall later see. [Fol. 7b] *The Noble cannot be recognized in the presence of the Poor*, as we have said; and wherever these hairs proceed downward, Judgments predominate, becoming increasingly exposed and destructive. (Exceptions: the beard and pubic hairs, which have the character of adornments generated by the "heart."[104]) This is why demons are hairy on the legs, where Judgments are most predominant.

From this you may grasp the nature of Esau.[105]

If his hair had been on his head alone, he would have been within Holiness. But inasmuch as his hair covered his entire body, the Judgments were predominant, thirsting entirely for destruction and shattering. So

---

102. Zohar, III, 290a (*Idra Zuta*): "The Holy Distant One, who is concealed, is called 'he.'" The language suggests the influence also of Zohar, I, 154b: "higher world, Jubilee, we call הוא (*Hu*), He, since all its matters are concealed" (trans. Matt, *Zohar*, who comments: "The third-person pronoun indicates *Binah*, who, being concealed, can be referred to only indirectly"). The author's reason for making this point is not yet apparent. It will become dramatically clear at the end of this section.

103. The primordial catastrophe in Lurianic Kabbalah, hinted at in the Zoharic references to the "death of the kings" (above, chapter 2, note 94). The author normally attributes the "Shattering" to the unrestrained potency of Grace, not of Judgment. He courts this inconsistency in the interest of what he wants to say here about the nature of "Esau."

104. I am not sure of the meaning of this sentence.

105. The Biblical name "Esau" (or "Edom") is used in medieval and early modern Jewish writing to represent Christianity and Christendom, and what the author is about to say about "the nature of Esau" (*sod 'esav*, literally "the secret of Esau") is an overture to his esoteric theology of Christianity, one of the core themes of his treatise. In what follows, he distinguishes between the visible ("exposed") Christianity—historical Christianity, experienced as harshly judgmental—and an invisible ("concealed") Christianity, a metaphysical entity of pure Grace, associated with the Holy Distant One and thus not only cognate to Judaism but actually superior. This extraordinary theory will unfold as we proceed.

the Bible says: *He came out all as a mantle of hair, ruddy-colored*,[106] meaning that Judgment and Mercy were mixed together without any Balance. That was why he was called "Esau," an anagram for *shoaʻ*, "Noble"; and, in its character as "reflected light," every anagram is Judgment.[107]

Isaac's whole purpose was for Mercy to master Judgment, and he therefore tried to bless [Esau] to *be lord over your brothers*,[108] meaning that the Mercies should dominate. *May your mother's sons bow down to you*—meaning the Judgments, whose nature is that of the female from whom all Judgments are aroused.[109] But the truth is that Isaac himself partook of the nature of Judgment,[110] and therefore lacked the ability to empower the Graces. Hence Jacob's need for trickery.

[p. 36] Jacob was *a smooth man*,[111] yet he did have hair on his head, for there it was in a state of concealment as has been said. That was why Esau's head was in Holiness and why Isaac *ate of his game*,[112] for he sensed holiness in that head. Luria tells us, accordingly, that Esau's head was buried with Jacob in the Cave of Machpelah, for that head was in Holiness.[113]

It has already been explained that "head" is a representation of the Distant One and is called "he."[114] This is the meaning of the verse *You must*

---

106. Gen 25:25, with some change in the word order.

107. "Reflected light" is a technical term drawn from the sixteenth-century Kabbalah of Moses Cordovero (*Pardes Rimmonim*, part 15; Scholem, *Kabbalah*, 115–16; Ben-Shlomo, *Mystical Theology*, 268–74). The upper *sefirot* shine masculine "direct light" (*or yashar*) upon the lower, who mirror it back up to them in weakened, feminine form as "reflected light" (*or hozer*). Since reflected light is a reversal of direct light—the light ray going backward, so to speak—its linguistic correlate will be the reversal or rearrangement of the letters of a Hebrew word, and the consequent change in its meaning. Thus, Esau's name is composed of the letters for "Mercy"—the anagram of *shoaʻ* and "Esau" works in Hebrew script, though not in transliteration. Yet the fact of their rearrangement puts them under the rubric of "reflected light," which by its nature is Judgment, and thereby contaminates the Mercy inherent in the word.

108. Gen 27:29, which Isaac spoke to Jacob presuming him to be Esau. The fact that Esau had only one brother encourages an understanding of "your brothers . . . your mother's sons" as allegorical.

109. This "female nature" being "your mother." Somewhat surprisingly, the Kabbalah takes Grace to be an essentially male trait, Judgment essentially female.

110. In Kabbalah, Isaac is the embodiment of *Gevurah*, the *sefirah* of strict Judgment.

111. Gen 27:11.

112. Gen 25:27.

113. Cf. Ginzberg, *Legends*, 2:154.

114. Above, note 102. The use of "head" in this passage will be reprised in the very

not loathe an Edomite for he is your brother.[115] "He" is used deliberately, precisely: *there* he is your brother, not in the rest of his body.[116] We know that when the Judgments prevail over Mercies, there are two drops of Judgment and one of Mercy; therefore *their third generation may enter into the congregation of the Lord.* For this same reason the Levites, representing Judgment, are required to shave their heads.[117] Understand.

---

last paragraph of the treatise, where the full mystery of Sabbatai Zevi's apostasy will be unveiled.

115. Deut 23:8.

116. In its invisible yet essential character, as opposed to its unattractive historical manifestation, Christianity is Judaism's "brother." The pronoun "he," as observed in note 102, conveys the "concealment" of this Christianity. The quote from Deut 23:9 that follows is a first hint at the universality of the author's Grace-based faith.

117. At the inauguration of the Levitic order in the wilderness (Num 8:7, Mishnah, m. Neg. 14:4). The association of the Levites with Judgment (the *sefirah Gevurah*) is standard Kabbalistic doctrine. The incongruous use of the present tense, however, may suggest a covert allusion to Catholic monks, called in Hebrew *gallahim*, "shaven-headed ones."

3

The Gestation of God

1. Another Contraction: The Self-Folding

[The male Shape, from which the Female has emerged as a discrete entity (chapter 2, section 3), folds himself up and enters her womb. The purpose of this is partly, as we learn in section 6, to filter out the traces of darkness with which the Shape is contaminated. But more significantly, as we are told right now, its aim is to restructure divinity as a system of vessels and "Interiorities," the former protecting but also concealing the latter as our essences are protected yet concealed by our skin and flesh.

The Shape thus becomes, fetus-like, in essence its "head," its "body" folded up around it. The Female (Shechinah), who will later become the male Shape's sex partner, now is his placenta (or perhaps embryonic sac), conveying nourishment to him from the Root while "sheltering him from the expansion of the Graces so that they not wash him away and obliterate him as a Shape."

(The destructive potential of Grace is a recurring theme in this treatise. If the cosmic evolution moves toward increasing definition, which is a function of Judgment, there is an ever-present threat that the overwhelming power of Grace may erase the process.)]

This is the reason—resuming our exposition[1]—why that Spot needed to have the quality of Balance, and why the "heart" needed to be in

---

1. Referring back to chapter 2, section 5: the Graces and Judgments were promiscuously mixed together in the Spot, so that, upon their extension downward, the

place, controlling the blood temperature (i.e., the effluence) so it would be neither hot nor moist.[2] When the heart functions properly, the head also can better function, since the heart draws into itself all the moisture and heat from the head, regulates them and sends them back, as the natural philosophers well know.

Furthermore, the worlds needed to be built as vessels and "Interiorities" (as the Bible says, *You clothe it with skin and flesh*).[3] This would not have been possible if the form of that Spot were not to undergo Contraction, and all that [the Root] emanated of its glory were to persist as Interiority. There were many other reasons as well, in Ein Sof's undifferentiated Will, why worlds could not exist within this form. And so he willed a Contraction that took the form of Self-folding.[4]

You may consult what Luria has written about the Shattering of the Vessels having been essentially an act of Self-folding, and his detailed account of how this Self-folding came to be and how, after the Self-folding, the Curtain was made. [p. 37] We need only say that when [Ein Sof] began to enact this improvement, he made within the Spot a Contraction and Self-folding, such that its entire form[5] was made into a sort of knot, all the body's limbs bound into one and subsumed under the category of "head," for all the body was folded around the head and made into a single aspect—head, heart, and all the limbs as one.

To understand this, take the concrete image of a fetus in the mother's womb, as described by Rabbi Simlai.[6] *To what may the fetus be compared? To a folded-up slate.* You will see from this passage that it is all one knot, all essentially the head, with the entire body ranged around it. So it was here, [the Shape] still in a kind of maternal womb, for prior to the

---

Judgments were bound to gain the upper hand and squeeze out the Graces—if not for the Balance.

2. In the Galenic theory of the four "humors," which was still accepted medical wisdom in the time when *Va-avo ha-Yom* was written, warmth and moisture are the natural properties of the blood. The author presumably means that these qualities are to be regulated so they are not present in excess.

3. Job 10:11, slightly altered. This is the author's first hint of a duality that will presently become central to his thinking, of "Interiority" (*penimiyut*) vs. "Enclothement" (*hitlabbeshut*): the "interior" divine entities, with which he has been exclusively concerned so far, require "enclothement" in lesser vessels that both protect and conceal them, as you and I require "enclothement" in skin and flesh to survive.

4. *Hitqappelut*.

5. That is, the Shape along with its now-distinct Female, who is presently to be made into the placenta for the male fetus.

6. In the Talmud, b. Nid. 30b, from which the following quotations are taken.

Contraction there was no *Tehiru*[7] and the "air" was not perceptible, as we know. For "air" alludes to the *Tehiru*, and the time before the Contraction was like the time before [the fetus] *goes out into the air of the world*, while it is still *Folded up* and all of it part of the head.

This is the deeper meaning of *The fetus may be compared to Mah* ["to what"]: it may be compared to *Mah*, "45," the Path of Emanation, which is the Shape described above.[8] It is the deeper meaning of, *Mi* ["who"] *will set me in the primordial months*,[9] *Mi* being the Root, which enacted all this and was the one who set me *in the primordial months*, which are the state of gestation as the Gemara says. The specific image of *a folded-up slate* is used to make allusion to *the heavens rolled up like a scroll*.[10] For it is known that "heaven" is symbolic of *Tif'eret* and the body,[11] which is rolled up *like a scroll*, all together. Hence *a folded-up slate* is specified; understand.

The Shechinah[12] surrounded it, enclosing it like a curtain, functioning as a *shilyah*, its placenta.[13] The *shil* part of the word is derived from *shelilah*, "negation," for it is denied participation in the name *Yah* [YH, *yod-hei*] as we have seen, for the Shape, vis-à-vis the extension and the

---

7. The *Tehiru*—variously rendered in the manuscripts as *Tehira* or *Tihra*—is one of the strangest and most paradoxical elements of our treatise. Its literal meaning is "purity"; in the Zohar it comes to mean "splendor," as in I, 15a, where *tehiru illa'ah* means "supernal splendor" (or "luster on high," as Matt translates it). In the Lurianic Kabbalah it comes to be the space left by Ein Sof's self-Contraction, sometimes equated with the *reshimu* (below), the light that remained behind. For Nathan of Gaza, who deeply influenced the thought of *Va-avo ha-Yom*, it takes on a demonic significance: the *Tehiru* is the abyss, dominated by the Mindless Light, which must be tamed and "mended" by the Messiah. So in Nathan's writings, as in this treatise, the "supernal purity" has become precisely the locus of impurity and demoniality, the place requiring purification.

8. Beginning of chapter 2, section 5. *Mah*, the Hebrew word for "what," has the numerical value of 45.

9. Job 29:2, quoted in Niddah 30b. The Root, the active component of Ein Sof, is equated with *Mi* ("Who") in chapter 1, section 5.

10. Isa 34:4.

11. *Tif'eret* is the central male *sefirah* of the sefirotic system, envisioned as the trunk of the divine body. Although the *sefirot* as such do not yet exist, the name is here applied to the "body" ("God of Israel") aspect of the Shape. *Tif'eret*'s equation with "heaven" (corresponding to Shechinah/*Malkhut* = "earth") is a staple of the traditional Kabbalah.

12. The "Higher Shechinah" described in chapter 2, section 3.

13. So it seems best to translate *shilyah*, in accordance with Biblical (Deut 28:57) and rabbinic usage, although the author may possibly have conflated it in his mind with the amniotic sac. His image of it as enveloping the fetus is perhaps influenced by the midrash (*Leviticus Rabbah* 14:4), which interprets the "garment" and "swaddling-band" of Job 38:9 as the sac (*shafir*) and placenta (*shilya*) respectively.

Root, has the character of *hei* alone, and the Root itself is the *yod*.[14] So it is called *shil-Yah*, "excluded from YH," and it enfolds the Shape which now has the aspect of "head," [p. 38] having the quality of a child.

This is what is written in Job: *The seal becomes like a homer,* [fol. 8a] *standing erect like a garment.*[15] The word *homer* has the sense of "gathering," as in *homarta de-filon,* "a cluster of balsam," or "expounding *ke-min homer,* as a sort of cluster," meaning a "gathering together" of spices or anything else;[16] or as in *homarim homarim,* "heaps and heaps,"[17] and *homer,* "heap," *of many waters.*[18] As for *seal,* everyone knows this represents the God of Israel, that is to say *Tif'eret* (as the Zohar interprets *all who call upon him in truth* as referring to THE SEAL OF THE KING'S SIGNET-RING, while in the Gemara *the seal of the Blessed Holy One is truth*).[19]

So what the verse intends to say is this: that the seal becomes erect-standing like "a gathering," its parts cleaving together so *they stand erect like a garment,* this last word referring to the Shechinah which "clothes" him like the placenta and which partakes of the nature of clothing, as we well know. (Thus the Bible: *He clothes himself in righteousness.*[20])

Homer, moreover, is an anagram for *rehem,* "womb," he having been at the time as though in his mother's womb. The natural philosophers write, as is well known, that the placenta shelters the fetus, protecting it from being harmed by excessive heat or excessive blood. The placenta gathers everything to the fetus, which is nourished from it (say the philosophers) as though a nipple extends from the placenta to the fetus's navel in the form of a thick vein. This is what is meant by *its navel is*

---

14. And the Shechinah, now distinct from the male Shape it encloses, is neither. The pairing of "extension" and "Root" is imprecise, for the "extension" of the Will throughout Ein Sof *is* the "Root." The interpretation given here of the letters *yod* and *hei* is inconsistent with those in chapter 2, sections 3 and 4.

15. Job 38:14. Cf. the very different but cognate interpretation of this verse in chapter 9, end of section 1.

16. Talmud, b. Shabb. 62a and Git. 69b, Qidd. 22b and Sotah 15a, following Rashi to Shabbat and Qiddushin.

17. Inexact quotation of Judg 15:16. Having established the meaning of *homer* from Talmudic usage, the author proceeds to Biblical.

18. Hab 3:15.

19. Zohar, III, 297a, quoting Ps 145:18; Talmud, b. Shabb. 55a, Yoma 69b, Sanh. 64a. *Emet,* "truth," is a standard Kabbalistic epithet for *Tif'eret.*

20. Isa 59:17; "righteousness" is Kabbalistic code for the Shechinah.

open,²¹ and it "eats" from what its mother eats, for the placenta functions as a mother from whom the navel sucks.

The Shechinah is called "measuring line,"²² sheltering him from the expansion of the Graces so that they not wash him away and obliterate him as a Shape. That is why she receives everything from the Root and through her the embryo is nourished, and why she is called "placenta" in her role as a mother. The Bible hints at this: *A bundle of myrrh is my beloved to me, he shall lodge between my breasts*,²³ meaning that my beloved is a spice-cluster of the sort that might be called *homer* as above. *Between my breasts he shall lodge*, lodging there, sucking nourishment from between the breasts. The same is implied in the verse *Lodging in a secret place, in the protection of my breasts*;²⁴ understand.

2. *Tehiru* and "Insolent Waters"

> [When the Shape enters the womb, it leaves behind a space called *Tehiru*, within which a trace of its light remains. This light is a mingling of Mindful and Mindless Light, the latter yearning to merge once more with its source in Ein Sof and thereby to nullify the process of creation. The Mindful Light, by contrast, remains conscious of its role in creation, and seeks to maintain it.
>
> The clash of the two Lights produces an infinity of circles, the spinning "wheels" of the Hebrew alphabet, which are also the vessels in which the "Interiorities" will eventually be housed. This preliminary stage of the sefirotic system's emergence is what the Talmud calls *Ma'aseh Bereshit*, a preliminary sketch for the eventual full system that the Talmud calls *Ma'aseh Merkavah*. But with this inchoate structure an enduring antistructure also comes into being: the "Insolent Waters" of Ps 124:5, which will continue to surround and menace "the structure of the Merkavah."]

[p. 39] Now, when the Contraction²⁵ took place, the *Tehiru* or "internal air" came into being in the place where his body had stood. (This is

---

21. From Rabbi Simlai's description of the fetus in the Talmud, b. Nid. 30b, quoted above: its mouth is closed, its navel open.

22. See the beginning of chapter 2, section 3.

23. Song 1:13.

24. Ps 91:1. *Shaddai*, normally translated "the Almighty," is here understood as "my breasts."

25. Referring to the "Self-folding," while "his body" refers to the Shape that has

the *Tehiru* mentioned in Luria and in the Zohar.) "The Shechinah does not budge from its place without leaving a mark,"[26] and thus a light or imprint of that form remained in this *Tehiru*. This light was conscious of its own lack, of the departure of its light,[27] and therefore strove to go downward, upward, to reunite with its source. Know that this imprint contained the light that extended itself without any colors,[28] and it was this that sought to couple with its source and return everything to chaos. But there was also an imprint of the light that had extended itself *with* colors, namely the Mindful Light, and this was not in such a hurry to reverse its course, for it bore within itself the Root's intention to remain in a place of world-building.

And so the lights became mixed in a confused tangle, spawning an infinite multitude of circles and a number of alphabetic combinations and wheels, each one following a crooked path. This produced circles beyond counting, in all sorts of combinations and combinations of letters.[29] This was the essence of *Ma'aseh Bereshit*, "the Work of Creation": circles and combinations of this sort, made in the initial stage before the "straight line" was extended.[30] From these circles the vessels for the *sefirot* were made—for we know that any light near Ein Sof will move in its own circle, choosing its own individual path—and from this emerged the essence of the ten *sefirot*.

Call this the "sketch." Just as an artist will apply paint to his canvas as a sort of preliminary sketch that will later take on the shape of the portrait,

---

folded itself up in order to enter the Shechinah-womb. The space that remains after the folding is the *Tehiru*.

26. See above, chapter 1, note 71.

27. That is, the greater light of which it was a trace.

28. The Mindless Light, substrate of Ein Sof.

29. Reflecting the Kabbalistic doctrine, derived from the enigmatic ancient text called *Sefer Yetzirah* ("Book of Creation"), that the letters of the Hebrew alphabet not only possess tangible reality but were the building blocks of creation. The "wheels" are alphabet wheels, whose spinning yields all sorts of letter combinations.

30. The author here introduces the antithesis of *Ma'aseh Bereshit* and *Ma'aseh Merkavah* ("Work of Creation" and "Work of the Chariot"), which appear in the Talmud as designations of two esoteric and highly restricted studies, rooted in Gen 1 and Ezek 1 respectively. (See both Gemaras on Mishnah, m. Hag. 2:1). The author explains *Ma'aseh Bereshit* as designating to that which was made (*na'aseh*) in the "initial stage" (*be-reshit* in ms. Jerusalem 2491, *be-rishon* in the other mss.). *Merkavah*, though in its origin a reference to Ezekiel's "chariot," will presently be explained from another meaning of the root *rkv*, "to combine."

THE GESTATION OF GOD

before actually doing the portrait, just so here. These *sefirot* were made as a sketch, later to take on the structure of the Merkavah.

Know that *Hokhmah* and *Binah* were the key elements in this "sketching,"[31] and it was they that shaped all the *sefirot*, a vast multitude of circles. This is an additional sense of the verse *The Lord shaped the worlds through yod-hei:*[32] there [in those letters] all the worlds were sketched out, lacking only their Merkavah quality, for *yod-hei* refer to *Hokhmah* and *Binah*, shapers of it all.

In this *Ma'aseh Bereshit* all the 231 two-letter combinations came into being in their multitude of circles, one facing the other (*Albam* and the like), to which nearly the whole of *Sefer Yetzirah* is devoted.[33] [p. 40] The light of the *Reshimu*[34] was here present in the form of water, Judgments thoroughly mixed in with it; and the water therefore froze and became as it were frost and ice. Then, as the Judgments' heat [fol. 8b] gained the upper hand, these waters became savagely turbulent and came to be called "the Insolent Waters."[35]

---

31. These two *sefirot* were at once products of the *sefirah*-forming process and tools for its completion.

32. Isa 26:4; see above, chapter 2, note 75.

33. The 22 letters of the Hebrew alphabet are capable of generating 231 two-letter combinations (*aleph-bet, aleph-gimel, aleph-dalet* and so forth), with the second letter of each pair different from the first and at a later position in the alphabet from the first. The mysterious *Sefer Yetzirah* (2:4) speaks of these letter combinations as building blocks of reality: "Twenty-two basic letters fixed in the wheel in 231 gates, the wheel turning forward and backward.... How did [God] weigh them and transmute them? *Aleph* with each of the others and each of the others with *aleph*; *bet* with each of the others and each of the others with *bet*; and going backward, resulting in 231 gates." This image of alphabets in rotating "wheels" or "circles," letters facing each other and combining with one another, gave rise to the practice called *Temurah*, of interpreting Hebrew words by substituting one letter in a pair for its partner; e.g., replacing the first letter *aleph* with the twelfth letter *lamed*, the second letter *bet* with the thirteenth letter *mem*, and so forth. This specific technique is called *Albam* (אלב״ם), the acronym for *aleph-lamed-bet-mem* (Trachtenberg, *Jewish Magic*, 263–64). (In two mss., Oxford 976 and Jerusalem 2491, האלב״ם is followed by what appears to be an abbreviation, מרכ״ז. I do not know what this is supposed to mean.)

34. An Aramaic term used in Lurianic Kabbalah for the trace of light left behind at Ein Sof's self-Contraction (above, note 7). Our author uses it to designate the "imprint" of which he has earlier spoken.

35. Thus, without fanfare, the author introduces a soon-to-be-pivotal element of his cosmos: the "Insolent Waters" (language taken from Ps 124:5), the forces of chaos and destruction that continually menace the "structure of the Merkavah."

All this took place in this *Tehiru*; and it is self-evident that the light[36] should take the form of a circle like this ○, inasmuch as the Contraction at the Spot had a circular quality like the Ein Sof that surrounded it, from which the Contraction was made into circles.[37] No further detail is required, given that Luria has also written of the circular quality of the Contraction-Spot.

3. The Circle Made Square

[Now something happens inside the womb. The circular entity within pulls itself into a square, leaving four cavities between itself and the walls of the encompassing Ein Sof. What will come to be called "Creation-Human" (below, section 6) will make its home in the topmost of these spaces. The function of the other three is unknown and, at least for the present, unknowable.

The square then splits into two half-squares, rather like brackets with extended legs. The purpose of this splitting is to induce the Mindful Light to collect itself in one half-square, the Mindless Light in the other, and thus to thwart the Mindless Light's uncontrollable impulse to merge with its source—equated, confusingly, with the Shechinah-womb and the Shape contained within it—or, a new thought, to draw down upon itself light from these entities.

(The reader will note some inconsistency over whether the Lights are located outside the womb, in the *Tehiru* as in section 2, or within it as here.)]

All, then, was circular. Yet it was the will of the God of Israel (who had at the time the character of "Distant One," the Will of Ein Sof contained within him)[38] that the sides of the circle extend themselves[39] so that it be transformed from circle into square, like a square within a circle, thus:

36. Of the *Reshimu*.

37. For a detailed discussion of the text from here to the end of section 5, see Lefler, "'When They Came,'" 216–22; and cf. Wolfson, "*Malkhut Ein Sof*," 65–71.

38. "God of Israel" is used here in its original, broader sense of the Shape that had emerged within the Spot (above, chapter 1, note 67 and chapter 2, note 34). The Shape is now curled up in a fetal position, "all one knot, all essentially the head, with the entire body ranged around it" (above, section 1). The Distant One, and not the "God of Israel" in its narrower sense, is the Shape's "head," which therefore now characterizes the Shape as a whole.

39. From arcs into straight lines. The somewhat paradoxical result of this "extension" is a square that fits inside the circle, as the author's diagram makes clear.

THE GESTATION OF GOD

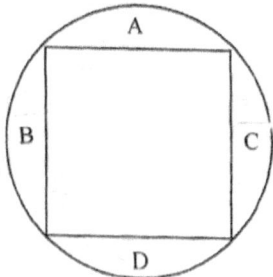

The sides of the circle, in other words, stretched themselves and drew near each other to transform into a square, withdrawing themselves from the walls of Ein Sof that surrounded them. Only their corners touched it.

And so they met together, drawing near each other, transforming themselves from a circle into a square. The entirety of the light-trace[40] shaped itself into a square, leaving four empty spaces beside the four walls—four gaps, perfectly void, between them and the Emanator.[41] In the uppermost of these empty spaces (the one marked A) the worlds were constructed in the character of "Primordial Creation-Human."[42] As for the remaining three spaces, we are in complete ignorance as to what they may have served and are not authorized to say anything about them.

These four spaces were what our sages of blessed memory had in mind when they spoke of *what is above and what below, what is before and what after*.[43] The head partakes of the quality of *before*-ness,[44] the right of *above*-ness, while the left side is the *below* side, as in the phrase "*below over against Grace.*"[45] The point opposite the *before* is the *after*. [p. 41]

---

40. *Roshem* (in all mss. except Oxford 955), the Hebrew equivalent of Aramaic *Reshimu*.

41. Ein Sof.

42. *Adam Qadmon di-Veri'ah*, a flawed entity who will appear again and again on the following pages; opposed to *Adam Qadmon da-Atzilut*, "Primordial Emanation-Human."

43. Mishnah, m. Hag. 2:1: "He who contemplates four things—what is above, what is below, what is before and what is after—it were a mercy for him if had not come into the world." The Talmudic passage quoted below is a comment on this mishnah.

44. *Panim*, "before," also means "face." The cavity marked with the A is evidently conceived as the "head," inasmuch as it is at the top of the diagram.

45. A Talmudic phrase, from b. Rosh Hash. 17a, conveying that where the scales of judgment are evenly balanced, God inclines (*matteh*) them in the direction of mercy. The author reads *matteh* as if it were *mattah*, "below," and takes the phrase to mean

But the *what is before* clause, speaking of the worlds currently being constructed in the quality of "Primordial Human," bars us only from speaking of the time prior to Primordial Human's construction.[46]

This is the point of the Gemara's question: *It makes sense* [that I should be prohibited from examining] *that which is "above," that which is "below," that which is "after" my lifetime—but what is* [the point of prohibiting] *"before"? Whatever was—was!*[47] The Gemara replies that it is dishonoring to suppose absolute emptiness prior to the act of construction, and offers a parable to illustrate its point.[48]

All the Kabbalistic scholars have gotten themselves muddled on this issue, from not understanding what is meant by "above," "below," and the rest. *The King's Depths*[49] and many other Kabbalists have claimed that this refers to the Ein Sof, encompassing the world on all sides. But this is impossible. First, the Gemara's problem and still more its resolution would then be irrelevant, for [the Mishnah] would have spoken of a place in which there was never any construction.[50] Yet more problematic: what bearing would this have on *Ma'aseh Bereshit*, the "work of Creation"? *One must not expound Ma'aseh Bereshit in the presence of two*, say [the Talmudic sages], *lest one come to contemplate what is above*, and so forth.[51] They did not say this of *Ma'aseh Merkavah*; and yet, if [the Kabbalists] are right, the question would have to pertain essentially to the teaching of *Ma'aseh Merkavah* and not *Ma'aseh Bereshit*.[52] Follow our explanation,

---

that "below" is the opposite of "Grace." Since Kabbalistic symbolism uses the "right" to represent Grace, it follows that Grace's opposite will be the "left."

46. As opposed to the other three spaces, BCD, concerning which "we are not authorized to say anything."

47. Talmud, b. Hag. 16a, commenting on the mishnaic prohibition quoted above.

48. "It may be compared to a human king who said to his servants, 'Build me a grand palace atop a garbage heap,' and they went and built it. The king has no desire that the garbage heap be remembered."

49. Naphtali Hertz Bacharach, *'Emeq ha-Melekh* (1648). Scholem calls this "[o]ne of the most widely read kabbalistic books in the time of Sabbatai Ṣevi" and says that it "gives a full and detailed account of Luria's system based on Israel Sarug's interpretation of it, and the author does not miss an opportunity to stress the messianic function of the doctrine" (*Sabbatai Ṣevi*, 56, 68–69).

50. That is, the Ein Sof itself, not the space within it where the worlds were created. The Gemara's resolution, which speaks of the building of "a grand palace," could not then apply to the Mishnah text it is supposed to interpret.

51. Presumably a very free citation of the final lines of the Talmud, b. Hag. 11b, which seem to equate expounding *Ma'aseh Bereshit* with the investigation of "what is above, what is below," and the rest.

52. Following the reading of ms. Oxford 976. It is not entirely clear to me why a

however, and it all makes sense. It contains a deep secret which [the sages] kept tightly guarded and which no one was authorized to reveal to me, yet by fleeting hints I have come to understand that Messiah ben David is destined to expound it openly. Wait for him.[53]

We now have the clue to the passage in the fortieth chapter of Isaiah, *He who sits above the circle of the earth*—alluding to its original circularity—and afterward *spreads the heavens like a curtain, stretching them like a tent to dwell in*,[54] i.e., pulls them from circle into square, [p. 42] tentlike. For all "tents" are square, inasmuch as whenever the Bible compares something to a tent, it refers (as the Zohar makes clear) to the Tent of Meeting,[55] which was square and not circular. That is why the Scripture can speak of "stretching," which applies, as we know, not to a circular object but to that which has length and breadth.

The shape of the final letter *mem*[56] having thus been assumed, the lights and combinations[57] drew near one another, their power greatly intensifying, both Mindful and Mindless Light extending themselves among them.[58] The Mindful Light [and Mindless Light][59] were conscious that the God of Israel would dwell with them and the Straight Line extend itself among them; yet the time was not yet ripe for this downward extension until the Mindful Light should separate itself from the Mindless. They greatly yearned to rise to their source, to attach themselves to

---

statement about Ein Sof would be properly part of *Ma'aseh Merkavah* and not *Ma'aseh Bereshit*. Because, to our author, *Ma'aseh Bereshit* refers specifically to a transitional phase ("initial stage") of the evolution of the Kabbalistic worlds (above, note 30) while Ein Sof remains permanent and unchanged?

53. This is the first explicit reference to the Messiah in the treatise. The "secret" presumably concerns the mystery of the three spaces left unused for purposes of creation.

54. Isa 40:22.

55. Moses's desert Tabernacle. Maciejko in his note *ad loc.* identifies the Zoharic reference as I, 52b.

56. This letter is shaped like a square (ם). There may be an allusion to the baffling final *mem* that occurs in the middle of the word לםרבה in Isa 9:6 (*le-marbeh ha-misrah*, meaning something like "the increase of dominion"), which had long tickled the Kabbalistic imagination.

57. Cf. above, note 33.

58. Following the reading of mss Oxford 976, Jerusalem 3100.

59. This insertion is unsupported by the manuscripts, yet seems required by the plural verbs and pronouns that follow, as well as by the exegesis of Gen 11 in the next section. The impulse to return to the source is normally attributed to the Mindless Light, not the Mindful; here the latter seems to be infected by its proximity to the former.

the Shechinah and the Distant One[60] with the aim of bringing down the Straight Line and the God of Israel's light [fol. 9a] in great abundance, for their revival and satisfaction.

They conceived the intention to make the ascent; and to frustrate their plan, the God of Israel split that final *mem* of theirs (□) in two, like this [ ], like two *bets* or two *hets* laid on their sides.[61] The Mindful Light would thus be separated from the Mindless, the Mindful Light remaining in the *het* where the worlds are now constructed, inasmuch as it possessed thought and intended to stay in the place of construction. The Mindless Light, however, went forth to the second *het* so as to extend itself every which way and become fused once more with its source. For in the *het* where the Mindful Light was, it was blocked by that Light from freely expanding, and therefore departed for the second *het* to fuse again with its source.

Its hopes, however, were disappointed. Some minute trace remained of the Mindful Light, which "does not budge from its place [without leaving a mark]."[62] It was thus blocked from fusing with its source and found itself wandering back and forth, up and down in crooked paths, never finding any place to rest.

[p. 43] This is the significance of the story of the "generation of the Division."[63]

4. The "generation of the Division"

> [The splitting of the square is described, in the Bible's symbolic language, in the story of what the ancient rabbis called "the Generation of the Division" but which is better known to us as "the Tower of Babel" (Gen 11:1–9). That "generation" is the Lights, Mindful and Mindless mixed together, who "journeyed" from Ein Sof into the square and schemed there to construct *sefirot*—the male "tower" and the female "city"—that would attract into them the power of what the author anachronistically

---

60. The "head" of the fetal entity ("God of Israel") enclosed within the Shechinah-sac; above, note 38. The active role taken by this "God of Israel" in the next paragraph seems incongruous.

61. Referring to the letters *bet* (ב) and *het* (ח); it is the *hets* that are "laid on their sides."

62. Above, chapter 1, note 71.

63. *Dor ha-pallagah*, the standard rabbinic designation for the builders of the Tower of Babel.

calls "the God of Israel." In a manner that is not wholly clear, this is a step toward achieving their goal of "ascending" back to their source and merging into it.

Hence the divine act of "dividing" the square, one of its halves allotted to the Mindful Light, the other to the Mindless. The latter is now equated with the demonic realm, the "Impure Merkavah." The first half-square, within which the "worlds" are to be constructed (and which is now identified, confusingly, with the *Tehiru*), thus lies open on one of its sides to the demonic. This is the deep meaning of a much-maligned midrash of the ancient rabbis.]

It came to pass as they journeyed from the Primordial, says the Scripture;[64] and the midrash understands this as "the Primordial One of the world."[65] The reference is to those Lights that journeyed from the place of their fusion with the Infinite, which were originally circular and "journeyed" from that to the place of the *mem*.[66] *All one language,* meaning they were fused together without any separation, as in their primal state; and they conceived the plan of making their ascent. They consequently said, "Let us make a tower," the sort of "tower that flies in the air,"[67] *with its top in heaven,* namely the God of Israel.[68] *And we will make a Name for ourselves,* meaning that they would take on the quality of the *sefirah Malkhut*, which is called "Name,"[69] and would in female fashion receive effluence from him.

They accordingly made the *sefirot*, namely *Tif'eret* and *Malkhut*, as vessels for the God of Israel to dwell therein.[70] That is the meaning of their building *a city*, representing *Malkhut*, and a *tower*, representing *Tif'eret*, in order *not to be scattered over the whole earth*. For they sensed that otherwise the lights would each go in its own crooked path to find

---

64. Gen 11:2. *Qedem* can mean both "east" (which is certainly the original meaning of the Biblical passage) and "antiquity, primordiality." Unless indicated otherwise, all Biblical quotations in this section are from Gen 11:1–9.

65. Midrash Genesis Rabbah 41:7, referring, however, to *qedem* in Gen 13:11, not 11:2.

66. That is, were transformed from circle to square (above, note 56).

67. A Talmudic phrase of uncertain meaning: b. Hag. 15b, Sanh. 106b.

68. "Heaven" is a standard Kabbalistic code term for the *sefirah Tif'eret*, here transferred to the "God of Israel."

69. A standard Kabbalistic equation.

70. The theme of super-sefirotic entities indwelling, or enclothing themselves in the *sefirot*, is a thread running throughout this treatise.

rest; whereas if the God of Israel were to dwell with them, they would already have achieved it.

When the God of Israel saw the activity of the *children of the human*—which the midrash explains as "the First Human," for [the Lights] were rooted in the Shape of Primordial Human of the Path of Emanation[71]—he said, *Come, let us go down and confuse their language . . . and the Lord scattered them*, meaning that he shattered them (as in *shatter your infants against the rock*).[72] *He confused their language* by dividing the *mem* [square]. The Light that was a trace of thought remained where it was, while the Mindless Light went forth and became *scattered over the face of the earth*.

Their intention was thus frustrated, and they were therefore called "the Generation of the Division,"[73] as in the verse *In his days the earth was divided*,[74] i.e., split, made into two *hets* or *bets*, and their plan thus came to naught.

This is the meaning of the world's being open on its north side,[75] which seems on the face of it so preposterous. Surely the sky encloses the world like a globe; what side might be left open? All the nations have ridiculed us for this—but in accord with what I have said it makes perfect sense, conveying an essential fact about the *Tehiru*. It lies open on its northern side, facing the Impure Merkavah.[76]

---

71. The "Shape" that had emerged within the "Spot"; see above, chapter 2, note 90. The midrash cited is Genesis Rabbah 20:11, 24:6 (which, however, interprets *benei adam* in 2 Sam 7:14, not *benei ha-adam* in Gen 11:5). The author will presently develop his distinctive take on the Lurianic concept of *Adam Qadmon*, "Primordial Human," which he reads into the rabbinic phrase *adam qadma'ah* (originally meaning simply "Adam," the first human being).

72. Treating *nippetz* in Ps 137:9 as if it were from the same root as *nafotz*, "to be scattered." The reference is to the breaking of the *mem*-square into two *hets* (or *bets*).

73. The standard rabbinic designation for the builders of Babel.

74. Gen 10:25.

75. Referring to the midrash *Pirqei de-Rabbi Eliezer*, chapter 3: "God created the northern corner [of the world] but did not complete it . . . and there is the dwelling of demons and horrors, ghosts and devils, lightnings and thunders, and from there evil comes forth to the world." This passage is influenced also by *Sefer ha-Bahir*, which explains the shape of the letter *het* as signifying that "all the directions are enclosed apart from the north, which is open to good and to evil" (quoted by Maciejko in his note *ad loc.*).

76. If the universe was created inside the split half of a square—the letter *het* laid on its side—it makes sense that one of its four sides should remain open. It faces the realm of the demonic, hinted at in *Pirqei de-Rabbi Eliezer*, which occupies the other half of the square.

5. The two *hets*

[So the "Self-folding," which our author originally used to refer to the Shape's entering within its Female's womb (above, section 1), is now redefined as the Mindful Light's folding itself up into its allotted half-square. This, the locus for the building of "worlds," is currently a watery *Ma'aseh Bereshit* (rough sketch for construction) but will eventually become the solid structure of *Ma'aseh Merkavah*. The atavistic "Insolent Waters" of *Ma'aseh Bereshit*, however, will continue to rage around its edges.

The Mindless Light's half-square, by contrast, is entirely desolate, the snake-infested abyss of the "Impure Merkavah."]

[p. 44] To return to those two *hets*: All of the truly Mindful Light, with a very slight admixture of the Mindless, had folded itself up and entered into the one *het*—this being the essence of the "Self-folding" that Luria speaks about in connection with the Garment-world[77]—doubling up from two *bets*[78] into a single *bet* (or *het*) in which the entire world was created as one, from start to finish.

This is the meaning of the "*ma'arat* of Machpelah":[79] it folded itself up, clung to itself, its name *ma'arat* indicating its self-adhesion, as in *each clinging [ma'ar] to its partner*.[80] It is sometimes called *field*,[81] for at the time it partook of the quality of a field, and it was "Ephron's"[82] in that *Binah* gives form to all things, and *Binah* has the quality of *'afar*, "dust" (as in *possessing dust of gold*[83]), while the *vav* indicates the Father's penis that enters *Binah*'s womb and the *nun* refers to the "fifty gates of *Binah*, of understanding."[84]

---

77. *'Olam ha-malbush*. Maciejko locates the author's source for this phrase in Bacharach's *King's Depths* (above, note 49), which in turn draws it from the version of the Lurianic system propagated by Rabbi Israel Sarug.

78. "Hets," in one manuscript (Jerusalem 2491). Since *bet* and *het* are used to represent the same split-square shape (above, note 61), it hardly matters which reading one adopts.

79. Normally translated "Cave of Machpelah," the burial place of the patriarchs and their wives (e.g., Gen 23:9, 25:9).

80. 1 Kgs 7:36, understood as in the Talmud, b. Yoma 54a–b.

81. "Field of Machpelah" in Gen 49:30, "cave of the field of Machpelah" in 23:19, 50:13.

82. In Gen 23 Ephron is the owner of Machpelah, who sells it to Abraham.

83. Job 28:6; but I do not understand the relevance. Is this passage understood in the Kabbalah to refer to *Binah*? (As verse 12 might imply.)

84. The name Ephron (עפרון) can be broken down into *'afar*, "dust" + the phallic letter *vav* + the letter *nun*, which represents the number 50. (The "fifty gates of understanding" derive from the Talmud, b. Rosh Hash. 21b and Ned. 38a.) The use of "dust"

[Ephron/*Binah*] *dwells amid the children of Heth*,⁸⁵ namely amid the rest of the *sefirot* of *Ma'aseh Bereshit*, which are called *children of Heth* because they were compartmentalized into this *ḥet*.

The contents of this *ḥet* are now built up as *Ma'aseh Merkavah*, [fol. 9b] albeit with the Insolent Waters of *Ma'aseh Bereshit*—useless for construction, savagely raging like the sea's waters to destroy what had been built—around its edges, as we shall presently explain in detail. Before the construction, however, everything in this site had the quality of water. In the second *ḥet*, meanwhile, all was desolation, the light extending itself in a variety of crooked paths, bent on destroying what had been built so that all might return to *formlessness and void*.⁸⁶

These are called "snakes," *the crooked serpent*;⁸⁷ and this is the platform on which the Impure Merkavah stands. It is called *tehom*, "abyss," and also *tohu*, "formlessness." The other *ḥet*, by contrast, which serves as platform for the worlds, is called *bohu*, i.e., *bo hu*, "he [God] is in it," for it contains construction and the light of the Merkavah.

This is made clear in the Zohar to the Torah portion *Bereshit*, fol. 16: Tohu—from the place of slime, nest of refuse. Bohu—purification performed from the midst of refuse, where habitation is possible.⁸⁸ Consult that text.

6. The emergence of "Creation-Human"

> [One of the half-squares, then, has become the locus of construction. What has become of the uppermost of the four compartments that were created when the square withdrew itself from the circle (above, section 3)? Now we find out.
>
> The female Shechinah, enclosing the Shape, conceives a longing herself to beget a humanlike entity modeled after that

---

to represent the *sefirah Binah* is unusual; conventional Kabbalistic symbolism assigns it to the lower *sefirah Malkhut*, and Job 28:6, "possessing dust of gold," is interpreted in the Zohar, II, 24a as implying a fusion of *Malkhut*, dust, with *Gevurah*, fire. But the author may understand the sequel in Job (verse 12) to imply an equation of dust = *Binah*. On the significance of *Ma'aseh Bereshit* and *Ma'aseh Merkavah*, and on *Binah*'s primordial role as shaper, see above, section 2.

85. Gen 23:10.

86. Gen 1:2, *tohu va-vohu*. In what follows, however, *tohu* and *bohu* are opposed, and *bohu* given a new meaning.

87. Isa 27:1.

88. Zohar, I, 16a, adapting Matt's translation in accord with our author's understanding of the passage.

Shape. She cannot do this through a sexual connection: her future sex partner is still a fetus inside her. So she brings that entity into existence by the force of her thought, aided by light from the Root and the complementary thought of the Distant One (who is currently the "head" of the fetus in her womb). Through a kind of virgin birth—it is hard not to read this as a commentary on Christianity—a thought-begotten entity called "Creation-Human" emerges from her and takes its place in the topmost of the four spaces.

The thought-begotten, however, are at a disadvantage compared to those born of sexual coupling. In them, the orgasmic "contraction" of sex has no opportunity to purge their dross and darkness. This fatal deficiency in "Creation-Human" will presently show its consequences.]

[p. 45] At that time—coming back to our subject—all partook of the quality of "the Distant One," represented by the letters *yod-hei*.[89] All *Ma'aseh Bereshit* was nourished from him. This is the meaning of *Let the entire desolation shine from Yod-Hei*:[90] *Neshamah* is synonymous with *shemamah*, "desolation" (cf. Rashi and Tosafot),[91] and *Ma'aseh Bereshit* was still desolate, receiving illumination from *Yod-Hei*. (*Tehallel* speaks of illumination, as in the phrase *yehellu oram*, "shed their illumination."[92])

And so, resuming our discourse, once that *Ma'aseh Bereshit* and that Spot were completed everything had the quality of matter,[93] of the nature of that Shape, the Shechinah encompassing and enclosing it. The Shechinah then desired to create a human being in the form and lineaments of that Emanation-Human. Inasmuch, however, as that entity was at the time in the Folded-up state, not yet properly developed into Human-and-His-Female, the begetting of a human through sexual coupling was impossible. It could take place only through the modes of thought and

---

89. The first two letters of the Tetragrammaton, the YH of YHVH, earlier said to represent the Distant One (chapter 2, section 3).

90. Ps 150:6, normally translated "Let every spirit [*neshamah*] praise [*tehallel*] the Lord [*Yah, yod-hei*]."

91. Presumably referring to the Tosafot to b. 'Erub. 18b (ד"ה כל), which cites Rabbenu Hananel's suggestion that the Talmud reads *ha-neshamah* in Ps 150:6 as though it were *ha-neshammah*, "the desolate" (Ezek 36:34–36); versus Rashi on this passage, who gives *ha-neshamah* its usual meaning.

92. Isa 13:10. This is a very forced interpretation of the verb in Ps 150, normally taken to refer to praise.

93. Awaiting the imposition of form? The author's point is not clear.

"seeing" (the word "seeing" used to convey the idea of thought, as we say "I see the words of So-and-so" or *he saw in his heart*).[94]

Thus the Shechinah conceived the urge to beget a human and through this urge and the power of thought, aided by light received from the Root, a human form took shape within her. The Distant One[95] saw this thought of hers and added his own thought, affirming and complementing hers. The force of his thought joined itself to hers—for in that place[96] all potentialities and thoughts are effective factors—his "seeing" and thought cooperating with her, reinforcing her intention, coming to her in the quality of male juices, "direct light," as is well known; while the form already present within her took on the quality of "reflected light," female juices.[97] And when these male and female juices encountered one another, this image was completed and came forth from the Female in the form of a human image, taking its stand beneath them in the empty space above *Ma'aseh Bereshit* of which we have spoken,[98] its *Malkhut* inhering within it.[99]

This is the Primordial Creation-Human[100] of whom the Zohar speaks. So does Luria in his book *Tree of Life*, whose lengthy disquisitions on the subject of this human shape you may consult. He is called "Creation-Human" by comparison with the Shape comprising the Distant One and the God of Israel, which is "Emanation-Human" and which Luria calls "Ein Sof" as we shall discuss below.[101] [p. 46] Luria calls [Creation-Human] "Primordial Human"[102] inasmuch as he is the

---

94. "I see the words of So-and-so" is a standard rabbinic idiom for "I agree with his opinion." "He saw in his heart" is apparently supposed to be a Biblical quotation, but I cannot locate anything corresponding to it.

95. Who, recall, is himself enclosed within the Shechinah, the "head" of the fetal Shape inside her womb.

96. The super-sefirotic realm, where thoughts and intentions have effective power.

97. See above, chapter 2, note 107.

98. Between the upper wall of the square and the circumference of the circle, marked A in the diagram above.

99. That is, incorporating its own female element.

100. *Adam qadmon di-veri'ah*. This title is our author's; the corresponding Zoharic and Lurianic designations for the same entity will be discussed in what follows.

101. This accords precisely with the usage of *Shem 'Olam*, where "Ein Sof" and "God of Israel" (in the broader sense of the term; above, chapter 1, note 67, and chapter 3, note 38) are alternative designations for the "first effect" of the First Cause—the same entity that is called "Shape" and "Emanation-Human" in this treatise. See above, chapter 1, note 3.

102. *Adam qadmon*.

most primal of all the emanated entities, antedating the self-extension and establishment of the God of Israel.[103] For this latter was at the time in the state of Self-folding, existing only as part of the Distant One as we have already seen.

This Primordial Human, you must understand, did not come into being through the process of sexual coupling. When something is made through coupling, the contraction inherent in sex—"love squeezing the flesh"[104]—strains out the judgments and the dross from the mercies. Even within the maternal womb, the drosses and the excesses are removed and the choice qualities absorbed. But Primordial Human had neither of these, neither contraction nor copulation.[105]

This, you must understand, is the essence of the drosses: that light partaking of the quality of *Elleh* and *Ein*,[106] namely the Mindless Light, is to be found within the space of the Shape. True, [the Shape's] root and father is in the *Mi*, the extension of light; yet it could not escape having some trace of Mindless Light, whose nature is darkness[107] as we have seen. This darkness was only minimally perceptible in the Shape of Emanation-Human, thanks to the magnitude of its light from the Root and the Mindful Light. It nonetheless required a Self-folding, so that when the God of Israel should extend himself afterward—as we shall discuss presently, God willing—the darkness would be yet more thoroughly separated.

This Primordial Human, by contrast, emerged prior to that Self-extension and without a proper coupling.[108] Add that it was the Female who took the initiative and aroused herself to give birth, and it will follow that much [fol. 10a] Mindless Light, dark in its quality, was mixed within him. He was, moreover, produced from the Distant One, who was himself in a state of admixture—*your head like karmel*, as we have

---

103. The "self-extension" is the subsequent emergence of the God of Israel from his "Folded-up" state. "Establishment" seems the best translation in this context of the protean word *tiqqun* (above, chapter 2, note 99).

104. Talmud, b. B. Meṣi'a 84a; see above, chapter 1, note 49.

105. In the light of the author's linking of the Distant One to Christianity, his reflections on the flaws inherent in any being created by thought alone, and not through sexual intercourse, take on a special significance.

106. The passive substrate of Ein Sof. The terminology *Elleh*, *Ein*, and *Mi* is explained at the end of chapter 1.

107. Or "that which is withheld from us"; above, chapter 1, section 5.

108. As might have taken place after the Self-extension between the God of Israel and the Shechinah.

seen[109]—and thus with much in the way of dross, its quality darkness, mixed in with him. But since [the Distant One] stood in this lofty place, truly near his Root, the dross could not predominate within him and was indeed imperceptible, having the character of hairs.[110] He owed this to his exalted position, his nature being pure mercy in consequence of his august station, as the Kabbalists tell us. Yet in fact, as we well know, he was contaminated with darkness and much dross.[111]

This Creation-Human is normally called "Primordial Human"[112] in the Zohar, which [by contrast] designates the Primordial-Human-of-the-Path-of-Emanation as that "Primordial Light" of which *God said, Let there be light.*[113] So you may see from the Zohar to the Torah portion *Bereshit*, fol. 22.[114]

7. The Zoharic Evidence: I, 22a–b

[All well and good, but where is the evidence for any of this? The author pauses in the sequential unfolding of his cosmogony (theogony?) to provide a close analysis—which the modern reader is apt to find forbiddingly dense—of two passages of the Zohar that, in his view, presuppose his version of the primordial events.

The first passage, I, 22a–b, is actually from a late stratum of the Zohar called *Tiqqunim*, but the author does not distinguish it from the Zohar proper. The speaker is the Zohar's central figure, Rabbi Shimon ben Yohai, addressing a group of his "Companions." Our author notes a curious inconsistency in the passage's treatment of Gen 1:3 (*let there be light*) versus 1:26 (*let us make the human being*). In both Biblical texts, Rabbi Shimon assumes the presence of two entities: a male, whom he calls the "building's master," and a female, whom he

---

109. Above, chapter 1, section 4; and chapter 2, note 100, quoting Song 7:6. The equation "head" = Distant One is by now familiar.

110. Above, chapter 2, section 5.

111. A criticism of the God of Christianity?

112. So the author seems to understand the Zoharic phrase *adam kadma'ah*, which, however, normally designates the "first human" in the literal sense, the Biblical Adam.

113. Gen 1:3, expounded in the Zoharic passage that follows.

114. In the following section, the author gives an extended quotation from the Zohar, which he glosses in accordance with the system he has developed so far and which is thus made to provide "proof" for his system. He will do this several more times in the treatise.

calls "the artisan." Yet he supposes that the words *let there be light* are spoken by the male to the female, *let us make the human being* by the female to the male. Why?

Actually, the Zohar recognizes the presence of two male/female pairs, a higher and a lower. The higher male is the Will aspect of Ein Sof, while the higher female ("Supernal Mother") is its substrate, the Mindless Light. Having no will or capacity for thought,[115] she cannot address the male. The Bible must therefore be interpreted, contrary to its evident meaning,[116] as the male's speech to her, using her as a tool to execute his will (*let there be . . .*). Thus does the Shape, which the Zohar calls "the Path of Emanation," come into existence.

With Gen 1:26, we are on the lower level of the "Path of Emanation" itself. Here the female is distinct from the male, with mind and intention of her own. She can therefore approach the male with a proposal, *Let us make the human being*, and *Elohim* can be understood in its natural sense as the (female) speaker of these words.

The male's response is cool, and Rabbi Shimon's exegesis of Prov 10:1 explains why. The "wise son" is the Shape, Emanation-Human ("the Human of the Path of Emanation"). His "thought-begotten" and therefore flawed counterpart must be a distinct entity, explicitly called "Creation-Human" by Rabbi Shimon. Our author's seemingly eccentric nomenclature is thus shown to have solid grounding in the Zohar.

The anticipated objection to the author's cosmogony, that it makes no sense to speak of sexual differentiation within Ein Sof, is raised by Rabbi Shimon's "Companions." It is promptly refuted by Rabbi Shimon himself. The dichotomy of male and female is present *in nuce* at the highest, most primordial levels of existence—just as our author has said.

A flaw now shows itself in the author's Zohar exegesis. The dialogue between the Companions and Rabbi Shimon seems to assume that "Father" and "Mother," "building's master" and "artisan," are the same pair in Gen 1:3 and 1:26, with only the roles of speaker and addressee switched around. Emanation-Human and Creation-Human are direct offspring of the same "parents." How can the author square this with his theory that when Rabbi Shimon speaks of "the World of Division, i.e., the world

---

115. At least as far as creation is concerned. The discussion here is in some tension with chapter 1, section 5, which attributes to the Mindless Light "many thoughts, deep and lofty, that have nothing to do with creating worlds."

116. Assuming that *Elohim*, "God," must refer to a female element in divinity.

of discrete entities,"[117] he marks a change not only of scene but also *dramatis personae*? We are not told.]

[p. 47] HE[118] OPENED, SAYING: THIS MAY BE COMPARED TO A KING WHO HAD A NUMBER OF BUILDINGS TO CONSTRUCT. HE HAD IN HIS SERVICE AN ARTISAN, AND THIS ARTISAN WOULD DO NOTHING WITHOUT THE KING'S AUTHORIZATION. SO THE BIBLE SAYS: *I WAS AN ARTISAN IN HIS PRESENCE*.[119]

THE "KING" IS SURELY THE SUPERNAL WISDOM ABOVE, meaning the Root, which partakes of the quality of *Abba*, "Father," and of *Mi*, "Who,"[120] and is represented by the *sefirah Hokhmah*; this is why the Zohar reiterates SUPERNAL and then ABOVE.[121] WHILE THE CENTRAL COLUMN IS THE KING BELOW,[122] meaning the Shape of the Path of Emanation, which has the quality of Straight Line and Central Column.

ELOHIM, "GOD," IS THE ARTISAN ABOVE,[123] THIS BEING THE SUPERNAL MOTHER, meaning the one indicated by *Elleh*, "These," and *Ein*, "Nothingness"—the substrate of Ein Sof, having the quality of Mindless Light and darkness—WHILE *ELOHIM* IS THE ARTISAN BELOW, WHO IS THE LOWER SHECHINAH, namely of the God of Israel, enclosing him like the placenta, as we have described. A WOMAN HAS NO RIGHT TO DO ANYTHING WITHOUT HER HUSBAND'S AUTHORIZATION, SO FOR ALL THE STRUCTURES THAT CAME TO EXIST IN THE PATH OF EMANATION, FATHER WOULD SAY VERBALLY TO MOTHER, "LET IT BE THUS-AND-SO," AND AT ONCE IT WAS. THUS THE BIBLE SAYS: *HE SAID, "O ELOHIM, LET*

---

117. *'Alma de-feruda de-ihu 'olam ha-nivdalim.* "Discrete entities," *nivdalim*, is a technical term borrowed by the Zohar from medieval philosophy and radically reinterpreted. Originally it meant the spiritual entities "separated" from corporeality; the expression was reinterpreted by the Kabbalists to indicate the increasing differentiation one finds in descending from higher to lower levels of divinity.

118. Rabbi Shimon ben Yohai.

119. Prov 8:30.

120. See the end of chapter 1, section 5, above.

121. The original intent of the Zoharic passage is surely to equate the "king" of the parable with the *sefirah Hokhmah*, often called "Higher Wisdom" by contrast with *Malkhut*, the "Lower Wisdom." For our author, the "king" is a yet higher entity, a component of Ein Sof, toward which the *sefirah Hokhmah* points. He finds support for this reinterpretation in the seemingly redundant repetition of "Supernal" and "above."

122. Originally the *sefirah Tif'eret*; now reinterpreted as the Shape that emerged from the Spot (above, chapter 2, section 5).

123. Answering the question posed at the beginning of this section of the Zohar: who is the "God" who said, "Let us make the human being" (Gen 1:26)?

THE GESTATION OF GOD

THERE BE LIGHT!"[124] AND THERE WAS LIGHT; I.E., HE SAID, "LET THERE BE LIGHT" TO ELOHIM. THE BUILDING'S MASTER WAS THE ONE WHO SPOKE, AND AT ONCE THE ARTISAN CARRIED IT OUT.

IN THIS WAY, EACH AND EVERY STRUCTURE IN THE PATH OF EMANATION CAME INTO EXISTENCE. "LET THERE BE A FIRMAMENT," HE WOULD SAY, OR "LET THERE BE LUMINARIES," AND ALL AT ONCE IT WAS COMPLETED.

To interpret this passage, the first thing we need to understand is why it represents Father as speaking to Mother. The Biblical verse after all, does not mention Father at all. It says only, *Elohim said*,[125] and we have already established that *Elohim* represents Mother, "the artisan above." In the sequel, moreover, with respect to *Let us make the human being*,[126] it is written that *Elohim said* and this is interpreted as Mother speaking to Father, *Elohim* being a standard designation for Mother.[127] Yet here, with respect to the divine speech *Let there be light*, we are told the reverse.

The key is this: it is Ein Sof that is here under discussion.

We have already explained that within Ein Sof there is no division or juncture and no distinct names, other than that the thought of Ein Sof, its Will to create the world, is "the Light That Possesses Colors" and is called Father, while the substrate of Ein Sof is the Mindless Light and is called Mother. We know, moreover, that the verb "speaking" conveys thought or intention (as in the Bible's *When you say in your heart*[128] or the Zohar to *Bereshit*, fol. 16b).[129] [p. 48] *Elohim said*, therefore, must be understood as *Elohim thought*, and therefore must be applied to the Color-possessing Light within Ein Sof. For with regard to the Mindless Light one cannot speak of "thinking," since it has no such capacity.

---

124. A thinkable but very strained way to construe Gen 1:3. Our author will presently query why the Zohar goes to such lengths in stretching the Bible's language.

125. The more natural understanding of the verse should remain the default option. If the Zohar identifies *Elohim* with Mother and accordingly interprets Gen 1:26 as recording Mother's speech to Father, why does it insist on doing the reverse in 1:3?

126. Gen 1:26. The Zohar's exegesis of this verse is quoted below.

127. Throughout the Zohar, the divine name Elohim tends to be applied to the female aspects of divinity, particularly the Shechinah.

128. Deut 7:17, 18:21.

129. A cryptic passage, the key sentence of which Matt translates as: "ויאמר (*Va-yomer*), *Said*—a power raised ... rising, silently from the mystery of *Ein Sof*, in the origin of thought." Our author seems to imply an equation of "saying" with "thought." See Perlmuter, *Rabbi Jonathan Eibeschuetz*, 276–77, which compares the identification of "saying" and "thinking" in *Shem 'Olam*, 190.

The "thinking" therefore must be applied to the thought of Ein Sof, which has the "Father" quality, while *Elohim* must indicate the undifferentiated substrate of Ein Sof, which has the quality of "Mother."[130] From this the act was performed: the Spot came into being.

Quite properly, then, does FATHER SAY VERBALLY TO MOTHER. We might think of it this way: when a person performs a given act, who induces him to do it? His will, surely, or his intention. It follows that his intention, which induces and indeed directs him to act, functions as "Father" and "building's master," while the person himself who does the act is "Mother" and "artisan." When we see a certain individual doing an action, it was his *thought* that has directed him to do so, while his *body* (or the person himself[131]) actually does it.

Thus it is with Ein Sof, which lacks any distinction between these two. When it intends to do something and actually does it, its *thought* (i.e., Father) provides the inducement while the *substrate* of Ein Sof (i.e., Mother) carries it out. FOR ALL THE STRUCTURES THAT CAME TO EXIST IN THE PATH OF EMANATION, says the Zohar, FATHER WOULD SAY VERBALLY, meaning "in his thought," AS THE BIBLE SAYS: HE SAID, "O ELOHIM, LET THERE BE LIGHT!" *He said* means that [fol. 10b] his thought said to *Elohim*, namely the substrate of Ein Sof; for thought is the ruler and director of the human body. This the Zohar states explicitly: THE BUILDING'S MASTER WAS THE ONE WHO SPOKE, as we have just explained.

Such is the situation with Ein Sof. But when we come to speak of the God of Israel and His Shechinah, we find them in a state of division, she being an independent Shape with her own independent mind. So when we see the words *Elohim said* in this context,[132] we must take them as describing the Female's thought without any reference to the Male's.

Thus the Zohar says: WHEN IT CAME TO THE WORLD OF DIVISION, I.E. THE WORLD OF DISCRETE ENTITIES, IT WAS THE ARTISAN WHO SAID, LET US MAKE, TO THE BUILDING'S MASTER. This means that when it comes to treat of the emanated entities made by the God of Israel and his Shechinah—who are "discrete" in character and mind, male and female—*Elohim said* is used to convey that the Shechinah spoke (or thought) this to the God of Israel, who is the building's master, she

---

130. And therefore the Zohar has no choice but to understand Gen 1:3 as "he said [i.e., thought], 'O Elohim, let there be light!'"

131. *'Atzmut adam*, parallel to *'atzmut ein sof*, "substrate of Ein Sof," in the next paragraph.

132. Gen 1:26: "Elohim said, 'Let us make the human being.'"

being the one who is called *Elohim*, and the verb *said* referring to her thought, for she is capable of thought.[133]

THE BUILDING'S MASTER SAID: "SURELY IT IS GOOD TO MAKE HIM. BUT HE WILL SIN AGAINST YOU BECAUSE HE IS *KESIL*," AS IT IS WRITTEN, *A WISE SON IS HIS FATHER'S DELIGHT, BUT A SON WHO IS* KESIL *IS HIS MOTHER'S* TUGAH.[134] In other words: because you have taken the initiative [in his begetting] he will sin against you, for it is well known that whenever a woman initiates relations with her husband, her children do not turn out properly.[135] BECAUSE HE IS *KESIL*, the Zohar says; and the reason he is termed *kesil* is because, as we have said, he [Creation-Human] emerged from thought and not from sexual coupling.[136] (*Kesil* is a term indicating thought, as the Bible says, *They set* kislam, meaning "their thoughts," *on God*; cf. the entry for *kesil* in the *'Arukh*.[137]) And when it says, *A thought-begotten son*[138] *is his mother's* tugah, the word *tugah* is from the root *hogeh*, "contemplation," indicating ideation and thought (as in, *At daybreak I shall contemplate you*).[139]

---

133. Our author interprets the Zohar to interpret the Bible as follows: The consultative verb *Let us make*, in Gen 1:26, shows that we are dealing with a different sort of operation from the *Let there be*'s earlier in the chapter. No longer is the Will of Ein Sof addressing its own substrate, summoning additional entities into existence. Rather, one of these "discrete" entities, the Female, consults with the Male about bringing into being yet another entity, whom we will presently see to be the "Creation-Human" of section 6, above.

134. Prov 10:1. The last phrase is normally translated, "a foolish son is his mother's grief." But, as we will see, our author takes the key words *kesil* and *tugah* as having entirely different meanings.

135. Ms Jerusalem 2491 attributes this to "the Gemara," possibly referring to 'Eruvin 100b—which, however, seems to say the opposite, that when a woman initiates sex "she will have children unmatched even in the generation of Moses."

136. Above, section 6. The Biblical verse of course speaks of the creation of Adam, and this is apparently also what the Zohar means by "Creation-Human" (below). It is our author's innovation to turn "Creation-Human" from an inhabitant of the physical world into a flawed cosmic entity begotten by the Shechinah.

137. Ps 78:7. The medieval Hebrew lexicon called the *'Arukh* (by Nathan ben Jehiel, ca. 1105) quotes three rabbinic interpretations of *kislam* in this verse: "their thoughts," "their stupidity," and "their confidence" (s.v. *kesel*, in Kohut, *Aruch Completum*, 4: 273–74). Our author follows the first of these; most modern translators the third.

138. So the author has established to his own satisfaction that *ben kesil*, normally rendered *a foolish son*, ought to be understood.

139. Ps 63:7, using the verb *ehgeh*, "contemplate," from the same root. The second part of Prov 10:1 winds up meaning—or at least is understood by the Zohar as meaning—"a thought-begotten son is his mother's contemplation."

SAID SHE ... HE DROVE OUT THE MOTHER WITH HIM.[140] Here is not the place to interpret this passage; I shall presently offer a full explanation of the sin of Primordial Creation-Human, in its several aspects.[141] THIS IS WHY SCRIPTURE SAYS, A WISE SON IS HIS FATHER'S DELIGHT, REFERRING TO THE HUMAN OF THE PATH OF EMANATION (i.e., the God of Israel, who is the Shape of Emanation),[142] WHILE A THOUGHT-BEGOTTEN SON IS HIS MOTHER'S CONTEMPLATION, REFERRING TO CREATION-HUMAN (i.e., that Primordial Human of whom we have just spoken).[143]

THE COMPANIONS ALL ROSE AND SAID: "RABBI, RABBI![144] IS THERE INDEED SUCH DIVISION BETWEEN FATHER AND MOTHER, THAT THE ONE FROM FATHER'S SIDE IS IN THE PATH OF EMANATION WHILE THE ONE FROM MOTHER'S SIDE IS IN CREATION?" By this they meant that in Ein Sof there is no trace of any division to which the designation of "Father" versus "Mother" might be applied. Rather, these designations first emerge in the Path of Emanation itself,[145] with the God of Israel, who dwells in Emanation,[146] as we shall presently see, and his Shechinah, who has the quality of a Mother making her nest within Creation, as we all know.[147]

[p. 50] "NOT SO, O COMPANIONS!" SAID HE. "EMANATION-HUMAN IS BOTH MALE AND FEMALE, FROM THE SIDE OF FATHER AND MOTHER. THIS IS THE MEANING OF *HE SAID, 'LET THERE BE LIGHT!' AND THERE WAS LIGHT*[148]—LET THERE BE LIGHT FROM FATHER'S SIDE, AND THERE

---

140. Here is the full text of the Zohar passage: "Said she—after his sin was made the Mother's responsibility and not the Father's—'I wish to create him in my image.' So it is written, 'God created the human in his image' [Gen 1:27], the Father having no wish to be associated with him. When he sinned, what does Scripture say? 'For your sin was your Mother banished' [Isa 50:1]. The King said to the Mother, 'Did I not tell you he was going to sin?' Thereupon he drove him out, and he drove out the Mother with him." See below, chapter 6, section 7, note 201.

141. Below, chapter 6, section 6.

142. Using "God of Israel" in its broad sense, to refer to the Shape that had emerged from the Spot.

143. The Zohar seems to use the phrase *adam di-veri'ah*, "Creation-Human," to speak of the historical Adam. Our author re-interprets it as referring to a divine entity in his burgeoning pantheon.

144. Addressing Rabbi Shimon ben Yohai, who has been the speaker up to this point.

145. That is, among the entities emanated from Ein Sof.

146. *Ha-shokhen ba-atzilut*. This is the first use in the treatise of the key word *shokhen*, "dwelling," later to become a leitmotiv of the text: the higher entities "dwell," that is embody themselves, within the lower.

147. At least, so say the Companions.

148. Following ms. Jerusalem 3100, omitting the word *Elohim*—which, as we have

WAS LIGHT FROM MOTHER'S. THIS WAS ANDROGYNOUS HUMAN, WHO, HOWEVER, HAD NEITHER 'IMAGE' NOR 'LIKENESS.'[149] YET THE HIGHER MOTHER HAD A CERTAIN DESIGNATION, ITS NUMERICAL VALUE EQUAL TO THAT OF *ELOHIM*, WHICH DESIGNATION WAS LIGHT AND DARKNESS. IT WAS THE DARKNESS WITHIN THAT DESIGNATION THAT OCCASIONED FATHER'S PREDICTION THAT HE WOULD SIN AGAINST EMANATION-HUMAN ... AND IT WAS ON THIS ACCOUNT THAT HE SAID, *LET US MAKE THE HUMAN BEING IN OUR IMAGE*, NAMELY THAT LIGHT, *AFTER OUR LIKENESS*, NAMELY THAT DARKNESS THAT IS THE LIGHT'S GARMENT."

This means that the designations "Father" and "Mother" are indeed proper to Ein Sof itself. For Emanation-Human's male/female dichotomy—the God of Israel and his Shechinah—mirrors the Father/Mother dichotomy that is of the essence of Ein Sof.[150] So it is written: *He said, "Let there be light!"*—namely Father, the Mindful Light—*and there was light*, namely the instrument, Mother, whose quality is Mindless Light. These had, strictly speaking, NEITHER "IMAGE" NOR "LIKENESS." Yet inasmuch as she is the substrate of Ein Sof, as earlier explained, we attribute to her a "Mother" quality.

She is said to have HAD A CERTAIN DESIGNATION. I heard once what this "designation" was and have forgotten, but can reasonably conjecture that it was *Mehetabel*, which has the same numerical value as *Elohim* (provided the word *Elohim* itself is added to the total) and figures in the Zohar as a name for the Shechinah in the doctrine of the Shattering of the Vessels.[151] The name *Mehetabel*, מהטבאל, moreover, is

---

seen, might be either the speaker or the addressee of "Let there be light."

149. *Adam du-partzufin*, literally "two-faced human," referring to the rabbinic tradition (rooted in Plato) that God originally created the human being with male and female fused back-to-back. In the Zohar, it seems to be Emanation-Human (= the Androgyne) who has neither "image" nor "likeness." This statement would make more sense, however, if applied to the higher entities from which Emanation-Human emerged, and so our author seems to understand it.

150. Emanation-Human could not have emerged dichotomous as male and female, unless this were rooted in a prior dichotomy (Father and Mother) latent in Ein Sof.

151. *Elohim* has the numerical value of 86; "Mehetabel"—the wife of the last of the pre-Israelite "kings of Edom," in Gen 36:39 and 1 Chr 1:50—is 87. Count the name *Elohim* itself as an additional 1, and the two are equal. (This last move is one of a wide range of devices used in Kabbalah to make gematrias come out the way expositors want them to.) Unfortunately, as the author will go on to (half) concede, this gematria requires that Mehetabel's name be misspelled. On the doctrine of the Shattering of the Vessels and Mehetabel's role in it, see below, chapter 4. Readers may judge as they will the likelihood of the author's claim that he once "heard what this 'designation' was and have forgotten."

a compound of הטב and אלם, the former pointing toward Mercy and Light, the latter toward Judgment—as in the expression *kol da-alam gevar*, "whoever strong-arms the other wins"—which has the quality of Gevurah and darkness.[152]

(Admittedly, the name is spelled in the Pentateuch מהיטבאל, with the letter *yod* added. In the book of Chronicles, however, the *yod* is absent.[153])

This is why the Zohar says, THAT DESIGNATION WAS LIGHT AND DARKNESS. [Fol. 11a] Primordial Creation-Human was light and darkness, as we have seen, in that he was still contaminated with drosses. Hence he was spoken of as being *in our image, after our likeness*.[154]

8. The Zoharic Evidence: II, 167b

[So far we have established (1) the presence of a "mindless" female component within Ein Sof and (2) the emergence of a pair of entities, Emanation-Human and Creation-Human, of which the former (= the "light" of Gen 1:3) is preferred over the latter (= the "human being" of Gen 1:26). The author now takes up a second Zohar passage, proposing to identify what it calls the "Human image" with Emanation-Human, and the "design" or "engraving of the Human image" with the inferior entity modeled after him.

The speaker, called "the young man,"[155] wrestles with the problem of the absence of any suitable female womb within which the "engraving of the Human image" (= Creation-Human, according to our author) might have been gestated. Neither the "Supernal Mother" nor the Shechinah will fit the context. The "young man's" resolution: there was no womb. In its place was a "Measure," identified by our author with the Shechinah in her

---

152. The author divides the six letters of "Mehetabel" into two groups of three, apparently understanding הטב as *hativ*, "to do good" to someone. The phrase *kol da-alam* [דאלם] *gevar* is modified slightly from the Talmud, b. Git. 60b, B. Bat. 34b. Gevurah is the *sefirah* of harsh judgment.

153. Since the letter *yod* has the numerical value of 10, its addition to the name in Gen 36:39 ruins the author's arithmetic. Unhappily, contrary to his claim, the *yod* is present also in 1 Chr 1:50.

154. He takes after his Mother—who, as Elohim, is the speaker in Gen 1:26—in that he is light and darkness mixed together. In this respect, he can be said to be "in the image" of a formless entity. On Creation-Human's "drosses," see the end of section 6, above.

155. He is identified by name only at the end of the Zohar's story about him.

placental mode, where "letters" produced by "thought" were conjoined as a sort of ersatz sperm and ovum.

Only later, when the male had emerged from his fetal dependence on the Shechinah and Shechinah herself become something more than placenta, could they have full sex (at his initiative). He would then impregnate her with "the structure of Emanation"—what appears in Kabbalah as the system of *sefirot*—engendered in his image. We have already learned from Gen 1:26, in which the female *Elohim* is the speaker, that Creation-Human came into being at her initiative. We will presently see that, as the "structure of Emanation" is represented in the Bible by Adam's son Seth, Creation-Human is represented by Eve's son Cain.]

[p. 51] Taking up from where we left off,[156] we may say that Creation-Human—the "Primordial Human" of the Lurianic writings—was created and emanated[157] from the God of Israel and His Shechinah by thought alone, in the absence of sexual coupling. He is therefore called *kesil*, "thought-begotten," as has been shown;[158] and this is the esoteric meaning of the verse *Better a poor and wise child than an elderly, thought-begotten king*.[159]

For the God of Israel was then in a Folded-up state inside the Female, in the quality of a child. He was then *poor*, sucking at his mother's breasts, called *poor* because he had nothing of his own,[160] yet for all that, he was *a wise son*.[161] Creation-Human, by contrast, was completely formed and therefore called *an elderly king*, inferior to the childlike God of Israel. Understand this.

Primordial Human's emergence without any Female, as described above, is clarified in the Zohar to the Torah portion *Terumah* (fol. 167b) in the question posed by the young man:[162]

156. At the end of section 6, before the lengthy excursus on Zohar, I, 22a–b.
157. The author seems to see no contradiction between these two verbs.
158. Above, section 7. The more normal meaning of *kesil* is "fool."
159. Eccl 4:13.
160. *Let leh mi-garmeh k'lum*, a phrase regularly used in the Zohar to convey the "poverty" of Shechinah, who has nothing but what she gets from her male partner *Tif'eret* (as the moon has no light of her own, but only reflects the sun's). The gender reversal here is very striking: it is the male "God of Israel" who "has nothing of his own," other than what he gets from Shechinah.
161. Returning to Prov 10:1, quoted and discussed in the previous section.
162. The passage that follows is part of an extended story (Zohar, II, 165b–69b) in which Rabbi Hiyya and Rabbi Abba, staying at an inn, encounter a seemingly unlettered

WELL AND GOOD WHEN THIS[163] HAPPENS WITHIN A WOMAN'S WOMB, SINCE SEED ACQUIRES DESIGN ONLY IN THE WOMB OF A FEMALE, THE HUMAN IMAGE EXPANDING INTO IT. BUT HERE,[164] IF THESE FIVE RUNGS ARE A HUMAN IMAGE, IN WHAT PLACE WAS THIS IMAGE DESIGNED AND EXPANDED IN THE MIDST OF THESE WATERS? The essential design of the fetus, in other words—the completion of its anatomy, the shaping of its limbs—takes place exclusively within the female's womb, she being the "measuring line" that allots him life and determines its tempo. Yet here nothing of the kind obtained.[165]

Now keep in mind that this Primordial Creation-Human is termed "design of the Human image" or "engraving of the Human image," the "Human image" itself being the "Path of Emanation" of which [Creation-Human] is the "engraving."[166] Thus the [young man] continues: IF YOU SAY, THEY WERE IN THE FEMALE, NAMELY THE WORLD THAT IS COMING[167]—by which he means, in the midst of Ein Sof's substrate, which is called "mother" and is the Supernal Mother as we have seen, and all were contained there—NOT SO! FOR DESIGN AND IMAGE DID NOT BEGIN TO TAKE SHAPE UNTIL LETTERS EMERGED AND AFTERWARD TOOK MATERIAL FORM. "Design" and "image," in other words, only came into being with the emergence of the Shape of the God of Israel,[168] with which "design" and "image" had their inception. (And [the young man] speaks of "letters" because all divine emanation has the quality of letters, as we find

---

young man who turns out—as the apparently unlettered often do in the Zohar—to be a scholar of dazzling erudition and profundity. (This translation is adapted from Matt, trans., *Zohar*).

163. The formation of the humanlike structure of the *sefirot*, represented here by "five rungs." If the analogy with the human body is to be maintained, there must have been a female womb in which that structure took on its shape and design. The womb of which female?

164. At the inception of the sefirotic system, described allusively in the first chapter of Genesis.

165. Since, as the young man will go on to explain, there seems to have been no suitable Divine Female within which the Human image might have been shaped.

166. The Shechinah, bringing Creation-Human into existence, models him after Emanation-Human ("the Path of Emanation," i.e., the Shape that emerged from the Spot). The author wants us to understand how the Zohar's terminology may be translated into his own.

167. Normally understood to refer to the *sefirah Binah*, but, for our author, a pre- and super-sefirotic entity.

168. Using "God of Israel" in the broad sense of the totality of the Shape.

throughout the Zohar, e.g., in the passage AT THE BEGINNING OF THE KING'S DECREE in the Torah portion *Bereshit*.[169])

FURTHERMORE, THE WORLD THAT IS COMING WAS THE ARTISAN, AS IT IS WRITTEN, HE SAID, "O ELOHIM! LET THERE BE LIGHT!" That is to say, she functioned as "artisan" vis-à-vis the creation of Light and not of the Human as here, as we have earlier explained at length.[170]

[p. 52] BUT IF YOU SAY, IN THE LOWER FEMALE, i.e. the Shechinah of the God of Israel, who in relation to the substrate of Ein Sof is "the Lower Female"—NOT SO! FOR SHE DID NOT YET EXIST, i.e., she did not yet exist as a Female but only as a placenta, so to speak of sexual coupling would be entirely out of the question. AND WHEN THIS HUMAN IMAGE EMERGED, HIS FEMALE EMERGED WITH HIM, meaning that when the God of Israel extended himself[171] (as discussed below), his Shechinah went forth also to become his partner in sex, and speaking of "Human image" and not "design of the Human image," for it is the God of Israel, the "Human image," that is here intended.

IF SO, IN WHAT PLACE WAS THIS SEED DESIGNED AND ENGRAVED, TO BECOME THE ENGRAVING OF THE HUMAN IMAGE? ([The young man] chooses his words carefully: intending now to speak of Creation-Human, he calls him "engraving of the Human image."[172]) THE FACT IS, THIS MYSTERY OF PRIMORDIAL HUMAN—referring to Primordial Creation-Human, made without sexual coupling—WAS DESIGNED AND ENGRAVED WITHOUT ANY FEMALE. THE SECOND ONE WAS ENGRAVED AND DESIGNED FROM THE POTENCY AND SEED OF THIS ONE, WITHIN A FEMALE.

What this means is as follows: "The second one" refers to the structure of the World of Emanation, which was fashioned and given its solidity at a later stage, as part of the process of mending the Shattered Vessels.[173] IT WAS ENGRAVED AND DESIGNED FROM THE POTENCY AND SEED OF THIS ONE, i.e. Creation-Human, in that it was he who emanated the ten vessels

---

169. The passage beginning on Zohar, I, 15a, which speaks of the divine "seed" as "engraved letters, mystery of Torah."

170. Referring to the preceding section. Our author has identified the "light" of Gen 1:3 with Emanation-Human (end of section 6, above). The young man's singling out of this verse suggests that the activity of the substrate of Ein Sof (= Supernal Mother) had to do with the generation of Emanation-Human, not Creation-Human. The question of whose "womb" Creation-Human was formed in, therefore, remains unanswered.

171. That is, emerged from the Shechinah's womb, at which point the Shechinah was transformed from his nourishing placenta to his Female.

172. And not "Human image," as before.

173. As described in chapter 5.

of Emanation that were shattered, the finest [of their fragments] absorbed into Shechinah and refashioned by her, through sex with the God of Israel, into the shape and structure of the World of Emanation wherein he desired to dwell,[174] as we shall explain at length below. All this was from the potency and seed of Primordial Creation-Human.

[The young man] proceeds to explain that PRIMORDIAL HUMAN, THE ENGRAVING [fol. 11b] OF THE DESIGN, WAS NEVER INSIDE A FEMALE. HE WAS DESIGNED AND ENGRAVED BELOW THE WORLD THAT IS COMING, WITHOUT MALE OR FEMALE. The following, rather, was the manner in which he was given his design: THOSE LETTERS TOOK ON MATERIAL FORM INSIDE A MEASURE, AND BY THEM WAS DESIGNED AND ENGRAVED THE MYSTERY OF THE HUMAN previously mentioned.

We have already explained that all the effluence, all the seed, is contained within "letters." What [the young man] speaks of, then, is the Shechinah's thought and intention having become a kind of action, those "letters" taking on material existence as an equivalent of female juice inside the Shechinah. The latter was at the time in her placenta-state, called "Measure" in that she was the measuring line that nourishes the fetus according to its need and nature, as has been said; and it was this intention, this thought of hers, that inscribed within her the Human design that functioned as her female juices.

THE LETTERS, IN A STRAIGHT PATH AND IN THEIR ORDER FROM THE MYSTERY OF PRIMORDIAL LIGHT,[175] BEGAN TO BE ENGRAVED AND TO TAKE ON DESIGN AS LETTERS, AND THIS LIGHT WAS SOWN WITHIN THIS MEASURE. That is to say, when the God of Israel perceived the Shechinah's intent, he resolved to concur and to fulfill her wish. His [complementary] intention functioned as male juice and direct light, and Human design was inscribed in [the letters] in the role of male juices. [p. 53] This is what [the young man] means by saying that THE LETTERS, IN A STRAIGHT PATH (i.e., as direct light) IN THEIR ORDER FROM THE MYSTERY OF PRIMORDIAL LIGHT (i.e., from the God of Israel) BEGAN TO BE ENGRAVED AND TO TAKE ON DESIGN AS LETTERS. As we have said: the intent to form the design of a

---

174. Speaking of the God of Israel and alluding to Ps 132:13, "the Lord chose Zion, desired it for His dwelling." This is the text's first adumbration of what will become a central theme, that the *sefirot* of the classical Kabbalah are "externalities," rather like suits of armor, within which the superior entities (like "the God of Israel and His Shechinah") choose to encase themselves.

175. Which the author has earlier explained as the Zoharic designation for Emanation-Human, the "Shape" that is the God of Israel in the broad sense of the term.

Human was inscribed and actualized in him as well, and the force of that intent came to the Female as seed and male juice.

Hence THIS LIGHT WAS SOWN WITHIN THIS MEASURE, i.e., within the Shechinah, AND WHEN IT REACHED INTO THE MEASURE, IT TURNED INTO WATER INTERMINGLED WITH WATER, AND A FIRM EXPANSE STRETCHED ITSELF OUT: THE DESIGN OF A HUMAN IMAGE. When his intent reached her, in other words, the equivalents of male and female juices mingled and stretched themselves out together; and when male and female juices fuse, the outcome is THE DESIGN OF A HUMAN IMAGE AS IT OUGHT TO BE.

AFTER THE FEMALE WAS ADORNED FOR HIM AND THEY TURNED face-to-face, THIS HUMAN IMAGE CAME TO LUST FOR HIS FEMALE, AND SOMETHING LIKE HIMSELF WAS ENGRAVED AND DESIGNED THERE. OF THIS IS WRITTEN: *HE ENGENDERED IN HIS LIKENESS, IN ACCORDANCE WITH HIS IMAGE.*[176] THIS ONE ACQUIRED ITS DESIGN INSIDE THE FEMALE, AS THE FIRST ONE HAD NOT, FOR THE FIRST ONE WAS FORMED INSIDE HER BY MEASURING WITHIN THE MEASURE, AS HAS BEEN SAID. This means that, when the time came to construct the World of Emanation about which we have spoken, the God of Israel was in a state of Self-extension,[177] the Shechinah herself a complete Shape. She was decked out with her adornments and so forth; their connection was FACE-TO-FACE, in the mode of sexual coupling; and the God of Israel's lust was stirred up for her, he seeking her out and not as before in connection with Primordial Human, when it was she who sought him. THIS HUMAN IMAGE CAME TO LUST FOR HIS FEMALE, it says, AND SOMETHING LIKE HIMSELF WAS ENGRAVED AND DESIGNED THERE—"like" the God of Israel, who was engendered through sexual coupling, autoerotic, as we have seen, within Ein Sof—and of this the Bible says, *He engendered in his likeness, in accordance with his image,* referring to what we shall speak of below, that Seth symbolically represents the structure of Emanation. This came into being INSIDE THE FEMALE, AS THE FIRST ONE (i.e., Primordial Creation-Human) HAD NOT, for his designing took place through intention and ideation alone, a self-performed "measuring" inside the Female.[178]

176. Gen 5:3, speaking of Adam's begetting of Seth.

177. That is, no longer folded up inside the Shechinah's womb.

178. The author cannot quite shake off the inconsistency in his argument, that Creation-Human was shaped "inside" the Shechinah yet at the same time not really "inside" her. We might reconcile by saying that he was begotten only "inside" her mind, lacking the solid physicality of having originated from within her womb. This will

The Zohar's words are thus made coherent and intelligible; and—to repeat the point made earlier—the Zohar designates Primordial [Creation-]Human as "Primordial Human" while calling the Shape of Emanation by the name "Primordial Light."

9. Esau Revisited—"The Serpent Lives"

[The dual meaning of the Aramaic designation *adam qadma'ah*, "Primordial Human"[179] and the "Adam" of Genesis,[180] invites our author to see the primordial pair of "Adam" and "Eve" as representing the Shape and the Shechinah that was split off from the Shape's male element and, transiently, turned into its maternal womb. One aspect of that Shape, the Distant One, is now given a name closely related to "Adam": "Edom," the fierce enemy of Biblical Israel, which came in medieval Jewish usage to stand for Christendom and the Christian religion.

The author proposes a surprising etymology for "Edom"—"silence." The name conveys that, on account of "Edom's" lofty mystery, we have no right or ability to speak of it. In its nature, "Edom" is pure Grace and Mercy—the familiar characterization of Christianity. Yet the absolute and undiluted character of "Edom's" Mercy, lacking any proper balance with Judgment, paradoxically breeds chaos and havoc.

As the treatise unfolds, the author will show how, in the metaphysical *Heilsgeschichte* of the universe, Christianity had to be superseded by the inferior religion of Judaism, embodied in "the God of Israel" (now conceived as antithesis to the Distant One). Only through the messianic act performed by Sabbatai Zevi, the "holy Serpent" who has enduring "life" in the domain of Esau/Edom, will the religion of the Distant One reclaim its rightful place as the faith of all humanity.]

Returning to our exposition, we may say that the Path of Emanation was in the nature of an "Adam"[181] comprised of the God of Israel and the Holy Distant One, with "Eve" as his Shechinah; and that this situation obtained while he was in his Folded-up state of raw matter, all of him "head."[182] [p. 54] The Distant One was called "Edom," inasmuch as we

---

explain the vulnerability on which our author lays such stress.

179. *Adam qadmon* in Hebrew.
180. *Adam ha-rishon* in rabbinic Hebrew.
181. Or, "Primordial Human," *adam qadma'ah*.
182. As fetus inside the Shechinah's womb. The characterization of the fetal deity as

THE GESTATION OF GOD

are not authorized to discuss him in detail as we do with the rest of the Shapes—called *Edom* from the root meaning "silence," as in the verse in Job, *I shall be silent, eddom, I shall not step outside the door.*[183]

At the time, moreover, he was in the state of a child in its mother's womb, its mouth sealed, and this speechlessness was another reason for calling him "Edom." The Root is called "Seir"—i.e., *se'ar*, "hair," as we have said[184]—and also "Esau" in that, as building's master, he gives the orders that "you must do, *'asu*, such-and-such."[185] Furthermore, "Esau" has the same numerical value as *nahash hai*, "the Serpent lives," inasmuch as sleep and entrancement are wholly absent from that place.[186] This is what the Bible means by speaking of *Esau the father of Edom*:[187] [the Root] is father to the Distant One.

The Distant One is Mercy. Yet, since he lacks the Balance and has the nature of *karmela*,[188] the Judgments are stirred up as he stretches himself downward, as I have written earlier concerning the significance of the hair.[189] The copious outflow of Mercies from him, moreover, brought

---

"raw matter" (*homer*), as yet without form, is unexpected.

183. Job 31:34. "Edom," which has the same consonants as *adam*, "human," but is vocalized differently, is used in the Bible to refer to the non-Israelite (and normally hostile) people descended from Jacob's brother Esau), in rabbinic literature to mean Rome and in medieval Hebrew to mean Christianity. The author's revaluation of the "Edomite" enemy, begun in the final section of chapter 2 and extended here, is astonishing.

184. The Bible regularly uses "Seir" as a designation for the territory of the Edomites (e.g., Deut 2:4, "the children of Esau who dwell in Seir"). Taking his cue from Gen 25:25, 27:11, the author treats it as another name for Esau, and as equivalent to *se'ar*, "hair" (from the same Hebrew root). He has established the Root = hair equation in chapter 2, section 3.

185. The imperative verb "do" (*'asu*) is graphically identical to the name "Esau." The characterization of the "Root" (= the Will of Ein Sof) as "building's master" is developed in section 7, above. *Se'ar*, "hair," the alternative designation for the Root, is a slight revocalization of "Seir."

186. *Nahash*, "serpent," is an allusion to Sabbatai Zevi, who used the snake as his emblem and was often called "the Holy Serpent" by his followers. ("Serpent" and "Messiah" have the same numerical value in Hebrew.) By equating "Esau" with "the Serpent lives"—both have a value of 376—the author conveys that Sabbatai Zevi, who historically converted to Islam, maintains a conscious existence in the upper spheres that are the metaphysical realm of Christianity. Sabbatai's messianic role, in the redemption and ultimate triumph of a radically reconfigured Christianity, is a concealed thread running through the treatise. Here it comes to the surface.

187. Gen 36:43.

188. Above, chapter 1, section 4.

189. Above, chapter 2, section 5. Hence the paradox of Christianity: in theory it is pure mercy and love; in reality, at least as experienced by Jews, it tends to be cruel

about the Shattering of the Vessels and the destruction and devastation of the worlds,[190] from which the Judgments and drosses are known to derive their existence. This is why the Zohar says that judgments are stirred up within Edom, especially given that Mindless Light was mixed in with him[191] until after the Self-extension, as we shall discuss presently.

This is the esoteric significance of the verse *For you silence is a praise-song*.[192] The word *lekha*, "for you," designates Ein Sof, in that the letter *lamed*—"tower flying through the air"[193]—symbolizes the Root, while the substrate of Ein Sof [fol. 12a] functions as its Female, and all females are represented by the letter *kaph* (in this case the extended *kaph*, corresponding to its absolute extension).[194] [Ein Sof] is therefore called *lekha, lamed-kaph*; and the Distant One, as we know, functions in the higher realms as its female, receiving its effluence. All this, however, is in the realm of potentiality. When the Distant One afterward conveys effluence to the Shechinah, she is the actualizing-vessel that brings him to completion.[195]

So *lamed-kaph silence is a praise-song* conveys that the Distant One, who is "silence," is for *lamed-kaph* [= Ein Sof] the female represented by the word *tehillah*, "praise-song." *Lamed-kaph in Zion*, i.e., in his female, *is made complete*, meaning that he is finished and emerges into actuality.[196]

---

and oppressive.

190. Discussed in chapter 4.

191. The Distant One = Edom. The Zoharic dictum, paraphrased from III, 135a, 142a (*Idra Rabbah*), 292a (*Idra Zuta*), is turned on its head: "Edom," which etymologically means "red," is no longer the blood-red sphere of Judgment as in the Zohar, but the realm of Mercies par excellence, whose excessive and uncontrolled Mercy paradoxically gives the Judgments occasion to arise.

192. Ps 65:2, the second part of which our author seems to misread as ולך בציון ישלם נדר and to understand as *lamed-kaph in Zion is made complete, vow-like*. His exegesis is, to put it mildly, forced. Its advantage for him is that it reinforces his connection of "Edom," the Distant One, with the idea of "silence" (*dumiyyah*, in the Psalms passage), as well as the female serving as transition from "airy" insubstantiality to tangible reality.

193. A cryptic phrase found in the Talmud, b. Hag. 15b, Sanh. 106b, and traditionally applied to the tower-like letter *lamed* ל (Rashi to Sanh. 106b). The author will soon emphasize the "airy," intangible quality of the "Higher World" of Ein Sof, where existence remains in potential.

194. *Lekha* is composed of the two letters *lamed-kaph* (לך), the *kaph* in its final ("extended") form. These two letters, the author thinks, represent Ein Sof in its two aspects: male Will (= Root) and female substrate.

195. I take this difficult sentence to refer to the Shechinah's acting as womb for the divine fetus whose essence is the "head," the Distant One. See the next note.

196. From a slight misreading of the rest of the Psalms verse the author implies that

That is why the verse goes on to say, *vow-like*, indicating that it speaks of the Higher World, as we well know; compare the expressions *released vows fly in midair* and *a vow applies to that which has no substance*.[197] For the Higher World is by its nature airy, intangible.[198]

Ein Sof emerged "completed" through his "female" (= the Distant One, who normally functions as male) from potentiality into actuality. The process is analogous to what happened at a lower level, when the Distant One emerged from the "actualizing-vessel" of the Shechinah's womb.

197. The first quote is from Mishnah, m. Hag. 1:8. The second is a slightly but significantly distorted quotation of Zohar, II, 115b (*Ra'ya Mehemna*): "a vow applies *even* to that which has no substance." The rabbinic literature flatly contradicts this assertion, declaring that a vow, unlike an oath, can apply only to a concrete, tangible object (Talmud, b. Ned. 13b and Rashi *ad loc.*; cf. Tishby, *Wisdom*, 1:55). By privileging the Zohar's ruling over the Talmud's, is our author hinting at its superior authority?

198. Reading, against all the mss., *avir* instead of *or*.

4

The Shattering of God

1. **The Riddle of the Eighth King**

   [The Zohar had interpreted the Bible's list of "kings who reigned in the land of Edom, before there reigned any king over the children of Israel" (Gen 36:31–39) as hinting at a system of *sefirot* that preceded our own, yet collapsed or was destroyed. Isaac Luria followed the Zohar's lead, expanding its cryptic allusions to the "Death of the Kings" into a full-blown myth of the "Shattering of the Vessels," the *sefirot* of what had been the "Point-world." Our author now undertakes to detail and explicate this crisis in the prehistoric life of God.

   He begins in good scholastic fashion, by pointing out obscurities and inconsistencies in the received accounts of the Shattering. Luria had identified the first seven Edomite kings, the ones said to have "died," with the seven *sefirot* from *Da'at* through *Malkhut*. But who was the eighth king, Hadar, about whose death Genesis is silent? Of whom the Zohar says that he did not die like the others because "male and female were present together"? A part of the story remains hidden; our author undertakes to unveil it.]

[p.55] Primordial Creation-Human at his emergence is symbolically represented by Cain. This is why Eve said, *I have acquired a man with the Lord*,[1] meaning that it was she through whom his birth was achieved,

---

1. Gen 4:1.

she who had begotten him. Hence the Bible says that *she bore* him: the birth was dependent on her.² Of Abel's birth we shall speak presently.

First, however, we must take up certain difficulties involved in the doctrine of the Shattering of the Vessels.

The Eighth King, the one indicated by the words *King Hadar reigned*,³ is said in the Lurianic writings⁴ to represent *Yesod*, which is symbolized (as the Zohar indeed attests) by *peri 'etz hadar*, the "fruit of a splendid tree," i.e. the citron.⁵ ([*Yesod*] is consequently called *Hadar*, "desirable for eating," as the Targum has it, the very word conveying the idea of desirability.⁶) Yet the Lurianic texts imply also that *Yesod* was

---

2. Referring to the account of Creation-Human's emergence in chapter 3, section 6. Eve = the Higher Shechinah, through whose volition Creation-Human came into existence; "the Lord" = the Distant One, to whom the designation "God of Israel" in its broader sense will shortly be applied, and who affirmed and reinforced that volition; and "Cain" = Creation-Human. Unlike Seth in Gen 5:3, Cain owes his existence essentially to Eve/Shechinah, not to Adam. This is why the Bible gives her full credit for his birth.

3. A free quotation of Gen 36:39. The context of this verse lists eight "kings who reigned in the land of Edom before there reigned any king over the children of Israel." Seven of these—Bela, Jobab, Husham, Hadad, Samlah, Shaul, Baal-hanan—are each said to have "died," while no death is mentioned in connection with Hadar, the eighth. (At least not in Genesis; the parallel list in 1 Chr 1:41–51 does speak of the Eighth King's death, as our author will soon observe.) The first seven kings, in the Lurianic Kabbalah, are symbolic of the seven lower *sefirot* that perished in the primordial catastrophe known as "the Shattering of the Vessels": *Da'at, Hesed, Gevurah, Tif'eret, Netzah+Hod* (considered as "two halves of one body," an eccentricity that will presently occupy our author), *Yesod*, and *Malkhut*. (Vital, *Sha'ar ha-Haqdamot*, 87; cf. Vital, *'Etz Hayyim* viii.4, 38c–d.) But given these equations, who might the Eighth King be?

4. Vital, *'Etz Hayyim* viii.4, 38c (מ"ב); ix.8, 47a; x.3, 48d (מ"ב).

5. The citron (*etrog*), used in the ritual for the Sukkot festival, is traditionally identified with the "fruit of a splendid tree" (*peri 'etz hadar*) of Lev 23:40: Talmud, b. Sukkah 35a. Our author connects *hadar* ("splendor") in this verse with the name of the Eighth King, a linkage for which the Zohar provides a precedent in III, 292a (*Idra Zuta*): "King Hadar" is identical with the "splendid tree" of Leviticus. The Zohar citation probably refers to II, 186b, where the "splendid tree" is equated with *Yesod* as well as with the human penis; versus the "fruit" of that tree, which the Zohar consistently represents as a symbol for the female *sefirah Malkhut* (I, 220a–b, III, 24a–b, and Tishby, *Wisdom of the Zohar*, 3:1249–50, 1308–14). I am tempted to delete the word *peri*, found in all the mss., and to translate: "... symbolized, as the Zohar indeed attests, by the splendid tree that is [i.e., yields] the citron."

6. The Aramaic phrase *regig le-mekhal*, "desirable for eating," is not in fact used by the Targum to translate *hadar*, but is a free quotation of Targ. Gen 2:9, referring to all the trees of Eden, and 3:6, referring specifically to the Tree of Knowledge. The author perhaps implies a further association of Hadar = *Yesod* with the Tree of Knowledge, inferring from the language of Genesis that the tree itself, and not only its fruit, is "desirable for eating." He may also allude to the story in Zohar, II, 13a–b, where a traveler

shattered, as *'Etz Hayyim* says, forfeiting that which he received on his own behalf but not that which he received on behalf of *Malkhut*.⁷ Hard to understand!—for once his vessel was broken, everything should have been shattered and fallen.

Also problematic: given that whatever any of the *sefirot* received on *Malkhut*'s behalf survived and was transmitted to *Malkhut*—for, as we know, it was precisely because of the plenitude of the effluence she received that she was effaced, and the *Book of Concealment* testifies that THE PRIMORDIAL KINGS DIED AND THE EARTH WAS EFFACED—it follows that *Malkhut* alone must have been the sole survivor [of the Shattering].⁸

The *Idra* claims that [the Eighth King] was not shattered because *male and female were present together*,⁹ which is also hard to understand. The Balance did not yet exist;¹⁰ how could there have been male and female? Hard to understand, too, why the *sefirot Netzah* and *Hod*, the "two thighs of truth," should be treated as "two halves of one body" and counted as one [king], while the "two arms," *Hesed* and *Gevurah*, are counted as two.¹¹

And why does the Pentateuch not speak of death in connection with King Hadar, while the book of Chronicles does?¹² Luria has indeed

---

in the desert sees "a tree desirable to look at [*meraggag le-mehze*], with a cave beneath it" which seems to be the entrance to Eden.

7. See above, note 3, where *Yesod* is "Shaul of Rehoboth by the River," the sixth of the dead kings. Vital, *'Etz Hayyim* viii.4, 38d, adds that after the Shattering "one light remained within the vessel of *Yesod* . . . in order to vivify the vessel of *Malkhut* which had nothing of her own . . . remaining concealed there for *Malkhut*'s benefit."

8. The Eighth King, who did not die, therefore ought to have been *Malkhut* and not *Yesod*. The *Book of Concealment* (*Sifra di-Tzeni'uta*), a brief and cryptic text found in Zohar, II, 176b–79a, opens with the words: "It has been taught: The Book of Concealment, a book balanced on scales. For until there was a balance, they did not gaze face-to-face, and the primordial kings died and their weapons vanished and the earth was effaced." (Adapted from Matt's translation; Matt renders the final word as "nullified.") "Earth" is understood to be a symbol of *Malkhut*, whose fate was apparently different from that of the Kings. Our author assumes that the difference is that they were annihilated ("died"), while something less drastic befell her.

9. Free quotation of Zohar, III, 135b (*Idra Rabbah*).

10. As the Book of Concealment attests; above, note 8.

11. The phrase "two thighs of truth," referring to the sefirotic body of which *Hesed* and *Gevurah* are the arms and *Netzah* and *Hod* the thighs, is drawn from *Tiqqunei Zohar* 21 (46b). "Two halves of the body" is from Vital, *Sha'ar ha-Haqdamot*, 87; Vital, *'Etz Hayyim* viii.4, 38d, which inconsistently treats *Netzah* and *Hod* as a single king but *Hesed* and *Gevurah* as two. The author will answer the question posed here in chapter 6, section 6.

12. Gen 36:39 vs. 1 Chr 1:51.

tried to explain away the contradiction; yet the problem remains unresolved, and his interpretation demands an interpretation of its own. The Zohar also contradicts itself, saying at times that the two cherubim that were on the Ark symbolize Little-face and his Female, at other times identifying them as *Netzah* and *Hod*.[13]

[p. 56] To make sense of all these difficulties, you must pay close attention to what I am about to say.

2. Cain and Abel

[The God of Israel remains in the fetal state he entered in chapter 3. The Shechinah, symbolized in the Bible by "Eve," has begotten—by pure mentation, without sexual intercourse—a Primordial Creation-Human (Cain) who stands above the chaos-waters of the *Tehiru* that the Shechinah wanted him to purify. She now begets, in the same asexual (and therefore flawed) way, a second being, who will enter the *Tehiru*, his soul infusing the sefirotic "bodies" that Cain had already emitted into it. His name is Abel.

Besides his location within the *Tehiru*, Abel has another advantage over Cain in the task of purifying it: he has two females, while Cain has only one. One of Abel's "twin sisters" (who are also his wives) enters the *Malkhut* of the Point-world as a female normally ought, there remaining barren and sexually undeveloped. The other shares a sefirotic vessel with the Point-world's *Yesod*, and thereby turns the phallic *Yesod* into

---

13. I am not sure which Zoharic passages our author has in mind, and the issue is complicated by a textual uncertainty: two manuscripts (Oxford 976 and Jerusalem 2491) speak of "the two cherubim," while the other two (Oxford 955 and Jerusalem 3100) speak instead of "the two tablets" (*luhot*) that were placed inside the Ark. Moses Cordovero, in the *Sha'ar 'Erkhei ha-Kinnuyim* section of *Pardes Rimmonim*, observes that "cherubim" in the Zohar is normally to be taken at face value, as referring to angels situated beneath the *sefirah Malkhut*. Where the two cherubim—winged creatures who spread their wings over the Ark-cover, in Exod 25:17-22; 37:6-9—do function as sefirotic symbols, they seem most often to be *Netzah* and *Hod* (III, 236a, *Ra'ya Mehemna*). A passage from *Tiqqunei Zohar Hadash*, however, suggests that they are fundamentally *Tif'eret* and *Malkhut* (= Little-face and his Female), but in the several aspects of their bodies representing other *sefirot*, including *Netzah* and *Hod* (Cordovero, s.v. *keruvim*). As for the two stone tablets containing the Ten Commandments, which Moses placed inside the Ark (Deut 10:5), they are explicitly equated in the preface to *Tiqqunei Zohar* (11b) with *Netzah* and *Hod*; yet *Tiqqunei Zohar* 55 (88b) identifies them with the last two letters of the Tetragrammaton, representing *Tif'eret* and *Malkhut* (Cordovero, s.v. *luhot*, which harmonizes the two positions). The upshot: the author's statement is defensible regardless of which reading we adopt.

an androgyne. These two females figure in the Bible as the two wives of Lamech (Gen 4:19). Their duality will prove the key to the riddle of the Eighth King.]

Once the construction of Creation-Human was complete—this being the Primordial Human symbolized by Cain, the bottom of his *Malkhut* reaching down to the *Tehiru* that was *Ma'aseh Bereshit*,[14] as I have written earlier—the Shechinah conceived a desire to beget another human being that should actually be within the *Tehiru* and *Ma'aseh Bereshit*. The quality of *Ma'aseh Bereshit* was that of a preliminary sketch,[15] frozen water; she therefore wanted a human to be in its midst, purifying those frozen waters, repelling the Mindless Light, Judgments, and all refuse from the Mindful Light and leaving [that Mindful Light] as purified gold and silver, vivified, restored clean and pure to the place from which it was taken. The intended purpose was that the entire locus of *Tehiru* and *Ma'aseh Bereshit* be converted into *Ma'aseh Merkavah*; which indeed did happen, but not at once. It took place only after the Shattering, as we shall presently describe.

For that reason did [the Shechinah] beget a human being to be in the place that Emanation[16] now occupies; and this is how it came about.

The "sketch" that was *Ma'aseh Bereshit* similarly[17] possessed ten *sefirot*. Yet these were in the nature of a garment, like a nutshell vis-à-vis its kernel. (This is the meaning of "the shell preceding the kernel":[18] *Ma'aseh Bereshit* preceded *Ma'aseh Merkavah*.) Into this "garment" of *Ma'aseh Bereshit*, Primordial Creation-Human then emitted ten spots that were to serve as "bodies," vessels for the *sefirot*, and this was the

---

14. *Malkhut* is the lowest *sefirah* of a sefirotic body. It was Creation-Human's nethermost extremity alone that reached down as far as the *Tehiru*.

15. Above, chapter 3, section 2.

16. The sefirotic system that came into being in response to the Shattering.

17. "Similarly," that is, to the later sefirotic system.

18. *Ha-qelippah qademah la-peri*, a Kabbalistic maxim that condenses the idea expressed at greater length in the Zohar, II, 108b: "In all actions performed by the blessed Holy One, He begins with the external, and then the kernel within. . . . For every shell derives from the Other Side, and kernel from kernel. The Other Side always precedes: growing, developing, protecting the fruit" (trans. Matt, *Zohar*). In Kabbalistic usage *qelippah*, "shell," like "Other Side" (*sitra ahra*), normally indicates the demonic, but can at times function neutrally, indeed protectively, in the divine economy (Tishby, *Wisdom of the Zohar*, volume 2, 454–55). Our author seems to intend no demonic overtone for *qelippah*; his point is simply that, as in the Zohar passage just quoted, the outer layers have chronological precedence over the inner: first "garment," then "bodies," then "interiority and intelligence."

"Point-world" of which Luria spoke.[19] Yet the organs of intelligence, the inner light essential to any *sefirah*, was placed within them by the God of Israel's Shechinah through acts of mentation. As earlier with Primordial Creation-Human, so here: [a second entity] was begotten of her mental activity and that of the God of Israel, to serve as interiority and intelligence within the Point-world vessels emitted by Cain.

He was thus named Abel, "vapor," the mere "vapor within the bones"[20] of the bodies that Cain had provided. Abel was Cain's "brother," born likewise of the Shechinah and the God of Israel. Know this also: that the Shechinah, having invested more of her desire in him [fol. 12b] for the mending of *Ma'aseh Bereshit*—and given that the essential agent of mending is the female—placed two females within him. Unlike Primordial Human, who had only *Malkhut* for his female, he had two females.

This is the significance of the "additional twin sister born with Abel," with regard to whom the Bible says that [Eve] *additionally bore Abel*,[21] using the word *additionally* to convey that the females were two.[22] [p. 57] Yet the vessels numbered only ten *sefirot*.[23] One of those females consequently took up residence within the *Malkhut* of the Point-world,[24] this being her proper place, while the other female dwelt with Abel's *Yesod* in one location, namely his genital organ. The two of them thereby *became one flesh*,[25] androgynous, male and female.

---

19. In the Lurianic cosmogony, the "Point-world" (*'olam ha-nequdim*) is the second stage of the evolution of the *sefirot*, when they exist as individual entities but, not having yet undergone the Shattering, have not been organized into the system of "shapes" (the third stage).

20. Applying the phrase from Zohar, III, 169a, to the interpretation of Abel's name.

21. A slight misquotation of Gen 4:2, which ms. Jerusalem 2491 corrects in accord with the Biblical text.

22. Midrash Genesis Rabbah 22:7: "An additional twin sister was born with Abel" and the brothers, grown to manhood, quarreled over her, "one saying, 'I will take her because I am the elder,' the other saying, 'I will take her because she was born with me.'" ("Additional," because Cain and Abel each already had one twin sister who was to be his wife.) Our author takes an exegetical path different from that of the midrash, inferring Abel's second twin sister from *va-tosef*, "additionally," in Gen 4:2, but carries over the midrash's essential point: Cain was born with one sister-wife, Abel with two. For the range of rabbinic traditions about the girl-children born with Cain and Abel, see Ginzberg, *Legends*, 5:138.

23. So where were Abel's two females to be lodged?

24. The sefirotic system emitted by Cain, the "body" for which Abel is to be the inner intelligence.

25. Gen 2:24.

The lower female, the one in *Malkhut*, needed to remain barren and sexually undeveloped, so that the Insolent Waters might not penetrate her womb and belly. For that reason, barrenness must be her nature. The female located within the genital, by contrast, was sexually open; inasmuch as she was together with the male *Yesod*, she was in the category of "a woman protected by her husband,"[26] who stops up her opening (as it were) so no strangers can get into her. This is the significance of the men in the generation of the Flood—symbolizing the Point-world, for the Flood is a representation of the Shattering of the Vessels, as Luria has written[27]—having taken two wives, one barren and the other not.[28] Understand this.

A close reading of the Biblical text reveals an explicit enumeration of the vessels, the sefirotic bodies that Cain emitted. *Cain made love to his wife and begat Enoch*,[29] this being a title for the *Keter* of the Point-world, the place where the name *YHVH* began to be revealed and where it found its rest. (*YHVH* has the numerical value 26, *kaf-vav*; hence Hanokh, *nah kaf-vav*, for that was where *kaf-vav* rested.)[30] *And Enoch built a city*,[31] i.e., *Hokhmah*, where *Keter* has his dwelling; and inasmuch as *Hokhmah* and *Keter* are combined as one and share a single name, the Bible says that *he named the city after his son Enoch*.

Hokhmah emitted *Binah*, and this is *Irad*, "city of David" and also "city of *dalet*," inasmuch as *Malkhut*, symbolized by the letter *dalet*, resides there.[32] *And Irad begat Mehujael*, who combines *El*, "God," and *hayyim*,

26. *Ishah ba'alah meshammerah*. The expression is found nowhere in the rabbinic literature, but perhaps alludes (as Maciejko suggests) to Talmud, b. Qidd. 86a, where a woman is permitted to be alone with a man provided that her husband is in town. Alternatively, this may be a misquotation of *ishah ba'alah mesammehah* ("a woman's husband provides her joy," b. Qidd. 34b, Rosh Hash. 6b), which graphically is nearly identical (משמרה vs. משמחה).

27. Vital, *Etz Hayyim* viii.4 (38c-d, מ"ב), quoting Gen 7:19–20 in support of the claim that "the Flood alludes to the Shattering of the Vessels."

28. According to *Midrash Genesis Rabbah* 23:2, each man of the antediluvians would take two wives, one for procreation and the other for pleasure; a contraceptive potion would keep the latter in a state of barrenness. The author introduces the idea, foreign to the midrash, that "barrenness" implies being sexually closed.

29. Hebrew *Hanokh* (חנוך); see the next note. All quotations in this and the following paragraphs are from Gen 4:17–22. The Biblical text speaks of Cain's wife doing the "begetting"; our author finds it convenient to shift this action to Cain.

30. *Nah kaf-vav*, "*kav-vav* rested" (נח ד"ו), is an anagram of חנוך, *Hanokh*.

31. Misquotation; the Bible makes clear that the city's builder is Cain, not Enoch.

32. The first three Hebrew letters of the name of Enoch's son Irad spell *'ir*, "city." The fourth letter, *dalet*, represents *Malkhut* in Kabbalistic symbolism; or, alternatively,

"life," and thus stands for *Gedullah*, for *Hesed*.³³ For [the divine name] *El* is proper to *Hesed*; [p. 58] and the Biblical verse provides the alternative spelling *Mehijael* for *Mehujael*, the letters *vav* and *yod* being interchangeable (as when Eve, *havvah*, is called "mother of all living," *hai*).³⁴

Next comes *Methushael* who is *Gevurah*. *Methusael* is an anagram for *shammot el*, "God's devastations," he being the smasher, the destroyer (as in *making devastations in the earth*³⁵). *Methushael begat Lamech*, i.e., *Tif'eret*, who is King of the World,³⁶ and *Lamech took two wives, the two females*,³⁷ *Adah* and *Zillah*. Adah was the one who dwelt in *Malkhut*, as implied by the Aramaic meaning of *Adah*, "she turned aside"—turned aside from her husband, lived in a vessel of her own—while Zillah, the second female, lived "in the shade," *tzel*, of her husband in a single vessel; see Rashi's Pentateuch commentary.³⁸ *Netzah*, *Hod*, and *Yesod* were contained within [the two females], once the interiority that was Abel had descended from above.³⁹ (So it was after the Mending, when the Shechinah enclothed the God of Israel up to his *Tif'eret*, fusing herself with his *Netzah*, *Hod*, and *Yesod*.)

And so Adah bore *Netzah*, symbolized by *Jabal*, "conveyer"⁴⁰ of the effluence. Hence the Bible says that he was *father of those who dwell in tents with flocks* [Gen 4:20]: the priest is known to stand for *Netzah*, and he is *father of tent and flock* in allusion to the sacrifices made by him from the flock.⁴¹ *His brother's name was Jubal*, i.e., *Yesod*, who is known to be

---

stands for "David" who also is *Malkhut*.

33. Alternative names for the *sefirah Hesed*.

34. *Mehijael*, as a gloss in ms. Jerusalem 2491 points out, is an anagram of *hayyim el* (אל + חיים = מחייאל); the forms *Mehujael* and *Mehijael* occur side by side in Gen 4:18. Eve's name *havvah* is derived from *hai*, "living," in Gen 3:20. Cf. above, chapter 1, section 4, where the replacement of *yod* with *vav* is given a meaning beyond randomly interchangeable letters.

35. Ps 46:9.

36. *Melekh*, "king," is an anagram of *Lamekh*.

37. Who were said above to have been given to Abel.

38. Rashi, in his comment on Gen 4:19, gives the etymologies of *Adah* and *Zillah* that our author employs here, though naturally without the Kabbalistic reference to "vessels." Their ultimate source is Midrash Genesis Rabbah 23:2.

39. *Netzah*, *Hod*, and *Yesod* of the Point-world were not "emitted" from *Tif'eret*, as each of the earlier *sefirot* was from its predecessor. (The Bible never credits Lamech with "begetting" Jabal, Jubal, Tubal-cain and Naamah.) Rather, they were infused by the indwelling Abel-spirit into his two females.

40. *Movil*, from the same root as "Jabal."

41. Also alluding, as the author surely intends, to the "Tent of Meeting" that was the

called *Jubal. He was the father of all who handle harp and pipe*, because "harp," *kinnor*, is the coupling of male and female, *ku ner*: he "handles" coupling in that he is the one who performs it.[42]

As for *Hod*, who is *Tubal-cain*, it was within Zillah that he was contained. His quality is Judgment, and thus he *forges iron and bronze*.[43] The sister of Tubal-cain was Naamah, the one from whom *Ma'aseh Bereshit* might suck its nourishment.[44] And Abel, who emerged from the God of Israel and his Shechinah in the manner described above, functioned as interiority [for them all].[45]

Given: [1] that Abel emerged from the quality of "head," which at the time was the quality of the Distant One[46] and had nothing of Balance—rather, Judgment was incorporated within Mercy and all the Mercies were stretched to their fullest extent, with no limitation whatever; and given [2] that Mindless Light, which is pure destruction inasmuch as it lacks any thought directed toward building, was still mixed in;

[p. 59] and given [3] the absence of Balance—

given all this, the Judgments that were there could not but become absolute, untempered Judgment upon their extension downward,[47] as we have remarked earlier.

---

wilderness prototype of the Jerusalem Temple.

42. *Yesod*, the penis, is the organ that "couples" male and female. The point of the analysis of *kinnor* into *ku ner* is not clear; Maciejko suggests that *ku* (כו, *kaf-vav*) is "26," the numerical value of *YHVH* (= male), while *ner* ("lamp") is a representation of *Malkhut* (= female). I find this rather strained but cannot think of anything better. The root of the word translated "pipe," *'ugav*, has strong overtones of sexual desire, which the author presumably has in mind although he does not say it explicitly. I do not know on what basis he says that *Yesod* "is known to be called *Jubal*."

43. Instruments of war; the Biblical text is slightly misquoted.

44. Presumably *Malkhut*, the lowest of Cain's *sefirot* and the one in closest contact with *Ma'aseh Bereshit*.

45. So paradoxically, Abel is the spirit dwelling within the generations of Cain.

46. The Distant One is the "head" of the Shape that entered Shechinah's womb (above, chapter 2, section 1), and it was the Distant One's thought that collaborated with the Shechinah's to produce "Cain" (= Creation-Human; above, chapter 3, section 6). Earlier in this section, the author has spoken of "Abel" being produced by "her [Shechinah's] mental activity and that of the God of Israel"; he uses "God of Israel" in its broader sense of the entirety of the Shape, including the "head" that is the Distant One. Here, he connects the begetting of "Abel," like that of "Cain," specifically with the "head."

47. As "Abel," into the sefirotic vessels provided by "Cain." All of these factors together account for Abel's fragility.

Had sexual coupling been in play, the result would have been far different. Through coupling, contraction is achieved; through contraction, Mindless Light is separated out. When light contracts itself together, Mindless Light will not go along [fol. 13a] with it, expansion rather than contraction being its natural bent. The Mindless Light therefore pulls itself away. Contraction, by its nature, partakes of Judgment; yet Mercies are mixed in with this Judgment, Judgments are sweetened and mixed with Mercies, and through the very act of contraction they are pressed together and intermingled. Most crucially: when the Female receives effluence, she acts as measuring-line, granting proportion, sweetening and mingling [its elements], as the mother does for the fetus and for whatever enters within her.

Here,[48] however, all this was lacking. There was no sexual coupling except in thought and imagining, as in a spermatic emission.[49] Had the male-female Balance been operative in the Point-world, this still would have been remediable: the effluence that reached them would have been sweetened upon arrival. But these "points" as well did not "look at one another face to face,"[50] and consequently were in every respect vulnerable to Shattering.

Yet all the effluence that reached them did so via Primordial Creation-Human who stood outside the *Tehiru*, and the potency of the effluence diminished as it fell from his mouth. This turned out to be their salvation, allowing them to survive and some remnant of them to persist in the *Tehiru*. The Abel-shape, meanwhile, was in the midst of the *Tehiru*, standing amid the *Tehiru*'s Insolent Waters and frozen waters. Upon the Abel-shape's arrival there the waters shifted themselves to the side, leaving space for the Merkavah and then raging to destroy it—very much as, when a structure of any kind is erected in a place of water, the waters will

---

48. In the generation of Cain and Abel, who embody the Point-world.

49. *Zera' le-vattalah*, literally, "wasted seed." The phrase derives from the Talmud, b. Nid. 13a, referring to masturbation. It will recur frequently in what follows, and will normally be translated "uncontained ejaculate."

50. From the beginning of the *Sifra di-Tzeni'uta* (Zohar, II, 176b): "For until there was a balance, they did not gaze face-to-face, and the primordial kings died" (trans. Matt, *Zohar*). The subject of "they" is the male and female aspects of divinity; the Vilna Gaon, in his commentary on *Sifra di-Tzeni'uta*, applies the statement specifically to the higher divine couple *Hokhmah* and *Binah*. It is possible that our author shares this understanding, and this is the point of his "as well." Not only did *Hokhmah* and *Binah* fail to "look at one another face to face" in the absence of the Balance, but the rest of the entities of the Point-world shared this deficiency.

rage to destroy it, tumbling every which way. They were not able to do so—yet. But at a later time they would, as we shall presently see.

3. Excursus: The Nature of the Waters

> [Since the Insolent Waters that fill the *Tehiru* are a menace to Abel, whom they surround, and also an object of his benevolent attention, the author pauses to give an account of their nature. This requires him to get ahead of his story, and to describe the Shechinah's ministrations to these waters in a later time—indeed, in our own time.
>
> The "Shechinah" spoken of here is not the Higher Shechinah with whom we have until now had to do, but one of the Lower Shechinahs "born" with Abel—specifically, the undeveloped virgin who dwells in *Malkhut*. Night after night she enters among the inchoate, undeveloped human souls that are the Insolent Waters, purifying them with her fire and lifting them up to the supernal realms. In their upward flow, symbolized by the sacrificial cult of the Pentateuch, they serve as "female juices," stimulating the downward flow of the "male" effluence.
>
> All this is far in the future. But like some modern thinkers who regard consciousness as a primordial element of the universe, our author locates the human soul near the beginning of all existence. Only, it is "soul" in a flawed and polluted state, a mortal menace therefore to the divine entities that dwell among it.]

[p. 60] If we seek to understand the sacrifices offered in the supernal realms by the ordinary priest, the deputy high priest, and the high priest—the Shechinah represented by the last of these, *Netzah* by his deputy, and *Gedullah* by the ordinary priest[51]—the crux of the matter is that the *Tehiru*, which is the *Ma'aseh Bereshit* and frozen waters described above, consists essentially of souls and light in a state of incompletion. For it is, in its entirety, a light-impression from the God of Israel and his Shechinah, manifesting as flooding or frozen waters.

---

51. The assumption that the Temple priests stand for the *sefirah Hesed* (= *Gedullah*) is a staple of Kabbalistic symbolism. I am not aware of any other source that associates the different ranks of the priesthood with different *sefirot*—paradoxically, the lowest *sefirah* (*Malkhut*, the Shechinah) with the high priest, the higher-ranking *Netzah* with the deputy high priest, and the still higher *Hesed* with the ordinary priest. On the meaning of "Shechinah" in this section, see the introductory summary.

The Shechinah's task is to walk into these waters night after night, plucking from them whatever may be worthy, walking with the power of fire to purify them. Like water that is unfit for drinking, yet when heated will expel its pollutants and retain its select elements, so it is here: she takes those Insolent Waters and, by virtue of the fire that she receives from Judgment, purges and purifies them. Much of that water, dried by the power of her fire, is swallowed up in the ground through the force of the heating and it turns to dust; for dust is *Malkhut*'s nature.[52] But when it turns to clear water, the "priest" (who is *Hesed*) showers it with graces,[53] vivifying it, purifying it.

Hence the command that *a perpetual fire shall be kindled on the altar, never allowed to die out*,[54] admonishing that it must burn all night long. For by night she goes to the *Tehiru*, as Scripture says, *in a pillar of fire by night to give them light*[55] (on which see below), fashioning them into worthy souls and intelligences. Afterward, when she is done with them, they rise as female juices up to *Netzah*, from there to *Gedullah*, and onward to the Root of Ein Sof.

The Zohar says this explicitly with regard to the sacrifices: THEY RISE TO EIN SOF, TO THAT CONCEALED ONE HIDDEN WITHIN IT, namely to the Root, which is the Will and intention of Ein Sof concealed within Ein Sof's substrate, as we have seen.[56] The *'olah*, the "ascending" sacrifice,[57] symbolizes those hyperselect that make the full ascension; while that category of souls and intelligences that remain blocked from

---

52. *Malkhut* being the "ground" of the sefirotic system.
53. *Hasadim*, the plural of *hesed*.
54. Lev 6:6.
55. Exod 13:21.
56. Zohar II, 239a, quoted imprecisely; cf. I, 65a. *Shem 'Olam*, 132, gives a more exact quotation of a small part of the Zohar passage, arguing from it that "'Ein Sof' is a term comprising both the 'image of the ten *sefirot*' [i.e., the first "effect"] and the First Cause," while " 'that Concealed One' means the 'image of the ten *sefirot*,' concealed within the First Cause in the most absolute secrecy." As Perlmuter points out in his important discussion of the parallel (*Rabbi Jonathan Eibeschuetz*, 290-91), *Va-avo ha-Yom* and *Shem 'Olam* use different terminology to express the identical thought: "Ein Sof's substrate" in *Va-avo ha-Yom* = "First Cause" in *Shem 'Olam*; "Root" or "Will" in *Va-avo ha-Yom* = "image of the ten *sefirot*" in *Shem 'Olam* (which, confusingly, also speaks of this entity as "Ein Sof," without qualification). Cf. above, chapter 1, note 3. Perlmuter rightly takes this as proof that *Va-avo ha-Yom* and *Shem 'Olam* are the work of the same author, Rabbi Jonathan Eibeschuetz.
57. The type of sacrifice that is burned in its entirety on the altar (Lev 1). The term *'olah*, normally translated "burnt-offering" or "whole-offering," literally means "ascending," i.e., to the Deity.

ascending[58]—the heights being reserved for the hyperselect, those represented by the *'olah*—stay attached [p. 61] to the distinct *sefirot* mentioned earlier, according to their rank and value. They are thus represented by the *hattat*-sacrifice that is eaten by the priests and does not rise upward in its entirety.[59] We shall presently have a great deal more to say about this.

All of these [raised souls] function in the supernal realms as female juices. The Root then pours out male juices toward them in accord with the quality of their female juice; for the more copious the female juices, the more copious the corresponding male. This we know well: IN ACCORD WITH THE AROUSAL FROM BELOW [fol. 13b], SO IS THE AROUSAL ABOVE.[60]

4. Why Abel Died

[Casual readers of the Bible are apt to come away with the impression that Cain murdered Abel. This is an error. Cain was indeed partly responsible for his brother's death, but his role in the catastrophe was inadvertent and stemmed from hasty judgment rather than malice.

The author has already spoken of Abel's advantages over Cain in the project of purifying the *Tehiru*. It is no wonder that Abel's "offering" was superior, and called forth a greater quantity of effluence from above. Cain therefore conceived the desire to plunge into the *Tehiru* and fuse himself with Abel, that he might enjoy success like Abel's.

The "God of Israel" warned him not to do that. By staying in his proper place he would assist Abel, shielding him from the devastating downpour of divine effluence. Without that shield, and without the solidity of a sexual begetting, Abel would be vulnerable to Shattering. But Cain would not listen, and went down into the *Tehiru*. The Shattering was the result.

---

58. *De-ishta'er behon de-la salqi*. This sounds like a quotation from the Zohar, but I have been unable to track it down.

59. The "*sefirot* mentioned earlier" are presumably *Malkhut*, *Netzah*, and *Gedullah*. Each is represented by a different rank of the priesthood; the priests' consumption of prescribed portions of the *hattat*-sacrifice ("sin-offering," Lev 4:1–5:13, 6:24–30 [Heb. 6:17–23]) therefore symbolizes the inferior soul-material's adhesion to these *sefirot* (versus the "select" that ascend all the way to the Root). I am not sure of the sense of the word *behinot* that qualifies *sefirot*; "distinct" is my best guess.

60. Zohar I, 164a, 235a, II, 32a; the same thought, in slightly different language, in I, 88a, 244a, II, 184b.

(It seems incongruous that the God of Israel, still a fetus in the Shechinah's womb, could be an active conversation partner as described here. Perhaps the author conceives that the fetal God can communicate with other entities but cannot control them. He can warn Cain not to make the descent, but cannot stop him from doing it.)]

Cain (i.e., Primordial Creation-Human), standing above the *Tehiru*, touched only the edge of the *Tehiru* with the base of his *Malkhut*.[61] He could absorb from the *Tehiru* only that which could be absorbed by his *Malkhut* at that point of contact, absent the rest of his *sefirot* and limbs. Abel, by contrast, stood with his whole body, all his limbs, in the midst of the *Tehiru*, and was therefore able to receive copiously of its most select elements.

This is the inner meaning of the Scripture, *It came to pass at the end of days*.[62] *Days* stand for the "Days of Creation,"[63] from whose extremity *Cain brought a gift to the Lord from the fruit of the earth*, namely that which had been absorbed by the ground of *Malkhut*, which is called "earth."[64] These were of no very high quality, partaking rather of Judgment, which is why [Cain's offering] is said to have been flax, which stands for Judgment.

Abel, however, was in the midst of the *Tehiru*. All of his *sefirot* could absorb and properly purify, with waters of perfect Mercy as the outcome. This is what is meant by *the firstfruits of his flock*, for "flock" is known to represent the *sefirot* of Little-face, which was then Abel's place; *firstfruits of his flock* in that they were fully ripened and perfected, as firstfruits are. They were the choicest, Mercy by nature, and so the text says [that Abel offered] *of their fat*, of the most select. "Fat," moreover, is symbolic of Mercy.

The female juices being more copious [in Abel's offering than in Cain's], the male juices also came in greater quantity, as we have seen. Hence *the Lord responded favorably to Abel and his gift*, bestowing upon him plentiful effluence, while *he did not respond favorably*—so plentifully—to Cain. [p. 62] It was very upsetting to Cain, not to receive effluence like his brother. He longed to be within the *Tehiru* so he could

---

61. The lowest of his *sefirot*.

62. Gen 4:3. Unless indicated otherwise, all Biblical quotations in this section are from Gen 4:3–8.

63. Kabbalistic code for the *sefirot*, the lower "extremity" of which is *Malkhut*.

64. A staple of Kabbalistic symbolism.

pour forth female juices as his brother Abel had, and so he sought to make a descent into the *Tehiru*'s midst. (This would have been a "fall," for any descent from one rank to another is a "falling." Hence *his face fell*, in his seeking to descend.)

Abel had another advantage in that he had two females, and thus could perform the act of collection more effectively. This also was a source of jealousy, as the Zohar and midrash tell us: "He envied him for his additional twin sister."[65]

The God of Israel told [Cain] he must not descend.[66] He would augment the power of the Insolent Waters, and Shattering would be the result. *If you do well* by staying in place, he told him, then *lifting up*: you will be able to lift your brother's burden and keep him standing, unshattered. *But if you do not do well, sin lurks by the opening.* The Insolent Waters, lurking at the edges, will gain the upper hand and work Shattering, *and it is you that they desire. But you can dominate them*—if you will only stay where you are!

Cain, however, was set upon his desire. He went ahead and clothed himself in the *Tehiru*, Abel extending from his navel and upward in erotic embrace, [Cain] seeking to make [Abel] his female and to absorb female juices from him. Thus the Bible speaks of "pledging" in the erotic sense, as in *you have pledged yourself to the Lord this day*:[67] *Cain pledged himself to Abel his brother*,[68] employing the selfsame erotic idiom.

You must realize that Abel, having initially been under [Cain's] feet, now stretched upward, taller, from his navel. Yet he was also enclothed within him, and he now entered from below and *rose upon him.*[69] The effluence consequently came to [Abel] in great quantity.

---

65. Combining Zohar, I, 54b, with *Midrash Genesis Rabbah* 22:7; see above, note 22.

66. Speaking from the Shechinah's womb? On the incongruity, cf. below, chapter 6, note 30.

67. Deut 26:17.

68. *Va-yomer kayin el hevel ahiv*, literally, "Cain said to Abel his brother"—problematic, since Cain does not appear to "say" anything. The interpreters, going back to the Greek Septuagint, often resolve the difficulty by supplying words like "Let us go into the field." The author suggests a drastically different resolution.

69. The pronouns are ambiguous. It would appear that Abel is "enclothed" within Cain—that is, as "interiority and intelligence within the Point-world vessels emitted by Cain" (above, section 2)—while Cain himself makes his disastrously unwise descent and "rises" upon Abel. The language is taken from Gen 4:8, "Cain rose upon Abel his brother and slew him," but the author envisions a "slaying" far more indirect and unintended than a casual reading of the Biblical text would suggest.

We have spoken at length of [Abel's] vulnerability to shattering from any and all causes, shielded only by this Primordial Creation-Human who is represented in Cain. But now, [Cain] having descended from his proper place,[70] the effluence fell heavily upon him. And so, *while they were in the field*—for the *Tehiru* is called "field of Machpelah,"[71] as we have seen—in *rising* upon him [Cain] then *killed him*, meaning that the Shattering befell him.

The Shattering consisted of great cracks being made in the vessels, light flowing out through those cracks and openings, [p. 63] and the Insolent Waters thus empowered to surge upward. Between the two,[72] the "garments" of which we have spoken were shattered while the "bodies" and inner lights fell into the Insolent Waters.[73] These latter, in consequence, gained in power and became flood-like, tempestuous.

5. The "Kings of Edom"

[The author pauses to remind us that only the seven lower *sefirot* of the Point-world were devastated by the Shattering—standard Lurianic doctrine, which will take on some importance in the author's treatment of the figure of Balaam. He adds that the Shattering occurred in the "territory and dominion" of the Distant One, which he identifies with the Bible's "land of Edom." This equation is unknown to the earlier Kabbalah, and is the fruit of the author's engagement with the historical "Edom," the Christian Church. The God of Israel is not yet on the scene, still the fetus in the Shechinah's womb, whose dominant "head" is the Distant One. (He seems to be able to engage in dialogue with the principals of the action, in sections 4 and 9, but he cannot control them in any way; in both instances his will is thwarted.) Hence: "before there reigned any king over the children of Israel."]

---

70. And no longer able to function as an intervening shield; above, section 2.

71. Above, chapter 3, section 5; which, however, does not make clear that the *Tehiru* is intended. For the Biblical source of the phrase, see chapter 3, note 81.

72. The cracking of the vessels on the one hand, the surge of the Insolent Waters on the other.

73. As explained in section 2 above, the "garments" are the inchoate *sefirot* of *Ma'aseh Bereshit*, the "bodies" the vessels emitted by Primordial Creation-Human (= Cain), and the "inner lights" the Abel-spirit within these vessels.

Only the seven lower *sefirot* were shattered.⁷⁴ The three prime *sefirot* in the higher domain experienced Shattering only in that *Ma'aseh-Bereshit* "garment" of which we have spoken, to which Luria alludes when he says that only the "rear portions" of the upper three were shattered.⁷⁵ This is the meaning of the passage, *And these are the kings who reigned in the land of Edom.*⁷⁶ For the Shattering was caused by the effluence of the Distant One, expanding without anything to stop it; and with the words *who reigned in the land of Edom* the Bible indicates the Distant One's territory and dominion, called *the land of Edom*, as we have seen.⁷⁷

He was then ruler in this *land*, for the king of Israel, namely the God of Israel, had not yet emerged. All was still in its Folded-up state, all subsumed within the Distant One, as we have seen;⁷⁸ therefore Scripture says, *before there reigned any king for the children of Israel*, since [the God of Israel] had not yet emerged in his proper form. *And these*, says the Bible, implying that [the kings about to be enumerated] were "additional to what was prior," namely Primordial Human who also was a king, his Balance entirely dependent on the Distant One.⁷⁹

---

74. The seven *sefirot* from *Da'at* down through *Malkhut* (*Netzah* and *Hod* counted as a single entity), said in the Lurianic literature to have experienced the Shattering. See above, note 3.

75. The author refers back to his tripartite division of the *sefirot* of the "Point-world" into "garments," "bodies," and "inner light" (above, section 2). He interprets accordingly the Lurianic doctrine that the "upper three" *sefirot* of *Keter*, *Hokhmah*, and *Binah* were mostly unscathed by the Shattering, losing only their "rear portions" (*ahorayim*), now identified with the "garments." See Tishby, *Doctrine of Evil*, 32–33, citing Vital, '*Etz Hayyim* ix.2, 41a (מ"ת).

76. Gen 36:31.

77. Above, chapter 3, section 9, which establishes the identity—unknown to the earlier Kabbalah—of the Biblical "Edom" with the Kabbalistic "Distant One." This equation will have momentous consequences for the author's understanding of the "Shattering of the Vessels" (= the "death" of the Edomite kings).

78. Above, chapter 3, section 1: when the Shape entered the Shechinah's womb, all its limbs were "bound into one and subsumed under the category of 'head'"—that is, the Distant One—"for all the body was folded around the head and made into a single aspect—head, heart, and all the limbs as one."

79. Who therefore was a "king of Edom" like those eight listed in Gen 36:31–39. The author asks why the Bible prefaces "these are the kings" with the seemingly superfluous "and." He replies, invoking a midrashic principle stated, e.g., in *Midrash Genesis Rabbah* 12:3 and 30:3, that the conjunction hints at a prior "king" to whom "these" are additional, and he identifies this king as Primordial (Creation-)Human. His reference to the latter's "Balance" (*matqela*) seems anachronistic; the Balance did not come into existence until after the Shattering.

6. The Shattering Impends: Num 22

[The camera now zooms in for a close-up of the Shattering's victims, the *sefirot* of the Point-world. These are the "Moabites" and "Midianites" of the book of Numbers, the former being the *sefirot* of Grace, the latter those of Judgment. In the Bible they are the villains, the would-be destroyers of God's people. But the author presents their dilemma dispassionately and indeed sympathetically.

The menace posed by the "children of Israel," symbolic of the effluence about to deluge the *sefirot*, is real. To resist it, the *sefirot* try to engage in sex with the female *Malkhut*, expecting that copulation can give them the solidity they need to survive. The effluence itself, however, blocks their efforts. Led by "Balak, king of Moab" (= the *sefirah Hesed*, "Grace"), they turn to the phallic *sefirah Da'at* (= "Balaam"), hoping he may able to ward off the deadly, paralyzing effluence and enable their sexual connection. Their hope is vain.]

Returning to the Shattering of the Vessels: [Fol. 14a] When they saw the vast quantity of effluence that was about to overtake them, they trembled greatly. *The kings assembled*, says the Bible, *they passed together*; and the Zohar expounds this verse with reference to the Shattering of the Vessels.[80] They sought to copulate with the female and thereby to achieve the Contraction of which we have spoken, for there are multiple reasons why it is copulation that grants life to all.[81] In this way, they thought, there might be hope. But the effluence poured plenteously from above like a swollen stream, separating the light and making copulation impossible.

[p. 64] All the *sefirot* therefore turned to *Da'at*, the very essence of sexual "knowing" and coupling,[82] to seek his aid in performing the sex act. That was the purpose of the "assemblage" in which they *assembled*

---

80. Ps 48:5, applied to the Shattering in Zohar III, 292a (*Idra Zuta*), which equates the "kings" of the Psalms verse with those of Gen 36:31. Ps 48 continues, *They saw and were astonished; they were terrified, in a panic; trembling seized them*—thereby providing the author with his vivid picture of the "kings'" consternation. He goes on to expand the exegetical web in an unprecedented manner, by drawing Num 22 into it and understanding the "Moabites" and "Midianites" as symbolic of the doomed *sefirot* and the "children of Israel" as the unstoppable, devastating effluence flooding down from above.

81. Text and meaning of this sentence are uncertain.

82. *Da'at* means "knowledge," and to "know" a woman in Biblical idiom is to have sexual intercourse with her.

together, and the object for which the elders of Moab and those of Midian sent to Balaam.[83]

Mercies and Graces are called "Moab"—*me-av*, "from a Father"—for all Graces derive from the Father.[84] The Judgments are called "elders of Midian," as in *the ones who sit at judgment*;[85] while the effluence is called "children of Israel," children of that Supernal Israel who is the Distant One. Thus the elders of Moab, i.e., the Graces, said *to the elders of Midian*, i.e., the Judgments, *Now this mob will lick up everything around us*, i.e., devastate it, which is what in fact happened.

Balak represents Grace. He is one with Jobab, called "Jobab" from the word that signifies wailing—his wailing over what was done to him—as when *Sisera's mother let out a wail*.[86] "Balak" is the equivalent of *mevullaqah*, "devastated";[87] and he is called *son of Zerah*,[88] i.e., "son of Grace," for Grace is called "Zerah" from the "shining forth," *zerihah*, of the light, and also *son of Zippor* from [Aramaic] *tzefar*, "dawn," this being a quality of Father Abraham.[89] He was therefore *king of Moab at that time*, meaning that he was the first of the Graces. For we have already seen that Moab is called *Hesed*, "Grace."

He sent to the *sefirah Da'at*, who is represented by Balaam son of Beor, as Luria has said with regard to the Death of the Kings. We know

83. As described in Num 22:2–12, from which the remaining quotations in this section are taken unless indicated otherwise. In this sentence I combine the readings of ms. Jerusalem 2491 and ms. Oxford 955.

84. Cf. above, chapter 2, section 3, drawing on the etymology of "Moab" implied in Gen 19:37. I am not sure whether the "Father" is understood here to be the Root, as in the earlier passage. At this point in his argument, the author is less interested in establishing the "Father's" identity than in demonstrating that the Biblical "Moab" is symbolic of the *sefirot* of Grace and Mercy.

85. Judg 5:10, as understood by the Targum and the Talmud, b. 'Erub. 54b. *Middin*, the word understood as "judgment" in the rabbinic sources, is spelled identically with "Midian."

86. Judg 5:28, where the verb *va-teyabbev* seems to mean that "she wailed" and provides the author with a clue to the meaning of the name of the Edomite king called *Yovav* ("Jobab") in Gen 36:33, whom the Lurianic tradition identifies with the *sefirah Hesed* (above, note 3). Jobab "wails" over what is done to him in the Shattering. Balak, whom the author declares to be identical with Jobab, is the king of Moab in the book of Numbers.

87. Nah 2:11, with a possible allusion to Isa 24:1, as the addition of *ha-aretz* ("the earth") in two of the mss. might suggest. The root of *mevullaqah* as the same as that of the king's name.

88. Gen 36:33, referring to Jobab.

89. Who, in the Kabbalah, embodies the *sefirah Hesed*. Balak is introduced as *son of Zippor* (*tzippor*, the same root as Aramaic *tzefar*) in Num 22:4.

that *Da'at* corresponds to and takes the place of *Yesod* on the lower plane, being the superior *Yesod* that connects *Hokhmah* and *Binah*. Hence the Bible says, *to Pethor*.[90] Joseph is known to be the *poter*, the "solver"—*Joseph was the one who solved*[91]—and the verse goes on to specify, *who was over the river of the land of the children of his people*, i.e., that he was higher than *Yesod*, which is called the *river* of *Malkhut*, who in turn is *the land of the children of his people*. He [*Da'at*] is higher than [*Yesod*], yet corresponds to him.

He summoned him, saying: A people—the effluence, that is—*has come forth from Mitzrayim*, namely the narrow place, *metzar*, of the *Shechinah* which is called *yam*, "sea."[92] The verse takes care to speak of *metzar*, "the narrow place," in order to convey that she had not experienced intercourse:[93] [the effluence] came forth from her "narrow place" and was hers alone. [p. 65] *Behold it has covered the eye of the land*: it has covered that lower place in *Malkhut*[94] so they could perform no act

90. "Pethor" in Num 22:5 is normally taken to be a place-name, Balaam's hometown. Our author understands it as a designation for Balaam himself, linking him to Joseph, the "solver" of dreams (*poter*, from the same root as "Pethor") and embodiment of the phallic *sefirah Yesod*. *Da'at* is on a higher level than *Yesod*, yet "corresponds to him" in that he is also a phallic entity, "the very essence of sexual 'knowing' and coupling" (above).

91. The author seems to regard this as a Biblical quotation, yet it occurs nowhere in Scripture. (Gen 40:8 and 41:15 are perhaps the closest.) Mss. Oxford 955 and 976 read *u-forat yosef* for *u-foter yosef*, apparently alluding to Gen 49:22, but this makes no sense in context.

92. Reading *Mitzrayim*, the Hebrew name for Egypt, as though it were two words, *metzar yam*, "the narrow place of the sea." The wordplay goes back to a letter, preserved in autograph, written by Sabbatai Zevi a few months before his death in 1676: adapting the language of Gen 45:13, Sabbatai speaks of an unspecified "angel" (or "messenger") who "will tell you all my honor in *metzar yam*, the narrow place of the sea." He seems to have intended this "narrow place" to refer to the coastal town of Dulcigno in Albania, to which he had been exiled; what symbolic overtones he attributed to it is anybody's guess. In the eighteenth-century hymns of the Dönmeh—the descendants of Sabbatian Jews who became Muslims in 1683, preserving their messianic Judaism under a thin veneer of Islam—the "sea" is taken as symbolic of the Torah or the Jewish faith, whose "narrowness" Sabbatai had widened. The web of associations in these hymns seems further to connect the "sea" with the Shechinah, as here, and this equation is in any case a Kabbalistic staple. See Halperin, trans., *Sabbatai Zevi*, 209–11; Liebes, *On Sabbateaism*, 280–81.

93. Which would have widened the Shechinah's vagina. The author makes this same point over and over: "effluence," produced without the limiting and protecting function of completed sex, is dangerous to all it touches.

94. The vagina of *Malkhut*, who, as we have seen, is the "land." The massive outflow of effluence, stopping up her opening, makes sex impossible.

of coupling, the specific words *eye of the land* being used to indicate that place that is the nether "eye." He therefore *sits to tear me*, meaning that this is why I will be shattered, that he "sits"[95] with the purpose of cutting me off. (For *mi-muli* has the sense of tearing into pieces.)[96]

We know that "cursing" is a term for pursuing, expelling, driving off. Hence [Balak] told him to *come now, curse*—you who are in the person of *Da'at, come curse this people*, meaning that he should pursue them so that *perhaps I will be able to knock at him*,[97] i.e., that we will be capable of copulation. For sexual intercourse is represented as "knocking," as in the rabbinic expression *until the knocking be healed*.[98] Afterward *I will drive them from the land*, for all will have the quality of Contraction and Balance.[99] For *I know that whoever you bless is blessed*, which, as we know, conveys the idea of adhesion, inasmuch as "blessing" has the sense of combination or adhesion (as we speak of "grafting"[100] one tree to another), and whoever *is blessed* is in a state of coupling and adhesion; while whoever you expel and drive out and *curse, is cursed*.

And so all the Graces and Judgments, *the elders of Moab and the elders of Midian*, went to [Balaam] *with chips of wood in their hands*,[101] stoking and fire being essential for copulation as is well known. (This is the hidden meaning of "chip of wood," which has the same letters as the root meaning "red."[102]) Their hope, however, was doomed to frustration. The Blessed Holy One sought otherwise—Luria has said that "thus was the Will of Ein Sof"—and he therefore said [to Balaam]: *Do not go with them* [the "elders"], *do not curse* or expel them [the effluence], for they

---

95. Over *Malkhut*'s genital opening.

96. *Mi-muli* is normally understood as "opposite me." Our author, however, takes it as derived from the root *mul*, "to circumcise," which involves an act of tearing and is used in Ps 118:10-12 for the "cutting off" of enemies.

97. More commonly understood as *perhaps I will be able to smite him*, in the sense of military defeat.

98. Mishnah, m. Nid. 10:1, referring to the bruise left by the taking of an underaged bride's virginity.

99. As a check on the unrestrained flow of the effluence.

100. *Mavrikhin*, from the same root as *berakh*, "to bless."

101. The author understands *qesamim* ("divinations") in Num 22:7 as equivalent to rabbinic *qismim*, "chips of wood."

102. The author reinforces his point with a philological observation: *qsm* is an anagram for *smq*, the Aramaic root meaning "red." He alludes to the redness of burning coals, and, as the next section will suggest, of sexually aroused genitalia.

are in a state of adhesion, which is what he meant by saying *for he is blessed*. Yet *Da'at* paid no attention, and went.[103]

7. The Shattering Erupts: Num 31

> [All the *sefirot* are doomed—first the "Judgments" and then, in their turn, the "Graces" (or "Mercies"). The executor of their annihilation is the *sefirah Tif'eret*, who will perish last of all in the general catastrophe. In the Biblical narrative, *Tif'eret* is represented by Moses, who is commanded to wreak vengeance on the Judgments ("Midianites") and does so, paradoxically, through a wound inflicted on his own body. "At the last, you shall be gathered to your people," i.e., you yourself will die.
>
> "Balaam" also dies, unnecessarily. As *Da'at*, the phallic connector between the male *Hokhmah* and the female *Binah*, he could like *Hokhmah* and *Binah* have stood safely above the destruction. But he chose, at "Balak's" invitation, to go down among the lower *sefirot*, and he shares in their demise.
>
> Amid the slaughter, the females are spared. This also is attested in the thirty-first chapter of Numbers, and applies to "Abel's" two wives: the sexually undeveloped *Malkhut*, and also the second female, the one sharing the sefirotic vessel with *Yesod*, who flees into her like Noah into the Ark. Sheltered like Noah within her, he also is saved.]

[p. 66] When the God of Israel embarked upon total devastation, the Shattering of *Tif'eret* and the Graces had to be preceded by that of the Judgments included among the Mercies. Afterward would come the Mercies' turn to be shattered; for were these to have been shattered together with the Judgments the result would have been a great jumble, its cleaning no easy matter. The Judgments would have had the upper hand [fol. 14b] by far, as we have seen that *the Noble cannot be recognized in the presence of the Poor*,[104] and their fall would have been severe indeed. That was why the Judgments had to be shattered first, and only then the Mercies.

You must be aware that the Shattering was executed in its entirety by *Tif'eret*, he being the Central Connector[105] with power over all. This

---

103. With disastrous results for himself, as we will shortly see.

104. Job 34:19, as interpreted above, chapter 2, section 5.

105. Drawing on the Zoharic equation of the "central bar" of Exod 26:28 with *Tif'eret*, but substituting the author's own coinage (*qosher emtza'i*) for the Biblical

is why God told Moses to *wreak vengeance on the Midianites*, that is to say on the Judgments, of which we have seen the "Midianites" to be symbolic representations.[106] Moses himself stands for the *Tif'eret* of the Vessel-Shattering,[107] for we know that Moses is symbolically equivalent to Abel and that Abel's body represents *Tif'eret*. At that time, the Balance not yet existing, *Tif'eret* was a Grace[108]—*Gedullah*[109] a Mercy, *Gevurah* a Judgment, *Tif'eret* a Mercy—and was therefore ordered first to wreak vengeance on [the Judgments] and kill them, and at last himself to be killed. Hence the Bible says, *at the last, you shall be gathered to your people*.

Twelve thousand did he dispatch;[110] for "thousand" is a known symbol for the effluence, while "twelve" are the depths contained within *Tif'eret*, corresponding to the twelve permutations of the Tetragrammaton

---

ha-beriah ha-tikhon. *Tif'eret* is the "Central Connector" in that he not only harmonizes and synthesizes the opposing forces of Grace and Judgment (= the *sefirot Hesed* and *Gevurah*), but is the primary nexus for the entire sefirotic system.

106. Num 31:2-18, from which all the quotes in this section are taken unless indicated otherwise. The Midianite war of Num 31—the most appalling case of sacralized mass murder in the entire Bible—was an object of particular horror and loathing to the eighteenth-century freethinkers who were Eibeschuetz's contemporaries. (Thomas Paine, *The Age of Reason*, 92: "Among the detestable villains that in any period of the world have disgraced the name of man, it is impossible to find a greater than Moses, if this account be true.") Can it be an accident that our author chose just this passage to turn into an allegory of the Shattering, purged of its genocidal content?

107. That is, of the Point-world that was destroyed by the Shattering. That Moses is an embodiment of *Tif'eret*—like Jacob, but to a higher degree—is standard Kabbalistic doctrine. According to Lurianic teaching, Moses reincarnated the highest and purest element of Abel's soul (Vital, *Sha'ar ha-Gilgulim*, *haqdamah* 29, 77-81), while Abel and his twin sister were modeled after *Tif'eret* and *Malkhut* (*Sha'ar ha-Gilgulim*, 77). Cf. section 4, above, where Abel's "place" is said to have been in "the *sefirot* of Little-face," the Lurianic "shape" corresponding roughly to *Tif'eret*. Yet the Moses = *Tif'eret* equation is so widespread and familiar, as compared to Abel = *Tif'eret*, that the author's insertion of Abel as the link between Moses and *Tif'eret* seems strange and unmotivated. Is he hinting at something not evident on the surface?

108. The point seems to be that *Tif'eret*'s subsequent role, as synthesizer of Grace and Judgment, did not yet exist. The *sefirot* of the Point-world were divided into "Graces" and "Judgments" without a third category in between. *Tif'eret*, enrolled among the Graces, was an appropriate tool for the destruction of the Judgments.

109. An alternative name for the *sefirah Hesed*.

110. Or, "Twelve [= *Tif'eret*] dispatched Thousand [or Aleph; = the effluence]"; see the next note. The language is taken from Num 31:5-6.

and also the twelve tribes.[111] That is why he sent [the effluence] *la-matteh*, i.e., *le-mattah*, "below," to the place of their stations.[112]

They made war against Midian and killed them and the five kings of Midian, who are the Judgments.[113] *Hokhmah* and *Binah* were spared Shattering by virtue of their lofty position;[114] had *Da'at* only remained concealed within them,[115] he also would have remained unshattered. He had left them, however, and gone down below. He therefore was shattered like the others, and hence the Bible says that *also Balaam the son of Beor they killed with the sword*, he having descended into their midst. The book of Joshua adds the detail, *Balaam the son of Beor the sorcerer*,[116] thereby conveying that inasmuch as he enclothed himself in Judgment and redness to effect copulation, he became one of those Judgments that the Blessed Holy One had doomed to slaughter.

[p. 67] The Shattering was done in its entirety by the *sefirah Tif'eret*, who is Moses. This is why the Bible says of Hadad the son of Bedad, who symbolizes the *sefirah Tif'eret*, that *he smote Midian in the field of Moab*: he wrought slaughter, as we have seen, among those "Midianites" who had mixed themselves in with the Mercies.[117] This is the inner meaning of *he smote Midian in the field of Moab*: the *field of Moab* means, upon

---

111. The author perhaps intends the "symbol for the effluence" to be the letter *Aleph*, its name spelled the same as *elef*, "thousand." By "depths" (*'omaqim*) he seems to allude to the beginning of *Sefer Yetzirah*, where the "ten *sefirot*"—which may or may not be identical with the *sefirot* of the later Kabbalists—are said to possess the infinite "depths" of beginning and end, good and evil, above and below, east and west and north and south. The four letters of the Tetragrammaton YHVH can be arranged in twelve distinct anagrammatic sequences: YHVH, YHHV, YVHH, etc.

112. Num 31:6: "Moses sent them *elef la-matteh*," normally understood as "one thousand for each tribe." Our author vocalizes *le-mattah*, "downward": in his ultimately suicidal assault on the Judgments of the Point-world, *Tif'eret* sends the killer effluence down to where they are located.

113. The author envisions a schema, difficult to correlate with the actual ten *sefirot*, in which five Graces are balanced by five Judgments. The latter are symbolized in the Bible story by the five kings of Midian.

114. In the sefirotic hierarchy; see above, note 75.

115. As the phallic connector between male *Hokhmah* and female *Binah*.

116. Josh 13:22. *Qosem*, "sorcerer," is an anagram of *someq*, "redness," pointing toward both the symbolic redness of Judgment and the red color of an aroused genital.

117. Gen 36:35. Hadad son of Bedad is the fourth of the Edomite kings listed in Gen 36, corresponding in the Lurianic exegesis to the *sefirah Tif'eret*; see above, note 3. The Bible's claim that *he smote Midian in the field of Moab* is genuinely cryptic, and the author's interpretation of it in the light of Num 31 is strikingly ingenious—so much so, that one is tempted for a moment to wonder if it might possibly be true.

the Shechinah, which is called "field of Moab" through the symbolism of "field."[118] Their Shattering was indeed effected through the making of a wound or puncture in the *sefirah Tif'eret*. The effluence then poured forth in a torrent, destroying and shattering the Judgments that were *in the field of Moab*, i.e., the place of the Shechinah, for their plan had been to copulate with the female, as we have said earlier.

This is the intent of the verse *the windows of heaven were opened*,[119] and why Lamech, symbolic of *Tif'eret*, says that *through my bruise I have killed a man*.[120] This "man" is *Da'at*, whose identity as "man" is hinted at in *a woman who has known man* or in *living man*,[121] and *I killed him through my bruise*—the "bruise," that is, inflicted on me.[122] *And a boy through my wound*, this "boy" symbolizing *Netzah* and *Hod*, as the Zohar interprets *the boys with whom God has graced your servant*;[123] and *through my wound* means, by the force of the "wound" inflicted on me.

Once the Judgments had been shattered and slaughtered, it was the Mercies' turn to be slain. Therefore the Mercies are generally spoken of as "living ones": they did not hasten to die as the Judgments did. (So Luria has said with reference to *Yesod*, as you may discover.[124]) Yet all the Graces were shattered as well, even *Tif'eret* falling into the Insolent Waters, the depths of the abyss. Only *Yesod* was spared death inasmuch as the female was incorporated with and within him,[125] for it was the will of the God of Israel that the female not be slain.

---

118. A Zoharic code word for the *sefirah Malkhut*. The "Shechinah" here is not the Higher Shechinah of which the author has mostly spoken up to now, but the *Malkhut* of the Point-world.

119. Gen 7:11, describing the outbreak of the Flood, which is understood as a representation of the Shattering. "Heaven" is a standard Kabbalistic designation for *Tif'eret*. Its "windows" are the punctures made in *Tif'eret*'s body.

120. Gen 4:23. The Lamech = *Tif'eret* equation is made above, section 2.

121. Num 31:17, 2 Sam 23:20. In the first of these passages, and possibly also in the second, "man" can be understood as a term for the phallus ("living man" = erect penis?). The "man" killed by Lamech/*Tif'eret* is thus *Da'at* (= Balaam), whose phallic character has already been noted. (*Da'at* is from the root *yada'*, the sexual "knowing" of Num 31:17.)

122. As just stated, it was the "wound or puncture" inflicted in *Tif'eret* that brought about the death of *Da'at* and the rest of the Point-world's Judgments.

123. Gen 33:5, quoted in Zohar, III, 202b–203a, which, however, does not interpret it with reference to *Netzah* and *Hod*.

124. I do not know what passage in the Lurianic literature the author refers to. *Hai*, "the Living One," is however a standard epithet for *Yesod*.

125. As described in section 2, above. I follow the text of ms. Jerusalem 2491.

So we find with respect to Midian, that the females were to be spared. They erred only in this regard, that each *sefirah* has within it a *Malkhut*-aspect, and they supposed this also was to be left alive.[126] That is why Moses became angry—*have you kept every female alive?*—and why he said that those adhering to a male[127] must die. Only *Malkhut* itself—infant-like, immature, barren, never having *known man*[128]— would be allowed to live.

[p. 68] Such was the case with the females of "Midian,"[129] *Malkhut* being classed among the Judgments. *Yesod*'s female, by contrast, is accounted one of the Graces and is thus a "Moabite female," entirely acceptable.[130] The Point-world *Yesod*, sensing this, went running to his female and shut himself up inside her. She became his shelter and concealment, that the waters might not sweep him away.[131]

8. The Eighth King Identified

> [Now the riddle of the Eighth King is solved. "King Hadar" is really a she: "Abel's" second female, the Ark that, along with the *Yesod*-Noah within her, survives the Shattering symbolized by the Flood. She survives intact, unlike her co-wife *Malkhut*, who indeed lives on but with "multiple breaches made in her, the Insolent Waters breaking into her and rising to flood all existence." These "breaches" are the subject of Rabbi Hizkiah's discourse at the beginning of the Zohar.]

---

126. It is standard Kabbalistic doctrine that each *sefirah* has a full set of ten *sefirot* within it, and so on (in theory) ad infinitum. "They"—the Israelite army of Num 31, symbolic of the "effluence" that executed the Shattering—falsely imagined that they were to spare the female aspect (*Malkhut*) of each and every *sefirah* of the Point-world, and not just the Point-world's *Malkhut* itself. Hence the wrath of Moses (= *Tif'eret*), described in Num 31:14–18.

127. That were the *Malkhut*-aspect of an essentially male *sefirah*.

128. Section 2 above: "The lower female, the one in *Malkhut*, needed to remain barren and sexually undeveloped, so that the Insolent Waters might not penetrate her womb and belly."

129. I.e., Judgment.

130. See above, chapter 2, note 62. "*Yesod*'s female" is said in section 2, above, to have been "sexually open; inasmuch as she was together with the male *Yesod*, she was in the category of 'a woman protected by her husband.'" The equation of "Moab" with the Graces (or Mercies) is set forth in section 6 above.

131. Ms. Oxford 955 reads "the Insolent Waters." But the reference seems to be, not to the Insolent Waters below, but the divine effluence flooding from above.

Yesod is quintessentially male, and he is "Shaul of Rehoboth by the River," as Luria has said.¹³² He indeed experienced death, for even though he escaped by entering the female's womb, ANY DESCENT IN RANK IS CALLED A DEATH, as the Zohar says in the *Idra*¹³³—most especially [fol. 15a] in that he went inside the female's womb, enveloped by her. So the saying goes: *There are three whose life is no life . . . he whose wife rules over him.*¹³⁴

"King Hadar" is the female dwelling in *Yesod*, for that reason named "Hadar" from *peri 'etz hadar*, the "fruit of the splendid tree"—that is the citron, as discussed above¹³⁵—and for that reason never said [in Genesis] to have died. (Chronicles does say that he died, a point I shall elucidate below, vis-à-vis the post-Mending.¹³⁶) *And the name of his wife was Mehetabel*,¹³⁷ that is the Shechinah, the second female who dwelt by herself, barren, as we have said, and symbolized by Lamech's wife Adah.¹³⁸

This is the significance of Noah's being a representation of the Point-world's *Yesod*, who went into the "Ark" that is the female and, sealed up inside her, was saved by her from the Shattering of the Vessels represented by the Flood. The Zohar accordingly makes plain that Noah is symbolic of that Righteous One who is the world's *Yesod*, its foundation, while the Ark symbolizes the Shechinah—a problematic claim, for [aboard Noah's Ark] there was no sexual coupling.¹³⁹ On our understanding, however, the problem is resolved. He was in hiding

---

132. Above, note 3; *Yesod*, the divine phallus, is as "quintessentially male" an element of divinity as one could find. "Shaul of Rehoboth by the River" is the sixth of the dead Edomite kings in Gen 36:37–38. Our author explains why, in spite of what he has just said about *Yesod*'s escape from the Shattering, the Bible nevertheless asserts that Shaul died.

133. A free quotation from the *Idra Rabba*, Zohar, III, 135b.

134. Talmud, b. Besah 32b.

135. Above, note 5. The author deftly explains the paradox that Hadar is at once the "quintessentially male" *Yesod* and the female citron.

136. Below, chapter 8, end of section 13.

137. Gen 36:39.

138. Above, section 2. Hadar and Mehetabel are thus the two females "born" with Abel; Hadar is treated as a male "king" because of her fusion with *Yesod*.

139. *Tzaddiq yesod 'olam*, understood as "the Righteous One is the world's foundation," is taken from Prov 10:25 and understood by the Kabbalists to refer to the *sefirah Yesod*. Thus *Yesod* = the Righteous One, a title applied to Noah in Gen 6:9, 7:1. The Noah = *Yesod* and Ark = Shechinah equations are "problematic" in that according to rabbinic tradition there was no sex aboard the Ark (Talmud, b. Sanh. 108b; Midrash Genesis Rabbah 36:7), while "sexual coupling" is precisely what *Yesod*'s relation to the Shechinah is about. Unless, of course, we suppose with our author that Noah/*Yesod* entered the Ark/Shechinah not as a lover but as a refugee.

inside the female dwelling in *Yesod*, he himself dwelling inside her, and she functioning as his rescuer. Inasmuch as all now rested on the water, she was the one who could float on that water.[140]

This was the Zohar's intent in the *Idra*, in saying that King Hadar did not die because MALE AND FEMALE EXISTED AS ONE,[141] [p. 69] that is to say, because male and female dwelt in one vessel, one *sefirah*. EXISTED AS ONE—employing AS ONE precisely, to convey that they were fused into a single body.[142] Now you will understand why *Yesod* is called "the Living One."[143] Not because he did not hasten to die—neither did any of the Graces[144]—but because he truly did live. He entered within the female and, safeguarded, lives for ever.[145]

The *Malkhut* that was the second female, meanwhile, did not die but was "effaced."[146] Know that multiple breaches were made in her, the Insolent Waters breaking into her and rising to flood all existence.[147] This is the meaning of *all the fountains of the deep were broken open*:[148] breaches were made in her. These breaches were thirteen in number and are alluded to in the Shechinah's being called a ROSE; see the Zohar to the Torah portion *Bereshit*, RABBI HIZKIAH OPENED HIS DISCOURSE, LIKE A ROSE AMONG THORNS [. . .] A ROSE OF THIRTEEN LEAVES, and so forth.[149] We shall presently have more to say about this, God willing.[150]

---

140. I am not sure of the point of this sentence. Perhaps that in the "shattered" ruin of the Point-world, flooded by the watery effluence, only females and those sheltered by females could "float" and survive?

141. Zohar, III, 135b (*Idra Rabba*). Contrary to the author's assumption, the words "as one" are not found in the Zohar text.

142. Literally, "they became one flesh," using the language of Gen 2:24. But the author's point is that male and female were not merely joined sexually, as in Genesis, but fused into a single hermaphroditic entity.

143. *Hai*, a standard Kabbalistic designation for *Yesod*.

144. Ms. Oxford 955 adds "yet they are not called 'living ones,'" which seems to contradict what the author has said at the end of the preceding section.

145. Following ms. Jerusalem 3100, *ve-nishmar ve-hai le-'olamim. Hai le-'olamim*—or *le-'olam* in the other mss.—probably alludes to the Kabbalistic epithet *hei ha-'olamim*, "life of the worlds," for *Yesod*. ('*Olam* has the two meanings "world" and "eternity.")

146. Following the *Sifra di-Tzeni'uta*; above, note 8.

147. *Yequm*, the word used in Gen 7:4, 23 and often translated "living substance."

148. Gen 7:11.

149. The very beginning of the Zohar (I, 1a), applying Song 2:2 to the *sefirah Malkhut*.

150. Below, chapter 6, section 4.

9. Cain Shirks His Duty

[And now "Cain" once more makes his appearance. His brother "Abel" has died without offspring. The levirate duty prescribed in Deut 25:5–10 therefore falls upon Cain: as Abel's brother, he must descend into the *Tehiru* where Abel was, take one of Abel's wives—the "breached" *Malkhut* of the Point-world—as his own, and thereby raise and redeem the fragments of the shattered *sefirot* of the Point-world (who, collectively, are Abel) from the dominion of the Insolent Waters.

But Cain, once so eager to take the plunge into the *Tehiru*, now shrinks back. The same flaws that made Abel vulnerable to Shattering are present within him as well; like Abel (and Jesus) he was begotten asexually, through an act of mentation alone. Not unreasonably, he fears for his own life.

The book of Ruth describes these events in typically veiled, symbolic language. Cain appears there as *Peloni Almoni*, "the Hidden and Concealed One," the "Primordial Creation-Human" of Lurianic tradition. He ought to marry Ruth-*Malkhut*, but is too afraid—of the Insolent Waters, and of the eventual appearance of the God of Israel within the *Tehiru*, which he knows will devastate him. He gets out of his obligation by yielding his own *Malkhut*, the "shoe" of Deut 25:9–10. This will be used to build a "house" for the God of Israel, namely the sefirotic system as we know it.

But if *Peloni Almoni* will not marry and "redeem" Ruth, who will? The Bible gives the answer: "Boaz," the God of Israel, ready at last to emerge from his fetal state and become lover to the Higher Shechinah, now a fully developed female Shape. "Worlds" that can endure will be the result.]

When these[151] fell, the Insolent Waters were empowered, having absorbed additional energy from both the Mindless and the Mindful Lights. The levirate duty[152] thereupon fell on Cain, who was Primordial Creation-Human.

---

151. The shattered *sefirot* of the Point-world.

152. Imposed by Deut 25:5–6 on the surviving brother of a man who died childless: "If brothers dwell together, and one of them dies without having begotten a son, the dead man's wife shall not go outside to [marry] a strange man. Her brother-in-law shall come upon her [i.e., have intercourse with her] and make her his wife and perform the levirate duty with her, and her first-born son shall carry the name of the dead brother, that his name not be erased from Israel." As discussed below, the denouement of the book of Ruth is based on this custom.

He was Abel's brother; his brother Abel had died, leaving no sons behind him but only a wife in the person of the female. It devolved on him to discharge the levirate duty by descending into the *Tehiru* to take his brother Abel's place, there to build up the worlds, there to receive the Shechinah and lift her from her collapse. He would thereby gather the sparks from his brother's fragments and lift him up as well.

This is the meaning of *her brother-in-law shall come upon her*—literally, that he shall descend into the *Tehiru* to take her and to raise up his brother's name, gathering all his brother's fragments, upraising them as a part of himself. This is the principle of the levirate duty, that the brother's soul becomes a part of the brother-in-law,[153] and it was in force here. *The dead man's wife*, i.e., his female, *shall not go outside to a strange man*, i.e., the Insolent Waters that flooded her,[154] the essence of the Unclean Merkavah, called *a strange man*.

Thus it was that God said to Cain, who was then in the brother-in-law's role: *What have you done? The voice of your brother's blood cries to me from the ground*,[155] meaning that she[156] had received all the "blood," the effluence of *Abel your brother*, as we learn from the Lurianic writings that all the effluence fell upon *Malkhut*, crushing her in the receiving of it. [p. 70] *Cursed is attah*, he said, referring to *Tif'eret* of the Point-world—*attah*, "you," being *Tif'eret*[157]—*from the ground that opened her mouth [to receive your brother's blood]*, meaning that *Tif'eret* was shattered, banished, driven away from *Malkhut*, having been shattered and taken prisoner by the Insolent Waters.[158]

When you work the ground—that is, when you sacrifice and offer worship to *Malkhut*, the Shechinah, still functioning as placenta[159]—

---

153. The language echoes the discussion of the levirate in the *Sava de-Mishpatim* section of the Zohar (II, 99b–101b), though the idea is rather different.

154. Following ms. Jerusalem 2491 and the conclusion of the preceding section. The other mss. have "him."

155. Gen 4:10–12, quoted and given a phrase-by-phrase interpretation in this and the following paragraph.

156. *Malkhut*, Abel's "second female" (section 8 end), symbolized by the "ground."

157. As opposed to the simple interpretation of the Biblical verse, in which *attah* is "you," namely Cain. The identification of the masculine second-person pronoun with the *sefirah Tif'eret* is widespread though not universal in the Kabbalah; see the end of the Fifth Gate of Gikatilla, *Sha'are Orah*, 240–46.

158. Reversing the familiar Kabbalistic motif of the exile of the Shechinah, where it is the female aspect of God that is driven out, exiled from the male.

159. Confusingly, the author seems to conflate the Lower Shechinah, the *Malkhut* of the Point-world about which he has been speaking up to this point, with the Higher

Tif'eret is no longer her strength on your behalf.[160] Her whole intention was concentrated on Abel and the purification of the *Tehiru*, for which purpose she granted him an additional twin sister.[161] But [fol. 15b] now that this world has been shattered, *Tif'eret is no longer her strength on your behalf.* Hence the levirate duty: he must descend from his place to that of the *Tehiru*, take his brother Abel's wife as his own, perform with her the levirate act. *A migrant and wanderer,* says the verse, *shall you be in the earth*: he must migrate and wander from his place into the *Tehiru*, to take *Malkhut* who is called "earth" to be his wife.

This is the secret meaning of the book of Ruth.

"Boaz" stands for the God of Israel, as we well know, and "Ruth" is the Shechinah. "Boaz" thus asks of "Cain"—represented by *Peloni Almoni*,[162] "the Hidden and Concealed One," as the Targum renders it,[163] for he is indeed hidden and concealed, as Luria tells us—asking him whether he intends to "acquire" the "field," symbolic of *Malkhut*, that was sold by "Naomi," the first female who was within *Yesod*, as we have seen. (She was wife to *Yesod*, who was *Tif'eret*'s brother and

---

Shechinah, womb (but soon to be sex partner) for the God of Israel. *'Avodah*, "worship," is from the same root as *'avad*, to work the soil.

160. *Lo tosef tet kohah lakh*, ordinarily translated "she shall no longer give you her strength." But the author understands תת (*tet*), not as the verb "to give," but as an abbreviation for the *sefirah Tif'eret* (ת״ת). The male of the Point-world can no longer be the female's "strength," coupling with her on Cain's behalf. Cain must therefore do the job himself.

161. As described in section 2, above.

162. Normally translated "So-and-so" or the like, the unnamed "near relative" (*go'el*, literally "redeemer") of Ruth 4:1, who has prior right (3:12) to "redeem" the field sold by Naomi and to perform the levirate act with Ruth. It is when *Peloni Almoni* relinquishes his right that Boaz steps in.

163. Referring to the Aramaic translation, not of Ruth 4:1, but of 1 Sam 21:3 and 2 Kgs 6:8, where *meqom peloni almoni*, "such-and-such a place," is translated *atar kasi ve-tamir*, "a concealed and hidden place." The author replaces the Targum's *kasi ve-tamir* with the essentially synonymous *temir ve-ne'elam*, using the wording of the popular Kabbalistic intention-formula, "I am ready and prepared to fulfill such-and-such a commandment, *for the sake of the unification of the Blessed Holy One and his Shechinah, through the agency of that Hidden and Concealed One*" (Horowitz, *Shnei Luhot ha-Berit*, e.g., *Massekhet Yoma, Perek Derekh Hayyim* #32; cf. Hallamish, *Kabbalah in Liturgy*, 45–70). The "Hidden and Concealed One" is apparently the *sefirah Keter*, called "Hidden One" in the Zohar. Our author shifts the allusion upward, to Primordial (Creation-)Human. Maciejko in his note *ad loc.* suggests that the allusion to "Luria" that follows is to the Sabbatian commentary on Ruth called *Tzaddiq Yesod 'Olam*, which circulated under Luria's name.

therefore called "Ahimelech," "king's brother,"[164] and it was she who floated as the Ark upon the Insolent Waters. Ruth, representing the second female, *clung to her*.[165])

["Cain"] was therefore asked whether he wanted to acquire her in marriage, and in truth would have been glad enough to do so, given how he hankered after the two females.[166] [p. 71] But when the God of Israel told him he would need to go down into the *Tehiru*, into the midst of the female, and *raise up the dead man's name over his ancestral portion*[167]— meaning, as we saw, that he descend to Abel's place to gather up the shattered sparks, raising them on his brother's behalf—when he heard this, that he must descend, he feared for his life. What if he should suffer the fate of his brother Abel, brought into existence without sexual coupling by the Distant One, whom "Edom" represents (as we have seen) and consequently shattered and inundated by the Insolent Waters? The same could happen to him if he were to wander far from the place where he had settled himself beside the Shechinah—in her role as placenta, as we have seen—and come to dwell in the midst of the *Tehiru*. His brother Abel's fate would then befall him.

So he said: *I do not want to marry her*[168] and perform the levirate duty with her. *I cannot act as redeemer*, he said, *lest I devastate my own ancestral portion*,[169] that is to say, lest in making the descent he devastate his portion and die like his brother. Cain said the same thing: *You have banished me today from upon the ground*, referring to his adhesion to the Shechinah,[170] *and from your face shall I be hid*, meaning that he

---

164. A strange error, found in all the mss. and indeed necessary for the author's exegesis. Naomi's husband in the book of Ruth is Elimelech, not Ahimelech. Perhaps the author is thinking of Ruth 4:3, which calls Elimelech "our brother."

165. Ruth 1:14.

166. The twin sisters born with Abel; above, sections 2 and 4.

167. Ruth 4:10.

168. Deut 25:8. Note the irony: Cain had insisted on going down into Abel's place in the *Tehiru* when the God of Israel warned him not to (above, section 4). Now that the God of Israel wants him to make the descent, he balks.

169. Ruth 4:6.

170. That is, the Higher Shechinah, currently in her role as placenta. The text translated is that of ms. Jerusalem 2491, which accurately quotes Cain's words from Gen 4:14. But mss. Oxford 955 and Jerusalem 3100 have, in place of Genesis's "from upon the ground," the words of 1 Sam 26:19, "from attachment to the Lord's ancestral portion." Ms. Jerusalem 3100 adds that the Shechinah "is the Lord's ancestral portion." The copyist of ms. Oxford 976 originally followed the reading of ms. Jerusalem 3100 but corrected it to that of ms. Jerusalem 2491, in the process crossing out the

will be in the *Tehiru*, which is called "hidden place" in that he will be enveloped there by the Insolent Waters. *And All, finding me, will kill me.* He knew that the God of Israel—who functions as *Yesod* vis-à-vis Ein Sof, as we have seen, and is therefore called *kol*, "All"[171]—would eventually establish his presence in the *Tehiru* as in the place of Emanation, and upon finding me and establishing his presence within me *will kill me* through the massiveness of the effluence and through my own weakness. For he was created asexually, as we have said.

Having refused his levirate duty, [Cain] was obliged to perform the rite of shoe-removal.[172] First, of course, the God of Israel had to try to convince him to perform the levirate act; the court must urge [the brother-in-law] to act in the levirate manner toward his brother's wife and not undergo the shoe-removal, for the levirate duty takes precedence. But when he continued to refuse the levirate role, then *his brother's widow shall approach him*, and so forth.[173]

Luria's teaching in *The Tree of Life* is well known: the *Malkhut* of Primordial Creation-Human descended into Emanation, and this is what is called *Holy Distant One*. (Granted, we have earlier said that "Holy Distant One" is a name applicable to Interiority, whereas [Luria] speaks here of Enclothement. [p. 72] The Distant One of Interiority is properly named *Distant One Holiest of All the Holy, Most Hidden of All the Hidden*; yet at times he is called simply "Distant One," as we find throughout the Zohar.[174]) The *Hokhmah* of Primordial Creation-Human, in other words, beamed light into Creation-Human's *Malkhut*, and his *Malkhut* descended into Emanation to build up the structure of Emanation.

---

statement that the Shechinah is the Lord's ancestral portion. It is hard to explain these features except by supposing that the author originally quoted Cain's words from memory and imported 1 Sam 26:19 into them, later correcting his error. The mss. reflect both stages of the text.

171. A standard Kabbalistic code term for *Yesod*.

172. *Halitzah*, prescribed in Deut 25:7-10.

173. Deut 25:9: "His brother's widow shall approach him in the elders' presence and pull his shoe off his foot and spit in his face, and say: 'Thus shall be done to the man who will not build up his brother's house.'"

174. The author apologizes for having earlier used the term "Distant One" imprecisely, to refer to an entity different from the one to which Luria applies the term. He remarks, anticipating a point that will be developed more fully below (chapter 5, section 5), that the Zohar consistently does the same thing. The distinction between "Interiority" (*penimiyut*) and "Enclothement" (*hitlabbeshut*), first adumbrated here, will take on considerable importance as the treatise unfolds. For now, the reader can best understand this paragraph by skipping over the words in parentheses.

The "shoe" is a familiar symbol for *Malkhut*, as in *a garden enclosed is my sister bride*.[175] "Spitting," *yaroq*, stands for *Hokhmah*, hinted at by *yeraqraq harutz*.[176] *His brother's widow accordingly draws near and goes up to the gate*,[177] namely to the Root, *and to the elders*, symbolizing the Distant One, who is elderly, "Ancient of Days."[178] *My husband's brother refuses*, she says; whereupon *the elders of his city summon him*, meaning, as we have said, that the God of Israel (who was then equivalent to the Distant One[179]) tried to persuade him to perform the levirate act with her. But when he said *I do not want to*, then *his brother's widow approached him and pulled his shoe*, namely his *Malkhut*, *off his foot* to which it clung, and drew it down into the structure of Emanation.

She shall spit in his face, referring to *Hokhmah*'s inner lights, *and shall say, Thus shall be done to the man* [fol. 16a] [*who will not build up his brother's house*]. *And his name shall be called in Israel*—that is, in the structure of Emanation, called "Israel" and "Jacob"—*his name shall be called the house of the pulled-off shoe*. For this[180] [structure of Emanation] is a *house* for the God of Israel, constructed from that *pulled-off shoe* that is *Malkhut*, "pulled off" from Creation-Human.

This is the meaning of the passage in Ruth: *So it was in prior time in Israel, over Redemption and over Exchange*.[181] This refers, like *before there reigned any king*, to the time prior to the Self-extension of the God of Israel.[182] *Over Redemption and over Exchange*: higher than the two

---

175. Song 4:12, applied to *Malkhut* in, e.g., Zohar, I, 32b, II, 4a, and linked to Ruth 4:7. *Na'ul*, "enclosed," is from the same root as *na'al*, "shoe."

176. A phrase from Ps 68:14, normally taken to mean "greenish gold" or the like. For reasons I do not understand, the author assumes this refers to the *sefirah* Hokhmah. He goes on to connect *yeraqraq* of Ps 68 with the verb *yaraq*, "to spit," used in Deut 25:9.

177. Combining Deut 25:7 and 9.

178. *'Attiq yomin*, from Dan 7:9. Cf. above, chapter 2, note 15. The author has earlier (chapter 2, section 1) chosen to understand *'Attiqa Qaddisha* as "the Holy Distant One" rather than "the Holy Ancient One," as most would. Now he finds it convenient to draw on the understanding he once dismissed.

179. Or "the Ancient One," appropriately symbolized by Deuteronomy's "elders."

180. The structure of Emanation. This passage expresses our author's conception of the Emanation-world as an external structure, housing the "Interiority" that is the God of Israel.

181. Ruth 4:7.

182. From his fetal state. Ruth's *le-fanim* ("in prior time") is interpreted in accord with *lifnei* in Gen 36:31, "before (there reigned any king over the children of Israel)."

Shechinahs,[183] the females of whom we have spoken. The Zohar makes clear that the one dwelling in *Yesod* is called "Redemption," *Yesod* being the "Redeemer,"[184] while the second female is "Exchange," as the Zohar interprets *do not exchange him*;[185] and this takes place higher than both. *To uphold everything*, i.e., that it may endure eternally—for the male is called *every* and the female is called *thing*, as in *the end is "thing"*[186]—*a man would pull off his shoe and give it to another*, just as we have seen that Cain gave his *Malkhut* as described in the sequel, *He pulled off his shoe*.[187]

This done, and [*Malkhut*'s] descent completed, the God of Israel undertook to perform the levirate act, to bring out those vessel fragments that were of the Point-world[188] (as Luria says), the God of Israel playing the part of the deceased's brother. [p. 73] "What can come of this?" they all cried out.[189] Everything partook, after all, of the quality of the Distant

---

183. The author follows the exegesis of Ruth 4:7 in *Tiqqunei Zohar* 21 (60b–61a): "*Over Redemption*: this is the Higher Shechinah . . . *and over Exchange*: this is the Lower Shechinah, who is *exchanged* with the one of whom it is said, *do not exchange me for him*" (Talmud, b. Sanh. 38b, interpreting Exod 23:21 in reference to the angel Metatron). But while the writer of *Tiqqunei Zohar* intended the "Higher Shechinah" as the *sefirah Binah* and the "Lower" as *Malkhut*, our author reinterprets them as the "two Shechinahs" of his own system. (*Tren shekhinatin*; I cannot recall having seen this plural [or dual?] of "Shechinah" anywhere else.) See the following two notes.

184. The Zohar equates *Malkhut* with *ge'ullah*, "Redemption" (I, 228b, II, 156a) and also *go'el*, "Redeemer" (I, 205b). III, 95b makes clear, however, that she is called "Redeemer" only via the higher *sefirah* that "stands above her and beams light into her," i.e., *Yesod*, to whom the title properly belongs. Cf. Gikatilla, *Sha'are Orah*, Second Gate, 74.

185. EXOD 23:21, the verb *tamer* interpreted, following b. Sanh. 38b, as from the same root as *temurah*, "exchange." The *Tiqqunei Zohar* and *Ra'ya Mehemna* (III, 281a) strata of the Zoharic literature develop the Talmud's exegesis, understanding the *temurah* of Ruth 4:7 as the "Lower Shechinah" concealing herself within Metatron. Cf. Zohar I, 232a, II, 125a, and the discussion in Cordovero, *Pardes Rimmonim*, part 16 (שער אבי"ע), chapter 4.

186. Hyperliteral translation of Eccl 12:13, conveying that the female, who as *Malkhut* is the "end" of the sefirotic system (e.g., Zohar, III, 256b, *Ra'ya Mehemna*), can also be called "thing." Its combination with the masculine "every" points to a system of sexual pairings, which, unlike the "virgin"-begotten Abel, has the ability to endure.

187. Ruth 4:8. Our author imagines the sentence continuing: ". . . and gave it to the God of Israel" (= Boaz).

188. Ms. Oxford 955 adds here *la-torah*, "for the Torah," mss. Oxford 976 and Jerusalem 3100 *ve-torah*, "and Torah," linking the *sefirot* of the Point-world (*niqqudim*) to the vowel signs (*niqqud*) of the Biblical Hebrew text. This association, entirely gratuitous here, will be taken up in chapter 5, section 8.

189. The vessel fragments are unable to trust that their elevation will accomplish anything useful or enduring.

One: no coupling of male and female, as we have said, but only seed which for a variety of reasons had no prospect of survival.

Yet they had a remedy—when the Human of the Path of Emanation should stretch himself out from his Self-folding and resume the "heart" aspect of which we have spoken, in the character of God of Israel; when the Shechinah, too, should become a fully developed female Shape, not just a placenta as before. The whole structure would thus have the capacity to endure.

5

The Restoration of God

1. The New World Emerges

[The world that emerges from the Shattering, the divinity that emerges from the Shechinah's womb, is filled with paradox. The Shechinah is no longer a nurturing placenta but a fully developed Female, sex partner for the God of Israel (identified now as the God of the Hebrew Bible). Yet she also manifests in a form closer to that of the placenta, as the curtain[1]—the Zohar's *parokhta*—that separates the God of Israel from the higher Distant One, the God of Christianity.

Two distinct deities, it would seem. Yet they are also one, "heart" and "head" of the divine entity variously known as the Shape of the Path of Emanation or Primordial Emanation-Human (= "the God of Israel" in the broader sense of the term). The "heart" is now in control, its tripartite "Balance" of Grace and Judgment granting stability to the entire structure, serving as guarantee that the divine energies will be distributed in proper measure and that the Shattering will not recur.

The God of Israel (in the term's narrower sense of the "heart") pays periodic visits to the loftier realm above the *parokhta*. He has left his imprint on the superior "head"; his three chambers and the head's one are represented in the four compartments of the phylactery (*tefillin*) that the male Jew wears on his head during worship. But the head is also crowned

---

1. Her simultaneous existence as a curtain and as a female Shape is rationalized in section 4, below: the curtain is not actually the Shechinah, but only the "mark" she has left in the higher realms.

by something associated at once with the mitre worn by the Biblical high priest and the turban that for the Sabbatians was the symbol and embodiment of Islam.

The Distant One is Christian, but less in the sense of a distinct religion than in the otherness ("Distant") of pure Grace. The Islam to which Sabbatai Zevi converted, thereby stepping into his high priestly (turban-wearing) role, is part of the Distant One's domain.[2] Sabbatai's salvific act of conversion is what will enable the Distant One's eventual triumph, if a victory so pacific and benign can be called by that name. For now, the day belongs to the God of Israel.]

The reason is this: When [the God of Israel] extends himself as a line, as a straight Human, through that act of Self-extension the Mindless Light will separate itself from him, given the Mindless Light's tendency to extend itself upward to cling to its source. Only the Mindful Light remains.

At the higher level the Mercies are great, unmixed with Judgment and without any Balance.[3] But in his condition of Self-extension, functioning as "heart,"[4] he has three cavities[5] which constitute the Balance: Judgment, Mercy, and the Central Column that mingles them. The heart is known to be centrally located like a king within his country, granting lawful measure to all. We have earlier spoken at length of the heart's royal character: to govern justly, lawfully, without deficiency or excess, each receiving what it requires.

Male and female, moreover, could couple in reality and not just thought and mentation;[6] and their coupling would involve Contraction, which (as earlier discussed) would provide all the structures with

---

2. A connection no doubt encouraged by the Sabbatian practice, its precise origin and significance unclear, of speaking of Islam as *torat hesed*, "the Torah of Grace," as opposed to the "Torah of Truth" (*torat emet*) that is Judaism. See Scholem, *Sabbatai Ṣevi*, 813, 863–64; Liebes, *On Sabbateaism*, 32–33; Halperin, "Son of the Messiah," 181.

3. And therefore dangerous.

4. Above, chapter 2, section 1; as opposed to the fetal state in which "the body's limbs [were] bound into one and subsumed under the category of 'head,' for all the body was folded around the head and made into a single aspect" (chapter 3, section 1).

5. The three-chambered heart is Aristotelian: *Historia Animalium*, I, 17, which seems to treat the left and right ventricles and the left atrium as the heart's three "cavities," while understanding the right atrium—the fourth chamber in modern anatomy—as a dilated vein and not a part of the heart. See Van Praagh and Van Praagh, "Aristotle's 'Triventricular' Heart."

6. Like the mental activity that produced the fatally flawed Cain and Abel, while the God of Israel was confined to his fetal state. "Contraction" here seems to be conceived as orgasmic.

solidity and stability. The Female also would receive it[7] and give it out in proper measure, for she is Measuring Line, the Artisan by whom it is firmly established.

So the God of Israel willed; and he stretched himself out from his Self-folding and from "head" made himself into "heart." And since he is extended as Straight Line from the beginning—from the place where the Distant One emerges from the Root—through the place where *Tif'eret* of Emanation was to be built and then downward from there to the place of the Shechinah's building, he is called *Israel, yashar el*, "the straight one of God" because he is the Straight Line; and he functions as "heart" for this Shape, king in his country. He is the name YHVH, blessed be he; and throughout the Torah, Prophets and Writings he is called "the Lord," for he is our God and we his servants.[8]

The Distant One and the Root are sometimes also called "the Lord," for in truth he, the Distant One, and the Root are all one, a single Shape, as we have earlier explained at length.[9] Yet inasmuch as he is Director and Builder of all—concerning which we shall presently reveal a secret—the name YHVH is essentially his, [p. 74] while the others are called "above the Lord" or by the name *El*, "God," since they are pure Grace. The Root is normally called *Elohim*, "God," for he is the Thought of Ein Sof (which is called *Mi*) and its substrate (called *Elleh*), and *Elohim* is the combination of the two.[10]

[The God of Israel], as already indicated, functions as "heart." He modifies the Distant One who is the "head," separating the Mindless

---

7. "It" here is presumably the semen-like effluence, while later in the sentence "it" refers to the structure in the process of being built up.

8. Echoing Ps 100:3, "YHVH is God; he made us and we are his, his people and the flock he shepherds." The God of Judaism has just been defined, "Israel" (ישראל) etymologized as a compound of ישר אל, "the straight one of God." The "Straight Line" (*qav ha-yosher*) is a Lurianic technical term for the ray of light emitted by Ein Sof into the spherical cavity left by Ein Sof's earlier withdrawal. Its identification with the God of Israel, found also in *Shem 'Olam*, 187, seems to have been unique to our author. See Perlmuter, *Rabbi Jonathan Eibeschuetz*, 295–96, and cf. above, chapter 2, section 3.

9. Chapter 2, section 4, developed in section 3 below. In this account of the tripartite Shape, an alternative to the one set forth in chapter 2, section 1, and normally presupposed, the Root functions as "head," the Distant One as "heart," and the God of Israel as "penis."

10. The letters of *Mi* ("Who") and *Elleh* ("These"), combined and rearranged, spell *Elohim* (מי+אלה=אלהים). The equation of the Root with both Thought and substrate of Ein Sof is peculiar, and seems to contradict the author's definition of the Root as specifically the Will of Ein Sof, its masculine *Mi*-aspect; above, chapter 2, section 2, cf. chapter 1, section 5.

Light out from him; this is the heart's nature, to accomplish the thought and intention of others.[11] He absorbs the moisture while expelling the "head's" wastes, leaving it in a state of pure Grace and therefore to be called the "nose" that breathes life into everything that lives. (Not so the God of Israel, who has the quality of "heart" and also the penis with its two apertures, and is therefore called *erekh appayim*, the one who is "long [fol. 16b] of two noses," "long-suffering" with the wicked and the righteous alike.)[12]

The Shechinah correspondingly made herself from a placenta into a fully developed Female, a complete Shape, as we have seen. She is represented by the final letter *hei* [of the Tetragrammaton],[13] and they by the two millennia that are the two alphabets, the great and the small.[14] The great alphabet stands for the God of Israel in that all the letters are written with *vav*, like this *aleph* א, thereby symbolizing the God of Israel, who is

11. A difficult sentence, in which "others" refers to the mind of the same individual, modified and its goals thus rendered attainable by the activity of his or her heart. I follow mss. Oxford 955 and Jerusalem 3100, *le-hafiq*, "to accomplish," vs. *le-hafig*, "to cause to disappear," of mss. Oxford 976 and Jerusalem 2491. The latter reading evidently refers to the elimination of the Mindless Light.

12. The Biblical idiom *erekh appayim*, usually translated "long-suffering" or "patient" (e.g., Exod 34:6), literally means "long of nose"; and the Hebrew word for "nose" is a dual form, literally meaning "two noses" (the nostrils?). The Talmud plays with this grammatical duality, inferring that God is "long-suffering" not only with the righteous, but the wicked as well: b. ʿErub. 22a, B. Qam. 50b, Sanh. 111a-b. Our author pulls in the Talmudic midrash, apparently not noticing that it confuses his distinction of the Distant One, who is a single "nose" (*hutma*) and therefore unmixed Grace, vs. the "double-nosed" (*appayim*) God of Israel, who acts with Judgment as well as Mercy. See below, chapter 9, section 5, where the distinction is made more clearly and consistently. On the two apertures of the penis—one for urine, one for semen—see below, chapter 8, section 5.

13. A standard Kabbalistic association.

14. "They," the God of Israel and the Shechinah, are symbolized by the "great" and the "small" Hebrew alphabets, that is, the exceptionally large and exceptionally small letters sprinkled here and there through the traditional Masoretic Text of the Bible. (For example, the oversized *bet* of *bereshit* in Gen 1:1 and the ʿ*ayin* and *dalet* in Deut 6:4, versus the undersized *aleph* of *va-yiqra* in Lev 1:1.) These "great" and "small letters" are given theosophical significance in the Zohar; see Matt's note 22 to II, 180b, and I, 159b, where the "great" and "small letters" seem to correspond to male and female, as here. Cf. Lipiner, *Metaphysics*, 344–45. Playing on the Hebrew word *elef*, which means "one thousand" but also points toward *alfa beta*, "alphabet," the author further identifies these two "alphabets" with "two millennia," presumably those spoken of in the Zohar, III, 128a (*Idra Rabba*; quoted and explicated below, section 8), in which the Torah is hidden for two thousand years after its creation. Cf. also the Talmud, b. Sanh. 97a: "The world will last for six millennia: two millennia of chaos, two millennia of Torah, and two millennia of the Messiah's days."

represented by the *vav*. The small alphabet, written with *yod*s like this *aleph* א, stands for the Shechinah, which, as is well known, is called *yod*.¹⁵

It is this "heart"-aspect that expels, through the mouth and other orifices, the breath upon which (as Luria's writings teach us) the supernal worlds depend. This it is that grows the "head's" hair and beard for the purpose of spreading out the moisture,¹⁶ as is also well known. This is the God of Israel, who caused to grow upon the Holy Distant One that holy beard from which the Thirteen Adornments of the Beard depend.¹⁷

Inasmuch, moreover, as neither the Shechinah nor any other sacred entity can *budge from its place without leaving a mark*,¹⁸ some trace of the "heart" aspect remains above in the Holy Distant One's place, beside the mouth and the forehead. So it was [when the Shape was] in the state of Self-folding, and although it has since stretched itself out, that mark remains in place. All had then functioned as "head," as we have seen; for [the Shape] was then in a state of infancy, its brain soft, all in a state of uniformity.¹⁹ [p. 75] This is the symbolism of the phylactery worn on the head. The heart has three chambers and the skull one, four chambers in all, and these are the phylactery's four compartments, which must be placed *on the spot where the infant's brain is fragile*,²⁰ just as we have said.

---

15. That is, the "great" *aleph* is composed of long vertical strokes like the letter *vav* (ו), the "small" *aleph* of tiny strokes like the *yod* (י). The Kabbalistic equation of the phallic *vav*, the third letter of the Tetragrammaton, with the male aspect of Deity is indeed "well known." But I am not aware of *yod* being connected with the Shechinah.

16. Said above to have been "absorbed" by the God of Israel. Cf. above, chapter 2, section 1: "When the heart functions properly, the head also can better function, since the heart draws into itself all the moisture and heat from the head, regulates them and sends them back, as the natural philosophers well know." In the divine organism, even those features associated with the "head"/Distant One—breath, hair, beard—originate with and are regulated by the "heart"/God of Israel.

17. Thirteen features of the beard of the Distant One, described at length in the Zohar's *Idra Rabbah* (III, 130b-135a) and identified with the "thirteen attributes of mercy" listed in Exod 34:6-7, through which pure Mercy flows downward from the highest level of divinity. See Hellner-Eshed, *Seekers of the Face*, 208-45, who calls the beard "a personified expression of the figures of rivers, streams, channels, and rapids that transmit the divine flow from its source into external reality. We can think of the beard as a primordial mode of transmission, a kind of nervous or electrical system that conveys and regulates the flow, full of Love, from 'Attiqa's brain into the cosmos." For our author, the fullness of that Love is itself fraught with danger.

18. See above, chapter 1, note 71.

19. That is, without any distinction of "head" and "heart."

20. Talmud, b. 'Erub. 95b, Menah. 37a, referring to the placement of the head-phylactery (*tefillin*), which is indeed worn close to the spot of the anterior fontanelle. See Preuss, *Biblisch-talmudische Medizin*, 48-49. The head-phylactery's small hollow

The placenta that once enwrapped [the Shape] now took the form of a curtain separating the Distant One from the God of Israel. The Zohar sometimes calls this the *parokhta*,[21] and it is symbolized by the *tallit*, the prayer shawl that enwraps one's head and the greater part of one's body,[22] functioning as the Shechinah once did. This is why the *tallit* represents the Shechinah, as the Zohar makes clear.[23]

On weekdays the God of Israel receives effluence via this *parokhta* and via the phylactery's compartments. They reach the "heart" as one and therefore are together as one in [the phylactery worn on] the arm,[24] which is beside the heart. On Sabbaths and festivals, however, he is in a state of coupling, that is, the "Deep Sleep" of which we have earlier spoken.[25] When that happens—when the Root encounters and couples with the Shape of the Path of Emanation—then "Deep Sleep" comes upon him and he is as it were in that dream-state of which we have spoken. His light then rises above the *parokhta* and receives emanation. This explains why one need not wear phylacteries [on Sabbaths and festivals].

This is the meaning of *your splendor upon your head* and *a crown of splendor, tif'eret, upon their heads*—i.e., that *Tif'eret* remains, as a trace, within the "head," as we have seen.[26] It is why the phylacteries are called "splendor," which we have seen to be a term for *Tif'eret*.

---

box, unlike that of the phylactery worn on the left arm (below), is divided into four compartments, each one containing a short Biblical passage written on parchment; its structure and placement, our author thinks, are relics of the divine Self-folding. On the heart's three chambers, see above.

21. E.g., II, 99a: "As he approaches, she begins to speak with him from behind a curtain [*parokhta*] she has drawn, words suitable for him, until he reflects little by little" (trans. Matt, *Zohar*). In the Bible, *parokhet* is the curtain separating the Holy of Holies from the outer sanctuary.

22. The language is taken from the Talmud, b. Menah. 40b.

23. Possibly implied in III, 226b (*Ra'ya Mehemna*), as Maciejko suggests. I am not aware of any other Zoharic source for this equation.

24. Which unlike the head-phylactery has only one compartment, with the four Biblical passages written on a single strip of parchment.

25. Above, chapter 2, sections 2-3, and especially note 25.

26. Ezek 24:17—the precise form of the quotation influenced by verse 23—and 23:42, slightly misquoted. The Talmud understands "splendor," *pe'er*, in the former passage to refer to the head-phylactery (b. Sukkah 25b, Mo'ed Qat. 15a). Our author extends this meaning to the synonymous *tif'eret* in the latter passage, which he understands as the Kabbalistic *Tif'eret*; like *pe'er*, the trace imprinted by *Tif'eret* (= the "heart" aspect of the Folded-up Shape) on its "head" is represented symbolically by the phylactery. He explains on this basis the Talmud's assumption that Ezekiel's *pe'er* must be the head-phylactery.

*From my flesh I can visualize my God.*²⁷ In the state of Folding-up, the intestines occupied a higher position than the heart, covering the head in the place where the hair would be, sweetening the Judgments and the waste matter [p. 76] so that it should not mix in. They are symbolically represented by the high priest's mitre, which is like the turbans of the Muslims (as Rabbi Abraham ben David points out in his critique of Maimonides, "Laws of the Temple Paraphernalia"), resembling, as we know, the intestines wrapped around.²⁸ It is well known that the God of Israel is represented by the high priest, those intestines by his mitre; therefore the high priest who stands for the God of Israel wears the mitre while an ordinary priest does not.

This is the meaning of the verse in Job, *he turns himself all around in his ropes*; for they are ropelike, and when he "turned" to fold himself up, he was encompassed "all around" by them.²⁹ It is the meaning likewise of, *I wore righteousness; it enclothed me like a cloak*, alluding to the Shechinah, which is called Righteousness, which enclothed him like a "cloak," as we have seen, she being symbolized in the prayer shawl.³⁰ *And his justice like a turban*³¹—just as we have said, that it is the intestines that sweeten the Judgments, and they are turban-like.

When he is above the *parokhta* he is called by the name YH, for when he is above he takes on the identity of the Distant One, who is

---

27. Job 19:26, with *elohai*, "my God," substituted in all the mss. for the Biblical *eloah*, "God." See above, chapter 1, note 13.

28. The mitre (*mitznefet*) is mentioned several times, though not described in detail, in Exod 28. The twelfth-century French scholar Abraham ben David, dissenting from Maimonides's effort to distinguish it from the headgear worn by other priests (*Mishneh Torah, Hilkhot Kelei ha-Mikdash* 8:2), asserts that "the *mitznefet* is very long, wrapped around multiple times like the Muslims' turbans, while the 'headgear' is like our caps, narrow at the top and short." The distinction between turban and cap, incidental and illustrative in Abraham ben David, takes on enormous symbolic significance in the present text. For Sabbatai Zevi and his contemporaries, the turban was the symbol of Islam; "donning the turban" (*tzanif* or sometimes *mitznefet*) meant converting to Islam, repudiating one's Jewish "cap" (Halperin, *Sabbatai Zevi*, 111, from Joseph Halevi). Now we are told: divinity itself has donned the turban.

29. Job 37:12, giving *tahbulot*—usually taken as "guidance" or "direction"—the meaning of *havalim*, "ropes," from the same root; and understanding them as the intestines by which the divinity's "head" is encompassed.

30. This and the following quotation from Job 29:14. The use of *tzedeq*, "righteousness," as a code term for the Shechinah is a Kabbalistic staple.

31. "His justice" is a misquotation of the Bible's "my justice." On the symbolic freight of *tzanif*, the Biblical word translated "turban," see above.

above it; while below it his name is VH, indicating the God of Israel and his Shechinah.³²

2. Torah and Commandments

You must realize that the Root imposed the doing of the commandments on the Shape of the Path of Emanation, yet with their full obligation falling entirely on the God of Israel, who is called *Qadosh barukh hu*, "Blessed Holy One." At the higher level all has the quality of *qodesh*, "holiness," without the letter *vav*; whereas the God of Israel, for whom the *vav* serves as emblem, is called *qadosh*, "holy," with the *vav*.³³ This is the meaning of *the Blessed Holy One puts on phylacteries*:³⁴ as the "heart" made up of Judgment and Mercy, the duty is his alone, and he must observe the commandments.

The Distant One, by contrast, has no need to perform the commandments or uphold the Torah. The God of Israel draws and separates from him all his wastes, leaving pure Grace behind. [The God of Israel,] moreover, acts as female vis-à-vis the Root, [fol. 17a] and Torah and commandments are the female's adornments to arouse sexual desire.³⁵ *A woman asks for sex with her heart*,³⁶ as we all know, and all the Torah's commandments, all its injunctions, therefore depend on the heart. *The Merciful One*

---

32. In the traditional Kabbalah the first two letters (YH) of the Tetragrammaton represent the fusion of the higher sefirot *Hokhmah* and *Binah*, while the last two (VH) are the central male deity (*Tif'eret*. "Little-face," "Blessed Holy One") + his Female (*Malkhut*, Shechinah). The subject of the sentence is presumably the God of Israel.

33. See above, chapter 2, note 12.

34. Talmud, b. Ber. 6a. Our author takes the "putting on" (literally, "laying" on himself) of the phylacteries as symbolic of taking on the yoke of the commandments, and links it to the epithet "Holy One" (*qadosh*, spelled with a *vav*) which is used for God in this passage. (And also throughout the rabbinic literature, but our author prefers not to mention that.) Maciejko notes a parallel from *Tzaddiq. Yesod 'Olam*, a Sabbatian commentary on the Book of Ruth claiming Isaac Luria as its author: "The body that puts on the phylacteries has the quality of the *vav*."

35. The Zohar speaks frequently of "adorning" the divine female (Shechinah) for lovemaking by such acts as propounding fresh interpretations of the Scriptures (I, 8a) or putting on phylacteries (I, 132). Here the God of Israel, turned female in relation to the Root (above, chapter 2, section 2), takes the Shechinah's place.

36. I.e., silently (Talmud, b. 'Erub. 100b); but our author understands "heart" with strict literalness.

seeks the heart,[37] and similarly *you must love the Lord your God with all your heart* and so forth, with no mention of the head.[38]

[p. 77] This is the meaning of the infant in his mother's womb—i.e., above the curtain, which is called *mother's womb*, as we have seen[39]—being *taught the entire Torah*, as it is written, "He taught me and said to me, Let your heart maintain my words; keep my commandments and live."[40] The text singles out *your heart*, which we have seen to represent the God of Israel. The verse *in the mystery of God over my tent* is likewise quoted;[41] it speaks of the Root, whom we have already seen to be called "God."[42] *Over my tent*—this is the curtain of which we have spoken, which for the infant is like a tent.

Know also that he partakes of the nature of a bridegroom while in the higher realms. We are explicitly told, in reference to the higher realms where the curtain is symbolically the bridal canopy, that the newborn is like a bridegroom;[43] in those higher realms, therefore, he is a bridegroom inside his canopy. This is the meaning of *above All*—i.e., the God of Israel—*Glory*—i.e., the Shechinah—*is a canopy*,[44] and also, *like a bridegroom shall Splendor act as priest*.[45] For he is represented by both "priest" and "Splendor," as we have seen.

---

37. Zohar, III, 281b; but the idea goes back to 1 Sam 16:7.

38. Deut 6:5: "you must love the Lord your God with all your heart, all your soul, all your might." The passage of which this is a part occupies a central place in the Jewish liturgy. (It comes immediately after the Jewish credo, the *Shema*.) In all these quotes our author takes "heart" literally as referring to the "heart" of the divine Shape, the God of Israel, in opposition to its "head."

39. Referring to section 1 above, where the Shechinah as placenta is transformed into the Shechinah as curtain separating the Distant One from the God of Israel.

40. Talmud, b. Nid. 30b, quoting Prov 4:4. The Talmudic passage is the continuation of Rabbi Simlai's account of the fetus in the womb, quoted and discussed by our author in chapter 3, section 1.

41. Job 29:4, one of several texts from the beginning of Job 29 invoked by Rabbi Simlai. I translate it the way our author seems to have understood it: the God of Israel is taught the Torah ("mystery") by the Root ("God") in the realm above the curtain ("over my tent").

42. Above, section 1. The word used for "God" in the Job passage is *Eloah*, however, and not *El* or *Elohim* as above.

43. Probably referring, as Maciejko suggests *ad loc.*, to the Talmud, b. Ned. 32a. The Talmudic simile allows our author to view the God of Israel at once as a newborn infant and as a young man, ripe for romance with his newly wedded Shechinah.

44. Isa 4:5, the words stretched almost beyond recognition to evoke the image of the God of Israel and his bride the Shechinah standing beneath their canopy.

45. Isa 61:10. *Pe'er*, "splendor," is from the same root as the *sefirah Tif'eret*, a

While he was above, when he was in that "bridal canopy," he was commanded the Torah. So says the Scripture, *Go forth and look, O daughters of Zion, upon King Solomon on his wedding day*, alluding to the giving of the Torah.[46] For it was then that the Torah was commanded to him.

3. The Alternative Anatomy Revisited: Dawn and Morning, Noon and Evening

[Our author now reintroduces the "alternative anatomy" of chapter 2, section 4, in which the Shape's "head" is the Root (and not the Distant One), its "heart" the Distant One (and not the God of Israel), while the God of Israel is now its "penis."

The realities of male sexual arousal illustrate how these three aspects are distinct and yet one. So do the transformations of the twenty-four-hour day, in which "dawn" (= the Root) morphs into "morning" (= the Distant One) and that into "noontime" (= the God of Israel). "Evening" in this schema is the female Shechinah, toward which the "penis" that is the God of Israel—or, the penis (*Yesod*) of the God of Israel—extends itself. So we can observe, as the afternoon wears on and the shadows lengthen.

From "evening" (*'erev*) and "west" (*ma'arav*), the author comes to explicate a more mysterious word from the same root: *'Aravot*, which appears in the Talmud as a name for the highest heaven. This is the Shechinah, both in her placental state (prior to the Self-extension, when the Shape was still a fetus within her, and persisting as an imprint even after the Self-extension) and in her present existence as a fully developed female. She is thus the first female *hei* of the Tetragrammaton (YHVH, *yod-hei-vav-hei*), partnered with the *yod* that is the Distant One, and also the second, partnered with the *vav* that is the God of Israel. Only, as first *hei* the Distant One is *inside* her, while as second *hei* the God of Israel is *atop* her.

How do we know? Because only on this basis will a difficult passage in the Zohar yield itself to interpretation.]

You must understand the following principle and fix it in your memory: In the three-tiered Shape wherein the Root functions as "head," the manifestation of the God of Israel.

---

46. Song 3:11, with its standard midrashic interpretation (e.g., Talmud, b. Ta'an. 26b) of the "wedding day" as the lawgiving at Sinai.

Distant One as "heart," and the God of Israel as "penis,"[47] all are one in a single Shape. These are the entities we speak of as "each incorporated within the other."

When the head conceives a thought—to give a concrete example—where does that thought go? To the heart, to be given the subtleties of planning, such that the head's thought is incorporated in the heart. The heart's thought then proceeds into the penis to work its effect, so that whenever one entertains erotic thoughts, he experiences an erection. The heart's thought has become incorporated within the penis.

[p. 78] Three levels, in other words, incorporated within one another. They are essentially a single Shape; yet, as our example allows us to understand, they may properly be considered one individual incorporated within another. We accordingly speak of the Distant One as being incorporated within the God of Israel and called his "soul," and the Root is spoken of as "within" the Distant One and called his "soul," whereas in reality it is all one, a single Shape.

These three levels manifest themselves in the day's three transformations.

In the Root there is no distinction whatever between male and female, but all are as one. It is therefore called *one*, in that it is in a state of perfect unity, alluding also to its being comprised of the Graces and Judgments in which male and female are inseparably contained (*ehad*, "one" = *ah*, "brother" + the letter *dalet*, i.e., male + female);[48] they dwell together, wholly indivisible. It is symbolized by *karmela*, as we have seen,[49] and it is the *Dawn*.

Thus the Zohar (on the Torah portion *Terumah*) explains that the dawn does not yet shine as it ought and requires mending in order to shine.[50] The reference is to the Root, which was at the time a mingling of Graces and Judgments; the Human Shape of the Path of Emanation

---

47. The alternative anatomy set forth in chapter 2, section 4.

48. A play on the *Shema*'s word *ehad*, "one" ("the Lord is one"), found in the late strata of the Zohar, e.g., II, 116a (*Ra'ya Mehemna*), *Tiqqunei Zohar* 34. אחד=אח+ד; the "brother" (אח) represents the male *sefirah Tif'eret*, the letter ד the female Shechinah.

49. Above, chapter 1, section 4: "Above, in the place of that 'head' to be discussed presently, Graces and Judgments cannot in practice be distinguished. Graces and Judgments, male and female elements, are mingled; and this is *karmel*, the intermingling of the aspects."

50. Zohar, II, 140a. Matt, trans., *Zohar* translates: "For the light abiding in darkness does not shine until enhanced [literally, "mended"] below." Our author understands the Zohar's *be-shahruta*, not as "in darkness," but "in the dawning."

mends it, clearing away its waste products and Judgments, purifying and mixing them to illumine properly. The Zohar consequently says that WHOEVER MENDS THIS LIGHT, BLACK THOUGH IT IS, MERITS THE WHITE LIGHT[51] that symbolizes the Shape of the Path of Emanation, represented as white light.

The Bible says, *Those who perform the Dawning-operation on me will find me*;[52] and the Zohar points out that THE TEXT DOES NOT SAY, FIND ME, BUT FIND THE TWO ME'S:[53] TWO LIGHTS, THE SHINING MIRROR AND THE ONE THAT DOES NOT SHINE. In other words, the Root emits the God of Israel, [p. 79] symbolized as "Shining Mirror," and the Shechinah, who is symbolized by the "Mirror that Does Not Shine."[54]

This is the meaning of *his locks are curly*—referring to the Root, whom we have seen [fol. 17b] to be symbolized by hair[55]—*and dawn-like as a raven*.[56] It is well known that the raven uses the spittle from its mouth to inseminate,[57] and we have already explained that at the level of the Root it was Father who said, *O Elohim, let there be light!* to Mother (refer back to what I have previously written on this subject).[58] [The Root] is therefore like a raven in that all is done through its mouth—a point you must thoroughly grasp.[59]

We have earlier explained that Abel came into existence while the Shape of the Path of Emanation was folded up and in the character of a child, begotten of its thought with the Root's aid.[60] This is the meaning

51. Here and in the next paragraph, our author condenses his Zohar quotations.

52. Prov 8:17, following the Zohar's understanding of *meshaharai* (as this is interpreted by our author), not as "those who seek me," but as "those who do the act of Dawn [*shahar*] upon me," i.e., who "mend" the dark light of dawn.

53. Where we would expect the verb "find me" to be spelled with one letter *nun* (ימצאוני), the Bible uses two *nuns* (ימצאנני), hinting at a double "finding."

54. A familiar Kabbalistic symbolism for the *sefirot Tif'eret* (male) and *Malkhut* (female).

55. Above, chapter 2, sections 3 and 5.

56. Song 5:11. The author's understanding of *shehorot* as "dawn-like" (deriving the adjective from *shahar*, "dawn"), rather than "black" as it is universally translated, is very forced.

57. Talmud, b. Sanh. 108b, as explained by Rashi.

58. Above, chapter 3, section 7.

59. The words that follow "raven" in this sentence are found only in ms. Oxford 955. The overall point is clear, although we are apt to think it is not very convincing: through the symbolism of both "hair" and "raven," the Root is linked to the dawn.

60. This is not quite what is said about Abel's origin in chapter 4, section 2, where the Shechinah has the central role and the Root is not even mentioned. The parallel

of the verse *childhood + dawn-hood = Abel*,[61] conveying that he was born of the two of them; also the meaning of *his bringing into being is solid as the dawn*,[62] for the one that brought him into being was the Root, "solid" indeed as the Dawn.

The Distant One is represented as *Morning*. This is light that is clear, shining, most exceedingly pleasant, for such is the Distant One: pure Mercy without any Judgment whatsoever. He is the entity designated, at the level of Interiority,[63] by the name "Abraham" which conveys pure Mercy. He is called the "Primordial Light" that the Root emitted before anything else, as we have seen: *he said, "O God, let there be light!"*[64] Consequently the Zohar throughout declares "morning" to represent the Primordial Light that is pure Mercy, symbolized by Abraham, who at the level of Enclothement stands for the *sefirah Gedullah*, as we all know, but at the level of Interiority for the Distant One.

This is the meaning of the verse *To you I cried, O Lord, and with the Morning my prayer transcends you.*[65] This "Lord" is the God of Israel, [p. 80] and when I pray to the "Morning," who is the Distant One—we shall presently see who these are and at what time one might pray to the "Morning"[66]—then my prayer "transcends you," rises higher than you, takes precedence over you. For this is the meaning of "transcends you," and it is the reason why the Bible consistently links "Grace" with "morning," e.g., *your grace in the morning*[67] and other expressions of this kind.

---

account of Cain's begetting, however, says that "the Shechinah conceived the urge to beget a human and through this urge and the power of thought, aided by light received from the Root, a human form took shape within her" (chapter 3, section 6).

61. Eccl 11:10, more normally translated, "childhood and youth are vanity."
62. Hos 6:3.
63. "Interiority," *penimiyut*, is the author's term for the super-sefirotic entities to which his treatise has until now been devoted. Its contrast with "Enclothement" (*hitlabbeshut*), the sefirotic structure designed post-Shattering to conceal and protect the "Interior" beings from any such future calamity, will be developed in the coming sections. Here he remarks that although at the level of "Enclothement" the Biblical figure of Abraham represents the *sefirah Hesed* (a.k.a. *Gedullah*)—a standard piece of Kabbalistic symbolism—at the deeper level of "Interiority" it stands for the Distant One. Both *Hesed* and the Distant One share the quality of absolute Grace.
64. Full discussion above, chapter 3, section 7.
65. Ps 88:14, as understood by our author.
66. And thereby transcend the God of Judaism.
67. Ps 90:14, 92:3, 143:8.

The Morning extends to *the Sixth Hour*,⁶⁸ for the God of Israel is known to be represented by the heart, which corresponds to the Six Points.⁶⁹

The Bible therefore says that *Moses was in six*,⁷⁰ conveying that the number six is his representation, for Moses is symbolic of *Tif'eret* and the God of Israel, as I shall explain below. (So the Zohar, which you may consult, understands Moses's being *in six*: his rung was *in six*.⁷¹) The sun of noonday heat stands for the God of Israel, who is that "Sixth Hour," shining most brilliantly; for he is symbolically represented by the sun.⁷²

The sun has the dual nature of drying out the moist and moistening the dry. Put something that is frozen in the sunshine and it will melt—as the Bible says, *it melted when the sun grew hot*⁷³—while anything wet will be dried out. Such is the God of Israel, who has within him the Balance of Judgment and Mercy, granting to each according to merit and represented therefore as "double-nosed," as we have seen.⁷⁴

He is also *the sun for whom a tent has been placed within them, who like a bridegroom emerges from his canopy*.⁷⁵ When he partakes of "Morning" quality, he is in the higher realms, inside the *parokhta*, inside the bridal canopy.⁷⁶ When he takes on the quality of "sun," however, he *emerges from his canopy* and from the *parokhta* to a place revealed,⁷⁷ there to beam forth his light. In him, as we have earlier explained at length, there is no admixture of Mindless Light whatever. All is done with thought, be it for Judgment or Mercy—thought brought to completion, with perfect lucidity. That is why the passage says that *Nothingness*,

---

68. I.e., noon.

69. In the traditional Kabbalah, the "Six Points" are the cluster of six *sefirot* (*Hesed, Gevurah, Tif'eret, Netzah, Hod, Yesod*) dominated by *Tif'eret*. These are the "heart," or more accurately the trunk, of the sefirotic man, the totality of the male aspect of God.

70. Exod 32:1, reading *boshesh*, "tarried," as *be-shesh*, "in six"—a midrashic reading that goes back to the Talmud (b. Shabb. 89a) and is employed by the Zoharic passage our author goes on to cite.

71. Paraphrasing Zohar, II, 191b. "Rung" is Matt's standard translation of *darga*, used by the Zohar for the *sefirot*.

72. Standard Kabbalistic symbolism for the *sefirah Tif'eret*.

73. Exod 16:21, referring to the manna.

74. Above, note 12.

75. Ps 19:5–6.

76. Taking up the image of the God of Israel as bridegroom; above, section 2.

77. *Atar de-itgalya*, a Zoharic phrase (II, 29b; cf. I, 64b, II, 164b, 227b) whose meaning for our author will be elucidated in the next section.

i.e., the Mindless Light, *is hidden from his solarity*.[78] It is "hidden" from him in the sense that he is entirely untainted by it.

[p. 81] The *Evening Shadows*,[79] which come into being as the sun inclines westward, stand for *Netzah, Hod,* and *Yesod*.[80] Most essentially they are the *Yesod*, phallus,[81] of the God of Israel, which is represented as a shadow and extends itself toward the West, i.e. the Shechinah. This accounts for what we have observed [fol. 18a] earlier, that the Shechinah who dwells in Abel's *Yesod* is named Zillah;[82] for *Yesod* is called *tzel*, "shadow," and the evening is symbolically equivalent to the Shechinah. She is called *ma'arav*, "west," and also *'Aravot*, both falling within the category of *'erev*, "evening."[83]

Realize that it is not only the Shechinah[84] that is called "evening." The placenta, represented, as we have seen, by the bridal canopy and the prayer shawl, is also symbolically equivalent to *'Aravot*. She is quintessentially female, having been the Shechinah that once enfolded [the divinity] like a placenta and even after descending[85] left her mark above, which therefore retained its female character. But note also a crucial distinction. The God of Israel in relation to his Shechinah would be called *rider upon 'Aravot*—two rungs, one atop the other. The Distant One in relation to

---

78. Ps 19:7, normally translated, "Nothing is hidden from its heat."

79. A phrase from Jer 6:4. While the subsequent identification of "West" with the Shechinah is standard Kabbalah, Jeremiah's "evening shadows" are more commonly connected with *Gevurah*, the *sefirah* of stern Judgment (e.g., Zohar, I, 132b).

80. The three *sefirot* that, in the traditional Kabbalah, are the two thighs and the penis of the divine human form.

81. This being the element of the male anatomy that elongates in the presence of the female.

82. Above, chapter 4, section 3. Cf. chapter 4, section 8, where this female entity is identified with the Eighth King of Gen 36. The term "Shechinah," originally used primarily for the "Higher Shechinah" who is the partner of the God of Israel, is increasingly applied to these lower females as well.

83. *'Aravot* is normally used in the Bible for "steppes" or "desert plains." The strange usage in Ps 68:5, where God is called "the rider in *'Aravot*," prompted the Talmudic rabbis to understand *'Aravot* as the name of the seventh, highest heaven (b. Hag. 12b); this interpretation inspired the Zoharic passage that our author will analyze in the next section. Here he makes the reasonable observation that *'Aravot* and the Hebrew word for "west" are both from the root *'erev*, "evening." *'Aravot* can thus be understood, like the other two words, as symbolically indicating the Shechinah.

84. In her aspect of fully developed female.

85. To take on discrete existence.

the placenta, by contrast, is *rider in 'Aravot*,⁸⁶ for he dwells within the placenta that envelops and conceals him, as we have seen.

Moreover the Shechinah, as final *hei* [of the Tetragrammaton], is female partner to the *vav*. The curtain of which we have spoken, however, is a higher female, whose relation is with the Distant One, and who is represented within the letters *yod-hei*, as I have earlier written.⁸⁷

With this, we have the key to understanding the Zohar on the Torah portion *Terumah*, fol. 165b.

4. The Zoharic Evidence: II, 165b

> [Rabbi Eleazar (son of Rabbi Shimon ben Yohai, one of the central characters in the Zohar) professes himself baffled. When Ps 68:5 speaks of *the Rider in 'Aravot*, it apparently refers to the God of Israel. But the God of Israel should ride *on* the Shechinah, not *in* her. And why does the psalm speak of the deity's "name" (i.e., female) as "in Yah"? We think of the Shechinah as occupying a lower level of divinity, in *vav-hei* and not *yod-hei* ("Yah").
>
> But Rabbi Eleazar knew what our author now reveals: that the Shechinah is also placenta for the higher divinity called the Distant One. He—"the Most Distant of All the Distant, Most Hidden of All the Hidden"—is therefore the "Rider" inside her. And Rabbi Eleazar tells us more, in cryptic, allusive language that only our author's system allows us to decode. The Shechinah is "the primordial mystery that emerges ... from that unknown hidden one," namely the Root, which begot the Higher Shechinah through sex with the Shape (also the Root's offspring). After the Self-extension she both is and is not the placenta that the Zohar speaks of as *parokhta*, "curtain," a paradox encoded in Rabbi Eleazar's puzzling language. Only our author's theology provides a proper context for understanding it. If the Zohar is true, then, that theology must be true as well.]

---

86. Ps 68:5. The hypothetical phrase *rider on Aravot* occurs nowhere in the Bible.

87. In the traditional Kabbalah, the four letters of the name YHVH represent the *sefirah Hokhmah* (*yod*), the higher female *sefirah Binah* (*hei*), the *sefirah Tif'eret* (*vav*), and the lower female *sefirah Malkhut* (the Shechinah, the final *hei*). The *vav* and the final *hei* are sex partners; so, in a steadier and less tumultuous relationship, the *yod* and the first *hei*. Our author transfers this symbolism from the world of Enclothement—the traditional *sefirot*—to that of Interiority.

Rabbi Eleazar said: This verse is problematic, *Exalt the Rider in 'Aravot*.[88] It should read, *upon 'Aravot*; why *in 'Aravot*?

In the preceding context, the Zohar has understood these words as applying to the God of Israel. The words *be merry before him*[89] are referred to the Distant One, whose realm is pure Mercy and where joy and lightheartedness are requisite, for there is no Judgment and no need for fear; hence *before him*, as in *before there reigned any king*.[90] This is the point of Rabbi Eleazar's question. If the passage intends the God of Israel and his Shechinah, who is called *'Aravot*, it ought to have said, *upon 'Aravot*, for he is superior to her.

[p. 82] *In his name Yah? It should read, In Yah, he*.[91] "His name" has the quality of the female who is called "name," as in *to make for you an eternal name*.[92] Hence Rabbi Eleazar's perplexity: what has the Female to do with the name *Yah*? Surely *Yah* stands for the Distant One and not for the Shechinah, who is at a lower level, represented within *vav-hei* rather than *yod-hei*. The verse ought to have said, *in Yah, he*; for the pronoun *he* is known to indicate the Distant One, the place that is utterly unrevealed.[93] Of this [Rabbi Eleazar] says: But this verse speaks of the Most Hidden of All the Hidden, the Most Distant of All the Distant, the One entirely unrevealed and unknown who is the Rider in

---

88. Ps 68:5. The text of the Zohar quoted here is slightly different from that of the Mantua edition; I have translated accordingly.

89. From the end of Ps 68:5, shortly after "exalt the Rider in *'Aravot*."

90. An abbreviated quote from Gen 36:31, "These are the kings who reigned in the land of Edom before there reigned any king for the children of Israel"; see above, chapter 4, section 5. In Ps 68:5, "him" refers to the God of Israel and "before him" to the "Edomite" domain that is both prior to ("before") and higher than the God of Israel. For our author, "Edom" (Christianity) is the sphere of the Distant One, of divine Grace; when one leaves the God of Israel and enters into this sphere, the effect is joy and merriment.

91. Continuing Rabbi Eleazar's questioning in the Zohar, with the words "in his name Yah" that immediately follow "exalt the Rider in *'Aravot*" in Ps 68:5. "Yah" (*yod-hei*) is commonly used in the Bible as a shortened form of the Tetragrammaton; the Kabbalists understood it to refer specifically to the higher levels of divinity. Rabbi Eleazar's awkward "in Yah, he" will be elucidated below.

92. Slight misquotation of Isa 63:12: God is the possessor of an "eternal name," i.e., the Female who shares his eternity. The understanding of a divinity's "name" as a distinct entity, the female partner to that (male) divinity, is a Kabbalistic staple.

93. *Atar de-la itgalya*; from the Zohar, II, 207a. The use of the third-person singular pronoun as code for the arcane, inaccessible levels of divinity derives from the traditional Kabbalah: Zohar, I, 49a ("*He*—hidden of all hidden, concealed of all concealed, called *He*, unknown by any name," trans. Matt, *Zohar*); Gikatilla, *Sha'are Orah*, 245.

'Aravot—namely the Distant One, whom the curtain represented as *Aravot* envelops as a placenta, and who is appropriately called *Rider in 'Aravot* and not *upon 'Aravot* because he is inside that curtain.

BUT WILL YOU SAY THAT HE COMES AND RIDES IN IT? IF SO, EVEN THOUGH HE IS HIDDEN, HE STANDS IN A PLACE REVEALED. This means that we need not be concerned lest the reference be to the God of Israel,[94] who at times ascends above the curtain and then can also be spoken of as *Rider in 'Aravot*. That is why [Rabbi Eleazar] says, BUT WILL YOU SAY THAT HE, namely the God of Israel, who was earlier the subject, COMES AND RIDES in *'Aravot*, i.e., when he ascends above the curtain? And he says in response: IF SO, EVEN THOUGH HE IS HIDDEN when he ascends on high, when he comes back down to his proper location he has the quality of A PLACE REVEALED. Why then, should we praise him[95] when he is in that hidden place? Would it not be more proper when he is in the PLACE REVEALED?

The word *sollu*, "exalt," has moreover the sense of purely mental activity, suitable not for the place revealed but for that concealed, the essence of which is thought.[96] If the verse were speaking of the God of Israel, the language appropriate to his revealed locale would have been "praise" or "prayer." BUT RATHER, EXALT THE RIDER IN *'ARAVOT* WHO IS THE MOST DISTANT OF ALL THE DISTANT, MOST HIDDEN OF ALL THE HIDDEN, THE UNKNOWN.

AND IN WHAT DOES HE RIDE IN *'ARAVOT*? IN *YOD-HEI*, WHICH IS THE PRIMORDIAL MYSTERY THAT EMERGES FROM HIM, AND THIS IS HIS NAME FROM THAT UNKNOWN HIDDEN ONE; HIS NAME IS *YOD-HEI*—[p. 83] meaning: IN the Higher Shechinah, who, as we have seen,[97] is represented in *yod-hei*. She is THE PRIMORDIAL MYSTERY THAT EMERGES FROM HIM, whom we have seen the Bible to hint at when it says that

---

94. Who, as the author will shortly remind us, appears in the Zoharic context as the *Rider in 'Aravot*.

95. As the psalm calls us to do.

96. Cf. the role of the Distant One's "thought" in the emergence of Cain (= Primordial Creation-Human) and Abel; above, chapter 3, sections 6–8 and chapter 4, section 2. I do not know on what basis the author sees the verb *sollu*—normally used in the Bible of "lifting up" in a physical sense—as indicating specifically mental activity.

97. At the end of the preceding section. Rabbi Eleazar's problem—"what has the Female to do with the name *Yah*?"—resulted from his initial dichotomy of the Distant One versus the Shechinah who is partner to the God of Israel. He now recognizes a Higher Shechinah who belongs with the Distant One, in fact enfolds him; and she, like the Distant One, is indicated by the letters *yod-hei*.

God cast deep sleep upon the human and *indeed she is my sister, daughter of my Father* and so forth.[98] FROM THAT UNKNOWN HIDDEN ONE: this refers to the Root which is called UNKNOWN HIDDEN ONE; and it was through him that he [the Root] produced the Shechinah, for it was he with whom [the Root] copulated.[99]

She is called "his name"; the Bible therefore says, *In his name Yod-Hei*. True enough: when the Shechinah is below,[100] she has the quality of *vav-hei*. Yet here, where that *parokhta* is the subject, she[101] has the quality of *yod-hei* as already indicated.

NOT THAT IT IS HE,[102] BUT IT IS HE BY VIRTUE OF THAT PAROKHTA THAT IS SPREAD AND GOES FORTH FROM BEFORE HIM. YET THIS PAROKHTA IS HIS NAME—which is to say, essentially the Shechinah that issued from him.[103] Not truly the same, for after the Self-extension the Shechinah descended below as the final *hei*[104]—hence the text says, NOT THAT IT IS HE, the Shechinah—yet partaking of Shechinah-nature BY VIRTUE OF THAT PAROKHTA THAT IS SPREAD AND GOES FORTH FROM BEFORE HIM. During his Self-folding, in other words, the Shechinah was like a placenta, a PAROKHTA SPREAD BEFORE HIM, the choice of words conveying that as placenta she encompassed him on all sides, his head included, just as we have seen. Even after the Self-extension, when she went down to take her place as final *hei*, her mark remained where it had been; and, remaining there, it shared her essential designation as the "Higher Shechinah" that had emerged from the Shape of the Path of

---

98. Gen 2:21, 20:12. See the next note.

99. Above, chapter 2, section 3, where both Genesis verses are understood as referring to the Root (= "God" and "Father") begetting the Higher Shechinah through a sex act with the Shape (= "the human"). The object of the Root's erotic attention seems here to be understood specifically as the Distant-One aspect of the Shape; but its earlier identification with the totality of the Shape (above, chapter 2) will soon be resumed.

100. Shechinah *qua* fully formed female shape (*hei*), sex partner to the God of Israel (*vav*).

101. Shechinah *qua* curtain (*parokhta*), who can properly be called the "name" of the Distant One.

102. Rabbi Eleazar apparently takes up his earlier objection that the Scripture ought to have said, *in Yah, he*, rather than *in his name Yah*; what he does with it is very unclear. Our author understands *he* as the Shechinah, and the point to be that the curtain (located in the upper realms) is not fully identical with the Shechinah that has descended below.

103. From the Distant One, after coupling with the Root.

104. Of the Tetragrammaton.

Emanation.[105] It was called "his Great Name," for everything there has the quality of Mercy, and it was consequently called *gadol*, "great." For "greatness," *gedullah*, is known to be the quality of Mercy.[106]

The words of the Biblical verse thus make perfect sense. We are to *exalt* the Distant One, who is *the Rider in 'Aravot*, the bridal canopy of which we have spoken, and *in his name Yah*, that name[107] that has the quality of *yod-hei* and not the final *hei*, her mark persisting in the higher place.[108] This you must understand.

5. First Modification: The Enclothement

[From Zohar exegesis, our author returns to his narrative. What shall the God of Israel do to ensure the survival of divine structures just emerging from the harrowing catastrophe of the Shattering, which—unless preventive steps are taken—might recur at any time?

The answer: provide these structures with a suit of armor, protective clothing, which our author calls *hitlabbeshut*, "Enclothement."

The three highest *sefirot* of what was once Abel have, as Luria taught us, survived the Shattering in flawed but fixable condition. Using the raw energy that proceeds from the Distant One, the God of Israel builds these up into the Lurianic Shapes of Long-face (*Arikh Anpin*), Father, and Mother. Long-face will from now on serve as Enclothement for the Distant One, while Father and Mother function as devices for purifying the shards of Abel's shattered lower *sefirot*—the first stage of their reconstruction.

These fragments then enter the womb of the Higher Shechinah. She is pregnant with them; a new deity takes form inside her, solid and durable thanks to its origin in sexual comingling. This is the "Six Points" of the classical Kabbalah, *Tif'eret* and its five satellite *sefirot* (= the Lurianic Little-face), which from now on will be the Enclothement of the God of Israel, the suit of armor that he wears and dwells inside. Little-face's Female (= *Malkhut*, the lowest *sefirah*) will be the Enclothement of his Shechinah.]

---

105. As described above, chapter 2, section 3.
106. Hence the *sefirah Hesed* ("Grace") is also called *Gedullah*, "Greatness."
107. I.e., female.
108. The realm of the Distant One, above the curtain.

When the God of Israel—to resume our narrative—set about constructing the World of the Mending and the World of Emanation, and repairing Abel's fragments, he resolved on two modifications[109] to ensure the Mending's permanence.

The danger of Shattering concerned him deeply. Abel's vessels had undergone shattering even in the absence of sin. How much greater would be the vulnerability when, as he now foresaw, human beings would sin and thereby inflict multiple injuries on the Higher Merkavah—mutilating it, dividing it, [p. 84] and above all introducing into it the Mindless Light, which (as I shall presently explain) is sin's natural effect.[110] The Mindless Light causes breakage and division, due to its tendency to spread itself out. So he decided that modifications were required, and he made two of them.

The first was to interpose a screen separating Primordial Creation-Human (represented by Cain) from *Tif'eret* and the Six Points of Emanation (represented by Abel and the vessel fragments), so that the Mindless Light might not kill him or something similar befall. He aimed also at the mending of Abel's *Keter, Hokhmah,* and *Binah,* which had survived in a reparable state.[111] Observing, however, that these were still contaminated by wastes and Judgments without any semblance of Balance, the God of Israel did not wish to send them down from their place to enter the Shechinah's womb as embryos within the Female, there to be purified. This would not have been possible, for so drastic a descent would have exposed them to Shattering, which was hardly his intent. (He had other reasons as well.)

Instead, he rebuilt them into the form of the Head That Is Unknown and the Three Heads and the rest, familiar from the system of Enclothement of which Luria spoke (calling them "the Three Heads of Long-face"), and similarly the Shapes of Father and Mother.[112] All these did the God

---

109. *Tiqqunim,* the plural of the word translated "Mending."

110. The notion that human sin has a harmful effect on divinity, and thus on the entire universe, is a staple of Kabbalah.

111. On the survival of the three highest *sefirot,* see above, chapter 4, note 75; on Abel as a representation of *Tif'eret* and its satellite *sefirot* ("Six Points") and their destruction in the Shattering, above, chapter 4, section 7. The Abel of the "Point-world" has of course already been killed. The God of Israel's aim is to protect his successor in the "World of the Mending" from undergoing a similar fate.

112. The cryptic Zoharic text known as the *Idra Zuta* speaks of "three heads, inscribed within one another and above one another" as a feature of the entity whom our author calls "the Holy Distant One," and of "a head that is not a head, that does not

of Israel construct in his capacity as "heart," through the effluence and illumination conveyed as the breath from the Distant One's mouth and the other apertures of his head—for it is the "heart" that brings all this forth, yet as pure, sweetened Mercies [fol. 19a] without any Mindless Light, as we have seen[113]—and also through the effluence and illumination of the Distant One's holy beard.[114] It was the God of Israel who brought them forth, pure Mercies as the Lurianic writings tell us of the Thirteen Adornments of the Beard, that they are [p. 85] pure Mercies. (These, as we know, are called "the Dispenser.")[115]

With this effluence and illumination, then, did the God of Israel reconstruct them[116] as complete Shapes, in all those aspects that Luria has described at length. The *Malkhut* of Primordial Creation-Human enclothed itself within them through the shoe-removal rite, as we have seen.[117] All this was effected through the Distant One's effluence, as described above. That is why this effluence is known as the "Hidden Intelligence";[118] for "intelligence" means effluence, as represented by the intellectual organs, and it proceeds from the head of that Distant One who is called "Most Hidden of All the Hidden."[119]

---

know nor is it known what is in that head" (Zohar, III, 288a–b). The Lurianic writings wrestle with the definition of these "Three Heads" and "Head That Is Unknown," and how they relate to one another: Vital, *Mevo She'arim* III.ii.4–5, 120–26); *'Etz Hayyim* III.xiii.3–4, volume. 1, 180–83; Avivi, *Binyan Ariel*, 123–24, 193–95, 270, 393–95. All are understood as features of "Long-face"—probably understood as "the Patient One"—the Lurianic "Shape" (above, chapter 1, note 51) corresponding to the *sefirah Keter* of the older Kabbalah. For our author, the Lurianic Long-face functions as the "Enclothement" of the Holy Distant One, with the "Shapes" of Father and Mother (= *Hokhmah* and *Binah* in the older Kabbalah) as attachments.

113. Above, section 1.

114. Above, note 17.

115. On the Thirteen Adornments, see above, note 17. *Mazzala*, which normally means "constellation" but is understood here as "Dispenser" of liquid effluence (from the root *nzl*, "to flow"), is associated in *Idra Rabbah* and *Zuta* with the highest level of divinity (Zohar, III, 134a, 289a, 292b). Gikatilla equates it with the highest *sefirah Keter*, "from which living water flows down to all the dispensers" (i.e., *sefirot*), and applies to it a pseudorabbinic dictum that "everything depends on the Dispenser, even the Torah scroll in the Temple" (*Sha'are Orah*, 134–36). For our author, it is part of the "Enclothement" that the God of Israel is in the process of providing for the Holy Distant One.

116. Abel's *Keter*, *Hokhmah*, and *Binah*.

117. Above, chapter 4, section 9.

118. *Moha stima'ah*, a phrase taken from the *Idra* literature and understood in the Lurianic writings to refer to one of the Three Heads.

119. E.g., above, section 4.

The Three Heads previously mentioned, together with the Father, have the character of the Distant One's phylactery, the four chambers that remained imprinted, as we have earlier said.[120] They are the Holy Distant One's Enclothement over against his Interiority, and therefore can themselves be called "Holy Distant One." When, however, the Zohar treats of both together, it designates the Three Heads—which belong to the Enclothement of the Distant One, versus the Interiority—as *Holy Distant One* without qualification. By contrast, the Holy Distant One of Interiority—that which functions as the "head" of the Shape of the Path of Emanation—is called *Distant One Most Holy of All the Holy, Most Hidden of All the Hidden*; and you must attend carefully to this distinction. But when not speaking of the two together, the Zohar may at times call the Interiority simply *Holy Distant One* as well.

Afterward the God of Israel gathered Abel's fragments, raising and redeeming them from the Insolent Waters in a manner presently to be elucidated at length.

First they entered the Shape of Father and Mother to be freed of the wastes left by the Insolent Waters, washed and purified and nurtured so they might enter unharmed into the womb of the God of Israel's Shechinah. Having completed this process of building and nursing—described by Luria as the stages of Nursing and Maturity[121]—they entered the womb of the God of Israel's Shechinah, there to be her female juices. (So the Zohar tells us: the souls entering the Female function as female juices for her.[122]) [p. 86] The God of Israel then poured male juices down upon them and she became impregnated with them, and they grew.

This is what made them into a solidly established Shape: its having come into being through an act of full sexual intercourse between male

---

120. Referring to section 1 above, where the "heart" aspect leaves its imprint on the "head" aspect (= the Distant One) in the form of the four compartments of the head-phylactery (the three chambers of the heart + the one chamber of the skull). Here the four compartments are reinterpreted as the Three Heads of Long-face + the "Shape" of Father. The phrase *tefillin shel 'attiqa* ("Distant One's phylactery") is adapted from the traditional term *tefillin shel rosh* for the head-phylactery, since *'attiqa* ("Distant One") = *rosh* ("head").

121. Of the central male deity of the Lurianic system, the Shape of Little-face (*Ze'ir Anpin*, probably to be understood as "the Irascible One"). The Lurianic "mythos of God giving birth to Himself" in the form of *Ze'ir Anpin*, as Scholem describes it (*Major Trends*, 270–71), is elaborated at length in Vital's *'Etz Hayyim* IV.xvi-V.xxix.

122. Zohar, I, 60b, 235a, 244a-b, 245b: in the sexual connection between male and female elements of Deity, the souls of the righteous provide the female with her lubricant. This, mingled with the male's semen, produces the embryo.

and female, with all the advantages that construction through male-female intercourse entails.[123] This is the essence of Emanation's structure: the *Tif'eret*-and-Six-Points[124] that was made in the World of Emanation as a complete Shape. The Zohar and the Kabbalistic writers speak of it, for reasons presently to be elucidated, as *Little-face and His Female*.

This Shape is indeed unequalled for completeness among all the Shapes of Enclothement, possessing a solid male-female structure which, as we have seen, all the others lack entirely. It serves the function of "heart" to Enclothement, being the *Tif'eret*-and-Six-Points that corresponds to the Interiority of the God of Israel, who is the Shape of the Path of Emanation in Interiority. Of the Shechinah, and how it came to be fashioned out of those two females,[125] we shall presently have more to say.

Let this be your guiding principle:[126]

1. *The Three Heads of Long-face* correspond, in Enclothement, to *the Distant One Holiest of All the Holy, Most Hidden of All the Hidden*;

2. *Little-face* corresponds to *the God of Israel*; and

3. *his Female* corresponds, in Enclothement, to *the Shechinah of the God of Israel*.

Understand this also: Inasmuch as *Tif'eret* is superior in its completeness to all the other structures (as we have seen), it has even for its external designation the Tetragrammaton *YHVH*, which we have seen to be the sacred and essential name of [fol. 19b] the God of Israel. Not so the other Shapes, whose external designations are other names unrelated to the Tetragrammaton, such as *Ehyeh* or the like.[127]

Thus far the first modification.

---

123. As opposed to the flawed, "thought-begotten" Primordial Creation-Human (= Cain) and his equally fragile brother Abel; above, chapter 3, section 6, and chapter 4, section 2.

124. See above, note 69.

125. Who were created with Abel (above, chapter 4, section 2) and afterwards survived the Shattering, protecting the *Yesod* of the Point-world in the process (section 8).

126. For understanding the relation of Enclothement to Interiority.

127. The traditional Kabbalah identifies each of the ten *sefirot* with one or another of the Bible's sacred names, such that *Ehyeh*—"I am," the name God calls himself in Exod 3:14—functions as a code term for the highest *sefirah* Keter, while *YHVH* is associated specifically with *Tif'eret*. (See Tishby, *Wisdom*, 1:294.) Our author finds a superiority for *Tif'eret* in that, unlike the other elements of "Enclothement," it shares the name *YHVH* with the totality of divinity's "Interiority" (above, chapter 2, sections 1 and 3), while the others must make do with lesser names.

6. Second Modification: The Female's New Role

> [In addition to the Enclothement, the Shechinah is enlisted to provide a further layer of protection. Effluence from the higher entities is necessary for the maintenance of the lower ones; yet, if this comes to them directly in the form of "uncontained ejaculate," they are liable to Shattering. This is the case even when the effluence comes, not from the Distant One, but from the God of Israel. The solution is for the divine female to take on the role of mediatrix, receiving within her the effluence ejaculated by the God of Israel and dispensing it to the lower worlds in proper measure. The Shechinah's "Enclothement" *Malkhut*, though the lowest of the *sefirot*, thus becomes the pivot of the entire system.]

As to the second modification: I have written earlier that all the Cain-and-Abel worlds, in all ten of their aspects, flourished prior to the dominion of any Israelite king. They belonged rather to that *land of Edom* where the Distant One holds sway, and that is why they were shattered.[128] Even now, after the Self-extension, he remained Mercy-filled, and consequently the risk of shattering under his influence continued to hang over them. For he is pure Mercy, pure expansion, without anything to restrain or put a stop to it, Judgment being the restraining element.

[p. 87] A second factor was also at work. The Distant One's influence is exercised without any female, as uncontained ejaculate, and this is what causes shattering. (So Luria has written: the Shattering of the Vessels happened through uncontained ejaculate, the ten drops of sperm that Joseph emitted.[129]) Given this, his effluence would even now be in the form of uncontained ejaculate, and they would be liable to shattering as long as they depended on receiving it.

The God of Israel therefore removed from them any effluence that might come to them from the place of the Holy Distant One, providing them instead with effluence from himself; for his quality is that of the

---

128. See above, chapter 4, the beginning of section 5. The author draws his language from Gen 36:31. "Israel's king" is the God of Israel; the "ten aspects" of the Cain-and-Abel worlds are the ten *sefirot* of Primordial Creation-Human and of the original structures of Emanation that underwent the Shattering.

129. From his ten fingernails, when aroused beyond endurance by Potiphar's wife: Talmud, b. Sotah 36b; *Midrash Genesis Rabbah* 87:7. Luria equated these drops with the "Edomite" kings, who were destroyed "because the human entity was not yet perfected as male and female together" and the drops "went forth without a female, but only from the male" (Vital, *'Etz Hayyim* viii.3; translated and discussed in Wolfson, *Language*, 310–11).

sun, Judgment and Mercy balanced and mixed as we have seen, the God of Israel acting as a king in his country—marshalling his forces in orderly fashion, granting proper measure to all.[130] Nor did he stop there. The effluence might have taken the form of uncontained ejaculate, even with himself as its provider. To avert this, the God of Israel arranged that, dependent though they were on his spilling out the effluence to them, they should not receive it all. Rather, he would first spill it as male juices into the female who was the God of Israel's Shechinah. She would respond with her female juices; these would mix; her organs of intelligence would then be complete, perfected as male and female together.

All the worlds, all the structures, would then send forth elements of themselves into *Malkhut*, and she would grant effluence to each one in the pace and measure appropriate to it, for she is the Building Line, the Artisan designing each one according to its proper measure.[131] From these all the worlds would receive perfected intelligence, and through it become themselves entirely perfected. This is the meaning of the verse *Your Malkhut is the Malkhut of all the worlds*:[132] she sustains them all, above and below. It is the meaning of, *She sends forth her foliage*—i.e., branches, boughs—*as far as the sea* which is the Shechinah, *and to the river her sucklings*, these being the elements sent forth from all the worlds.[133]

[p. 88] As a result, when these elements descend into *Malkhut* to obtain effluence and nourishment, something of their character remains below inside *Malkhut*, for we have seen that they cannot depart from

---

130. Above, sections 1 (the image of the king) and 3 (the image of the sun).

131. Cf. section 1, where the Higher Shechinah is called "Measuring Line" and "Artisan." Here the reference is to the Shechinah's "Enclothement," the *sefirah Malkhut* of the World of Emanation. The female *Malkhut*, lowest of the ten *sefirot*, is assumed in traditional Kabbalah to receive nourishment from the *sefirot* above her, and to grant it to those entities—ourselves included—that are below. Our author gives this idea a new and remarkable twist. *Malkhut* receives effluence from the Higher Shechinah dwelling within her and is thus a fount of sustenance even for the higher entities, who send forth rootlike organs ("elements of themselves") into her to absorb that sustenance.

132. Ps 145:13, normally translated "your kingdom is an everlasting kingdom." (*Malkhut* literally means "kingdom," and *'olam*, which comes in post-Biblical Hebrew to mean "world," is used in the Bible for "eternity.")

133. Ps 80:12. The word usually translated "shoots," in the second part of the verse literally means "sucklings," and that is how our author understands it: like plants, the other *sefirot* ("worlds") send down their roots into *Malkhut*, to suck nourishment from her as from a mother. The use of "sea" as code for *Malkhut* is a Kabbalistic staple; e.g., Gikatilla, *Sha'are Orah*, 19–20.

a place without leaving some trace of themselves behind.¹³⁴ It follows that imprints of all the worlds remain throughout *Malkhut*. This is why the Zohar says that all the structures and designs are contained within *Malkhut*, and why *Malkhut* can, broadly speaking, be called by all the sefirotic appellations.¹³⁵

She is called *Keter*, "crown," as in *a worthy woman is her husband's crown*.¹³⁶ She is called *Solomon's Wisdom*, as the Zohar explains in several places, and she is indeed one and shares a single appellation.¹³⁷ As *Hesed*, she is called *priest*;¹³⁸ she partakes of the essence of *Gevurah* who is *Adonai* and of *Tif'eret* who is "king," by which name she also is called.¹³⁹ There are many other instances—the appellations given to *Netzah* and *Hod*, who are called *'arvei nahal*, "willows of the brook," while she is called *'aravit*, "evening"; and *Yesod* and *Malkhut* for the most part share a single appellation.¹⁴⁰ All these does she inherit, inasmuch as traces of all the *sefirot* remain within her.

7. Male Juices: Dew and Rain, Kissing and Copulation

> [The Distant One has no female, a lack which for the present must remain unfilled. His effluence, therefore, must be for the present be limited, incapable of bearing fruit, if it is not to have

---

134. On the principle that "the Shechinah does not budge from its place without leaving a mark"; see above, chapter 1, note 71.

135. Perhaps alluding to Zohar, III, 29a (*Ra'ya Mehemna*), which does not, however, speak specifically of *Malkhut*.

136. Prov 12:4, which the Kabbalists understood to speak of the *sefirah Malkhut*. The word for "crown" in this passage is *'atarah* rather than *keter*, but the link is clear.

137. With the *sefirah Hokhmah*, "Wisdom." See, e.g., Zohar, I, 248b, and Matt's n. 978 ad loc.: "*Shekhinah* is also the daughter of *Hokhmah* (Wisdom) and is known as 'lower *Hokhmah*' or *wisdom of Solomon*." The author skips over *Binah* and goes straight to the following *sefirah*, *Hesed*.

138. The Biblical "priest" is understood by the Kabbalists as a representation of *Hesed*. I do not know any source that uses it as a designation for *Malkhut*.

139. *Adonai*, "the Lord"—often used as a substitute for the Tetragrammaton, which is too holy to be spoken—is a name special to *Malkhut*, the female entity that encases the male YHVH = *Tif'eret* (Gikatilla, *Sha'are Orah*). I am not aware of it having any connection with *sefirah Gevurah*, as our author claims. *Tif'eret* is regularly called "king," while *Malkhut* appears in the Zohar (I, 30a, 199b) as the "lower king."

140. The "willows of the brook" of Lev 23:40 are equated with *Netzah* and *Hod* in, e.g., Zohar, II, 186b. On *Malkhut* (Shechinah) as "evening," see above, section 3; *'aravit* and *'arvei* are from the same Hebrew root. I am not sure what the author means by *Yesod* and *Malkhut* "sharing a single appellation."

disastrous consequences. The image used for it in the classical sources (Bible, Talmud) is "dew," as opposed to the fructifying "rain" of the God of Israel; "kissing," as opposed to the full sex act. This inability to absorb significant effluence from the Distant One is a serious flaw in the structure of the post-Shattering world dominated by the God of Israel (below, chapter 9, section 3), its mending left for the Messiah Sabbatai Zevi.]

We thus see that all the worlds, including even Primordial Creation-Human, depend on the Balance of the God of Israel to receive effluence, and they do so via *Malkhut*. There is a certain distinction to be made in this respect, however, and it is this:

You must be aware that when Luria writes (*'Etz Hayyim*, section 31, the exposition of Primordial Human) that embracing [fol. 20a] and kissing take place prior to sexual intercourse in order to expel a breath, and afterward comes the intercourse—this breath yielded by the kisses is far brighter and clearer than that produced in the coupling, yet has no capacity to beget offspring. It is the copulation-breath, rather, by which seed is sown and offspring produced, while the essence of the kiss is a vapor emitted by the mouth and the other apertures.

You must further grasp the [analogous] distinction between dew and rain. Dew indeed purer and more lucent than rain. Yet it is rain that nourishes seeds and makes them sprout, while dew can do no more than slightly moisten them, [p. 89] for it is the rain, you are to understand, that couples the male with the female seed. Our ancient rabbis hinted at this when they said that *for each and every drop that falls from heaven, two drops rise from the abyss to meet it*,[141] symbolic of the coupling of the male juices with the female. This is why rain is called *yoreh*, "the shooter," for *seed that does not shoot like an arrow will produce no offspring*.[142] You must understand this.

The spirit, the breath that goes forth from the mouth and the rest of the orifices and through the radiance of the Holy Beard,[143] is by contrast entirely without female participation. It partakes of the nature of dew, exceedingly pure indeed, for there[144] all is pure Mercy. But in the total absence of any male-female coupling, it can produce

---

141. A very free quotation of *Midrash Genesis Rabbah* 13:13.

142. Talmud, b. Hag. 15a. *Yoreh* is a common Biblical word, normally translated "the former rain" (as opposed to *malqosh*, "the latter rain," Deut 11:14).

143. Of the Distant One. See above, note 17.

144. In the sphere of the Distant One.

no offspring. Understand this; for the rabbis never said of the dew that anything comes forth from the abyss to meet it. Its nature is purely male, without any female component, and it is that which comes forth from the breath and spirit of the orifices and the Holy Beard, incapable of begetting, only moistening.

This is why it is called *tal*, "dew," which has the numerical value of the phrase "YHVH is one,"[145] indicating that it is produced solely of the male, without any combination of male and female. We have earlier said, moreover, that the Shape of the Path of Emanation can be represented by the numerical value of the spelled-out Tetragrammaton when its letters are written with *aleph*s, that is to say 45.[146] Given that this emerging breath is produced by the heart, i.e., the God of Israel, it follows that it is made through the coordination of the three letters *yod hei vav*, without the final *hei*, since he is not coupling with the Shechinah, who is symbolized by that final *hei*.[147] And [these three letters together] have the numerical value of *tal*, "dew."

This dew partakes of the nature of kissing, which is solely a matter of spirit, and just as dew requires rain, so kissing requires copulation.[148] True, Luria has written that both male and female spirits are present even in kissing.[149] But by this he referred to Father and Mother, those two COMPANIONS WHO NEVER ARE SEPARATED,[150] and not to this loftier realm where the only spirit and breath involved is that which the Holy Distant One emits to [the God of Israel] and which he then supplies to them.[151]

[p. 90] This is the dew that the God of Israel produces from the Distant One's orifices and the hairs of his beard. It descends from there via Creation-Human—who has no involvement in the construction process, as Luria has said; refer back to what we earlier said about his identification

---

145. *Tal* and *YHVH ehad* both have the numerical value of 39.

146. See above, beginning of chapter 2, section 5: when the letters *hei* and *vav* of the Tetragrammaton are both spelled with *aleph* (הא, ואו), the total value of the *millui* of the name is 45. When only the first three letter-names are counted, it comes to 39, the numerical value of *tal*.

147. See above, chapter 2, section 3 and the beginning of section 5.

148. If it is to produce offspring.

149. Versus our author's assertion that the kissing "spirit" is purely male. I do not know the source of the Lurianic quotation.

150. Zohar III, 4b; cf. the discussion in Tishby, *Wisdom*, 1:299–300.

151. The "Shapes" of Father and Mother, as the preceding context would suggest? Or, as seems more likely, all the entities of the Emanation world (the *sefirot* of the classical Kabbalah, the Shapes of the Lurianic)?

THE RESTORATION OF GOD

with *Peloni Almoni*[152]—but also via the Three Heads of Long-face, who manifests the Holy Distant One in the realm of Enclothement.[153] These receive the dew; *Tif'eret* with its Six Points in the realm of Emanation (called Little-face) receives it from [Long-face], and so does Little-face's *Malkhut*.[154] All receive it from them, the initial recipients who afterward spill it forth into the lower realms—now, however, in the form of rain, this being what the world requires for its continuing survival. The God of Israel spills it [as rain] into his Shechinah, and it is from her that all the worlds, all the Shapes, draw their nourishment and effluence.[155]

The God of Israel dwells within the *Tif'eret* of Emanation, the equivalent of Little-face, and his Shechinah within *Malkhut*, as I have earlier set forth.[156] This being so, he (i.e., the external *Tif'eret*) receives effluence in a measure greater than any of the worlds since he is nearest [to its source], for the higher this effluence ascends, the more it decreases and transforms itself into Judgment in its character as "reflected light."[157] Nevertheless, *Tif'eret* will at times receive rain-effluence[158] from the higher worlds and they from him, the aim being to ensure the survival of the lower worlds, out of concern lest the effluence be excessive and cause Shattering or that he himself will prove unworthy of it.[159] For that reason he directs the effluence upward, so that in rising

---

152. Of the book of Ruth; see above, chapter 4, section 9. By evading his duty to raise and redeem the fragments of the shattered *sefirot*, Creation-Human (= Cain, *Peloni Almoni*) has rendered himself irrelevant to the construction of the new sefirotic system.

153. Above, section 5.

154. The lowest *sefirah* of the traditional Kabbalah, the female sex partner of *Tif'eret*.

155. Again the paradox: the lowly Female is source of nourishment for the Shapes located above her in the sefirotic hierarchy.

156. This is the first occurrence in our text of the Sabbatian theologoumenon found, e.g., in the Dönmeh credo: the deity of their faith is "the God of Israel who dwells [*shokhen*] in *Tif'eret*." The corresponding verb for the Shechinah in the second part of the sentence is not the feminine form of *shokhen* but *shorah*, but I do not think a significant distinction is implied—*shoreh* is used for the God of Israel's "indwelling" later in the treatise, suggesting that the author employs the verbs interchangeably.

157. The behavior of the effluence is in accordance with Cordoveran theory, which predicts that reflected light will weaken as it ascends (above, chapter 2, note 107). But it yields the paradoxical result that the higher reaches of the world of Enclothement are less illuminated by it than the intermediate.

158. *Shefa' matar*, using the word *matar* for rain (and not *geshem*, as in the previous discussion), perhaps in anticipation of the subsequent quotation of Job 38:28.

159. And therefore suffer injury from the excess he receives.

it will take on the quality of Judgment,[160] and afterward he once more absorbs it and pours it forth. This is hinted at in the [Talmudic] saying *From your own do they give to you.*[161]

It was from this dew, in crystallized form, that the manna was made and brought down through the agency of the Distant One.[162] That is why the Bible says, *Your complaints are not upon us, but rather upon the Lord*, from which place your nourishment descends.[163] The word *'al*, "upon," is to be taken with absolute literalness:[164] [the nourishment] descends from a lofty place, superior to the entity designated *YHVH*, who is the God of Israel. [p. 91] Yet, in spite of this, it is the God of Israel who enacts it all. For he functions as the heart that brings forth the breath, and all is in [fol. 20b] his control, descending though it does from a place superior to him.

The guiding principle is that [1] just as *the Distant One Holiest of All the Holy Most Hidden of All the Hidden* is vis-a-vis Interiority, so in Enclothement is *the Three Heads of Long-face* (which in its totality can also be designated *the Holy Distant One*); [2] corresponding to Interiority's *God of Israel* is the *Tif'eret* of Emanation, who is called *Little-face*; and [3] corresponding to *the God of Israel's Shechinah* is *Little-face's Malkhut*.[165] Just as [in Interiority] there is a dividing curtain,[166] so in Enclothement a curtain separates the Distant One from Little-face. All the epithets, nearly all the specific details found in the Zohar contrasting the Distant One with Little-face in Enclothement, may be applied just as well in Interiority, to the God of Israel as contrasted with the Holy Distant One, Most Hidden of All the Hidden.

---

160. And, with Judgment's restraint, become less powerful and less potentially toxic.

161. Attributed to Ben Azzai in b. Yoma 38a–b.

162. Referring back to the dew described earlier in this section. The Bible story of the manna represents it as the residue of "a layer of dew round about the camp" (Exod 16:13–14), and the interpretation of the manna as the "dew" emanated by the Ancient/Distant One is drawn from the Zohar's *Idra Rabba* (III, 128a).

163. Exod 16:8, prior to the appearance of the manna. Three manuscripts add the gloss that Moses and Aaron, the "us" referred to in the Biblical verse, are symbolic of *Tif'eret*.

164. Attributing to "upon YHVH" (= "the Lord") the meaning "higher than YHVH."

165. Recapitulating what the author has said in section 5.

166. Between the Distant One and the God of Israel; above, section 1.

Hence the verse in Job, *The Yesh is father to the rain, while Mi has begotten the dewdrops.*[167] *Yesh*, as we know, stands for the God of Israel, as in *The Yesh, YHVH, is in our midst.*[168] He is consequently called "God of Israel," for he is the esoteric referent of the Torah, which is 231 gates, and also of *Yesh*; he is therefore *Yesh 231* = "Israel" (so I have heard).[169] He it is who produces the rain, while the Distant One, who is the esoteric referent of *Mi*—as is well known, and as I have earlier written[170]— is the one who produces the dew. Thus *the Yesh is father to the rain*, he being its father who brought it forth, while *Mi*, the Distant One who is called *Mi*, has begotten the dewdrops.

8. The Zoharic Evidence: III, 128a (*Idra Rabbah*)

[In this and the following section, the author offers a close though hardly dispassionate analysis of passages from the difficult Zoharic text called *Idra Rabbah* (III, 127b–45a). In these often cryptic pages, Rabbi Shimon ben Yohai and his inner circle of disciples discuss the qualities and interrelationships of the "Shapes" of Long-face, Little-face, and the Female; our author takes these as the "Enclothements" of the Distant One, the God of Israel, and the Shechinah. "You will be able to make sense of the holy *Idra*," he says at the beginning of section 9, "as treating in its entirety of Enclothement vis-à-vis Interiority." It thereby provides authoritative support for his account, set forth in this chapter so far, of the post-Shattering reconstruction.

Early in the discussion, the author takes up the first of the *Idra* passages (III, 128a) that invoke Gen 36:31, "These are the kings who reigned in the land of Edom, before a King reigned over the children of Israel." These "kings," the primordial

---

167. 38:28, more reasonably to be translated: "Does the rain have a father? Who has begotten the dewdrops?" The normal meaning of *yesh* is "there is." In the traditional Kabbalah, the word represents the *sefirah Binah*, or *Hokhmah*, or the two combined (Cordovero, *Sha'ar 'Erkhei ha-Kinnuyim*, s.v.).

168. Exod 17:7, usually translated "Is YHVH in our midst?"

169. The "231 gates" are the 231 possible two-letter combinations of the Hebrew alphabet, according to the second chapter of *Sefer Yetzirah*; our author chooses to identify them with the Torah. 231 is רל״א in the Hebrew numeral system; adding *yesh* to this number yields יש רל״א, an anagram for ישראל, "Israel." The author does not say from whom he "heard" this; one of his Sabbatian teachers, perhaps?

170. The allusion to "what I have earlier written" is strange. In chapter 1, section 5, *Mi* is said to represent the Root, which is the Will of Ein Sof, and this identification has been maintained more or less consistently throughout. In the traditional Kabbalah, *Mi* is the *sefirah Binah*.

sefirot destroyed in the Shattering, emerged from the thought processes of the Distant One, whom our author takes to be the principal actor at the beginning of the *Idra*'s story. Soon, however, the spotlight will shift to the God of Israel, the Distant One withdrawing into the role of passive recipient of the God of Israel's innovations ("mendings").

The "kings of Edom" recur on III, 135a; and here the author's exegetical talents are strained to the limits. The *Idra* depicts "Edom" as a blood-red sphere of stern, unmitigated Judgment (*adom* = "red" in Hebrew; see Gen 25:25, 30), whose unbending severity caused its collapse. This runs directly counter to the author's depiction of it, and the Christianity that it represents, as a realm of pure, unbounded Grace and Mercy. He must therefore twist the *Idra*'s language out of its plain meaning; or, where this is impossible, pass over it in silence.

But is pure Grace a good thing? The *Idra* draws on Exod 34:6 to suggest that there exist two YHVHs, both "perfect" but one more so than the other. But which is which? The less perfect, says our author, is the Distant One, who achieves perfection through his absolute Mercies—which, however, "make the act of construction impossible." It is not him but the God of Israel, with his all-important Balance, who at least for now is "perfect in all respects."]

Keep all this in mind, and you will have the key to understanding what the Zohar says in the *Idra*:[171]

> IT IS TAUGHT: IN THE TIME WHEN THE MOST DISTANT OF THE DISTANT ONES, MOST CONCEALED OF THE CONCEALED ONES, HAD NOT YET PREPARED THE KING'S MENDINGS AND THE CROWNWORK OF THE CROWNS, THERE WAS NEITHER BEGINNING NOR END, AND HE INSCRIBED [p. 92] AND CONCEIVED WITHIN HIMSELF.

The passage speaks of the Holy Distant One of Interiority, calling him by his proper title—replacing, however, *Most Hidden of the Hidden* by MOST CONCEALED OF THE CONCEALED, since he was at the time in

---

171. *Idra Rabbah*; Zohar, III, 128a. The text of the quotation differs slightly from our standard Zohar editions. I translate the passage, not as it would normally be understood in its Zoharic context, but as our author understood it; e.g., *'attiqa* rendered as "the Distant One" rather than "the Ancient One," *tiqqunim* as "mendings" or "modifications" (as above) rather than "adornments." Hellner-Eshed, *Seekers of the Face*, 174–84, quotes Matt's translation and provides an extended discussion.

a very high degree of concealment.[172] It speaks of a time prior to the establishment of THE KING'S MENDINGS [or MODIFICATIONS], by which it means the Enclothement, inasmuch as these were modifications required for the worlds' construction. Any Enclothement is considered female vis-à-vis its Interiority, since it is in the role of recipient from it, and we know that the female is called *crown*, as in *a worthy woman is her husband's crown*;[173] both MENDINGS and CROWNWORK OF THE CROWNS, consequently, refer to the Enclothement.

THERE WAS NEITHER BEGINNING NOR END—that is, everything was in its Folded-up state, having the quality of unformed matter. All had the aspect of "head," and consequently there was no beginning or end as there would be after the Self-extension, when beginning, middle, and end would be clearly delineated. The reason why the text specifies HE HAD NOT YET PREPARED, and does not say THEY WERE NOT YET IN EXISTENCE, is that while indeed the Self-extension had to precede the actual modification of the vessels, it was after the Shattering of the Vessels that [those future modifications] were "prepared" for the purpose of mending them.[174] It specifies that before he "prepared" them HE INSCRIBED AND CONCEIVED *WITHIN HIMSELF*, in order to convey that all this took place within the "head" aspect, the "conceiving" purely internal.

> HE SPREAD BEFORE HIMSELF A CURTAIN, AND ON IT HE INSCRIBED AND CONCEIVED KINGS AND MENDINGS. THIS IS WHAT IS WRITTEN, *THESE ARE THE KINGS WHO REIGNED IN THE LAND OF EDOM, BEFORE A KING REIGNED OVER THE CHILDREN OF ISRAEL*—A PRIMORDIAL KING FOR THE CHILDREN OF PRIMORDIAL ISRAEL. ALL THOSE THAT WERE INSCRIBED YET DID NOT ENDURE ARE CALLED BY THEIR NAMES, AND THEY DID NOT ENDURE UNTIL HE SET THEM ASIDE AND CONCEALED THEM.

The meaning is this: While in his Folded-up state, HE SPREAD BEFORE HIM A CURTAIN, namely the Shechinah, which partook of the nature of CURTAIN and placenta, as has been said.[175] [p. 93] Of his ideation

---

172. Explaining why Rabbi Shimon in the *Idra* chooses to call the Distant One *temira*, "concealed," rather than the more or less synonymous *setima* which would normally designate this entity (above, section 5), and supposing that *temira* indicates a higher degree of concealment.

173. Prov 12:4, regularly applied in Kabbalah to the female *sefirah Malkhut*.

174. And the *Idra* speaks of a time not only before the existence of the modifications, but even before their "preparation."

175. Above, chapter 3, section 1.

and INSCRIBING (i.e., his thought), the kings were born. These were they WHO REIGNED IN THE LAND OF EDOM, as has been said, BEFORE A KING REIGNED, this being the God of Israel, Primordial King for all THE CHILDREN OF PRIMORDIAL ISRAEL.[176] For he is represented as PRIMORDIAL ISRAEL, as has been said, and the vessels and worlds are his CHILDREN, under his direction and guidance.

All those that were "inscribed" and underwent Shattering were called by the names recorded in the Biblical passage concerning the kings of Edom; you may consult what Luria has said about the specific reason for each name. UNTIL HE SET THEM ASIDE AND CONCEALED THEM, meaning that he [the God of Israel] lifted [fol. 21a] the effluence and the spirit of Abel to a higher place, as we have earlier described.[177]

> AFTER A TIME HE LIFTED HIMSELF UP INTO THIS CURTAIN, AND BECAME MENDED THROUGH HIS MODIFICATIONS.

This means that the God of Israel, who is the Primordial King, lifted himself up INTO THIS CURTAIN—i.e., above it—from which he would descend *like a bridegroom emerging from his canopy,* as we have said.[178] HE BECAME MENDED THROUGH HIS MODIFICATIONS means that he established the garments, the Enclothement required for the world's repair. It further conveys that it was he, in his role as "heart," who caused to sprout upon the Distant One the Holy Beard that was [the God of Israel's own] modification.[179] Before the Self-extension, there was no beard. But afterward, in the process of Self-extension, he acquired his beard; and, as *one who has grown a beard,* he might *descend before the ark*—that is to say, downward before *Malkhut,* which we have seen to be symbolized by the ark. It is that act of descending, from a high place downward, that accounts for the specific use of the verb *descend.*[180]

176. Cf. above, chapter 4, section 5.

177. Above, section 5. Our author understands the subject of the *Idra*'s verbs to have shifted in the course of the paragraph, from the Distant One at its beginning to the God of Israel at its end.

178. Ps 19:6; above, sections 1–2.

179. Or, "adornment"; see above, note 17. Our author proposes two distinct but complementary meanings for the *Idra*'s *ittaqan.* The first treats the passive verb as though it were active, referring to the "mendings" (= modifications) instituted by the God of Israel to ensure the survival of the divine structures. The second lets it remain passive, and to refer to the "mending"—more conventionally understood as adornment—of the God of Israel himself: in the process of producing the Holy Beard of the Distant One, he acquires his own.

180. The "ark" spoken of here, in a very free quotation from the Talmud (b. Hul.

> It is taught: It arose within his will to create the Torah, and he brought it forth. Immediately it said to him: "Whoever wishes to perform mendings and to act, let him first mend himself." For two thousand years it was hidden.

In other words, when he conceived the wish to extract the fragments of the Vessels, which are symbolized by the Torah and its vowel signs, as we have said, they refused to come forth on account of the extended presence of the Mindless Light, until he should extend himself and undergo fundamental modification (as we have said).[181] The God of Israel and his Shechinah are represented as TWO THOUSAND YEARS, they being the greater and lesser alphabets, as we have said.[182]

> [p. 94] In the Concealed Book[183] it is taught: The Most Distant of distant ones, Secret of secrets, is mended and is present—which is to say, may be found and may not be found, not truly found and yet mended. No one knows him, because he is Most Distant of distant ones. Yet he is known through his mending as a certain Elder of elders, Distant of distant ones, Concealed of concealed ones.

24b), is the chest at the front of the synagogue that contains the Torah scroll, before which an individual from among the congregation stands to lead the congregants in prayer. Rabbinic sources occasionally speak of the prayer-leader as "descending" before the ark, a strange usage which our author explains as rooted in his theogony: the prayer-leader is a symbolic representation of the God of Israel, who does indeed "descend" to the *sefirah Malkhut*. (The rabbinic idiom continues to baffle modern scholars: Weiss, "Matai Hehelu") "We have seen" refers back to chapter 4, section 8, where Noah's Ark—the Hebrew word, *tevah*, is the same as for the synagogue ark—is equated with the divine female.

181. Referring back to the end of chapter 4, section 9: the Vessel fragments fear, reasonably, that they will again be shattered by the Mindless Light if no steps are taken to protect them. On their equation with the Torah and its vowel markings, see chapter 4, note 188.

182. Above, section 1, equating *elef*, "thousand," with *alfa beta*, "alphabet" (see note 14). The author leaves unclear how "hidden two thousand years," which occurs in an earlier position in the standard editions of the *Idra*, relates to the fragments' plaint.

183. *Tzeni'uta de-sifra*, literally "the concealment of the book." The reference is to the *Sifra di-Tzeni'uta*, a brief and cryptic text linked to the *Idra* literature, preserved in the Zohar, II, 176b–79a (Matt, trans., *Zohar*, 5:535–88). *Idra Rabbah* frequently quotes passages from this "Concealed Book," some of which—like this one—do not seem to occur in the extant versions of *Sifra di-Tzeni'uta*: Liebes, *Studies*, 95–98; Meroz, "Archaeology," 44–46.

This means that [the God of Israel] mended the Holy Distant One of Interiority by fashioning a corresponding entity in the sphere of Enclothement that is in the nature of his "mendings," namely the Three Heads of Long-face, which retained the character of "Distant One." Through this he MAY BE FOUND AND MAY NOT BE FOUND: it is altogether impossible to gain comprehension or recognition of him, inasmuch as he is THE MOST HIDDEN OF ALL THE HIDDEN, as we have seen in connection with the significance of "Edom."[184] Yet through the corresponding Enclothement he may be recognized in some small measure. A man, similarly, may be to an extent recognized through an engraved portrait of him, even though the recognition is not complete but only partial, through his likeness. So it is here. As MOST DISTANT OF DISTANT ONES, he is beyond all recognition. Yet through his "mendings," that is to say the Enclothement, he can be recognized to some small extent.[185]

When the text says MAY BE FOUND AND MAY NOT BE FOUND, YET MENDED, it means to convey that [the God of Israel] constructed, as a "mending," the Enclothement of which we have spoken. NO ONE KNOWS HIM at all, to have any real grasp of him. Yet he is known through his "mendings," i.e., the Enclothement, which is to say that we recognize him to some small degree through that to which he is likened, as though he were A CERTAIN ELDER OF ELDERS, and so forth. All this is in accord with our comprehension of the Enclothement; yet in his reality he is he is utterly unknowable other than through his likeness.

This is the inner meaning of the verse *Through the prophets do I form my likeness.*[186] When [the *Idra*] goes on to say that THROUGH HIS SIGNS HE IS KNOWN,[187] it refers to the mendings of beard and skull in Enclothement, by which he is known to that small extent that allows us to form a likeness of him, yet unknown in his proper essence. It then proceeds to enumerate those Enclothement-mendings of the Holy Distant One by which we may grasp some faint likeness of his reality.

---

184. Above, chapter 3, section 9.

185. It will be observed that the *Idra*'s claim of the higher divinity's unknowability makes more sense if our author's understanding of *'attiqa* as "Distant One" is adopted, as opposed to the conventional "Ancient One."

186. Hos 12:11.

187. Quoting a variant of our text, which has "through his mendings he is known."

9. The Key to the *Idra*: Enclothement Versus Interiority

You must give your closest attention to understanding this. Taking it as your starting point, you will be able to make sense of the holy *Idra* as treating in its entirety of Enclothement vis-à-vis Interiority, as Luria has said and as I have just told you. When the Zohar says that THROUGH HIS MENDINGS HE IS FINDABLE, knowable, this applies also to the *relation* of the Holy Distant One to Little-face, which corresponds to the relation in Interiority of the Distant One Most Holy of all the holy, Most Hidden of All the Hidden, to the God of Israel.

[p. 95] With this in mind, consider what [the *Idra*] writes on page 130:

> IT IS TAUGHT: NONETHELESS THE NAME OF THE DISTANT ONE IS HIDDEN FROM ALL, AND IS STATED IN THE TORAH IN ONLY ONE PLACE, IN LITTLE-FACE'S OATH TO ABRAHAM. IT IS WRITTEN, *WITHIN MYSELF I HAVE SWORN, IS THE UTTERANCE OF THE LORD*—THE UTTERANCE OF LITTLE-FACE.[188]

The meaning is as I have written above. The Holy Distant One is like a spirit within the God of Israel and can be spoken of as "inside him," even though they both constitute a single Shape, the "head's" thought going straight into the "heart."[189] The God of Israel is called "the Lord,"[190] and when he says, *within myself I have sworn*, he means that "I have sworn by what is inside me, by my Interiority, by my spirit"—this being the Distant One. Though the Zohar indeed speaks of Enclothement,[191] you can infer from it by analogy to Interiority. (The same thing, you will understand, is adumbrated by the verse in Habakkuk, *The Lord has sworn within his soul*.[192])

You can draw the same analogy on page 135:[193]

> IT IS TAUGHT IN THE CONCEALED [fol. 21b] BOOK: THE MOST DISTANT OF THE DISTANT ONES, IN THE TIME WHEN HE HAD NOT YET PREPARED HIS MENDINGS

---

188. Zohar, III, 130a, giving a hyperliteral reading of Gen 22:16 (more naturally to be understood as "by myself I have sworn").

189. As set forth at length in section 1, above.

190. The Tetragrammaton, YHVH.

191. And therefore identifies "the Lord" with Enclothement's Little-face.

192. There is no such verse in Habakkuk. Perhaps our author intends Jer 51:14 or Amos 6:8.

193. Of the *Idra*; Zohar, III, 135a. Cf. Hellner-Eshed, *Seekers of the Face*, 246–51.

—meaning, as we have said above, that the Shattering of the Vessels had not yet happened and the mendings and Enclothement were not yet ready, and using the word PREPARED precisely and deliberately[194]—

HE BUILT KINGS, GATHERED KINGS, RECKONED KINGS.

Luria has explained the specific use of these three verbs. BUILT refers to the realm of Emanation, which is the construction of the Merkavah; GATHERED refers to the World of the Bonded, which, as Luria has explained, were called "bonded" in that they were joined together with one another (as in the phrase "Isaac's binding");[195] while RECKONED KINGS alludes to Primordial Creation-Human, who, as I have written earlier, came into being only through ideation and thought and is therefore called *kesil*, "thought."[196]

THESE HAVING FAILED TO MAINTAIN THEMSELVES, HE PUSHED THEM AWAY, meaning that he shattered them,[197] AND HID THEM AWAY FOR A TIME. SO SCRIPTURE SAYS: *THESE ARE THE KINGS WHO REIGNED IN THE LAND OF EDOM*—IN THE PLACE WHERE ALL THE JUDGMENTS REMAIN. This means, as we have said, that that place partook of the nature of *karmel*, such that the Judgments REMAINED stable. They never became actualized, and they were mixed with Mercies.[198]

---

194. As discussed at the beginning of section 8.

195. In Lurianic Kabbalah, "the World of the Bonded" (*'olam ha-'aqudim*) refers to the initial stage in the differentiation of the lights emitted from the orifices of Primordial Human, to be followed by the "Point-world" (*'olam ha-nequdim*; see above, chapter 4, note 19) and eventually, after the Shattering, by the current sefirotic system. See Vital, *'Etz Hayyim*, I.vi.1, 74–75), where the *'aqudim /nequdim* terminology is rooted in the Hebrew text of Gen 31:10–12 and, as in our current passage, the familiar phrase *'aqedat yitzhaq*, "the binding of Isaac" (from Gen 22:9), is invoked to elucidate the use of *'aqudim*; Vital, *'Etz Hayyim*, I.vii.1, 91–94; Vital, *Sha'ar ha-Haqdamot*, 56–60; cf. Scholem, *Kabbalah*, 138. Our author proceeds in reverse chronological order, moving from the final "realm of Emanation," through the primordial "World of the Bonded," to the "Primordial Creation-Human" (= Luria's "Primordial Human"; above, chapter 3, section 6) from which the "bonded" entities have emerged. I do not know what Lurianic source he has for his distinction among the *Idra*'s three verbs.

196. Above, chapter 3, section 7.

197. Remarkably, our author here represents the Shattering as something performed deliberately by the Distant One, not a regrettable accident that befell his creations.

198. On *karmel* or *karmela*, see above, chapter 1, section 4; chapter 3, sections 6 and 9. By understanding the *Idra*'s "remain" as "remain stable," our author reverses what seems to be the natural meaning of the Zoharic text, that "the land of Edom" was a land dominated by Judgment and therefore doomed to Shattering. Rather, he says, "Edom" was the place where Judgment remained latent and inert.

THE RESTORATION OF GOD

NONE OF THEM COULD MAINTAIN THEMSELVES UNTIL THE WHITE HEAD, THE MOST DISTANT OF THE DISTANT, WAS MENDED—referring to that subsequent time when the God of Israel sprouted the Holy Beard, as implied by *one who has grown a beard may descend*, and so forth.[199] ONCE HE [the Distant One] HAD BEEN MENDED, HE [the God of Israel] WENT ON TO PERFORM ALL THE LOWER MENDINGS,[200] MENDING UPPER AND LOWER WORLDS ALIKE. FROM THIS WE LEARN THAT WHEN ANY LEADER OF A NATION, and so forth [HAS NOT FIRST BEEN MENDED, HIS NATION WILL NOT BE MENDED. IF HE IS MENDED, ALL ARE MENDED; IF HE IS NOT FIRST MENDED, THE NATION CANNOT BE MENDED. HOW DO WE LEARN THIS? FROM THE ONE REMOVED FAR FROM THE DAYS: UNTIL HE WAS MENDED WITH HIS MODIFICATIONS, NONE OF THOSE WHO REQUIRED MENDING COULD ACHIEVE IT, AND ALL THE WORLDS REMAINED DESOLATE]—which is self-explanatory.[201]

[p. 96] AND THERE REIGNED IN EDOM—THIS IS A MIGHTY SECRET, THE PLACE WHERE ALL JUDGMENTS ARE BOUND AND FROM WHICH THEY DEPEND. This is in accord with what we have earlier said: the SECRET is that of the Distant One, in whose realm ALL JUDGMENTS ARE BOUND, that is to say fastened to Mercies, mingled with them in the manner of *karmela*.

BELA, and so forth.[202] WHEN HE WENT UP TO SETTLE THERE—that is, for them [Bela and the other "kings"] to take on the nature of civilized settlement, dry land in the midst of the primordial waters that are the Insolent Waters—HE DID NOT ENDURE, NOR COULD HE HAVE ENDURED, meaning that they [the kings] had no capacity for survival. WHAT WAS THE REASON? the text goes on to inquire. BECAUSE THE HUMAN [= the God of Israel] WAS NOT MENDED, being then in his child-state, not having grown his beard. And of this the text says, WHAT WAS THE REASON?[203]

---

199. Above, notes 179 and 180.

200. Reading *taqqin kol tiqqunin diletatta*, with the standard Zohar texts, against the mss. *tiqqun kol tiqqunin diletatta*.

201. Supplying the elided text from the *Idra*, and translating the *Idra*'s *'attiq yomin*, not as "Ancient of Days"—its most natural understanding, following Dan 7:9—but the way our author has understood it (above, chapter 2, end of section 1). The Biblical quote, here and in the next paragraph, is from Gen 36:32.

202. The author skips over a chunk of the *Idra*'s text that interprets Bela, the first of the Edomite kings to be enumerated in Genesis, and the name of his city Dinhabah in a way characterizing "Edom" as a land of stern and savage Judgment—not exactly congenial to his line of interpretation.

203. This question is not repeated in the Zohar editions.

BECAUSE THE MENDING OF THE HUMAN IN HIS PROPER FORM CONTAINS ALL THINGS, meaning, as we have said, that the Human form is symbolic of the God of Israel, and upon him do all things depend.

AND BECAUSE THIS MENDING OF THE HUMAN WAS NOT PRESENT, i.e., he was not in a state of Self-extension, THEY WERE NOT ABLE TO ENDURE AND TO SETTLE, AND THEY CEASED TO EXIST [. . .] UNTIL THE ADVENT OF THE HUMAN'S MENDING, namely the Self-extension of the God of Israel, as we have said. BUT WITH THE ADVENT OF THIS FORM, ALL WERE INSCRIBED AND RESTORED TO A NEW EXISTENCE. This speaks of what we have described above: the God of Israel having extended himself, he gathered them[204] once more, and it was he who incorporated them within the female juices. SOME WERE SWEETENED, WHILE OTHERS WERE NOT SWEETENED AT ALL.

BUT PERHAPS YOU WILL OBJECT THAT IT IS WRITTEN, *AND HE DIED*, and so forth, IMPLYING THAT HE CEASED ENTIRELY TO EXIST?—the problem being that the *sefirah Yesod* survived [the Shattering], whereas we observe that the Bible says of him, *and he died*.[205] NOT SO! RATHER, WHENEVER SOMEONE SUFFERS A DEMOTION FROM HIS ORIGINAL RANK, WE SAY OF HIM THAT HE "DIED," and this is as we have said [of *Yesod*], that he entered within the Female and is thus said to have "died." (Consult what I shall write presently about King Hadar, who is said in the book of Chronicles to have died.[206] Like the others, he was demoted in rank.)

WHEN THE HUMAN WAS MENDED, referring to the modifications of the Human and the Self-extension of the God of Israel, THEY WERE CALLED BY OTHER NAMES, APART FROM THE ONE OF WHOM IT

204. The fragments of the shattered vessels.

205. Our author tampers with the *Idra* text to make it say what he needs it to say. In the Zohar editions, the Biblical *va-yamot* ("and he died") is repeated twice, and the verb "ceased to exist" is in the plural. The speaker is plainly troubled by the implication that *all* the sefirotic "kings"—not just one of their number—ceased entirely to exist. Our author suppresses the second *va-yamot*, marking its omission with the nondescript "and so forth." (So mss. Jerusalem 2491 and HUC 85; Jerusalem 3100 leaves out "and so forth," while mss. Oxford 955 and 976 "correct" in accordance with the Zohar editions while retaining the now meaningless "and so forth.") He also arbitrarily changes the plural verb to singular (mss. Oxford 976 and HUC 85; the other mss. "correct" his change). On the survival of "king" *Yesod* (= the Bible's "Shaul of Rehoboth by the River"), see above, chapter 4, sections 1, 8.

206. Gen 36:39 says nothing about Hadar's death, while the parallel in 1 Chr 1:51, calling him "Hadad," asserts that he did die. The apparent contradiction has been observed by our author (chapter 4, sections 1, 8), and will be elucidated in chapter 8, end of section 13. (The mss. here fluctuate between "Hadar" and "Hadad," the two names being graphically almost identical in Hebrew.)

IS WRITTEN, *THE NAME OF HIS WIFE WAS MEHETABEL*.²⁰⁷ FOR WHAT REASON? BECAUSE [p. 97] THESE DID NOT CEASE TO EXIST LIKE ALL THE OTHERS. AND WHAT WAS THE REASON FOR THAT?²⁰⁸ BECAUSE THEY WERE MALE AND FEMALE, LIKE THE DATE-TREE THAT IS ANDROGYNOUS BY NATURE. FOR THAT REASON, SINCE BOTH MALE AND FEMALE WERE PRESENT, THE BIBLE DOES NOT SAY THAT HE²⁰⁹ DIED. This is what we have described earlier, that female and male dwelt as one within the vessel of *Yesod*, and this is what enabled *Yesod* itself to find refuge within that Female that is symbolized by Noah's Ark.²¹⁰

BUT SHE WAS NOT SETTLED UNTIL THE HUMAN FORM WAS MENDED. This means that he was shut within the Ark and they could not busy themselves with the settlement of the world, as symbolized by Noah's having abstained from sex as long as he was in the Ark.²¹¹ But once the HUMAN FORM that was symbolic of the God of Israel was mended, then they were once again mended and Noah told to *go forth from the Ark*.²¹² This is the meaning of WHEN THE HUMAN FORM WAS MENDED, THEY WERE ONCE MORE ESTABLISHED IN A NEW EXISTENCE, AND PROPERLY SETTLED.

Consider this carefully, and you will surely understand what is said in the *Idra Rabbah* and *Zuta*,²¹³ that all that pertains to the Distant One has the character of holy dew. This is readily comprehensible on the basis of what we have earlier said, that the "dew" flows down upon the Distant One [of Emanation] and from there to the *sefirah Tif'eret* of Emanation.²¹⁴

207. Gen 36:39, 1 Chr 1:50, referring to King Hadar/Hadad, the only one of the Edomite kings said to have had a wife—and who, according to our author, was himself female (above, chapter 4, section 8, which should be consulted for the understanding of what follows).

208. Not in our Zohar editions.

209. I.e., Hadar. In the Zohar editions, "they."

210. Noah himself being symbolic of *Yesod*; above, chapter 4, section 8.

211. See above, chapter 4, note 139. Once again our author revises the *Idra*'s text, changing the plural "they were not settled" to feminine singular—ms. Jerusalem 2491 "corrects" back to plural—presumably with reference to the Female in which *Yesod* took refuge (though it is possible he intends the other Female, *Malkhut*). In the next sentence, "he" refers to *Yesod*, "they" to *Yesod* and the Female together; by "the settlement of the world," the author intends the restoration of the sefirotic system after the Flood = Shattering, with the modifications that are his current subject.

212. Gen 8:16.

213. Alluding to Zohar, III, 128b, 135b (*Idra Rabbah*), III, 288a, 292b (*Idra Zuta*).

214. Above, section 7, which speaks of the transmitter of the dew to *Tif'eret* as "the Three Heads of Long-face, who manifests the Holy Distant One in the realm of Enclothement." I remain uncertain just how the author links the detailed textual analysis that precedes with his earlier discussion of the dew.

In light of this, you will understand what [the *Idra Rabbah*] says on page 138:

> HERE TOO, THE BIBLICAL PUNCTUATION SEPARATES THE TWO OCCURRENCES OF THE NAME YHVH FROM ONE ANOTHER. THE FIRST [YHVH] IS PERFECT, THE SECOND PERFECT IN ALL RESPECTS.[215]

The Distant One, in other words, partakes of the quality of perfection through his absolute Mercies, [fol. 22a] yet is not PERFECT IN ALL RESPECTS since [precisely this feature] makes the act of construction impossible. Quite the contrary: it was wholly responsible for the Shattering! But the God of Israel is PERFECT IN ALL RESPECTS, in that he partakes of the quality of Balance, giving to each in its proper measure, be this augmentation or diminishment.

Just so, from all that has been said you will understand the *Idra Zuta*'s exposition (page 288) of *I am my beloved's and for me is his longing*.[216] You will observe how it says there that THE HOLY DISTANT ONE, MOST HIDDEN OF ALL THE HIDDEN, MADE A SPREADING-OUT[217] AND BECAME SEPARATED FROM ALL, meaning that he spread out the Curtain and thereby separated himself from everything, yet in reality HE MADE NO SEPARATION, FOR ALL CLEAVE TO HIM AND HE CLEAVES TO ALL, constituting a single Shape, as we have said.[218] [p. 98] When the text goes on to say that HE EMITTED NINE LIGHTS, this refers to the nine *sefirot* of the God of Israel, the Female being a Shape unto herself. Yet WHEN ONE DRAWS NEAR TO EXAMINE THEM [. . .] ALL IS ONE,[219] for all is indeed

---

215. Zohar, III, 138a, referring to Exod 34:6. The *Idra* takes the traditional Masoretic punctuation of the Biblical verse to suggest that *va-yiqra YHVH YHVH* should be understood, "YHVH called out: 'YHVH . . .' "; i.e., an inferior YHVH calling out to a superior YHVH. (Other Biblical examples of twice-repeated names have just been invoked to support this blasphemous-sounding interpretation; hence "Here too . . .".) Traditional Lurianic exegesis understands the superior YHVH to be Long-face, the inferior to be Little-face, and the former's superiority to lie in his perfect Mercy. Our author reverses this evaluation. The "inferior" YHVH is the perfectly Mercy-ful "Distant One," while the "superior" is the seasoned and balanced "God of Israel"; and perfect Mercy is a disadvantage for a deity rather than an advantage.

216. Zohar III, 288a, quoting Song 7:11.

217. Reading the first פריש in this passage as *pares* (with a *sin*), "he spread," and the second as *paresh* (with a *shin*), "he (did not) separate."

218. The Distant One, despite the "separation" imposed by the Curtain, remains part of the same Shape (*partzuf*) as the God of Israel.

219. Omitting a considerable portion of the *Idra*'s text.

THE RESTORATION OF GOD

one, without any separation among them, all sharing in the quality of the Shape of the Path of Emanation.

Understand this passage in the light of all that has been said, and no further commentary will be required. You will be able to comprehend the whole of the *Idra* along these lines, distinguishing those places where it speaks of Enclothement from those where it speaks of Interiority.

This is how you are to understand, on page 289, *Derekh Emet*'s textual emendation:[220]

> FOR THIS REASON THE HOLY NAME, THEY ARE HIDDEN AND REVEALED.[221] THE ONE THAT IS HIDDEN CORRESPONDS TO THE HOLY DISTANT ONE, THE MOST HIDDEN OF ALL; WHILE THE ONE THAT IS REVEALED IS ON ACCOUNT OF THAT REVEALED ONE SUSPENDED IN LITTLE-FACE.

The passage must speak of Interiority, for when it links the hidden name to the Distant One, it specifies him as THE MOST HIDDEN OF ALL, thereby hinting at Interiority, just as if it had said MOST HIDDEN OF ALL THE HIDDEN.[222] The name THAT IS REVEALED corresponds to the God of Israel, who is a REVEALED ONE; and when the text specifies that he is SUSPENDED IN LITTLE-FACE, this means that he dwells there. It does not say ON ACCOUNT OF LITTLE-FACE,[223] but ON ACCOUNT OF THE ONE SUSPENDED IN LITTLE-FACE, i.e., placed within Little-face. (As we say of the fourth day of Creation that *the luminaries were suspended*,[224] this being the language of placement.)

Page 289b speaks of [the Distant One] similarly: THIS HOLY DISTANT ONE, MOST HIDDEN OF ALL THE HIDDEN, GOES UNMENTIONED AND UNDISCOVERED—having the character of Interiority, that is—AND BECAUSE HE IS THE HEAD, LOFTIEST OF ALL THE LOFTY, HE IS MENTIONED

---

220. Zohar, III, 289a (*Idra Zuta*). *Derekh Emet* is a collection of textual notes on the Zohar, attributed to the seventeenth-century Kabbalist Joseph Hamis and published in Venice in 1658. The "emendation" here is *Derekh Emet*'s advocacy of the complex and difficult reading "the one that is revealed is on account of that Revealed One suspended," which we will see to be essential to the author's argument.

221. Literally translating the awkward sentence, which speaks of the "name" first as singular, then (in accord with the next sentence) as plural. The standard editions of the Zohar give the simpler reading "the holy name is hidden and revealed," and ms. Jerusalem 2491 "corrects" accordingly.

222. A distinguishing marker for the Distant One of Interiority, as we have seen.

223. Which would point to Enclothement, Little-face being one aspect of the Enclothement.

224. Paraphrasing the Talmud, b. Hag. 12a.

ONLY AS A SINGLE BODILESS HEAD, SUSTAINING ALL THINGS. This is in accord with what we have said, that his nature is that of Head. HE IS CONCEALED, HIDDEN, SECRETED AWAY FROM ALL, meaning that he is entirely beyond comprehension. Yet HIS MODIFICATIONS,[225] meaning his Enclothement (as we have said), HAVE BEEN CONSTRUCTED THROUGH THAT HIDDEN BRAIN OF THE ENTIRETY, WHICH EXTENDED ITSELF, and so forth. This accords with what we have earlier said, that it was through the influence of Abel, symbolizing the Hidden Brain, that his Enclothement was constructed. [The *Idra*] proceeds with an exposition of this subject, of which you will now understand a wealth of details that space does not allow to be put in writing.[226]

Along these lines, you will also be able to understand what is said in the first chapter of *The Book of Concealment*.[227]

[p. 99] THE PRIMORDIAL KINGS DIED, and so forth,[228] UNTIL THE HEAD, THE DESIRED OF ALL THE DESIRED—this is the Distant One, whose nature is Head; while the God of Israel partakes of "desire" in that all yearn for him while his own yearning is for the Distant One, who is therefore called DESIRED OF ALL THE DESIRED—CONSTRUCTED SPLENDID GARMENTS, namely the Enclothement, AND BEQUEATHED THEM, which is to say that he bequeathed his dominion to the God of Israel, who is in the role of his Son, as hinted at in the verse *Israel is my son, my firstborn*.[229] It is true that [the God of Israel] constitutes a single Shape [with the Distant One]. Yet we know that the *sefirot Keter, Hokhmah*, and *Binah*[230] play the roles of Father and Mother, with *Tif'eret* as their Son—and I have already explained the reason for his

---

225. Or "mendings."

226. And, perhaps, that are too esoteric to be written.

227. *Sifra di-Tzeni'uta*, a brief and very cryptic Kabbalistic text found in Zohar, II, 176b–79a. I translate the Zoharic text as the author understood it.

228. The author omits a few words that he does not think germane to his purpose: "and their adornments could not be found, and the earth ceased to be."

229. Exod 4:22. There is some inconsistency in the author's presentation: the God of Israel, earlier portrayed as the active agent in the construction of the Enclothement, here shifts to being its passive recipient. His "sonship," first mentioned here (apart from the parenthetical etymology in chapter 2, note 79), plays no further role in the author's thought.

230. The three highest *sefirot*, very roughly corresponding to the Distant One.

being called "Son"²³¹—to whom the Distant One bequeathed the kingship, for the settlement of the worlds.²³²

This is why the text goes on to say: THAT BALANCE WAS SUSPENDED IN A PLACE WHERE IT WAS NOT. Prior to this, the Balance had been suspended within the sphere of the Distant One, that of the "land of Edom," and from there did [the worlds] receive their effluence. But now it is from him that the effluence is received, and in him, the God of Israel, does the Balance of all worlds hang—SUSPENDED, therefore, IN A PLACE WHERE IT WAS NOT.

We now have the key to understanding the words of Midrash and Zohar: *The cedars that the Blessed Holy One had planted, he uprooted and replanted in a different place.*²³³ This refers to what we have earlier said, that before the Shattering they drew their sustenance [fol. 22b] from the Distant One. Now, however, it comes from the God of Israel through his *Malkhut*, which mixes it together as male and female juices.²³⁴

10. "Unto Us a Child Is Born"

[One more bit of evidence for the author's reconstruction of the Self-folding and subsequent rebirth of the God of Israel: assuming this scenario, an apparent contradiction in the Zohar's treatment of the Biblical figure of Issachar will resolve itself. Perhaps significantly, perhaps not, the author applies to the reborn Deity—who at the end of section 9 has been declared the "Son" of the Distant One and inheritor of his dominion—Isaiah's prophecy of "a child born to us," famously understood by Christians as speaking of Jesus Christ.]

This is the hidden meaning of the Biblical verse *Issachar is a* hamor garem, *crouching between the tongues. He saw that tranquility was good, and that the land was pleasant. So he stretched out his shoulder to bear, and became grantor of allotments.*²³⁵

---

231. Above, chapter 2, note 79.

232. Some mss. read here, "to direct the worlds."

233. A very loose paraphrase of *Midrash Genesis Rabbah* 15:1. I am not sure what Zohar passage our author has in mind; possibly I, 187b?

234. Something that the Distant One, lacking a female, cannot do.

235. Gen 49:14-15. *Hamor garem* is normally translated "large-boned ass"; the author will soon give his own interpretation of these words. The word *mishpetayim*, between which Issachar is said to "crouch" and which occurs only here in the Bible, is usually conjectured to mean "sheepfolds." The author derives it from the similar root *safah*,

Now, the Zohar suggests at one point that this alludes to the Distant One, for it says (in the section on the Torah portion *Va-yetze*), that Issachar IS LINKED TO THAT PLACE CALLED HU.[236] Subsequently, however, it says: *I HAVE SURELY HIRED YOU*[237]—IN YOUR BODY, TO BEGET A FORM,[238] implying that [Issachar] stands for the God of Israel.

But the fact of Issachar is this: he does indeed represent the God of Israel. In the Folded-up state, however, all had the character of "head,"[239] the *seal* [= God of Israel] transformed, as we have seen, into a *homer*, a "gathering," an assemblage of all its parts together.[240] So when the Bible says, *Issachar is a hamor*, it means that he was in a Folded-up state; and when it adds *garem*, it means that he was at the highest level, *gerem ha-ma'alot*.[241] He was *crouching between the tongues*, for I have already written that the heart [= God of Israel] [p. 100] made his dwelling place from the tongue and upward and was thus *the tongue of truth*—"truth" being a

---

"tongue," as he will go on to explain. The passage's final words, *va-yehi le-mas 'oved*, are normally translated "he subjected himself to servitude." Our author takes *mas* to be the object of the verb *'oved*—literally, "he became the doer of the *mas*"—and, for reasons he does not explain, understands *mas* not in its normal meaning of service imposed upon others (tax or tribute, in post-Biblical Hebrew) but as an allotment granted to them.

236. Very free quotation of Zohar, I, 156b, commenting on Gen 30:16, where "he lay with her that night" (describing how Issachar was conceived) might hyperliterally be translated "he lay with her in the night *Hu*." The Zohar identifies *Hu* (the pronoun "he") with "the Supernal World . . . that is hidden and not revealed"—standard Zoharic code for the *sefirah Binah*. For our author, this "hidden, unrevealed" world suggests the Distant One, and implies that the Biblical figure of Issachar functions as a symbolic representation of this deity.

237. Leah's words to Jacob in Gen 30:16, referring to the sex act that would produce Issachar.

238. Zohar, I, 157b–58a, drastically abbreviated and with *deyoqna* ("an image" or "form") in place of the Zohar's *deyoqnakh*, "your image." (Ms. Jerusalem 2491 "corrects" in accordance with the Zohar editions.) In interpreting *deyoqna*, the author alludes back to his earlier exegesis of *Idra Rabbah* (III, 135b), where *deyoqna de-adam*, "Human form," is said to be "symbolic of the God of Israel."

239. That is to say, the Distant One.

240. Above, chapter 3, section 1, where the "seal" of Job 38:14 is identified with the God of Israel and *homer* is explained as "gathering." The author now extends this interpretation to *hamor* in Gen 49:14, which derives from the same root. It does not mean "ass," as it is universally (and certainly correctly) translated, but rather refers to the Folded-up state in the womb, where the "head" and the "heart," the Distant One and the God of Israel, cannot be distinguished from one another.

241. Our author, no doubt influenced by Zohar, I, 242b, understands this obscure Biblical phrase (2 Kgs 9:13) to mean something like "the pinnacle of ranks."

designation for the *sefirah Tif'eret*—dwelling in the superior position.²⁴² Hence: *crouching between the tongues.*

Now, however, in order to bring forth the Torah—symbolizing the Point-world—[the God of Israel] has emerged from his Folded state. Thus Scripture says, *He saw that tranquility was good* (understood by the Zohar as referring to the Written Torah) *and that the land* (i.e., the Oral Torah) *was pleasant.*²⁴³ *So he stretched out his shoulder to bear,* i.e., extended himself from the Folded-up state. Previously his nature had been that of *a child about to be born to us, the rulership upon his shoulder,*²⁴⁴ for in the Folded state, the *sefirah Tif'eret* (symbolized by *rulership*) had been higher than his shoulder.²⁴⁵ But now he has emerged from that state and *become grantor of allotments,* abundantly giving measured allotments to all. For it is in him that the Balance now hangs.

---

242. The author's cross-reference is not exact. In section 1, he has made the point that in the Deity's Folded-up, fetal state, the "heart" was located where the "head" would be; thus, as he now says, "from the tongue and upward ... in the superior position." Previously, however, he has not specifically mentioned the tongue. Now he links the God of Israel to the tongue via the Biblical phrase *sefat emet* ("tongue of truth," Prov 12:19) and the Kabbalistic commonplace that *emet,* "truth," is a designation for the *sefirah Tif'eret,* the external manifestation of the God of Israel. By this extraordinarily convoluted path, he establishes the God of Israel as "crouching between the tongues," and the whole of the Genesis passage as an account of the Self-folding.

243. So expounded in Zohar, I, 242b. The notion of a special link between Issachar—the person, the tribe—and the Torah is rooted in rabbinic tradition, given a central role in the Zohar: Ginzberg, *Legends,* 5:368; Zohar, I, 156b–58a, 242a–43a.

244. Isa 9:5, normally understood by Christians as referring to Jesus Christ.

245. *Tif'eret* is the trunk of the divine body; yet, while God was in the womb, it was higher than his shoulder.

6

The Symbolisms of God

1. Prelude: The Emergence of God

[The author embarks upon an ambitious reconceptualization of Biblical narrative as symbolic of the activities of the God of Israel and his Shechinah, as he emerges from his Self-folding to repair the devastation of the Shattering and guide his reconstructed worlds. Hidden meanings buried within the stories of Cain (section 2), the youthful Moses (sections 3–5), and the Garden of Eden (sections 6–7), fill in the details of this process, which was sketched in general terms in the preceding chapter.

In this first section, which serves as prelude, the author analyzes the Song of Deborah (Judg 5) as describing the beginning of the God of Israel's distinct existence, through the Shattering—and makes the extraordinary claim, which he will presently take up, that the Biblical Pharaoh is a symbolic representation of the God of Israel.]

This leads us into the hidden meaning of the passage from the Song of Deborah in which *I sing, I hymn the God of Israel*.[1]

YHVH, in your going forth from Seir. This speaks of the beginning of the God of Israel's distinct existence from the Root, which is called *Seir*, as we have said—when it says *in your going forth*, it means that he was born.[2] *In your stepping forth from the field of Edom* refers to the

---

1. Judg 5:3–5. The author of course understands "God of Israel" in the technical Kabbalistic sense he has assigned to it, and the Biblical passage as an exposition of that deity's history and essence.

2. In addition to the obvious symbolism of birth as "going forth," the author perhaps

time when he folded himself up and departed from the *Tehiru*, which is called *field of Edom* as we have said,³ leaving it empty. Then *the earth quaked*, for *Malkhut*⁴ was nearly shattered, gashes made within it. (So the Bible says: *You have made the earth to quake, cracked it open*, and so forth.⁵) *The heaven also dripped*, as is well known and as we have said, that the Shattering of the Vessels took place when great holes were made in *Tif'eret*⁶ and the waters of effluence flowed out, as hinted in *the windows of heaven were opened*.⁷

The clouds too dripped water: these are the "Midianites" that are the Judgments, for it is known that "clouds" symbolize Judgments.⁸ As a result of this, *the mountains were liquefied*—shattered, melted—*before YHVH*, meaning, "prior to YHVH," who was then in his Folded-up state (as in, *before there reigned a king*).⁹ As for *this Sinai*, the *sefirah Tif'eret* is called by the name "Sinai"—

(The *sefirah Tif'eret*, when the God of Israel dwells within it, is called *qol*, "voice" [spelled out in full], for we know the God of Israel to be represented by the letter *vav*.¹⁰ When he is not settled within it, however, it is called *qol* without the *vav*, for the *vav* which is the God of Israel is absent. [p. 101] This is the esoteric meaning of the verse *And the voice*—*qol* without the *vav*—*was heard, namely the house of Pharaoh*,¹¹ this being the

---

intends a play on *tzet*, "going forth," and *metzi'at*, "existence." For the equation of the Biblical "Seir" with the Root, see above, chapter 3, section 9.

3. More exactly, that it is called "field"; above, chapter 4, section 4.
4. Regularly called "earth" in Kabbalistic symbolism.
5. Ps 60:4. The verse goes on to implore God to "heal its shatterings"—which, in our author's view, guarantees its relevance to the primordial Shattering.
6. "Heaven," in Kabbalistic symbolism.
7. Gen 7:11, referring to the Flood.
8. The author refers back—gratuitously, it would seem—to his interpretation of the "Midianites" of Num 22 and 31 as the *sefirot* of Judgment that were victims of the Shattering; above, chapter 4, sections 6–7. I do not know the basis of the author's claim that "clouds" ('avim) represent Judgments. Cordovero (*Sha'ar 'Erkhei ha-Kinnuyim*) gives the opposite symbolism for *'av*: it stands for *Hesed*, the *sefirah* of Grace.
9. Gen 36:31, the locus classicus for the Kabbalistic myth of the Edomite kings; see above, chapter 4, section 5; and chapter 5, section 8.
10. The Bible normally spells *qol*, the Hebrew word for "voice" or "sound," *qof-vav-lamed* (קול). At times, however, it appears defectively as *qof-lamed* (קל), and the author offers a Kabbalistic explanation for the inconsistency. The letter *vav* = *Tif'eret* is a standard Kabbalistic equation; our author extends it to the deity dwelling within *Tif'eret*.
11. Gen 45:16. The word "in," supplied by translators before "the house of Pharaoh," is missing from the Hebrew, and our author chooses to take "voice" and "house of Pharaoh" as being in apposition.

external *Tif'eret*. For "Pharaoh" is a symbolic representation of the God of Israel,¹² his name derived from *parua'*, "exposed," inasmuch as HE IS IN A PLACE THAT IS REVEALED, AND ALL THE LIGHTS ARE EXPOSED FROM THERE, as the Zohar says on the Torah portion *Va-yiggash*;¹³ and the external *Tif'eret* is *the house of Pharaoh* inasmuch as the God of Israel dwells in it. This is why the verse says, *And the voice*, the [defectively spelled] *qol*, which is "Sinai," both having the numerical value of 130.)

—so when [the Song of Deborah] says that *this Sinai* [was "liquefied"], it means that even *Tif'eret* was shattered at the last, as hinted at by *at the last, you shall be gathered to your people*.¹⁴ *Before YHVH the God of Israel*, meaning "prior to him," for he had not yet extended himself.

2. "Primordial Human" Restored

> [Among the first to be restored in the post-Shattering world is the being called "Creation-Human" (the "Primordial Human" of the Lurianic system), represented in the Bible by the figure of Cain. This "Cain," though diminished and allowed no part in the reconstruction of the sefirotic worlds that he was in part responsible for destroying, is nevertheless granted a secure continuation of existence—attached, not to the Distant One as before, but to the God of Israel and the Higher Shechinah. We are not, however, done with him. He will later reappear, in the Garden of Eden, in the form of the serpent.]

This is the inner sense of what God said to Primordial Human, symbolized by Cain: *Therefore "All" kills Cain*—followed by its remedy, *"Sevenfold" shall he be raised*.¹⁵ In other words, if he should receive effluence solely from

---

12. An extraordinary equation, rooted in the teachings of Nathan of Gaza (Scholem, *Sabbatai Ṣevi*, 225, 296), to be developed in section 3, below.

13. A very loose quotation of Zohar, I, 210a, which interprets "the house of Pharaoh" in Gen 45:16 as "the house from which all lights and sparks have been exposed [דאתפרעו, from the same root as "Pharaoh"] and revealed." (Matt, trans., *Zohar*, slightly modified; Matt explains that the Zohar understands "the house of Pharaoh" to be the *sefirah Binah*, and the defectively spelled "voice" to be the Shechinah which receives the light radiated from *Binah*.) The Zohar restricts this exegesis of פרעה, "Pharaoh," to this one Biblical occurrence of the word. The next step, of making the Biblical figure of Pharaoh a symbolic representation of the Deity, was left for the Sabbatians.

14. Spoken to Moses (symbolizing *Tif'eret*), in Num 31:2; see above, chapter 4, section 7. Moses is told to slaughter the "Midianites"—an allegory of the Shattering of the Vessels—after which he himself will "be gathered to your people." In other words, *Tif'eret*, the agent of the Shattering, is at last itself to be shattered.

15. On the author's understanding of Cain as symbolic for Primordial

"All," which is to say the *sefirah Yesod*, he will in that case have no female juices[16] and will similarly[17] be shattered. This is what the Bible means by *"All" kills Cain*. And the remedy? *"Sevenfold" shall he be raised*, meaning that the Shechinah, called "Sevenfold,"[18] shall raise him and grant him the effluence he requires, male and female juices mixed together.

And so it was. *He departed from Before-YHVH*, meaning that originally he had gotten his effluence from the Distant One, who is Before-YHVH. But now he has departed from that place, and *dwelt in the land of Nod*, meaning the God of Israel's Shechinah, who is called Nod [fol. 23a] (as implied in the phrase "a wineskin [*nod*] full of living water"[19]), and who is *prior to Eden*,[20] as will be noted below.[21]

It is the inner meaning of that which is said of Balaam—symbolic of the *sefirah Da'at* of the shattered vessels, as we have explained at some length[22]—that *he saw the Cainite*—symbolic of Primordial Human—*and he said, Stable is your dwelling*.[23] He prophesied of the Shattering of the Vessels; yet, [he told Primordial Human,] to you no Shattering will befall, for *stable is your dwelling*: you are in a lofty place, *your nest placed in the Rock* that is the Shechinah, and she will grant you effluence.

Yet Cain shall be consumed, the text goes on to say, meaning that [Primordial Human] will experience a certain demotion in that he will no longer receive effluence from the Distant One as he once did, and

---

Creation-Human (the "Primordial Human" of the Lurianic Kabbalah), see above, chapter 4, especially sections 2 and 4. The Biblical passage, Gen 4:15, is usually understood as "anyone who kills Cain shall receive sevenfold vengeance." The author reads it hyperliterally, seeing "All" (*kol*) as a designation for the *sefirah Yesod*, the divine phallus—this is standard Kabbalistic symbolism—and treating *yuqam*, "he shall be avenged," as though it were from the root *qum*, "arise." This discussion is linked to the preceding through its interpretation, also hyperliteral, of "before YHVH" in Gen 4:16 as "prior to YHVH."

16. Since *Yesod* is quintessentially male.
17. Like Abel before him (above, chapter 4, section 4)? Or, like the *sefirot*?
18. I do not know the basis for this identification.
19. I do not know the author's source. The midrash *Seder Eliyahu Rabbah* 14:2 compares human striving to "a wineskin filled with water," and possibly this is the allusion. But the midrash does not speak of "living water."
20. Normally translated, "to the east of Eden."
21. In section 6.
22. Above, chapter 4, sections 6-7.
23. Num 24:21. The "Kenites" (= "Cainites") appear in the Bible as an ethnic group friendly to the Israelites (e.g., 1 Sam 15:6), their name only coincidentally linked to that of Abel's brother. For our author, of course, nothing in Scripture is fortuitous.

this is a sort of death, when one descends in rank.[24] *Unto Mem-hei*, meaning that this [relationship with the Distant One] shall not continue. Rather, [he shall go] unto the God of Israel, represented by *Mem-hei*, Forty-five,[25] and *Asher*, namely the Shechinah—represented as the World to Come, which is known to be called *Asher*—she it is that *will settle you*.[26] That is to say, she will settle you, establish you, as we have seen: "Sevenfold" shall he be raised. [p. 102] And *Asher* is spelled with *vav*, in order to convey that it is through the coupling of male and female that he receives his effluence; hence the *vav*, symbolic of the God of Israel, is inserted into the word. Understand this.

3. The Rescuing of the Male

> [But if "Cain" bears some of the responsibility for the Shattering, so does the God of Israel for deliberately allowing it to happen. Somewhat unfairly, one cannot help feeling—was he not a fetus within the Shechinah-womb at the time of the Shattering?—the God of Israel is represented as acting as the cruel Pharaoh in the story of Moses, dooming the male *sefirot* to destruction in the Insolent Waters while sparing the females. Consequently, "Miriam" (the Eighth King from chapter 4) is safe from the waters, the *sefirah Yesod* ("Aaron") protected within her, while *Tif'eret*/"Moses" is cast into them. He is rescued by the Higher Shechinah, "Pharaoh's daughter," who takes him into her womb

---

24. Following Zohar III, 135b (*Idra Rabba*).

25. Num 24:22, *'ad mah* (עד מה), literally, "unto what," normally translated as "how long?" But מה can be read, not as the word "what," but as *mem-hei*, the numeral 45: the Tetragrammaton's value of Forty-five, which, in Lurianic Kabbalah, is equated with Little-face, *Tif'eret*, within which the God of Israel has his dwelling.

26. The exegetical gymnastics performed with the last two words of Num 24:22— *ashur tishbeka* (אשור תשבך), normally translated "Assyria shall take you into exile"—are remarkable even for our author. He reads *ashur* as though it were *asher* (אשר, without the *vav*). He then alludes to Zohar, I, 245b, where Jacob's son Asher is said to symbolize "the World to Come"—Kabbalistic code for the higher female *sefirah Binah*, sometimes called the "Higher Shechinah." (See Matt's notes, *Zohar, ad loc.*) But now the inserted *vav*, which transforms *asher* into *ashur* ("Assyria"), needs to be explained. The author accomplishes this by invoking the standard Kabbalistic use of the phallic *vav* to represent the masculine aspects of deity (see, e.g., the end of chapter 5, section 3, above), which, inserted within the female *asher*, conveys that it is from the sexual coupling of the two that "Cain" derives his effluence. As for *tishbeka*, the author derives it, not from the root *šbh* ("take you into exile"), but from *yšb* and as equivalent to *teyashevkha*, "settle you, establish you," in accordance with the use of "settle" and "settlement" in the *Idra Rabbah* texts expounded above, chapter 5, section 9.

to rebirth him as Little-face, in which capacity he will serve as Enclothement for the God of Israel.]

Up to this point, we have spoken in general terms of how the God of Israel and his Shechinah gathered the fragments from the Shattering and built them into the structure of Emanation from *Tif'eret* downward, and afterward generated the remaining worlds of Creation, Fashioning, and Making.[27] We must now go into the details.

It was Cain, to be sure, who caused the Shattering.[28] Yet it was the God of Israel's will that this should happen, as *Midrash Rabbah* on the Torah portion *Bereshit* explains, quoting Rabbi Shimon ben Yohai. *The mouth cannot utter this*, he says: it is like a king who stands watching one man kill another and does nothing to stop it. He himself is the killer; he wanted the killing to take place, for otherwise he could have prevented it.[29] This was the case with the God of Israel: he wanted it to happen.[30] Hence the Scripture says, *The voice of your brother's blood cries unto me from the ground*—yes, *unto me*, for it was I who brought it about; I could have stopped it. But in truth, it was just what he wanted.

Now, it is known that the God of Israel is symbolically represented by Pharaoh.[31] This is the key to understanding Pharaoh's decree that *"All," the son that is born, you shall throw into the Nile*[32] (taking "All"

---

27. From the later strata of the Zohar onward, the Kabbalists had postulated a series of four hierarchically arranged "worlds," from *Atzilut* ("Emanation") down through *Beri'ah* ("Creation") and *Yetzirah* ("Fashioning") to the lowest "world" of *'Asiyah* ("Making"), which is sometimes equated with our physical reality, sometimes placed above it. Each "world" has its own system of ten *sefirot*. (See Scholem, *Kabbalah*, 118–19.) The three highest *sefirot* of the world of Emanation, *Keter*, *Hokhmah*, and *Binah*, were not "shattered" in the cosmic catastrophe; therefore the rebuilding commences below them, with *Tif'eret*.

28. Above, chapter 4, section 4.

29. Paraphrasing *Midrash Genesis Rabbah* 22:9 (on Gen 4:10), which explains God's complicity in the killing of Abel with a parable of a king who watches two gladiators fight to the death and chooses not to separate them. The dying gladiator, reasonably, directs his blame against the king.

30. Has the author forgotten that, at the time of the Shattering, the God of Israel was in a fetal state and had, at most, a limited ability to control events? Hardly; he will presently speak of the God of Israel's Self-extension as having transpired *after* the Shattering. The inconsistency, the like of which we have noted before (chapter 4, section 4), is forced on him by the logic of his exegesis: if the Shechinah is the "daughter of God" and "daughter of Pharaoh" (*bat-yah*; below, note 50), then the God of Israel must be equivalent to Pharaoh and, as such, responsible for the Shattering.

31. Above, section 1.

32. Exod 1:22, normally translated, "Every son who is born you shall throw into

with absolute literalness, as we have seen in *"All" who finds me*).³³ *You shall throw him into the Nile*: shatter him, that is, and throw him into the midst of the Insolent Waters.

But "All," the daughter, you shall allow to live. This refers to [*Yesod*'s] two females, who were not to be put to death. I have earlier written that Moses is identical to Abel, and is also the *Tif'eret* that was Shattered. But this also you must grasp: that, as we have said, in the Point-world³⁴ one female dwelt together with Abel's *Yesod* in the same vessel.³⁵ That female was called "Miriam," in that *Yesod*, as a drop of the Graces, is called "dripper" inasmuch as he drips water into the Shechinah. This is *mar*, namely a drop, as in *a drop in a bucket*.³⁶ Add *yam*, "sea," and the result is her name "Miriam."³⁷

The male *Yesod* who dwells there is represented by Aaron. Aaron is known to stand for *Yesod*, and thus to be named "Ark of the Lord," for *Yesod* is the Ark.³⁸ [p. 103] In Luria's writings, which you may consult, *Yesod* became recipient of the Graces during the Shattering of the Vessels; he thereby [became] "Aaron the priest," who symbolizes the *sefirah Hesed*,

---

the Nile."

33. Gen 4:14 (normally, "everyone who finds me shall kill me"), but referring to the exposition to the exposition of "All" in verse 15 as the *sefirah Yesod* (beginning of section 2, above). The author interprets Exod 1:22 to mean that *Yesod* was particularly singled out for destruction; the circumstances of its being saved are described below.

34. That underwent the Shattering.

35. On Abel, *Yesod*, and the two females, and the equations Moses = Abel and Moses = *Tif'eret*, see above, chapter 4, sections 2, 7, and 8.

36. Isa 40:15.

37. *Miryam = mar + yam*, combining the seminal "drop" that is *Yesod* and the female "sea" that receives the drop. *Mar* as "drop" is found nowhere in the Bible except Isa 40:15; hence the author's citation of the lexical proof-text. *Mazal*, "dripper," is regularly used in Kabbalah of *Keter*, the highest *sefirah*, which "drips" effluence into all the rest. Its use for *Yesod* is logical, but as far as I am aware occurs nowhere else.

38. I.e., Aaron = Ark; *Yesod* = Ark; therefore Aaron = *Yesod*. The first equation makes some sense: "Aaron" (*aharon*, אהרן) is an anagram for "Ark of the Lord" (*aron h'*, ארן ה'). The second is highly eccentric. The Ark, the Biblical chest in which God's presence is manifest, is regularly used in the Kabbalah to represent the female *sefirah Malkhut* (the Shechinah); it hardly suits the quintessentially masculine *Yesod*. The author perhaps senses the weakness of this argument, and proceeds to his goal by an alternative path; see next note.

"Grace."[39] This is why Miriam is called *sister of Aaron* and not sister of Moses,[40] for it is with him that she is inseparably bound.

So, when the God of Israel thus willed,[41] *a man went forth from the house of Levi* who was the *sefirah Hokhmah* of the Point-world and was therefore called "Exalted People," *'am ram* = "Amram," inasmuch as he was from *the family of the Exalted*, namely the Holy Distant One;[42] while Jochebed, as we know, was symbolic of *Binah*. It was she who brought forth from her womb Moses, whom Luria has explained as representing the *sefirah Tif'eret*.[43] It was she who hid him inside her body *for three months*, symbolizing the three higher *sefirot*;[44] and *when she could no longer hide him*, she enclothed him within the sketch-*sefirot* of *Ma'aseh Bereshit*[45]—symbolized by *tar and pitch*[46]—and threw him into the Nile, which is to say, into the Shattering.

He was shattered. He fell into the Insolent Waters, the primordial waters, where it was the sketch-*sefirot* of *Ma'aseh Bereshit* that gave him protection, lest the Insolent Waters sweep him away.

Now, as he fell into the Insolent Waters, the *Yesod* that consisted of Aaron and Miriam was torn away from him[47]—Aaron on the inside, she floating upon the water's surface—and drifted some distance away from Moses. This is what the Scripture means by, *his sister stood at a distance*, namely Miriam, who was separated from him.[48] And with Moses's fall, all

---

39. The identification of Aaron and the Israelite priesthood with *Hesed*, the sefirotic embodiment of divine Grace, is standard Kabbalah. By inheriting "Grace," therefore, *Yesod* also inherits the Aaronic identity.

40. In Exod 15:20.

41. To allow the Shattering, as represented by "Pharaoh's" decree.

42. Combining Exod 2:1 with Job 32:2. In the story of Moses's birth, his parents are left unnamed; their names are given as Amram and Jochebed in Exod 6:20 and similar passages. Here they are held to represent the coupled *sefirot Hokhmah* (male) and *Binah* (female), near the top of the sefirotic hierarchy.

43. In the sefirotic structure, the "son" of *Hokhmah* and *Binah*. The *Tif'eret* = Moses equation is standard Kabbalah.

44. *Keter, Hokhmah*, and *Binah*. These "higher *sefirot*" escaped the Shattering; if *Tif'eret* could have remained sheltered with them, he might have been spared it as well.

45. See above, chapter 3, section 2; and chapter 4, section 2.

46. With which Moses's mother smeared the "ark" in which she placed him; Exod 2:3.

47. Which can be understood as: he lost his sexual organs.

48. Exod 2:4, which leaves Moses's sister unnamed.

the effluence that is symbolically represented as "the children of Supernal Israel"[49] fell into the Insolent Waters.

[Fol. 23b] When he fell, the Shechinah—whose Self-extension along with the God of Israel, after the fall and Shattering of the Vessels, has already been discussed at some length—went down to fetch him forth. This is the inner meaning of *Bityah, Pharaoh's daughter, went down to bathe in the Nile*,[50] speaking of the Shechinah, who is known to be *bat-yah*, "daughter of Yah"—*daughter of Pharaoh* and thus the daughter of the God of Israel, as has been seen, in accordance with the hidden sense of *my sister, daughter of my Father*.[51]

And she saw the ark, and she sent forth her amah—meaning, if one could possibly imagine it, that she received him into her genital, to become, as it were, pregnant with him.[52] She did not take into herself the vessels but only his Interiority, his Abel-nature; and this is what is meant by, *She opened it and she saw him*—the boy, and only *the boy*.[53] But the vessel and still more so the garment, which was the sketching of *Ma'aseh Bereshit*, remained below.[54]

---

49. See above, chapter 4, section 6.

50. Combining Exod 2:5 with 1 Chr 4:18, where one "Mered" is said, without any explanation, to have married "Bithiah the daughter of Pharaoh." The rabbinic midrash identified Mered as Caleb, and explained the name given to Pharaoh's daughter—who became converted to Judaism, and is the "Jewess" (*ha-yehudiyah*) mentioned at the beginning of the Chronicles verse—as *bat-yah*, "daughter of God." "The Blessed Holy One said to Bityah the daughter of Pharaoh, 'Moses was not your son yet you called him your son; just so, you are not my daughter yet I call you my daughter'" (Midrash *Leviticus Rabbah* 1:3, cf. Talmud, b. Meg. 13a). Our author builds on these midrashim but finds a more direct explanation of Bityah's name: she is daughter of Pharaoh and therefore daughter of God, because Pharaoh *is* God.

51. Gen 20:12, explaining that Sarah is Abraham's sister as well as his wife. See above, chapter 2, section 3, where, however, the Shechinah's "father" is not the God of Israel but the Root. The author uses the verse here, not quite appropriately, to make it seem plausible that the God of Israel's consort ("sister") should also be his daughter. (Ms. Oxford 976 ends abruptly at this point, in line 3 of f. 121b. F. 122a is from a different ms., starting at the end of section 2 above [ולכך נקט ב"י שהוא בסוד אלקי ישראל והבן], and catching up with where we are on 123b, l. 12.)

52. In its context in Exod 2:5, *amah* certainly means "maidservant." But in rabbinic Hebrew, a word identically spelled and almost identically pronounced comes to be used for the male sexual organ, and the author extends it—uniquely, as far as I am aware—to the female genital.

53. Understanding the slight pleonasm of Exod 2:6 as having a restrictive function: Pharaoh's daughter "saw him," but it was only "the boy" that she saw, and nothing else.

54. The "vessel" is the *sefirah Tif'eret*; the "garment" is "the sketch-*sefirot* of *Ma'aseh Bereshit*," earlier said to have protected *Tif'eret* from the Insolent Waters.

[p. 104] We know from the Zohar and Luria's writings that there are *tren nuqvin*,[55] two females, one having the nature of "essence" and the other of "flesh," *essence of my essences* referring to the first and *flesh of my flesh* referring to the second.[56] Now we shall add that the female dwelling in *Yesod* is the one called "essence," alluded to in *the essence of heaven in its purity*,[57] for she is exceedingly clear and radiant, possessing the quality of a drop of Grace; while the second female is the "flesh," the Mild Judgment known as *Adonai*, "the Lord."[58]

Know that *Yesod*'s having fled to within the female, and he fallen from there and she floating upon the Insolent Waters and they having thus endured no Shattering,[59] will yield the key to the passage that says that *Joseph died*:[60] he did indeed experience a sort of death, as explained above, in that he went down in rank and his wife gained mastery over him.[61] *And he was placed inside a chest*, symbolizing the female, who is called "chest,"[62] *in Egypt*, speaking of the Insolent Waters, which are called "Egypt," *Mitzrayim*, so exceedingly *metzerim*, "vexatious," are they. (Admittedly, we have earlier written that Egypt symbolizes the Higher Shechinah: *Mitzrayim* = *Metzar yam*, "the narrow place of the sea."[63] But this should occasion no surprise. It is a well-known feature of Kabbalistic terminology that one and the same term may bear contrasting meanings,

---

55. The author's statement is technically correct to this point, but grossly misleading. The phrase *tren nuqvin* does indeed occur with some frequency in the *Idra* literature of the Zohar (e.g., III, 131a). But its meaning is not "two females," as here, but "two apertures," specifically the nostrils, and there is no connection with Gen 2:23.

56. Gen 2:23, where Adam says of Eve, "This time she is *'etzem me-'atzamai*"—normally translated "bone of my bones"; *'etzem* can mean both "bone" and "essence"—"and flesh of my flesh."

57. Exod 24:10.

58. That is, she is the *sefirah Malkhut*, represented by the divine name Adonai, called in the traditional Kabbalah "the Mild Attribute of Judgment" and opposed to *Gevurah*, "the Severe Attribute of Judgment." Here, however, her antithesis is the Grace of *Yesod*'s female.

59. That is, he fell into the waters while still within her, with the result that both safely floated on the water.

60. Gen 50:26, interpreted in accordance with the standard Kabbalistic understanding of the Biblical Joseph as a representation of the *sefirah Yesod*.

61. Alluding to Zohar, III, 135b; Talmud, b. Besah 32b. See above, chapter 4, beginning of section 8, and chapter 5, section 9.

62. *Aron*, plainly meaning "coffin" in its Biblical context.

63. Above, chapter 4, section 6.

*one opposite to the other.*⁶⁴) And when the midrash has [that chest] *placed into the waters of the Shihor, which are the waters of the Nile,* this is as we have said, that he fell into the Insolent Waters.⁶⁵

Now, this female is called *essences of Joseph,*⁶⁶ she having the quality of "essence"⁶⁷ and Joseph, as *Yesod,* being inside her; she is thus appropriately called *essences of Joseph.* Joseph had made [the Israelites] swear, that when [God] should look after them and raise them, they should take with them his "essence," i.e. that first female.⁶⁸ And so it happened. When Moses was raised by the Higher Shechinah, he took with him the "essence" of Joseph, which was his sister Miriam. So says the Bible: *Moses took with him the essences of Joseph.*⁶⁹

This is why, when Bityah took [Moses], his sister came along with him, and it was [Miriam] who suggested that Jochebed be summoned to initiate with her (as we have said) [p. 105] the process of Nursing by cleansing him from the waste products of the Insolent Waters.⁷⁰ Only afterward did she *bring him* to the Shechinah, who was *Pharaoh's daughter, and he became a son to her,*⁷¹ meaning (as we have said) that he became a fetus within her, fully built up of both male and female juices, as we have said. He is the *sefirah Tif'eret* of Emanation, the entity known as Little-face.

---

64. Eccl 7:14, a Kabbalistic catchphrase meaning that the divine and the demonic are mirror images of each other. *Mitzrayim* thus can serve as symbol both of the Higher Shechinah (divine) and of the Insolent Waters (demonic).

65. Free quotation of the midrash in Talmud, b. Sotah 13a, *Midrash Exodus Rabbah* 20:19, Tanhuma *Be-shallah* #2, *Pesiqta de-Rav Kahana* 11:13, which has the Egyptians make an iron casket for Joseph and sink it into the Nile, from which Moses raised it at the time of the exodus. The midrashic sources speak of the river as the Nile (*nilus*); they do not identify it with the Biblical Shihor. Has our author been influenced by 1 Chr 13:5, where the Shihor is connected with the raising of a different "chest," the Ark of the Covenant?

66. *'Atzmot yosef,* more naturally translated "bones of Joseph." See above, note 56.

67. As described above.

68. Gen 50:25; Exod 13:19.

69. Exod 13:19.

70. As described in Exod 2:7-9. On "the process of Nursing," and its role in the rescue and reconstruction of the sefirotic fragments left from the Shattering, see chapter 5, section 5. The repeated parenthetical "as we have said"s in this paragraph seem to refer back to this earlier passage. The pronouns are somewhat confusing, and suggest that "Miriam" (= *Yesod*'s essence-female) is being "cleansed" along with "Moses" (= *Tif'eret*).

71. Exod 2:10.

This is why, even though he was Abel, she called him Moses: *because I drew him out of the water.*⁷² He had the quality of Seth, of whom we have already said—as is well known—that he was born of male and female and thus *in his likeness, in accordance with his image*, as the Zohar says in the Torah portion *Terumah*: born of male and female, he was truly *in his likeness.*⁷³ This is what we have earlier said with regard to the structure of the *Tif'eret* of Emanation, that he was the most select of all the structures, in that it was through male and female coupling that he came to be.

He was indeed the spirit of Abel, and the Bible consequently says that *God has set for me a different seed instead of Abel*, i.e., in Abel's place.⁷⁴ Yet he truly was *a different seed*, sown in a manner different from that of Abel, who came into being without any male-female coupling. Not so this one [Seth], who was born when the God of Israel extended himself downward to his proper place, where *Tif'eret* of Emanation currently stands.

We have already said that the external *Tif'eret* is represented by Sinai, with its numerical value of 130.⁷⁵ This is the significance of *Adam was one hundred and thirty years old*:⁷⁶ he was in the process of extending himself until he reached the place of *one hundred and thirty years* (i.e., *Tif'eret*), at which point *he engendered in his likeness* and so forth, through male-female coupling. This was in contrast with the prior situation, when he had not yet [fol. 24a] extended himself and could not have performed sexual intercourse. Once the Shechinah had absorbed Moses within her womb, he became her female juices, as it were, and the God of Israel came lusting for her; and from their copulation Moses was engendered as the *sefirah Tif'eret* of Emanation.

This is attested by the previously quoted passage from Zohar *Terumah*,⁷⁷ that with regard to Seth HE CAME TO LUST FOR HIS FEMALE, and it is therefore written *he engendered*, emphasizing that it was he

---

72. Exod 2:10. Our author understands the "water" of which "Pharaoh's daughter" speaks as the Insolent Waters from which she rescued "Moses," and the second syllable of *meshitihu*, "I drew him out," suggests to him the name *shet*, "Seth."

73. Zohar, II, 167b, quoting Gen 5:3 (speaking of Seth, whom Adam is said to have "engendered in his likeness, in accordance with his image"). See the full discussion of this Zoharic passage and its context in chapter 3, section 8.

74. So speaks Eve in Gen 4:25, explaining why she has named her new child Seth: *shet* from *shat*, "set."

75. Above, section 1.

76. When he begot Seth; Gen 5:3.

77. Zohar, II, 167b, discussed at length above, chapter 3, section 8.

who did the engendering—in contrast to the birthing of Cain and Abel, in which the Shechinah played the active role.[78] Yet, inasmuch as it was she who lifted [Moses/Seth] out from the Insolent Waters, his birthing is attributed also to her. This is why the Bible says in another passage that *she bore Seth*.[79]

We now can resolve an objection to the Zohar, that it makes a point of the Bible's saying *he engendered* in connection with Seth—yet does not the Bible also say, *she bore*?[80] In the light of what we have just said, the problem disappears.

4. The Rescuing of the Female

[In addition to the Higher Shechinah, there are two Lower Shechinahs within the sefirotic system (above, chapter 4, sections 2–3): the "Miriam" (subsequently also called "Leah") Shechinah who shelters *Yesod*, and the barren, sexually undeveloped "Rachel" Shechinah, who is the *sefirah Malkhut*. The latter survives the Shattering, though in a somewhat tattered state—symbolically perceptible in the architecture of the Jerusalem Temple—and must be rescued from the Insolent Waters (as "Zipporah") by the God of Israel (now as "Moses," embodied in *Tif'eret*). A complex and somewhat confusing distinction is made among this *sefirah*'s inner "intelligence," her "vessel," and her "garment." The last of these seems to remain below while the rest of her enters the womb of the Higher Shechinah, as did Moses/*Tif'eret*, to be rebirthed as the *Malkhut* of the reconstructed system.]

[p. 106] Once Moses had been completed, the God of Israel turned his attention to the rescue of the Shechinah who was the second female, the one symbolized by Rachel.

---

78. In Gen 4:1–2, the birthing of Cain and Abel is attributed solely to Eve.

79. Gen 4:25, freely quoted.

80. So the Zohar's apparent insistence, on the basis of Gen 5:3, that it was the male who was responsible for Seth's coming into being, is contradicted by another Biblical text (Gen 4:25), which credits Seth's birth to the female. To which objection—whether actually made by some critic or only hypothetical, is not clear—our author offers the resolution: yes, Seth/Moses was begotten of the sexual act of the male deity (*he engendered*), precisely as the Zohar says. Yet because it was the female who had originally taken Seth/Moses into her womb, the Bible credits the birth also to her.

THE SYMBOLISMS OF GOD

We have already written that she had the quality of being barren, sexually undeveloped.[81] *Rachel was barren*, says the Scripture, which the midrash interprets to mean that she was an *aylonit*, a woman who never develops sexual characteristics.[82] She had survived un-Shattered, yet she was in the midst of the Insolent Waters. Now the God of Israel sought to rescue her, in accord with the principle that *Scripture attributes the daughters to the males*—e.g., *his daughter Dinah—and the sons to the females*.[83] The [Lower] Shechinah was his daughter, and he was therefore to be her rescuer, while *the sons*, specifically *Tif'eret*, were saved by *the females*, for it was the [Higher] Shechinah who had rescued him.

The God of Israel therefore enclothed himself within Moses—representing *Tif'eret*—and descended and killed the Egyptian.[84] He also *fled to the field of Midian*,[85] which is to say to the place of Judgments; for it has already been explained that the Shechinah, being in the category of Judgments, was in the midst of "Midian."[86] God had ordered *the little ones who are female* to be kept alive;[87] [Moses] therefore descended to that place and rescued Zipporah (symbolic of the [Rachel-]Shechinah), and lifted her up on high. In the manner of Moses, as earlier described, she also entered into the womb of the [Higher] Shechinah in a sort of gestation; and thus there emerged, through male-female coupling, a complete

---

81. Above, chapter 4, section 2.

82. Gen 29:31. I am not aware of any midrash that explicitly calls Rachel an *aylonit*, but Tanhuma Buber *Va-yetze* #15 explains her "barrenness" to mean that she had no ovaries, and this is perhaps what the author refers to.

83. Talmud, b. Nid. 31b, which invokes the designation of Dinah as Jacob's daughter in Gen 46:15—versus her brothers, who are called "Leah's sons" in that same verse—in support of its notion that boys are conceived when it is the woman who climaxes first during the sexual act, girls when it is the man. Our author sees this folk belief as hinting at a gender crossing in the relations of the sefirotic to the super-sefirotic (parental) entities: Moses/Seth is "son" of the female Shechinah who is his rescuer, while the Rachel-Shechinah is "daughter" to the male deity who is hers.

84. Presumably representing the Insolent Waters, as in the preceding section.

85. A loose paraphrase of Exod 2:15, inserting the crucial word "field," a standard Zoharic code term for the *sefirah Malkhut* (= the Shechinah).

86. In the traditional Kabbalah the *sefirah Malkhut* (= the Shechinah) is considered to be under the influence of Judgment, and is sometimes given the title "Mild Attribute of Judgment" (as opposed to *Gevurah*, the "Severe Attribute of Judgment"). "Midian" is here understood as the collectivity of the "Midianites," who have earlier been explained as symbols for the *sefirot* of Judgment, "slaughtered" (as per Num 31) in the course of the Shattering (above, chapter 4, section 7). Moses-*Tif'eret* now rescues the "Midianite" female (Zipporah, Moses's Midianite wife in Exod 2:21) from that slaughtering, as indicated in the next sentence.

87. Num 31:18, referring to the slaughter of the "Midianites," i.e., the Judgments.

Malkhut-shape, built up likewise[88] of the coupling of male and female. This was the *sefirah Malkhut* of the World of Emanation.

Two things you must realize. All the *sefirot*[89] ascended only as intelligences, that is to say, in their "Abel" aspect. Their vessels, generated by Cain, and all the more so their garment of *Maʿaseh Bereshit*, remained below;[90] but since the female was never Shattered, her vessel stayed with her and she rose with it. You must realize also that her garment of *Maʿaseh Bereshit* should have risen as well. That garment was from *Maʿaseh Bereshit*, however, where the intelligences are mixed in with Mindless Light and Judgments, entirely without male and female. Consequently, they are wholly unfinished spirits, drastically in need of mending.

These are called *daughters of Heth*, for we have earlier written that the *Tehiru* is represented by [the Hebrew letter] *het*.[91] Hence, *daughters of Heth*: spirits that were left wholly unfinished, unmended. They are hinted at in the words, *I detest my life on account of the daughters of Heth*;[92] i.e., because of these spirits, inasmuch as they are not in a state of Mending.

[p. 107] Know, also, that when Abel's *Malkhut* descended below,[93] the Insolent Waters wanted to couple with her. She was utterly unwilling to receive them, however, and she concealed herself deep within her vesture, so that the Insolent Waters and the spirit of *the children of Heth*[94] might not penetrate inside her; she is consequently represented as Esther, who "concealed herself," *mistatteret*.[95] But the vesture of the *sefirah Malkhut*, being in the midst of the *Tehiru*, sought out its like and did admit the Insolent Waters, becoming thoroughly enwrapped in them.

When the God of Israel raised the Shechinah on high, he wanted to raise her as well.[96] She must, however, strip off the dung-befouled

---

88. Like Moses/*Tif'eret*.

89. Of the Point-world, raised from the Insolent Waters after the Shattering. On the distinction between the "vessels" and the "intelligences" of these *sefirot*, and the "Abel" character of the latter, see above, chapter 4, section 2.

90. Above, note 54.

91. Cf. above, chapter 3, sections 4–5.

92. Gen 27:46.

93. Above, chapter 4, section 9.

94. Gen 23:3, etc.; cf. the very different interpretation of the phrase in chapter 3, section 5.

95. Deriving "Esther" from the root *str*, "to conceal." The Talmud, b. Meg. 13a, gives a different etymology of the name from this root: she was called Esther "because she concealed her words."

96. Who is this "her"? The language is confusing, but it would seem that the author

garments[97] she had received and come before him naked, without her dungy clothing. This is the inner meaning of Ahasuerus—symbolizing the God of Israel—wanting Vashti to come before him naked.[98] But she was strongly attached to [those garments] and was unwilling to strip them off, and she therefore remained below, *no more coming before the king, and the king would give her royal status to another* [fol. 24b] *better than she.*[99] This was Esther, who was *better than she* in that she guarded her genital,[100] refusing to allow the Insolent Waters to come within her.

This is the symbolism also of Ruth and Orpah. Ruth clung to the Shechinah; Orpah, her name indicative of "turning one's back," was the one who remained below, *while Ruth clung to her.*[101] The one who remained below is represented as "First Eve,"[102] called "first" in that her quality is that of *Ma'aseh Bereshit*—while the Interiority [of *Malkhut*] ascended on high.

---

has split the Lower Shechinah ("Abel's *Malkhut*") into an "Esther" aspect and a "Vashti" aspect—parallel to the Ruth/Orpah dichotomy below—both of whom the God of Israel (= Ahasuerus) wishes to raise. Only, "Esther" is willing to discard her befouled clothing, "Vashti" is not. This passage has a deep Sabbatian background: the Sabbatians saw the Biblical Esther as a "type" of Sabbatai Zevi, and placed great emphasis on the impure (Muslim) clothing that their Messiah had been compelled to wear, and that he would eventually strip off.

97. Drawing on the language of Zech 3:3.

98. Talmud, b. Meg. 12b, presumably understanding "with the royal crown" in Esth 1:11 to mean: wearing only the royal crown.

99. Esth 1:19, freely quoted.

100. Literally, "she kept her covenant." The author regularly—and with precedent in post-Biblical Hebrew—uses *berit*, "covenant," to refer to the penis, the locus of the "covenant" of circumcision. Here he seems, uniquely, to extend that usage from the male to the female genital, parallel to his use of *amah* in section 3, above.

101. Ruth 1:14; "Naomi" in the Bible story is taken to symbolize the Higher Shechinah. (Her role in the elevation of "Ruth" does not sit well with the author's principle, at the beginning of this section, that the male rescues the females while the female rescues the males.) The author derives the name of Ruth's sister-in-law from *'oref*, which literally means "neck" but can be used idiomatically to speak of turning one's back; and *ahorayim*, "rear parts," which he couples with *'oref*, can be used in the Kabbalah to convey the notion of externality. Cf. his treatment of Ruth in chapter 4, section 9, above.

102. A mysterious figure mentioned in a cryptic passage of Midrash Genesis Rabbah (22:7), where one rabbi declares that Cain and Abel quarreled "over the First Eve," while another rabbi counters that "the First Eve had already returned to her dust." Clearly this is *not* the Biblical Eve, who was still alive when Cain killed Abel. But who it is remains entirely unclear; and our author mentions the "First Eve" only here.

It is the esoteric meaning also of Ezekiel chapter 16, addressed to "Jerusalem" as a symbol for the Shechinah.[103]

Your father the Speech-man: ha-emori, equivalent to *amar yah*, "the Lord spoke," he having been created, as has been said, through speech and thought.[104] *And your mother*, namely the Enclothement[105] which is like a mother[106]—the *Tehiru*, symbolized by the letter *het*. When the text says, *your mother a Het-woman*,[107] it points toward that which the *het* represents.

As for your birth, on the day you were born and so forth, *you were cast out upon the field*, meaning that she was immediately Shattered.[108] *I passed by you and I saw you wallowing in your blood.*[109] This alludes to what has earlier been said, that all the blood fell upon you, as hinted at in *your brother's blood crying to me from the earth.*[110] *And I said to you, In your blood, live*, meaning that he[111] rescued her, as has been described.

[p. 108] You must also know this: We have already said that thirteen gashes were made in the Shechinah, as symbolized by the rose.[112] This is what is meant by *you have made the earth to quake, cracked it*

---

103. The Lower Shechinah, the *sefirah Malkhut*.

104. The "Speech-man" is Abel, brought into being by an act of mentation without sexual coupling (above, chapter 4, section 2), and conceived as "father" to the *sefirot* of the Point-world. The quotation, from Ezek 16:3, is normally translated "your father was an Amorite, your mother a Hittite." But our author derives *emori* from the root meaning "to say" or "to speak," and points out that *ha-emori* (האמרי) is an anagram for *amar yah* (אמר יה).

105. The "vesture" of *Malkhut*, spoken of above. On the symbolism of the letter *het*, see above, chapter 3, sections 4–5.

106. Of the mss., only Oxford 976 gives the correct reading אם הי' הטהירא, the other four mss. corrupting אם into שם and omitting הי'. Moreover, the way אם is written in Oxford 976 easily invites the error. Will this suggest priority for Oxford 976 over the other mss.?

107. *Hittit*, normally translated "Hittite."

108. Abbreviated quotation of Ezek 16:4–5. The author will go on to make clear that *Malkhut* was not fully destroyed like the male *sefirot*, but left in a "gashed" state; and this presumably happened "immediately" upon her emergence ("on the day you were born").

109. Ezek 16:6.

110. Gen 4:10, as interpreted above, chapter 4, section 9, where "your brother's blood" is said to be Abel's "effluence" that fell upon *Malkhut*. "Earth" = *Malkhut* is standard Kabbalistic symbolism.

111. The God of Israel.

112. With its thirteen petals. The author alludes to the well-known passage at the beginning of the Zohar; the passage represents the *sefirah Malkhut* as a thirteen-petalled rose. See the end of chapter 4, section 8, above.

open,[113] meaning that he made of her a series of cracks. He [the God of Israel] did indeed lift her up on high, yet he did not fully *heal the shatterings:*[114] the cracks remained.

Yet within each crack the blood of virginity served as an obstruction, denying any point of entry to the Insolent Waters. This was the symbolic significance of the thirteen ruptures made in the Temple by the Greeks, representing the Judgments and the Insolent Waters. It was a *Soreg,* a "webwork," which is to say the blood of virginity—as the physicians say that the blood of virginity is like a weaving, i.e., a *Soreg*—and the Judgments, symbolically equivalent to the Insolent Waters, smashed their way through it. The Hasmoneans, who as priests symbolized Mercies, repaired it as the *Soreg.* Yet the ruptures remained as the thirteen Temple gates, while the *Soreg,* standing for the blood of virginity, kept the Insolent Waters from penetrating within.[115]

This is why this virginity-blood is in need of reinforcement, lest the Insolent Waters gain the upper hand. Consequently, in order to reinforce it, thirteen prostrations were instituted in the Temple, as described in Gemara and Mishnah.[116] Not until future times will these shatterings be healed, by *the One destined to heal the fracture of the sea,* referring to the Shechinah which is called "sea."[117]

Since the Mending, no trace of brokenness can be recognized in the other fragments of the Shattering, all of them having been most excellently mended. Only from the esoteric tradition, vouchsafed to the

---

113. Ps 60:4, understanding "earth" as the Shechinah. See above, section 1.

114. As the Biblical verse begs God to do.

115. Based on the Mishnah, m. Mid. 2:3: "Within it [the area of the Temple Mount] was a webwork fence [*soreg*] ten handbreadths high. Thirteen ruptures [*peratzot*] had been made there by the kings of Greece; and [the Hasmoneans] repaired them and decreed thirteen prostrations toward them." In m. Mid. 2:6, the Temple gates seem to be equated with the "ruptures"; cf. m. Sheqal. 6:1, 3. The *Soreg* marked the point on the Temple Mount beyond which Gentiles were not permitted to proceed, i.e., the boundary between the profane and the sacred. The identification of priests with Mercies (or Graces) is standard Kabbalistic symbolism. What supposed view of "the physicians" the author alludes to, I have no idea.

116. Mishnaic passages cited in the preceding note; I am not aware of any mention of the "thirteen prostrations" in the Gemara.

117. *Midrash Lamentations Rabbah* 2:17, Pesiqta de-Rav Kahana 16:3: "The One destined to heal the fracture of the sea—he will heal you" (expounding Lam 2:13, "your fracture is as great as the sea; who will heal you?"). The mysterious "One" is presumably understood by our author to be the Messiah Sabbatai Zevi. The "sea" = *Malkhut* equation is standard Kabbalistic symbolism.

God-fearing,[118] does one hear of any such thing having befallen them. In the Shechinah, however, the fractures and ruptures are still perceptible. This is the hidden meaning of the verse *The kings gathered together* and so forth, *with the east wind did you shatter the ships of Tarshish*, which, as the Zohar explains, speaks of the Shattering.[119] And the Bible goes on to say: *As we have heard* this—for they were already mended, and we therefore could have known [what had befallen them] only by report and not by sight—*so we have seen in the City of the Lord of hosts*: in the Shechinah (symbolized as a city), where the cracks are perceptible, might this yet be seen. Understand this.

5. Interlude: Moses and Messiah

[The figure of Moses, already multivalent, now takes on a fresh dimension drawn from the Sabbatian tradition. Exod 12:38 spoke of a "mixed multitude" (*'erev rav*) that went up with the Israelites from Egypt. Inspired by the later strata of the Zohar (*Ra'ya Mehemna*), Nathan of Gaza understood this "mixed multitude" to be the ancestors, or the source of the souls, of those unbelieving Jews who mocked and rejected the Messiah Sabbatai Zevi, of whom Moses was the "type." Normally Nathan, and the Sabbatian writers who followed him, denounced and condemned the *'erev rav* as infidels, Jewish only on the surface.[120] Our author, perhaps inspired by Hayyim Vital's uncommonly sympathetic understanding (see notes to this section), takes a more irenic stance.]

[p. 109] Returning to our discussion of how Moses lifted up the Shechinah on high: when he did so, the effluence, which we have seen to be represented as *the children of Israel*,[121] also took hold of his heel and rose to the heights. This is the inner meaning of *"Six hundred thousand at my foot"—on account of me you were all saved.*[122]

118. Drawing on the language of Ps 25:14. The reference is presumably to the Kabbalistic tradition as a whole—*qabbalah* literally means "tradition"—and not to some Sabbatian variant of it.

119. Ps 48:5–8, interpreted in Zohar III, 292a (*Idra Zuta*) to refer to the primordial "kings of Edom" who fell victim to the Shattering. The words omitted from the Biblical quote describe the "kings'" raw terror at the event.

120. Nathan's epistle to Joseph Zevi, translated in Halperin, *Sabbatai Zevi*, 63–69; Magid, *From Metaphysics*, 75–110; Maciejko, *Mixed Multitude*, 1–6.

121. Above, chapter 4, section 6.

122. Spoken by Moses to the Israelites in Talmud, b. Sotah 12b, quoting Num 11:21.

When these rose, certain souls from *Ma'aseh Bereshit* also grasped hold of him and rose. These were in fact still incomplete, and are the ones alluded to in the verse *Also a mixed multitude went up with them*.[123] They are the ones who remained [fol. 25a] unmended, and they did great damage—including to the one whose heel they seized.

For Moses was destined to be reincarnated in the Messiah's generation, as the Zohar tells us.[124] The mixed multitude would then rebel against him, betraying him with their words; and thus he would expel them from his compartment, from the place to which they had adhered. Yet the better sort would remain clinging to his place, while the worse would separate themselves in order to rebel against him (as the Zohar tells us), and this would be their mending.[125] He stands for the Messiah, inasmuch as Moses and Messiah are one. This is the hidden meaning of *At the Messiah's heels shall shamelessness increase*,[126] speaking of those who laid hold of his heel. Understand.

6. Genesis 3: The Sin of God

[The God of Israel and the Higher Shechinah, their work of reconstruction completed, settle into their places in the

---

The Biblical phrase properly means "six hundred thousand on foot," i.e., the adult Israelite males who left Egypt (Exod 12:37). But our author, taking his cue from the Talmud, understands *ragli* literally as "my foot": it was by grasping hold of Moses's foot that the "Israelites" (= the *shefa'*, the effluence) were redeemed.

123. With the Israelites from Egypt; Exod 12:38. See the introduction to this section.

124. Presumably referring to passages in *Ra'ya Mehemna* in which Moses is apostrophized as the "suffering servant" of Isa 53, applied to "the generation of the Last Exile" (Zohar, III, 282b), and Moses himself complains that "among the iniquitous *'erev rav* I am considered as a dead dog, stinking among them" (III, 125b-26a, cf. 276b, 280a). But perhaps our author's source for this paragraph is less the Zohar than Vital (quoted *in extenso* in Horowitz, *Shnei Luhot ha-Berit, Torah Or*, chapter 3, volume 5, 102-4), who speaks of Moses's being reincarnated "in every generation" and explicitly equates him with the Messiah as well as with Isaiah's "suffering servant."

125. This cryptic sentence surely speaks of divisions within contemporary or near-contemporary Sabbatianism, but its hints resist elucidation. Vital (quoted and discussed in Magid, *From Metaphysics*, 106-8) also knows the "mending" (*tiqqun*) of a portion of the *'erev rav*. But these are the penitent among them, not the rebellious, as here. Is their "rebellion" against Sabbatai Zevi (= Moses) expressed through their loyalty to traditional Judaism, which our author acknowledges as being in its own way virtuous, and thereby constituting their "mending"? A paradox so humane and tolerant would not be beyond his ability to conceive.

126. Mishnah, m. Sotah 9:15, normally translated, "in the footsteps of the Messiah," i.e., just prior to his coming.

Enclothement, the *sefirah Tif'eret* and the "Miriam" Shechinah respectively. The Root, whom we last saw briefly at the beginning of the chapter, now takes an active role in the "garden" that is the new architecture of the sefirotic worlds, as the "God" of Gen 3 giving directives to the "Adam" and "Eve" that are the God of Israel and the Higher Shechinah.

The God of Israel—and, by implication, his human adherents—must keep the Torah. Both he and the Higher Shechinah must abstain from sex with the Lower ("Rachel") Shechinah, at least during the daytime; this is the meaning of the prohibition of eating from the Tree of Knowledge. But Creation-Human, whom we last saw manifested as "Cain," steps in, in the form of the serpent. (He will long afterward reappear as the Messiah, with whom his name is numerically identical in Hebrew.) In his lust for the nourishing "female juices" such sex would evoke, he persuades the Higher Shechinah to violate the Root's command; and the God of Israel partakes with her. No longer virgins, they are newly vulnerable to the Insolent Waters and must clothe themselves. Meanwhile privileges once granted to Creation-Human as "Cain" are stripped from him as "the serpent."

(The chronological reversal of Gen 3 and 4—the "Cain" story prior to "Eden," as suggested by the Hebrew text of Gen 4:16—is to be noted.)]

To return to our prior subject: Once the structure of Emanation had been completed and Abel's first female, the one represented as "essences of Joseph," dwelt inside *Yesod* with the male *Yesod* in a single vessel, while his second female remained within a vessel all her own just as in the Point-world—when all this was done, the God of Israel came to desire a dwelling-place for himself.[127] He accordingly settled himself, as we have said, within the *sefirah Tif'eret* of Emanation.

This was the location most suited for him, inasmuch as, unlike anything else in the world, it was made from male and female together.[128] The Straight Line[129] indeed extended down through the entire world, but it concealed itself, and they were thus wholly incapable of receiving effluence from it. Only in *Tif'eret* did its hidden power become revealed, spilling into the Shechinah, from which all the worlds received it—as we have earlier explained at length.

127. Drawing on the language of Ps 132:13–14.

128. Above, chapter 5, section 5. By "the world," the author means the array of Kabbalistic structures.

129. Which was the God of Israel; above, chapter 5, section 1.

The Higher Shechinah, meanwhile, had no wish to descend and distance herself from the God of Israel by taking up her dwelling within the shape of the second female.[130] Rather, she settled within "Miriam" (or "the essences of Joseph"),[131] while *Malkhut*, symbolized by "Rachel," was at a level below them both. This is why the *sefirot Netzah* and *Hod* were "halves of a body," in contrast to *Hesed* and *Gevurah*.[132] For they were in fact body halves, one male and one female, at that time represented symbolically by Abram and Sarai—androgynous in character, maleness and femaleness together. She dwelt with the God of Israel in what was truly a single body, [p. 110] her nature that of the *uma* that surrounds the lung and embraces the heart, functioning as its female.[133] That was why Sarai was called *"princess" for her umah*—literally, the *uma*.[134]

We have earlier said that all the Six Points, excluding *Malkhut*, rose only as Abel-intelligences, without the vessels that are Cain's offspring.[135] This is why, as we have written above,[136] *Malkhut* descends by night into the midst of *Ma'aseh Bereshit*, equipped with Judgment's raging heat.[137] She goes as a virgin, that no strangers may enter her,

130. That is, the independent *sefirah Malkhut*. So, while the God of Israel dwelt in *Tif'eret*, the Shechinah did not correspondingly dwell in *Malkhut*, which remained "at a level below them both"—that is, beneath the God of Israel and the Higher Shechinah. (The author seems to contradict himself on this issue; below, note 141.) Ms. HUC 85 ends at this point, in midsentence, with the words אף שיורד.

131. Above, section 3, expounding the Exodus story of Moses's birth.

132. Replying to the question posed in chapter 4, section 1. The author's answer is not altogether clear. He seems to have envisioned the sefirotic cluster *Tif'eret-Netzah-Hod-Yesod* as having been, "at that time"—that is, the reconstruction in the wake of the Shattering—a single androgynous body, with *Netzah* and *Hod* together as the androgynous link between the God of Israel's dwelling and the Shechinah's.

133. *Uma* is used in medieval Hebrew for a part of the lung, connected to the lobes yet distinct from them (Tosafot to b. Hul. 47a, cf. the Soncino Talmud's note *ad loc.*); perhaps what is now called the diaphragmatic surface? Cf. Preuss, *Biblisch-talmudische Medizin*, 113–14. The image of the enclosing, embracing female is cognate to that of the Miriam-female as the Ark within which Aaron-*Yesod* takes refuge.

134. Talmud, b. Ber. 13a, etymologizes the name "Sarai" as "princess for her *umah*," plainly using *umah* in its ordinary sense of "people, nation." Our author rejects this obvious understanding of the Talmudic passage, insisting that it really intends the internal organ called the *uma*.

135. Above, section 4. In the traditional Kabbalah, the "Six Points" are the cluster of six *sefirot* whose nucleus is *Tif'eret*—*Hesed, Gevurah, Netzah, Hod, Yesod*, and *Tif'eret* itself—situated immediately above *Malkhut* in the sefirotic schema.

136. Chapter 4, section 3.

137. *Rut'ha* (רותחא), which in rabbinic Hebrew combines the meanings of boiling heat and Divine wrath. On *Malkhut* as an embodiment of Judgment, see above, note 58.

and she purifies and cleanses the intelligences worthy of purification.[138] This was the Root's intention, that *Malkhut* descend by night into the *Tehiru* and receive the Cain-begotten vessels that are Cain's offspring, then bring them up on high to partake of resurrection. In this way, the power of the Insolent Waters is greatly lessened.

This is what is conveyed by *YHVH God planted a garden*—that is, the structures of Emanation, Creation, Fashioning and Making—*through the agency of "Eden," out of the Primordial*.[139] For we have already written that the essential shape-giver in *Ma'aseh Bereshit* (= the *Tehiru*) is the *sefirah Binah*, which is called "Eden" as is well known;[140] and when it says, *through the agency of "Eden," out of the Primordial*, it speaks of *Ma'aseh Bereshit*, which is called "primordial."

And he caused to sprout from the earth, from *Malkhut* (which was Higher Shechinah and Artisan),[141] *every pleasant tree*, namely the *sefirot*, *and the Tree of Life*, symbolically representing the God of Israel's Shechinah, which is called "Higher Shechinah." She is *Tree of Life* in that every bit of her is Life, without any admixture of waste, for her quality is wholly that of Interiority, as we have said—versus the Lower Shechinah,[142] represented as *the Tree of Knowledge of Good and Evil*.

---

138. This must be an error: the "intelligences" have already risen, and in the next sentence it is (appropriately) the vessels that are beneficiaries of her purification. The sudden appearance of the Root in the following sentence is jarring, but we have need of him: he will appear in the Eden story of Genesis as "YHVH God."

139. Gen 2:8, normally translated "YHVH God planted a garden in Eden to the east." (*Qedem* can mean either "east" or "antiquity.") With these words, the author opens an extraordinarily inventive reinterpretation of the Eden story, with "YHVH God" = the Root, "Adam" = the God of Israel, "Eve" = the Higher Shechinah, the "garden" = the four Kabbalistic "worlds," and the "serpent" = the Messiah.

140. Referring back to chapter 3, section 2 (which gives the "shaper" role to both *Hokhmah* and *Binah*) and section 5. The "Eden" = *Binah* equation has some support in the traditional Kabbalah, but it is hardly unequivocal. (According to Cordovero, *Sha'ar 'Erkhei ha-Kinnuyim*, s.v."Eden" is more properly *Keter* or *Hokhmah*.)

141. A confusing statement of *Malkhut*'s role as "Enclothement" of the Higher Shechinah, both of which entities are called "Artisan" (*omana*) earlier in this chapter. Cf. the author's exposition of Zohar, I, 22a–b (above, chapter 3, section 7), where the "artisan above" and the "artisan below"—used by the Zohar for *Binah* and *Malkhut* respectively—are reinterpreted to refer to "the substrate of Ein Sof" and the Higher Shechinah. The inconsistency with the beginning of this section, where the Higher Shechinah does *not* take up residence within *Malkhut* but within the female dwelling with *Yesod*, remains troubling.

142. *Malkhut*.

And there he placed the Human,[143] representing the God of Israel, who dwells there,[144] as we have said. *And YHVH God commanded*: this is the Root commanding the God of Israel—for it is he who commands him—to keep the Torah, as is well known.[145] *From every tree of the garden you may eat*: including the Tree of Life. Not, however, from the Lower Shechinah (represented as the Tree of Knowledge); and "eating," as we well know, is a term for sexual intercourse.

The rationale is plain. It was only by day that he was prohibited from sex with her, for if they were to copulate in the daytime she would be sexually opened. He as well—if he were to ejaculate in the daytime, the Insolent Waters would have greater opportunity to attach themselves to him. The nighttime is different: Judgment and the raging heat of fire then hold sway, and the intensity of that fiery flame keeps them from drawing near. [p. 111] This is why the Scripture says, *In the day wherein you eat of it*—if you have sex in the daytime, that is—*you shall surely die*. You will be compelled, that is, to go up on high in order that the Insolent Waters not lay hold on you, and it is in a state of entrancement, as earlier said, that you will be obliged to ascend.[146]

Now, it is an established fact that "serpent" is symbolically equivalent to "Messiah." The two words have the same numerical value; and Luria has written in *'Etz Hayyim*, in his exposition of Primordial Human, that [the serpent] indeed represents the Messiah.[147] [Fol. 25b] He is above the *Tehiru, denuded of all Heth the field*,[148] for, as we have seen, the *Tehiru* is called "field" and also "Heth," and he is bare of it.

143. Free paraphrase of Gen 2:15.

144. Within the *sefirot*.

145. Following a widespread midrashic tradition that "to work it and to keep it" (Gen 2:15) means "to labor in the Torah and to keep its commandments" (Targum Pseudo-Jonathan; see Finkelstein, ed., *Sifrei to Deuteronomy: 'Eqev* section 41, p. 87, and Finkelstein's note *ad loc.*). On the obligation to keep the Torah and its commandments imposed specifically on the God of Israel, see above, chapter 5, section 2.

146. As described in section 7, below. On "entrancement" (*dormita*), see above, chapter 2, section 2, and especially note 25.

147. On the Messiah = serpent equation, which goes back to the beginning of the Sabbatian movement, see above, chapter 3, section 9, especially note 186. (I am not aware of anything in Vital's *'Etz Hayyim*, or anywhere else in the Lurianic writings, that might substantiate the claim that Luria propounded it.) Gen 3 is thus read as a primordial chapter in the biography of Sabbatai Zevi.

148. Gen 3:1, *'arum mi-kol hayyat ha-sadeh*, normally translated "more cunning than any beast of the field." *'Arum* can mean "naked" as well as "cunning," and חית, vocalized *hayyat*, "beast," can also be read as *het*, "Heth." Both "Heth" and "field" are designations of the *Tehiru*, (chapter 3, section 5; chapter 4, section 4; and section 4 of

Greatly does he desire female juices. And so he lusted for the Higher Shechinah to couple with *Malkhut* so that she would receive female juices—and he receive them as well; for it is from her, the Higher Shechinah, that his effluence derives, as we have learned from the verse *"Sevenfold" shall Cain be raised.*[149] He consequently asked her if she were not able to eat from the trees of the garden. To which *the woman*—symbolic of the Higher Shechinah—responded that *from every tree of the garden*, and so forth, but from the Tree of Knowledge *you may not eat.*[150] She made no mention of the Tree of Life, for she was herself the Tree of Life.[151]

To this, [the serpent] replied that *you will not die*,[152] meaning by this that the prohibition did not apply to her. On the contrary, he said: this act would bring about an increase in the female juices, which are now in a virgin state.

For it is known that the Shechinah has the equivalent of a penis, as Luria has written concerning the letter *'ayin* in the secrets of the alphabet;[153] and prior to first intercourse even the male is a bit like a female virgin in that a thin membrane seals off his seminal aperture. [The serpent] consequently said that, as matters stood, there was no way to absorb the organs of intelligence from *Ma'aseh Bereshit*, given that they were both sealed up.[154] But if they were to have intercourse, their nether "eyes" would be opened, and they would *be as God, knowing good and evil.*[155] They would be able, in other words, to distinguish good from evil and to choose out of the *Ma'aseh Bereshit* those intelligences well suited to be made into female juices, as the

---

this chapter) and the serpent is "bare" of the *Tehiru*'s filth. He is thus like Esther, unlike Vashti (above, section 4); and it is surely no coincidence that both Esther and the serpent served the Sabbatians as representations of their Messiah.

149. Gen 4:24; referring, however, to the author's exegesis of the very similar Gen 4:15 in section 2, above. There it is "Cain" (= Primordial Human) who needs the female juices supplied by the Higher Shechinah, and the serpent of Gen 3 is now identified with him (see below).

150. Combining Gen 3:2–3 with 2:16–17.

151. And thus a vexing question in the interpretation of Gen 3—why does Eve mention no prohibition of eating from the Tree of Life?—is neatly answered.

152. Free quote of Gen 3:4, using the plural verb.

153. I do not know what the author is referring to.

154. Which, it seems, could only be remedied if they were both to have sex as males with the hitherto virginal *Malkhut*—the God of Israel with his penis, the Higher Shechinah with her quasi-penis.

155. Gen 3:5.

THE SYMBOLISMS OF GOD

Root did when he separated evil from good.[156] She [the Shechinah] would thereby receive a plenitude of male juices.[157]

When *the woman saw that it was good for eating*—for female juices—*and desirable to the eyes*—[158]

for there is a distinction to be made, in that the male absorbs the female's juices visually. This is why the Bible says of the ritual fringe, which is female in essence, *you shall look upon it*,[159] and likewise *the Lord's eyes roam about the whole earth*[160] and other similar passages. [p. 112] Thus you may grasp the inner meaning of the verse *his eyes are like doves upon streams of water*:[161] when the Shechinah receives male juices, she will at times expel them like a woman who expels semen,[162] rejecting the excess; whereas the male, who receives visually, will not expel, for he receives only that purest and most luminous element which is absorbed through his sense of sight, and therefore will not expel anything whatever; and we learn from the Mishnah tractate *Parah* that the dove is the only bird that does not disqualify purification-water by drinking from it, *because it sips*, which Rashi explains to mean that all birds expel the excess [of what they drink] but the dove does not[163]—and thus *his eyes*, which do not expel, *are like doves upon streams of water*, which do not expel anything whatever. And thus, returning to our subject, he[164] receives through his eyes, and hence *it was desirable to the eyes*—

---

156. The reference is not clear; perhaps to the Root's dispatching *Malkhut* into the *Tehiru* to lift up the "Cain-begotten vessels," as described earlier in this section?

157. I think this must be an error for "female juices."

158. The author here breaks off the sentence—a slightly altered quotation of Gen 3:6—to explain why the Scripture seems to represent eating and seeing ("desirable to the eyes") as distinct modes of absorption.

159. Num 15:39, referring to the ritual fringe that an Israelite male is commanded to wear on his garment. The male subject absorbs the female essence from the fringe by the visual act of looking upon it.

160. Slightly free quotation of 2 Chr 16:9, understanding "earth" as code for the *sefirah Malkhut*: the male deity's eyes "roam about her," absorbing the female juices from her.

161. Song 5:12.

162. Following the language of the Mishnah, m. Shabb. 9:3 (cf. Ber. 3:6, Miqv. 8:3–4).

163. Mishnah, m. Parah 9:3, quoted in the Talmud, b. Git. 86b, where Rashi explains it as our author says.

164. The God of Israel = Adam.

—*then she ate*;¹⁶⁵ and inasmuch as [the God of Israel and the Higher Shechinah] were together in a single shape, he ate as well, for she had given to him,¹⁶⁶ and the sex with her [*Malkhut*] was his as well. Then *the eyes of the two of them were opened*,¹⁶⁷ virgins no longer; and the Insolent Waters raged upward and laid hold on them.

That was why they required covering. Previously they had been *naked, unashamed*,¹⁶⁸ the Insolent Waters having no hold on them. But now that they had copulated, they did obtain a grip on them, and they therefore covered themselves.

Over this did the Root grow livid, and he decreed the serpent's expulsion from the *Tehiru*. *Cursed are you from all Heth the field*, was what he said¹⁶⁹—expelled, that is, for "cursing" is a term for pursuit and expulsion. *On your belly shall you go*: you shall not receive the female juices that would enable male juices to be poured upon you from the Distant One.¹⁷⁰ Rather, *on your belly*—i.e., the Shechinah, known to be alluded to as *the one bringing me forth from the womb*¹⁷¹—upon her shall you go; from her shall you receive effluence.

Hence: *dust shall you eat all the days of your life*. Not male juices from the Distant One, not the female juices that are the water from the *Tehiru*,¹⁷² but *dust* alone shall be your food. In other words, you shall receive from *Malkhut* herself, not from that which enters into her of male juices and female. Previously¹⁷³ he had dwelt in the land of "Nod," the

---

165. Finishing the interrupted quotation of Gen 3:6.

166. Paraphrasing the Biblical text.

167. Gen 3:7, understood to mean that their genital apertures were no longer blocked.

168. Gen 2:25.

169. Gen 3:14, interpreted as above, and with the words *mi-kol behemah* ("from [= more than] all animals"), which would severely undercut this interpretation, conveniently omitted from the quote.

170. A handicap that, as we will see in chapter 9, Sabbatai Zevi was able to overcome through his apostasy.

171. *Gohi mi-baten*, Ps 22:10. The author associates *gohi* with *gahon*, the word used for "belly" in Gen 3:14; and *baten*—which can also mean "belly" as well as "womb"—can be used in Kabbalah as an epithet for *Malkhut* (Cordovero, *Sha'ar 'Erkhei ha-Kinnuyim*, s.v.). "Shechinah" here, as the context shows, is the Lower Shechinah, *Malkhut*.

172. Presumably, that which has been purified and raised through *Malkhut*'s nightly incursions into the *Tehiru*, as described near the beginning of this section.

173. *Mi-qedem*, alluding to Gen 4:16, where Cain is said to dwell in the land of Nod *qidmat 'eden*, understood by our author as "prior to Eden" (and cf. 2:8, where Eden is itself called *mi-qedem*).

wineskin filled with living water.¹⁷⁴ But now it is decreed that he must eat from the elements of *Malkhut*, who is symbolized by *dust*.

[p. 113] *I will set enmity*—suffering and hatred, that is—*between you and the woman*.¹⁷⁵ This is set forth in the Zohar to the Torah portion *Bereshit* (page 22), previously quoted at length,¹⁷⁶ where Creation-Human is called A THOUGHT-BEGOTTEN SON who is bound to SIN AGAINST YOU, and who therefore is HIS MOTHER'S GRIEF, this being their *enmity*. When in that passage Father says that [Creation-Human] is bound to cause sin for Emanation-Human, this refers to what has just been described—for it was he who caused her to sin, and him as well.¹⁷⁷

Between your seed and her seed. Had it not been for the sin, the vessels that are Cain's offspring¹⁷⁸ would have been at evening time¹⁷⁹ gathered into one, and risen to be mended. But now they remain below in the Insolent Waters, and they are enemies of the Holy Merkavah; hence *between the seed* of the woman, representing the structure of the Merkavah, versus *your seed*, the vessels and bodies of the above-mentioned *sefirot* of Abel.¹⁸⁰ *He shall bruise your head*, referring to *your seed*, whose head the Merkavah strikes, grinding down upon it; *and you shall bruise his heel*, for they are able to lay hold upon the heel of the God of Israel, as hinted

---

174. Gen 4:16, equating "Nod" with the Higher Shechinah; see above, section 2. "He" is now Cain, equated with the serpent on the one hand, and with "Primordial Creation-Human" on the other. In line with the author's understanding of *qidmat 'eden* (see the preceding note), and in flagrant contradiction to the Biblical sequence, the serpent's condemnation is treated as something coming *after* Cain's sojourn in "Nod."

175. Gen 3:15.

176. Chapter 3, section 7. *Tugah* in Prov 10:1, which the author has previously explained to mean "contemplation," is now taken in its more usual sense of "grief."

177. Taking the Zohar's *le-mehtei*, "to sin," as though it were causative. "Emanation-Human" is the Shape that emerged from Ein Sof (above, chapter 2), in its broadest sense incorporating the Distant One, the God of Israel and the Higher Shechinah, but normally used for the last two—as here, where "her" is the Shechinah and "him" the God of Israel—or for the God of Israel alone. "Father" is the God of Israel speaking to the Shechinah ("Mother"), the terminology drawn from Prov 10:1.

178. Above, section 4. Cain and the serpent being the same, "Cain's offspring" are the Biblical "serpent's seed."

179. *Le'et 'erev*; the language suggests the mysterious prophecy in Zech 14:7, "There shall be a day known to YHVH which is neither day nor night, and at evening time there shall be light." But it is unclear why the author invokes it here. Perhaps he is thinking of Gen 3:8, where God's confrontation with his disobedient creatures takes place in the evening? But the Hebrew is altogether different.

180. This reading, though found in all the mss., must be an error for "Cain."

at in *his hand grasping the heel*.[181] And who is the one who grasps Esau's heel? He is the one who grasps—and you must understand.[182]

7. Genesis 3: The Punishment of God

[The God of Israel has sinned against the Root; now he must atone. He must depart for the heights, to enter the asexual state of "entrancement," alienated from the Female with whom, in his violation, he had fused. Even when "mended" and returned to his place, as we shall see in the next section, his primordial nakedness is lost.]

To the woman he said, I will greatly increase [fol. 26a] *your difficulty*[183] *and your pregnancy*, inasmuch as her genital must be narrow so that the Insolent Waters not penetrate her, and she therefore gives birth with difficulty—as hinted at in *the doe, her genital is narrow*.[184]

And your desire shall be toward your man—to be interpreted presently.

To Adam he said, Cursed is the ground on account of you. This means that she was expelled,[185] for he had to separate from her in order that [the Insolent Waters] not be able to take hold of him. *With difficulty*

---

181. Gen 25:26: "Afterward his brother emerged, his hand grasping Esau's heel."

182. The allusion is deliberately cryptic. "Esau," as we have seen, is a symbolic representation of Christianity, both in its often hostile historical aspect and in its ideal aspect, as a religion of pure Grace, superior to Judaism (above, chapter 2, section 5 and chapter 3, section 9). Here he seems to be equated with the God of Israel, as well as with the Moses/Messiah of section 5, above. The mysterious "one who grasps" is presumably also the serpent-Messiah, Sabbatai Zevi.

183. *'Itzavon*, normally translated "pain" here and "toil" in the following verse. In both passages, I translate the word the way the author seems to have understood it: "difficulty."

184. Talmud, b. B. Bat. 16b: "The doe's genital is narrow; and when she crouches to give birth, I appoint for her a serpent [*draqon*] who bites her on the genital, and it relaxes so she can deliver" (cf. b. 'Erub. 54b, Yoma 29a). The Zohar (III, 249a–b; cf. II, 52b, 219b) develops this image into a powerful and resonant myth of the Shechinah (= *sefirah Malkhut*) as a doe journeying by night through the mountains. Ready to give birth, she finds herself closed up. She "moans and emits cry after cry," whereupon "the Blessed Holy One hears her and . . . brings forth a great serpent from among the mountains of darkness. It goes among the mountains, its mouth licking dust [cf. Gen 3:14], until it reaches that doe. It comes and bites her on that place twice." At the first bite, blood comes out; at the second, water, "and she is opened and gives birth." Our author understands the "suffering" and "pregnancy" of Gen 3:16 to allude to this myth.

185. Understanding "curse" to refer to expulsion, as in the preceding section, and the "ground" as symbolic of the Shechinah.

shall you eat her[186] *all the days of your life*, meaning that in order to mend this, to keep the external forces and the Insolent Waters from getting a hold upon him, he was compelled to enter into a state of entrancement, to ascend above the Curtain, as has earlier been said, and there to remain until he was mended.[187] This is the hidden significance of Adam's having sat *in the waters of the Upper Gihon*,[188] referring to the place of Ein Sof, of whom it is written that *he uses darkness as his concealment*;[189] and this is hinted at in *man knows not his burial*, as I have earlier explained at length.[190]

[p. 114] At that time, the Female received only "bread of shame" and *difficulty*-bread; and when the Scripture says, *With difficulty shall you eat her*, it specifies *all the days of your life*, i.e., before he ascended on high in the state of entrancement.[191] *Thorns and thistles shall she bring forth to* you, because she had absorbed the Insolent Waters, which were not yet suitable for the growing of plants and could yield only thorns and

---

186. Taking the Hebrew of Gen 3:17 hyperliterally: the Higher Shechinah ("ground") is the direct object of the verb "eat." As in the previous section, "eating" is sexual intercourse, for which the God of Israel is temporarily incapacitated.

187. On "entrancement" (*dormita*), see above, chapter 2, section 2, and especially note 25; and below, chapter 9, section 2. On the "curtain" that separates the Distant One from the God of Israel, see chapter 5, section 1. It will be observed that the Distant One takes no part in the action described in this rendering of the Eden story. As a detached observer to it? Or, as suggested in chapter 2, section 2 (note 34), incorporated within the God of Israel?

188. For seven weeks according to the midrash, doing penance for his sin, until his body became like a sponge (*Pirqei de-Rabbi Eliezer*, chapter 20; discussed in Ginzberg, *Legends*, 5:114–16).

189. Ps 18:12.

190. Chapter 2, section 2, where "knows not" (Deut 34:6) is understood as a negation of sexual coupling.

191. And he was as though dead. We learn here that the God of Israel's sexual incapacity predated his deathlike state, that even while still "alive," yet unmended from his sin, he could copulate only "with difficulty." The author's intention in the first part of the sentence is not fully clear. "Bread of shame" (*nahama de-kissufa*) is a post-Zoharic expression that entered Kabbalistic thought from the writings of Joseph Karo (1488–1575) and Eibeschuetz's younger contemporary Moses Hayyim Luzzatto (1707–1746), indicating sustenance granted out of unmerited grace, which shames the person consuming it. The author seems not to use it in this specific sense, but as a more general reference to the "shame" that infected the couple's relations after their sin (versus their initial freedom from it, Gen 2:25), and which induced or amounted to their sexual "difficulty." (The female's receiving "bread" is functionally equivalent to the male's "eating her.")

thistles—and plants, which are inferior to animals and rational creatures, in that the souls of the latter are more completely mended.[192]

Those Insolent Waters could in no way have served her as rain, as previously indicated.[193] Rather, all that she had in the way of male juices, which might allow the "ground" [= Shechinah] to yield her fruit, was in the way of sweat from the God of Israel; this must be her "rain," the male juices that would allow her to bear fruit, to beget offspring. This is the inner meaning of *Your heavens shall be like bronze*, which Rashi interprets to mean that [the sky] sweats and thus moistens the earth;[194] and such was the case here. Hence the text says, *With the sweat of your face shall you eat bread*.[195]

Until you return to the ground—that is to say, that higher region represented by *Elleh* and "Nothingness," and as darkness and as entrancement, from which he was taken.[196] *For you are dust*—referring to the God of Israel in his esoteric identity as "the Lord's dust" (and also Pharaoh)[197]—and therefore *you must return to dust*, namely that Nothingness of which we have spoken.

This is what is meant by, *YHVH God said, The Human has become like one of us, knowing* and so forth.[198] *And now, lest he extend his hand* to couple with the Higher Shechinah[199]—a coupling he could not possibly

---

192. This awkward addition to the sentence, apparently contradicting what has gone before, seems to be a comment on the words of Genesis that the author has left unquoted: "and you shall eat the herbs of the field."

193. In chapter 5, section 7, where "rain" represents the plenteous effluence ("male juices") the Shechinah would normally receive from the God of Israel.

194. Free quotation of Deut 28:23. Rashi's comment on the verse assumes that bronze, unlike the iron of the parallel Lev 26:19, is a metal that "sweats"; a bronze sky will therefore yield a certain small amount of moisture, though far short of a full rain. The equation of "heaven" with the male potency of divinity, "earth" with the female, is a staple of Kabbalah.

195. I.e., have sexual intercourse.

196. The passive, undifferentiated female substrate of Ein Sof, as explained above, chapter 1, section 5, with "entrancement" now added to the mix. "Ground" now refers, not to the Shechinah but to this loftier female, from which the God of Israel once emerged.

197. עפר ה׳, "the Lord's dust," is an anagram of פרעה, "Pharaoh." On the extraordinary equation of the Biblical Pharaoh with the God of Israel, see above, sections 1 and 3.

198. Gen 3:22, suppressing the words "good and evil," which are restored in ms. Jerusalem 2491.

199. Which Genesis calls "eating" from the Tree of Life. The author seems to take "extend his hand" to mean that he makes an attempt at sex which is doomed to fail, and

have achieved at that time, prior to his mending—he was therefore sent upward, to the place of Nothingness, *to serve the Ground from which he was taken* in a state of entrancement and death. [The Shechinah] also was driven from her place, and he [the Root] set above her *Netzah, Hod* and *Yesod*, which are (as we know) symbolized by the cherubim and the flaming sword.[200] This is the meaning of the words, *For your sin was your Mother banished*—which, as the Zohar tells us, is addressed to the "thought-begotten" entity, Creation-Human.[201]

(And note that the title *YHVH Elohim* is used throughout this passage, thereby indicating the Root, who is represented by both *YHVH* and *Elohim*, "God.")

8. Postlude: The (Homo)erotics of God

[Ensheathed now in skin, for fear of the Insolent Waters, the God of Israel must roll the skin from his penis for sex with his Shechinah. But he also engages in a different kind of sex, involving anal penetration, with the dominant male figure of the Root. This can take on a distinctly sadomasochistic character, the God of Israel liberally wounded in the course of what amounts to a rape by the Root, who unlike the God of Israel is unrestrained by any Torah or commandments.

The notion of wounds inflicted on the body of a divine being seems alien and bizarre in a Jewish text. I know of no parallel to it in any Jewish source, Sabbatian or non-Sabbatian, Kabbalistic or non-Kabbalistic. But it has a strong parallel in the contemporary Moravian veneration of the salvific wounds, vagina-like, inflicted on the crucified Christ by the phallic spear. ("Powerful wounds of Jesus, So moist, so gory .... You are so succulent, whatever comes near becomes like wounds

---

which must therefore be forestalled.

200. The trio of *sefirot* which stand between *Tif'eret* (the "Enclothement" of the God of Israel) and *Malkhut* (that of the Shechinah), here functioning to keep the two apart. Gen 3:24 represents them as the (two) cherubim and the "flaming sword," which "guard the path of (to?) the Tree of Life," the Higher Shechinah. The equation of the cherubim with *Netzah* and *Hod* is indeed rooted in the traditional Kabbalah; the "flaming sword" is more usually identified with *Malkhut*, but its phallic quality makes plausible an association with *Yesod*.

201. Isa 50:1, quoted in Zohar, I, 22a–b; above, chapter 3, section 7. In the Zohar, as here, Isaiah's בפשעכם is written without the *yod*, converting the plural "for your sins" into singular: the specific sin of Adam (Zohar) or the serpent = Creation-Human (our author).

I CAME THIS DAY TO THE SPRING

and flowing with blood. Juicy wounds of Jesus . . . I crawl to you."[202] And of the instrument of wounding: "I kiss the Spear . . . I lay myself in the Hole made by the Spear. . . . Soldier, for this Pricking with the Spear I give thee Thanks."[203]) In the Christian context, unlike the Jewish, the image is natural and meaningful. It seems most reasonable to suspect direct borrowing.

Anal sex, we are told, is part of our future in these lower realms, for the Shechinah and presumably others as well. A blatantly obscene "mending," performed or believed to have been performed by Sabbatai Zevi, has inaugurated or at least foreshadowed this development.]

Once [the God of Israel] had sat in that higher realm that is represented by *the waters of the Upper Gihon*, he and his Shechinah were mended. Once more they dwelt in their proper place, as they had originally. [p. 115] But now he must be clothed, that the Insolent Waters might not lay hold on him; and this was the *tunics of skin* (*'or*, spelled with an *ayin*) that at times were *of light* (*or*, spelled with an *aleph*), which we know to be the esoteric referent of *hashmal*.[204] The external forces, in other words, at times have a hold on him, and it is called *skin*, whereas at other times they have none, and then it is called *light* with an *aleph*, as is well known.

During sex, he rolls back[205] this skin from upon his penis, in order that the skin have no share in the reception of the holy semen; he

---

202. From the 1744 *Litany of the Wounds of the Husband*. See Atwood, *Community*, 102–8, 203–8, 233–40.

203. From a Moravian hymn ca. 1750: Schuchard, *William Blake*, 36.

204. Gen 3:21: "YHVH God made for Adam and his wife garments of skin and clothed them." *Midrash Genesis Rabbah* 20:12 quotes a variant, supposedly found in "the Torah of Rabbi Meir," which reads in place of "skin" (עוֹר, *'or*) the almost identical-sounding but differently spelled *or* (אוֹר), "light." Zohar, I, 36b, makes exegetical play with the two variants: "At first they were *garments of light* . . . and the supernal angels would come to bask in that light. . . . Now that they had sinned, they were *garments of skin*, in which the skin takes pleasure but not the soul." Our author takes a different tack: "Adam" = God of Israel (only he, and not Eve/Shechinah, seems to be envisioned in this connection) clothed himself after his sin in a garment that was sometimes of "skin," sometimes of "light." On *hashmal*, the mysterious word that occurs in Ezekiel's visions (1:4, 27, 8:2) and is usually translated "amber" or "electrum," see below.

205. *Matznif*, normally used for "enwrapping" or "veiling" something (like a human face: Rashi to Isa 3:19). The context here requires the opposite meaning, of unveiling or exposing—the skin, while protecting the God of Israel from "external" pollution, has acquired some of that pollution and therefore must not be recipient of the "holy semen." The choice of *matznif* to express this may be significant: the root (צנף) is that of *tzanif* and *mitznefet*, "turban," with all the turban's implications, for the Sabbatians, as a symbol of Islam. See above, chapter 5, note 28.

consequently rolls it, folds it back from his penis. This is represented by the act of *peri'ah* [in circumcision],[206] and it is done at the time of intercourse—and in secret, that the external forces may have no awareness of it. That is why [the skin] is called *hashmal*: because it is "circumcised," *niMAL*, in secret, *HASHai*.[207]

Now, when he has sexual connection with the Root, he must strip this skin away, as hinted at in *I have stripped off my tunic*.[208] At times, however, when earthly sinfulness predominates and the Judgments have the upper hand, the skin cannot be peeled off, as indicated in *their skin clung to their flesh*,[209] and in this event [the Root] copulates as if through a sheet.

This is as our ancient rabbis have said, that one makes a hole in the sheet and through it he copulates;[210] and in just this way [the Root] makes a wound, a perforation in the skin, and afterward performs the coupling. This is, as I have written above, the hidden meaning of *what are those wounds?*[211] It is the hidden sense as well of *beneath my skin this one was knocked*, this beneath-the-skin "knocking" referring to copulation, as indicated by the pronoun *zot*, "this one."[212] These words were spoken

---

206. An element of traditional Jewish circumcision, in which not only the foreskin must be removed, but the membrane beneath it that covers the glans peeled back as well.

207. No doubt inspired by Talmud, b. Hag. 13a-b, which similarly etymologizes *hashmal* by breaking the word into its component sounds and associating each one with a distinct word. The author's specific associations, however, are entirely original with him.

208. Song 5:3, spoken by the female, in whose role the God of Israel now finds himself. (The word used for "tunic," *kuttonet*, is the same as in Gen 3:21.) In chapter 2, section 2, the author has described the Root's sexual relations with the Shape, considered as a totality incorporating the God of Israel. Now the object of his lust is specifically the male God of Israel, and their connection explicitly homoerotic.

209. Misquotation of Lam 4:8 ("their skin clung to their bones; it was dry as wood"), corrected in mss. Oxford 955 and Jerusalem 3100 in accordance with the Biblical text.

210. Probably referring to Palestinian Talmud, y. Yebam. 1:1, where Rabbi Jose ben Halafta is said to have performed his levirate duties "through a sheet." The author's paraphrase of the Talmudic passage transforms a specific incident, idiosyncratic and therefore memorable, into something habitual and perhaps prescribed. The famous "hole in the sheet," customarily dismissed as urban legend (see, e.g., snopes.com), turns out to have been—at least in the eighteenth century—real after all.

211. Free quotation of Zech 13:6, where the question, "What are these bruises between your hands?" is answered, "It is where I was bruised in the house of my lovers." See above, chapter 2, note 19.

212. Job 19:26, substituting the feminine singular verb *niqefah* for the Bible's plural *niqefu*, and treating it as a passive with the feminine *zot*, "this one," as subject. Why

by Job, who, as the Gemara explains,²¹³ symbolizes the God of Israel: *Job was not*—i.e., he cannot be equated with *Binah*, who is represented by the word *hayah*, "was"—*and he was not created*—nor is he the Shechinah, who is a created Glory—*but he was a mashal*, i.e., *Tif'eret*, who is *moshel*, ruler of the earth, represented by the *mishlei*, proverbs of Solomon, the king to whom peace belongs.²¹⁴ Understand this.

This is what [Job] means when he says, *The one who is in hair*—i.e., the Root, who is represented by "hairs"—*bruises me*, which is to say, crushes me fine.²¹⁵ *Freely he multiplies my wounds*—"freely," unrestrained

---

zot should have overtones of copulation is unclear to me; but on the sexual sense of "knocking," cf. the British use of "knocking shop" as slang for a brothel. It is hardly coincidence that these words are followed immediately in Job 19:26 by the freighted passage *mi-besari ehezeh eloah*, understood by the Kabbalists as "from my flesh I can visualize God" and used by them (and by our author) to justify their anthropomorphic, sexualized depictions of the Deity. See above, chapter 1, section 1.

213. There follows a hyperliteral exegesis of a passage from the Talmud, b. B. Bat. 15a, that might more reasonably be translated: "Job never existed, but was a purely symbolic figure." The equation of Job with the male deity serves our author's purpose, in that it helps him identify the "God of Israel" as the passive recipient of the Root's sadistic sexual attentions. But it is also surely linked to the Sabbatian interpretation, developed by Nathan of Gaza in his *Treatise of the Dragons*, that treats Job as a "type" of the suffering Messiah Sabbatai Zevi: Scholem, *Sabbatai Ṣevi*, 308–10.

214. The thrust of this complex analysis of a fairly straightforward Talmudic text is that Job cannot be understood as standing for any of the female aspects of divinity—whether for the higher *sefirah Binah* (whose association with the verb *hayah*, "was," is unknown to me from any other source) or for the Shechinah/*Malkhut*—but rather for the central masculine figure of the sefirotic system, who *as a male* is object of the Root's lust. The characterization of the Shechinah as a "created glory" (*kavod nivra*) derives from the tenth-century philosopher Saadiah Gaon and the Hasidim of medieval Germany: Scholem, *Major Trends*, 111–16; Wolfson, *Through a Speculum*, 126–27. *Mashal*, in its Talmudic context, plainly means "parable." But our author uses two separate word associations to connect it with the male divinity: (1) *mashal* = *moshel*, "ruler of the earth" (or "the land," referring to Gen 45:8, 26, where the *moshel* is Joseph, representation of the quintessentially masculine *Yesod*); and (2) *mashal* = *mishlei*, "proverbs," linking it to Solomon. The explanation of the name "Solomon" (*shelomoh*) as referring to "the King to whom peace [*shalom*] belongs," i.e. God, goes back to the rabbinic midrash, e.g. *Midrash Exodus Rabbah* 52:5. The Kabbalists, followed by our author, took up this derivation and used it to make "Solomon" a symbol for *Tif'eret*, the male aspect of deity—especially in connection with the Song of Songs.

215. Job 9:17. In its context, *se'arah* certainly means "storm-wind." But a slightly different form of the word means "hair," and the author finds here a designation for the Root, whom he has earlier said to be represented by the "hairs" on the divine head that is the Distant One (above, chapter 2, section 3). The author draws his gloss on "bruise"—the same verb as in Gen 3:15—from Rashi to this passage, and he perhaps sees that "crushing" or "grinding" as a sexual metaphor (Job 31:10, as interpreted in the Talmud, b. Sotah 10a).

by commandments; for in the higher realms the commandments have no force. This is why it is called "wound" and "perforation."[216]

[Fol. 26b] Know: [the God of Israel] is at times the recipient [p. 116] of anal sex, as implied in the words *I made love to Israel, boy-fashion*.[217] Know also: in future time, when the Insolent Waters are gone from the earth and the *Tehiru* purified,[218] the Shechinah will engage in anal sex in the lower realms. This is the secret meaning of what the Gemara tells us, that *a woman will bear a child each day . . . and he showed him a hen*—which gives birth through the anus.[219] Understand.

And this was the symbolism of carrying the Torah scroll into the latrine. Understand.[220]

---

216. At the beginning of the preceding paragraph, though I do not understand why the author sees these specific terms as reflecting the sexual libertinism of the higher realms—on which see above, chapter 5, section 2—eventually to be bestowed upon a regenerated earth.

217. Hos 11:1, understood in a way that, even if the rest of this treatise were unobjectionable, would surely have been enough to get it banned.

218. An ironic turn of phrase: *tehiru* literally means "purity." It is not clear whether "earth" is intended literally or, as often in Kabbalah, as a symbol for the Shechinah.

219. Talmud, b. Shabb. 30b: when Rabban Gamaliel preaches that in messianic times "a woman will bear a child each day," a student mocks him. Gamaliel offers to show the student "an example of this in the present world," and produces a hen, which lays an egg every day. The contemporary hen is therefore a token of the messianic-age woman—and the hen, our author points out, lays eggs through her anus. She, and the female whom she betokens, may be supposed to copulate in the same way.

220. וזהו סוד הכנסת ס״ת לבה״כ והבן, *ve-zehu sod hakhnasat sefer torah le-vet ha-kisse' ve-haven*—ms. Oxford 976, supported by Jerusalem 3100—the symbolism too blatant for anyone to fail to understand. Ms. Jerusalem 2491 originally contained these words, but some shocked reader scraped them out of the text with a sharp instrument. Ms. Oxford 955 alters לבה״כ to the pointless לבהכנ״ס, "into the synagogue," and adds, "which mending he performed," plainly referring to Sabbatai Zevi. The addition is plausible enough, but I know of no other testimony that Sabbatai performed this specific act.

7

The Geography of God

1. The Seated God, Summoned to "Arise!"

[By which act the full luminescence of Divinity, currently confined to the World of Emanation, will shine forth in the messianic future upon these lower worlds as well.]

So, to resume, the worlds were mended.[1] The God of Israel dwelt in *Tif'eret* of Emanation, while the Shechinah, as we have seen, dwelt within *Yesod* in the character of Zillah.[2] You must realize that in the other three worlds of Creation, Fashioning, and Making, the God of Israel similarly dwells in *Tif'eret*. Yet there is a difference.

The God of Israel, as it were, sits upon a throne; and this is *Malkhut*, which is called "throne" inasmuch as it is common knowledge that the throne is her symbol. When a person sits on a throne, his feet below him, he looks like this ⌐, and so it is here. The Straight Line reaches as far as the floor of the World of Emanation, diffusing itself within the Shechinah much as a seated person would;[3] from there on down it remains diffused. The light does not reach [the lower three worlds] in the form of a straight

---

1. From the Shattering, and perhaps also from the subsequent "sin" of the divinities.
2. The female who dwells in the same vessel with the male (the name drawn from Gen 4:19), as opposed to the second female, who strikes off on her own in the *sefirah Malkhut*; above, chapter 4, section 2. On the Higher Shechinah's choice of this female for her "Enclothement," see above, chapter 6, section 6.
3. When I sit down, the vertical line of my body is disrupted by the bending of my joints. The Shechinah, dwelling in *Yesod* just above *Malkhut*, corresponds to the seat within which the hitherto vertical "Straight Line" becomes bent and thereby diffused.

line, and therefore is not one-thousandth as bright as in the World of Emanation, travelling as it does by a crooked path.

This is what the Bible means by *You, O holy one, sit enthroned upon the Praises of Israel*: the God of Israel is called "holy," and he sits upon the Praises of Israel.[4] But afterward, in the Mending,[5] he will rise to his feet and all the worlds will be equal. In the future Mending-time, therefore, all the worlds of Creation, Fashioning, and Making will be equal in their luminescence to the World of Emanation, and *on that day his feet shall stand upon the Mount of Olives*, his position erect.[6] This is why David prayed, *Arise, O Lord*; for when he rises, the World of Making shall become purified.[7]

[p. 117] From this, you will understand what the Zohar means by saying that the "tower that flies in the air" represents the God of Israel, symbolized by the letter *lamed* [ל]—as we have said, that he is in the shape of a reverse *lamed*, ך, with a hook at its top like the letter *yod* [י], which stands for the head of the Distant One.[8]

2. The Diagonal

> [We now consider more closely how the geography of the upper worlds relates to our own. There is a reversal of qualities between north and south, in the earth versus the divine structures. The lower one goes in those structures, moreover, the narrower the safe, built-up territory of the Merkavah becomes. All around rage the Insolent Waters, "like land encompassed by the sea," intercepting the effluence that descends from above except for a narrow line at the center, defined by the

---

4. Ps 22:4. The author's equation of "Praises of Israel" with *Malkhut* is rooted in the traditional Kabbalah.

5. Of the messianic future.

6. Zech 14:4.

7. The author understands the "World of Making" as our lower world, which will enjoy in messianic ("Mending") times the sexual liberties, currently restricted to the higher spheres, alluded to at the end of chapter 6. The call to "arise, O Lord" occurs repeatedly in the book of Psalms: 3:8, 7:7, 9:20, 10:12, 17:13, 132:8.

8. The reference is apparently to Zohar, II, 91a, which links the letter *lamed* that opens the prohibition in the First Commandment ("you shall have no other gods before me") to the Talmud's cryptic allusion to "a tower that flies in the air" (b. Hag. 15b, Sanh. 106b). But the Zohar's point is that the "tower" suggests the Tower of Babel and therefore idolatrous worship; it offers no support for the author's suggestion, which seems without basis in the traditional Kabbalah, that the *lamed*-tower represents the God of Israel.

point of contact between the *sefirot Yesod* and *Malkhut* . . . (to be continued in the next section).]

Know this also: that the structure of the worlds, vis-à-vis the *Tehiru*, is at a diagonal, thusly—

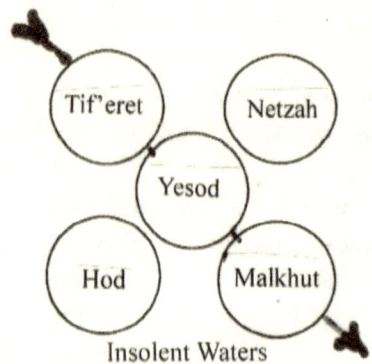

—for it is the Merkavah's way to descend diagonally, as a Straight Line indeed, yet at a slant.

You will understand from this how the Zohar can say that the north is THE PLACE OF THE POWER OF FIRE whereas here below, the northern regions are cold and moist. Along the same lines, the south is said to be the place of mercy, of water, whereas here below it is hot and dry; see the Zohar to the Torah portion *Va-era*, which seems at first wholly unintelligible, but in the light of what we have said makes perfect sense.[9] Inasmuch as all the Merkavah's lines are diagonal—for that is the way of the Merkavah, to descend on the diagonal—if you were to draw a line from the north like this \ and from the south like this / and then combine them, north and south would appear like this—

---

9. The author has given a very loose quotation of the Zohar, II, 24a: "Fire is on the left, toward the north; for fire has within it the power of heat, and its dryness is intense, and 'north' [being cold and moist] is the opposite of that. And the two are mingled together." The Zoharic passage—which is, as our author says, not easy to make sense of—reflects on the paradox that "fire," "left," and "north" are all symbolic of the *sefirah Gevurah*, yet in these earthly regions "north" is the very opposite of fiery.

North   South

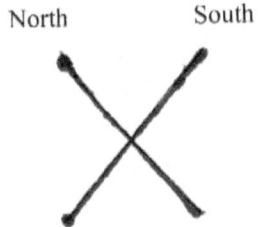

—such that the earthly region, which [as seen from] above is "north," receives the straight line from the south and is therefore moist. Similarly the reverse: that which [as seen from] above is "south," has on the ground the "northern" quality of heat. Understand this.

Now, there is a consequence to the Merkavah's being on a diagonal. Up above in the place of Emanation it occupies a broad area within the *Tehiru*, progressively constricting as one moves downward, to the point that in the World of Making, below, it[10] is exceedingly narrow, and the Insolent Waters swell upward until they literally are beneath the floor of Making's *Malkhut*.[11] Wherever the Merkavah is constructed, the waters retreat and clear the space. Yet they remain surrounding it, as we have seen, and therefore encircle *Malkhut* on all sides, like land encompassed by the sea—thus do the Insolent Waters encompass *Malkhut*.[12] Even on the floor [p. 118] of Emanation, *Malkhut* is beset by water on all sides, as may be seen from the diagram above; yet in that higher region the intense luminosity of Emanation prevents them from flowing with any great force.

You will understand from this that all the effluence that reaches *Malkhut* from *Netzah* and *Hod* must pass through the Insolent Waters. These intercept it and transfer it to the other half of the *Tehiru*, that which partakes of the nature of "abyss" and "formlessness."[13] This is the flow of

---

10. The subject must be the Merkavah. All mss. supply "the *Tehiru*" as subject, which makes no sense and must be deleted as a dittograph from the preceding *le-mattah*, "below" (למטה הטהי׳, in ms. Jerusalem 3100).

11. That is, the manifestation of the *sefirah Malkhut* in the lowest of the four "worlds."

12. "Land," in Kabbalistic symbolism.

13. As described above, chapter 3, sections 4–5. This earlier passage speaks of the "Impure Merkavah" but does not mention its "Princes"—a personification of the forces of destruction that rarely occurs in this text.

effluence to the Princes of the Impure Merkavah, and it is why all the Kabbalists assert that the Externals' point of attachment is at *Netzah* and *Hod*; for, as we have just seen, [it is there that] they receive all the effluence. It will follow that even as far as *Malkhut* is concerned, it is from her edges that the Insolent Waters receive what they do. At her center, by contrast—that is to say, her point of contact [with *Yesod*]—she receives without any involvement of the rest of the Insolent Waters.[14]

3. Exile and Its Healing

[... which point of contact corresponds, on our earth, to the Land of Israel—not the center of the world as the medieval maps depicted it, but corresponding to the sweet spot that is the center of the Merkavah's structure. Effluence from above, prayers from below, can only be transmitted directly through that sweet spot; elsewhere, they are intercepted by the Insolent Waters. This is the uniqueness of the Land of Israel, and the tragedy of Israel's exile from it.

So what is to be done?

Answer: take the battle to the enemy. The Shechinah—not the Higher Shechinah now, but the Lower one that is the *sefirah Malkhut*—must nightly enter the Insolent Waters "with the fiery heat of blazing Judgment." Not to punish or destroy them, for God "casts off no one," but to purify them and give them life. Our earthly experience, that the seas steadily shrink while the land grows ever larger, vouches for the ultimate success of her mission. It is a hazardous undertaking. But shielded by her virginity, as we shall see in the next chapter, she is supremely qualified to carry it out.]

With this, you will understand the distinction between the Land of Israel and the lands beyond.

On the ground, to be sure, the Land of Israel is not located at the center of the world.[15] But—prayers being the female juices that evoke the corresponding [fol. 27a] male juices [from above], and they travel upward along the Straight Line—when you extend that Straight Line from [the Land's] location, you will find it reaching the point of contact

---

14. I am not sure what the author means by "*the rest* of the Insolent Waters." But his overall point seems clear. The arrow in the diagram at the beginning of this section, as found in ms. Oxford 955, indicates the downward flow of the effluence through *Yesod* into *Malkhut*.

15. As depicted, e.g., in the famous Bünting Clover Leaf Map of 1581.

between *Malkhut* and *Yesod*, where the Insolent Waters have no adhesion. This is what makes the Land of Israel uniquely special; whereas the lands beyond it are distant from that point of contact, such that the effluence that comes to them must transit through the Insolent Waters which intercept and absorb it. This is the reality of Israel's exile, and the Shechinah's: that [the Insolent Waters] receive it all, leaving only a specimen for the Jewish people. Prayers, likewise, must pass through them and are blocked by them. Hence Scripture says, *You are sheltered within a cloud of yours [that prayer may not pass through]*,[16] referring to those Insolent Waters that are a *shelter of watery darkness*[17]—dark waters indeed; and they block *prayer from passing through to you*.

You will recall what we have earlier said, and now we shall extend the discussion: that the Insolent Waters have the character of *Ma'aseh Bereshit*, of souls not yet completely ripened.[18] The closer they are to the Land of Israel, symbolic of *Malkhut*, the fitter and more suitable they are to receive purification; but those waters that are distant, in the remote north, are known to be frozen solid into ice.[19] [p. 119] And it is in order to give them light,[20] to gather them under the Shechinah's wings[21] and grant them life—for God *casts off no one*[22]—that the Shechinah enters into these waters each night with the fiery heat of blazing Judgment. Thus does she purify the waters that are near her with the heat of fire.[23]

Like water that is no good for drinking or any other purpose, yet through the process of heating can be purified and made usable, so it is here: in her character as Judgment, and as fiery heat, she purifies them until they are fit to be good water. She then receives them; waters of Grace are poured upon them, and by this they are restored to life.[24] She

16. Lam 3:44.

17. Ps 18:12.

18. See above, chapter 3, section 2.

19. The varying condition of terrestrial seas is thus emblematic of the various states of the Insolent Waters that surround *Malkhut*.

20. *Le-ha'ir lahem*, from Exod 13:21, referring to the pillar of fire about which the author will presently speak.

21. A rabbinic expression for converting people to Judaism; e.g., Talmud, b. Sanh. 96b; *Midrash Genesis Rabbah* 39:16.

22. 2 Sam 14:14, following the interpretation of the medieval commentator David Kimhi.

23. As described briefly in chapter 4, section 3, and developed fully in chapter 8.

24. The syntax here is choppy, and the subject of the "pouring" left undetermined. The subsequent discussion of the Red Heifer, and the parallel in chapter 4, section 3,

does something similar with the waters that are close by the land, letting them be absorbed into it so that the waters become dry land and the land grows larger day by day. Thus it happens in the material world: each day the land grows larger while the sea progressively shrinks. Even in the far north, where all is frozen ice, she heats and burns it with the power of Judgment until it is made into dust, just as they do in the far north here below on earth, where they burn the ice and it turns into dust.

The Shechinah thus bestows life upon all. She purges the chaff from the wheat; she turns [the Insolent Waters] into souls. This is the esoteric significance of *the one who renews each day perpetually the Ma'aseh Bereshit*:[25] each night she enters there, gathers them and purifies them and makes new souls out of them and brings them to life. They then partake of the nature of sacred offerings; for those souls ascend from her, higher and higher, up to the Root of Ein Sof, as we have said—THAT CONCEALED PLACE of which we have earlier spoken at length.[26]

This is the significance of the Heifer, female in her character and also *adummah*, "red"—that is to say, deriving from the land of Edom, as we have said.[27] For this reason the priest burns her to *dust*, afterward empowering over [those dust-souls] the waters of Grace, which are *living waters*, in the *vessel* of *Malkhut*.[28] In that vessel they come to life, and through this process they are made fit to be pure and to receive purification. [p. 120] It is the secret sense of the Scripture, *And*

---

show that it is not the Shechinah herself—hers is the preparatory fire of Judgment, not the life-giving water of Grace—but the higher *sefirah Hesed*, represented by the "priest" of Biblical ritual. See above, chapter 4, note 51.

25. From the *Yotzer* prayer in the liturgy of the daily morning service, normally taken to mean that God daily renews his creation (Birnbaum, *Daily Prayer Book*, 71–72). Our author, however, assumes that the author(s) of the prayer understood *Ma'aseh Bereshit* as he does: a technical term for the chaotic world of the *Tehiru* and the Insolent Waters.

26. Above, chapter 4, section 3, alluding to Zohar, II, 239a.

27. The ritual of the Red Heifer (*parah adummah*) is set forth in Num 19: a red heifer is sacrificed and burnt to ashes, which are then placed into a vessel and water added; the resulting liquid is to be sprinkled on those who have become unclean by contact with the dead. In the author's symbolism, the Heifer is "the Female"— presumably the Higher Shechinah indwelling within the *sefirah Malkhut*—while the vessel in which her ashes are placed is *Malkhut* herself. Her coming from "the land of Edom" (the same Hebrew root as *adummah*, "red") conveys to our author that she derives from the sphere of pure Grace.

28. Following Num 19:17, where the Hebrew speaks of "dust" (and not "ashes" as in verses 9-10). Note the shift in symbolism: although the Heifer herself is the Female, the dust to which she is reduced represents the Insolent Waters burned by her fire.

YHVH—accompanied by his "court," meaning the Female—*went before them by day, and by night in a pillar of fire to give them light*,[29] namely to illuminate the souls and to bring them to life. It is the esoteric reason why each day [upon awakening] we bless *the one who restores souls to dead bodies*,[30] alluding to the *Ma'aseh Bereshit*, which is like dead bodies whom God restores, making them into living souls.

And it will explain for you why *the springs of water are hot in the nighttime*:[31] the Shechinah walks amid them in the power of fire.

---

29. Exod 13:21, omitting the pillar of cloud that went before the Israelites by day. It is a midrashic principle that the word "and," when prefixed to the divine name (*ve-YHVH*), means that God is accompanied by his court (*Midrash Genesis Rabbah* 51:2); the traditional Kabbalah goes on to equate that "court" with the Shechinah (e.g., Zohar, I, 64b).

30. Talmud, b. Ber. 60b.

31. Talmud, b. Pesah. 94a, which adduces this alleged fact in support of the opinion of the "Gentile scholars" that by night the sun travels beneath the ground back to its rising point in the east. (A distorted awareness of the Greek view that the earth is round and the sun revolves around it?) Our author's interpretation is yet more fanciful.

8

The Virgin of God

1. The Sin of the Blasphemer

[The "son of an Israelite woman" by an Egyptian father, according to Lev 24:10–23, perpetrated an unspecified "blasphemy" and was stoned to death for it. What was that blasphemy? Following the Zohar's interpretation of the Biblical passage, our author explains that the man defended his mother's adultery with the Egyptian by claiming it was no worse than what the Shechinah does every night, allowing herself to be penetrated by the Insolent Waters in violation of her pledge of virginity.[1] For casting this aspersion on the Shechinah, he was justly punished.]

Know this: that the Shechinah must partake of the quality of a virgin, *a sealed fountain*, that the Insolent Waters and the externals might not cling to her.[2] For if she were sexually open, the Insolent Waters would

---

1. The complex associations of this passage with the Lurianic literature, the writings of Nathan of Gaza, and the medieval anti-Christian polemics of the *Toledot Yeshu* genre are explored in two papers published as part of Maciejko's edition of *Va-avo ha-Yom*: Benarroch, "Piercing,"; Alleson-Gerberg, "Way of a Man."

2. Alluding to Song 4:12, where the Bride is called "a closed-up garden" and "a sealed fountain." The sexual symbolism of the Biblical verse is fairly transparent; and so the midrashic tradition, which understood the Bride as the people of Israel, took the passage as praise of the chastity of Jewish women and men as well (*Midrash Leviticus Rabbah* 32:5, *Song of Songs Rabbah* 4:12; cf. Rashi *ad loc.*). The Zoharic literature applied it to the Shechinah, "opened" to her husband, *Tif'eret*, only on Sabbaths (Tishby, *Wisdom*, 3:1226–27, quoting *Tiqqunei ha-Zohar*, *tiqqun* 36; cf. Zohar, I, 32b). The Catholic exegesis of the passage, its roots in antiquity but blossoming in popularity

gain entry to her womb and penetrate within her, and therefore she must be a virgin, a sealed fountain. Each day, therefore, as the Zohar explains, THE EARTH IS EXAMINED AS TO WHETHER SHE HAS KEPT FAITH,[3] that is to say, whether or not she has received the Insolent Waters within her. Each day she is examined—and she does keep faith. She does not receive them at all.[4]

You must also realize that the structure of Emanation is symbolized by wheat, which is equivalent to the twenty-two letters of the Torah.[5] Were it not for the sin [of Adam], wheat would be edible without requiring any preparation—as it will be in the [messianic] future, when fine *cakes will grow out from the earth*.[6] But the sin spoiled it, so that it became husks and enclothements[7] from which nourishment can be extracted only by a toilsome process of preparation. This is the straw and

---

in the later Middle Ages, understood it as referring to the perpetual virginity of Mary: Daley, "Closed Garden." This last seems the closest to our author's usage; may direct Christian influence be conjectured?

3. Zohar, III, 189a, using "earth" as standard Kabbalistic code for the Shechinah. The Zohar asks how this "examination" is carried out, and answers: through an offering of barley, as in the case of the wife suspected of adultery (Num 5:15). This reply is presupposed the discussion of wheat versus barley that follows; and in light of the sequel, the association with the doubtfully faithful wife is significant.

4. The situation of the mss. at this point is puzzling. Only ms. Jerusalem 2491 gives the full text. Oxford 955 and Jerusalem 3100 omit the next four paragraphs, following ואינה מקבלת כלל with והאי מגדף (Oxford) or והא מגדף (Jerusalem). Oxford 976 ends fol. 129v with ואינו מקבל כלל, indicating that the next page will begin with ודע. However, the continuation, on fol. 131r, is not ודע כי בנין האצילות, but ודע כי בזמן הגלות (which has a certain graphic resemblance to it), from much later in the text (beginning of chapter 9, section 2 = p. 154 in Maciejko's edition); the intervening material is skipped over. Between fols. 129 and 131 someone has inserted a sheet containing, on 130r, *precisely the passage omitted from Oxford 955 and Jerusalem 3100*, in a different handwriting from the rest of the ms.; and on the verso, in a handwriting different still, two paragraphs from an entirely different text offering explanations in terms of Kabbalistic sex for two Talmudic passages. It is very difficult to think of a hypothesis that will correlate all these variations.

5. That is, of the Hebrew alphabet. *Hittah*, "wheat," has the numerical value of 22; cf. Zohar, III, 188b, *Tiqqunei Zohar* 69.

6. Talmud, b. Ketub. 111b, imagining a return to pre-Adamic conditions when wheat "grew tall like the cedars of Lebanon" (*Midrash Genesis Rabbah* 11:7), bearing ready-made bread as its fruit. Cf. Ginzberg, *Legends*, 5:97–98, who points out that this midrashic fantasy rests on an equation of *het* (חטא), "sin," with *hittah* (חטה), "wheat." The author here presupposes the literal Biblical/midrashic understanding of Adam's sin, disregarding his own earlier exposition of its theosophic, cosmic significance.

7. *Qelippot ve-malbushim*, the words translated (in the singular) as "nutshell" and "garment" in chapter 4, section 2. On the overtones of *qelippah/qelippot*, see above, chapter 4, note 18.

chaff of the Torah, from which the food must be extracted and properly prepared. Hence the Gemara's dialectics in the Babylonian Talmud, as the Zohar explains.[8]

The entities of *Ma'aseh Bereshit*, by contrast, are symbolized by barley, fit to be eaten only by horses and donkeys, i.e., the dragons and serpents [of the *Tehiru*]. This was the point of Adam's complaint, *Shall I and my donkey eat from the same trough?*[9] inasmuch as the wheat had turned bad and required preparation as the barley did. And this, you must understand, is why the Shechinah, under scrutiny for the sin just mentioned—WHETHER SHE HAS KEPT FAITH—requires an offering of barley.[10]

But in fact the Shechinah did keep faith, and she gave God's honor to no one else. This is what Joseph told Potiphar's wife, *How shall I do this great evil, and sin* לאלהים, *lelohim?*—which [last word] the midrash interprets as, *Not so God who is with me.*[11] Joseph, in other words, asks in his role as the *sefirah Yesod*:[12] "How can I do this, to betray the Shechinah by fornicating with an alien woman? Not so God"—i.e., the Shechinah—"who is with me! She keeps her covenant, entering into the *Tehiru* yet receiving nothing from them."

[p. 121] This was the sin of the blasphemer, as the Zohar tells us—that, in defense [of his mother], he slandered the Shechinah.[13]

---

8. For the sources of this paragraph in the Zoharic literature, especially its later strata (*Ra'ya Mehemna, Tiqqunei Zohar*), see Giller, *Enlightened*, 90-91. Drawing on these sources, our author digresses from the line of his argument to suggest the inadequacy of the Torah, when taken as the traditional norms of Judaism. As it stands, it is unfit for human consumption. Like the wheat, it must undergo a process of *tiqqun* ("preparation," literally "mending") before it is edible.

9. Talmud, b. Pesah. 118a, describing Adam's reaction to being told that the earth would yield him "thorns and thistles" (Gen 3:18)—soothed, however, by the subsequent reassurance that he would "eat bread."

10. Representing the *Ma'aseh Bereshit* amid which she walks, and by which she might conceivably be polluted.

11. Gen 39:9, quoting Joseph's response to the seductions of Potiphar's wife. *Midrash Genesis Rabbah* 87:5 breaks the verse's final word *lelohim*, normally translated "against God," into the two words *lo elohim* (לא אלהים), "No, God"—evidently understood as an oath: "No, by God, I will not do this evil thing!" Our author takes his cue from the midrash. But, ignoring its simple interpretation, he expands *lo elohim* into *ve-lo ken elohim 'immi*, "not so God who is with me," i.e., which God who is with me would not do.

12. The divine phallus, symbolized in the traditional Kabbalah by the Biblical figure of Joseph.

13. Lev 24:10-23, as interpreted in Zohar, III, 106a, which sets out to explain why the Bible specifies that the blasphemer was the son of an Israelite woman and an Egyptian man, and what his quarrel with an "Israelite man" had to do with his

The blasphemer, we are there told, wanted to defend his mother, who had betrayed her husband and fornicated with an Egyptian man, becoming pregnant by him and giving birth to that blasphemer. "What of it?" he said. "Doesn't the Shechinah also go each night into the *Tehiru* and receive the Insolent Waters into her womb, [fol. 27b] growing them and bringing them to birth as fully completed souls?"—as we have said. He thereby denied that the Shechinah was a virgin, honoring her covenant, her "fountain" sealed. This is as the Zohar says, on the Torah portion *Emor*: HE PIERCED THAT WHICH HAD BEEN CLOSED UP.[14] She had been a virgin, her "fountain" closed and sealed; he made her as though her "door" had been opened, her virginity gone.[15]

The Zohar goes on to explain THE SECRET OF THE MATTER: THAT HE TOOK THE LETTER *HEI* OF THE HOLY NAME[16] AND CURSED, IN ORDER TO DEFEND HIS MOTHER. THIS WAS THE "PIERCING," THAT HE PIERCED[17] THE HOLY NAME; AND THIS IS SOMETHING SPECIALLY REVEALED TO THE LABORERS IN THE FIELD.[18] THE SECRET OF THE MATTER: *THIS IS THE WAY OF AN ADULTEROUS WOMAN*.[19] Meaning, as we have said, that he cursed and insulted [the Shechinah], likening her to an adulteress who goes each night to a different place, that is the *Tehiru*, there to receive the Waters of

---

blasphemy. In addition to the Zohar, our author has been influenced by the midrashic passages cited in note 2, which link the story of the blasphemer to the "sealed fountain" of Song 4:12.

14. The Zohar interprets the verb *va-yiqqov*, "he cursed" (Lev 24:11), on the basis of 2 Kgs 12:10, as "he pierced." Our author extends this to suggest that the blasphemer did in fact pierce, with his slanders, the virgin Shechinah's hymen.

15. Following the Talmudic expression "I found an open door" (b. Ketub. 9a–10a), spoken by a new husband who claims his bride is not a virgin.

16. The last letter of the Tetragrammaton, understood by the Kabbalists as symbolizing the Shechinah.

17. Our author omits from his quotation the following verb "and pronounced," which would not have suited his interpretation of the Zoharic passage. For him, the "Holy Name" *is* the Shechinah, quite literally—a standard piece of Kabbalistic symbolism—and the blasphemer quite literally "pierces" her by penetrating her virginity.

18. I.e., those expert in Kabbalah. The Zohar has earlier declared that the secret of the blasphemer "may be revealed only to those companions who are among 'the laborers in the field.' Blast the souls of those who come to reveal it to those who do not know!" This would surely suggest to our author that something peculiarly esoteric is involved here. The Zoharic passage is genuinely cryptic, and our author's understanding of it seems about as good as any.

19. Prov 30:20: "This is the way of an adulterous woman: she eats and wipes her mouth, and says, I have done no wrong." The image of wiping the lower "mouth" seems to be taken up by our author in the following discussion; see below, note 27.

I CAME THIS DAY TO THE SPRING

Creation.[20] HE PIERCED THE HOLY NAME by saying she had been sexually opened,[21] which was wholly untrue and spoken only to defend his mother, that she not be put to shame for having betrayed her husband.

This was why he was punished, why he was found culpable. She does indeed DRAW SUSTENANCE FROM TWO SIDES[22]—the male juices mentioned earlier, and the *Tehiru*-waters mentioned earlier. Yet her quality remains that of a virgin, and he was therefore punished [for saying otherwise]. Understand this.

2. The Curtain at the Portal

> [Yet the blasphemer had a point. How is the Shechinah to raise and redeem the waters of the *Tehiru* unless she takes them into herself, and how can she do that without allowing them to penetrate her? The answer is that she absorbs them into the cloth—the Talmudic *Vilon* or curtain—which she customarily spreads over her vulva. She then squeezes them into herself (or into the higher Female who has come to dwell within her, as we shall presently see) so that inside the womb they can be purified . . .]

Should you wonder how she in fact receives the Insolent Waters, you must be aware that she does *not* receive them with any of her elements, even her other limbs.[23] All such contact, even with her Enclothement, would lead to sexual intercourse. This is the symbolism of *those clothes in which one mixes the cup for one's master*—an allusion to sex, as we well know—*are not to be worn while cooking his dinner*, i.e., those *Tehiru*-waters of which we have spoken.[24]

[p. 122] So then: how does she receive them?

---

20. *Mei bereshit*, referring to the *Ma'aseh Bereshit* that the Shechinah redeems by absorbing within herself.

21. *Be'ulah*, the feminine passive of the verb meaning "to have sexual intercourse." The literal translation of *be'ulah* cannot be spoken in polite company.

22. Interpreting the cryptic remark with which the Zohar concludes its treatment of the blasphemer: "The final *hei* was the Female who draws sustenance from two sides, and on that account takes up the King's weapons and executes her revenge."

23. And not her genitalia.

24. Loose quotation of a proverb invoked in the Talmud, b. Shabb. 114a, 119a, Yoma 23b. The proverb's point is that cooking is a dirty job, and will befoul the fine clothing that ought to be used for serving wine. Our author understands this to mean that the Shechinah's Enclothement, which is the "clothing" she wears when she goes to make love with her "master" (the God of Israel), cannot be used for the dirty work of raising the polluted *Tehiru*-waters for their purification.

THE VIRGIN OF GOD

You must realize that the Shechinah has a sort of covering or curtain[25] over her genitalia, hinted at in the words *she covered her face*, namely her nether "face."[26] She removes it during sex, as we know, so that nothing should stand in the way; and after the sex is done—for, after sex, she is bound to expel some drops of male and female juices—she wipes herself with this curtain, which serves her as a napkin after a meal.[27] Those drops are absorbed into this napkin, and they are like mists and clouds, spermatic drops lacking full expulsive force.[28]

When the Shechinah goes by night into the waters of the *Tehiru*, she dips this curtain into them and, with the aid of the above-mentioned mists and drops of sperm, she absorbs the waters from the *Tehiru* and the Insolent Waters. She sweetens them until they have been made into water fit for use, and then squeezes them out into the Female,[29] into her genitalia. Once they are inside her she purifies them still further. They serve her as sacrificial offerings, as we have seen; also, as we have seen, as female juices.[30] Then the male juices are stirred up within the God of Israel, in the fullness of his desire; and thus she can nurture them[31] to the point that they can rise to lofty heights and be made into completed souls. Most of the souls of the converts to Judaism are of this sort.

25. *Parokhta*, the word used in chapter 5, section 1, for the curtain—there identified with the Higher Shechinah—that separates the Distant One from the God of Israel.

26. Gen 38:15, where Judah sees his daughter-in-law Tamar, thinks her to be a prostitute "because she had covered her face," and proceeds to have sex with her—as if the face-covering is a sign of sexual availability. Our author understands this "face" to be what Shakespeare called the woman's "face between her forks" (*King Lear*, Act IV, Scene 6).

27. As Benarroch points out ("Piercing," 266), the Shechinah's behavior is disturbingly similar to that of the adulteress of Prov 30:20, and it once again appears that the "blasphemer" may have had a point. There is an obvious tension between the Shechinah's sexual activity, reported in this passage, and the author's insistence on her strict virginity; but see below, section 16.

28. The language is awkward, and the author's point not entirely clear. That the drops in the cloth are indeed sperm, but not shot forth the way a spermatic emission would be, so that she can absorb them without losing her virginity? His calling the spermatic drops "mists" (*edim*) anticipates the exegesis of Gen 2:5-6 that he will presently undertake.

29. Into herself, perhaps; or, more likely, into that higher Female, the God of Israel's Shechinah.

30. Above, chapter 4, section 3; cf. chapter 7, section 3.

31. With the aid of the male juices, apparently. It is not absolutely clear who is doing the nurturing, the Higher (?) Shechinah, or the God of Israel. The feminine pronoun would suggest the former, the masculine verb the latter; and the former option seems the more likely.

This is the significance of *Vilon*:³² the curtain, the "sheet" over the portal to the womb, that *portal of the Lord into which the Righteous do enter.*³³ *It does not copulate at all,* since, as we have seen, it plays no role in the sex act, its sole activity being *to enter in the morning* into the Merkavah from the midst of the *Tehiru* and *to go forth in the evening* to the *Tehiru* to receive those waters. *It is of this* [*Vilon*] *that we say, "The one who renews each day perpetually the Ma'aseh Bereshit,"* daily gathering souls of Ma'aseh Bereshit, renewing and restoring them. *It is of this that we say*—taking care to convey that it is [*Vilon*] that does it all.³⁴

It is the symbolic meaning of what was done by Elijah, who represents the Shechinah: he took his mantle, representing *Vilon, and he threw it into the midst of the waters and the waters dried up*³⁵—this being an allusion to *Vilon*, as we have said. And when the Bible asks, *Who bound up waters in a garment?*³⁶ it hints at that wiping-napkin of which we have spoken.

3. The Curtain at the Portal, Continued

> [... and in their turn they benefit the Shechinah, supplying her with female juices to evoke the male juices she needs to bear the soul-fruits ...]

32. Literally "sheet" (Latin *velum*), the lowest of the seven heavens enumerated in the Talmud, b. Hag. 12b, which the author will proceed to quote and partly to misquote. "*Vilon* serves no function [*eno meshammesh k'lum*] except to enter in the morning and go forth in the evening, and each day to renew *Ma'aseh Bereshit*, the Work of Creation." Playing on a double meaning of the Hebrew verb *meshammesh*, our author understands *eno meshammesh k'lum* as "does not copulate at all" (!); he misrepresents the Talmud as asserting, not merely that *Vilon* daily renews the *Ma'aseh Bereshit*, but that the liturgical formula describing this activity (above, chapter 7, note 25) refers to *Vilon* and only to *Vilon*.

33. Ps 118:20, understood Kabbalistically to refer to the vulva, the "gateway" to be entered by the Righteous One, the phallic *sefirah Yesod*. There may be a Sabbatian allusion: the initials of *tzaddiqim yavo'u bo*, "the righteous enter it," are an anagram for "Zevi."

34. That is, the entire operation of gathering, renewing, and restoring. Unfortunately for the author—but would any of his readers have noticed?—the words "it is of this that we say" do not actually occur in the Talmud.

35. Very free quotation of 2 Kgs 2:8, in which Elijah strikes the Jordan River with his rolled-up mantle and the waters part so he and Elisha can cross "on dry ground." (I am not aware of any source for Elijah's being a symbol for the Shechinah.) Recall that the turning of water (or ice) to dust is, for our author, symbolic of strengthening the forces of divine order at the expense of those of chaos.

36. Prov 30:4.

[p. 123] This is the significance of, *There was no human being to work the ground*;[37] namely, that the Shechinah has two types of female juices. One of these derives from the souls of the righteous on earth, from the stimulus provided down here by the Jewish people, which serves in the higher realms as female juice.[38] But there is another sort of female juice, the one just described, in which the *Vilon* and the "mists" absorb *Tehiru*-waters and deposit them as female juices within the womb of *Malkhut*, sweetening them in the process. So when Scripture says, *There was no human being to work the ground*, it means, to pour out and prepare female juices, for humans were not yet here on earth.[39]

At that time *all the field's plants did not yet exist* for it had not yet sprouted them, inasmuch as [the Shechinah] cannot grow vegetation without male and female juices and the coupling of the two sexes, and there was then *no one to work the ground*, to provide within her the female juices that might evoke male juices—for without female juices, male juices will not descend. But this is what happened: *a mist went up from the earth*, namely that *Vilon* of which we have spoken, made up of "mists" from the drops of sperm it had wiped up. It had absorbed those Insolent Waters, mended them, and now *watered the earth*[40] with them as female juices inside her, in order to receive the male juices.

You now have the key to understanding the debate recorded in the Gemara and the midrash, whether clouds are from earth or from heaven[41]—and that both opinions are entirely correct, inasmuch as they are made from those drops of expelled sperm, which is both male and female in character.[42] You will likewise understand the question of whether

---

37. Gen 2:5. As usual, "ground/earth" (and presently "field") is understood as symbolic of the Shechinah.

38. Standard Kabbalistic doctrine: the acts of religious devotion and obedience performed by the Jews on earth rise as "female juices" to meet the "male juices" descending from divinity. It is the second kind of "female juice" that is the author's innovation.

39. And so the first kind of "female juice" was unavailable.

40. Gen 2:6, slightly altered.

41. Both rabbinic debates alluded to in this paragraph are found in *Midrash Genesis Rabbah* 13:10-11, though in reverse order; the second in the Talmud, b. Ta'an. 9b, where Rabbi Eliezer holds, against Rabbi Joshua—and invoking Gen 2:6 in support—that the earth "drinks from the waters of Ocean." Cf. Palestinian Talmud, y. Sukkah 5b.

42. I.e., the "drops of male and female juices" expelled by the Shechinah after sex and absorbed into the "curtain" that is *Vilon*. The male component of the "sperm" is represented by "heaven," the female by "earth," in accordance with standard Kabbalistic symbolism; the "clouds" consequently derive from both. The incongruity, of preserving the Shechinah's virginity by means that presuppose her wiping her genitalia after sex,

the earth[43] draws its moisture from the celestial waters[44] or from ocean waters, [fol. 28a] and that here also both views are correct.

For "the Ocean-Sea," i.e., the sea that encompasses the globe, is symbolic of the female juices received from the "mists," to which the rabbinic dictum applies that *the ocean's waters are salty*, being unfit for drinking.[45] Yet among the clouds, earth's upper waters participate in their sweetening, and consequently *they become sweetened in the clouds*. Once they have entered [the Shechinah's sexual organs] and been made into female juices, then male juices can be poured as rain—or, as the rabbis put it, "celestial waters"—from the God of Israel into the Shechinah. This is the meaning of *by the rain of heaven you shall drink water*;[46] and you must understand.

4. The Curtain at the Portal, Concluded

[. . . by which she and the God of Israel are nourished.]

[p. 124] We have earlier written that the Shechinah has thirteen ruptures,[47] and that these are symbolized by the [Temple's] thirteen gates; that, moreover, the barrier of the *Soreg*, the "webwork," functioned as blood of virginity. From all of these did sperm leak out, needing to be wiped away on all sides. This is the meaning of *Bathsheba wiped herself with thirteen napkins*, for all thirteen of the ruptures of which we have just spoken.[48] And this is why the Temple had the thirteen gates of which

---

is left unnoted.

43. Understood by our author to mean the Shechinah.

44. As asserted by Rabbi Joshua.

45. Quoting Rabbi Joshua's retort to Rabbi Eliezer, in the Talmud and midrash: the ocean's waters, salty as they are, would be unsuitable for irrigating the earth. To which Rabbi Eliezer responds: "They become sweetened in the clouds." Similarly, the waters of the *Tehiru* (corresponding to the ocean) are unfit for the Shechinah's absorption, until they are sweetened and "mended" within the "mists" of *Vilon*. (They are called here "female juices" in anticipation of their transformation.)

46. Deut 11:11, quoted by Rabbi Joshua in both the Talmudic and the midrashic texts, in support of his view that the earth draws its moisture from the celestial waters. Both Eliezer and Joshua, says our author, are right: the Shechinah's "moisture" comes from the formerly salt-polluted waters of the *Tehiru*, plus the "male juices" that these waters, once "sweetened," can call forth. As the Zohar says (above, end of section 1), she "draws her sustenance from two sides."

47. From the trauma of the Shattering; above, chapter 6, section 4.

48. Talmud, b. Sanh. 22a, meaning in its original context that the aged David had sex with Bathsheba thirteen times on a single occasion—the one mentioned in 1 Kgs

we have spoken, and the thirteen curtains enumerated in the Gemara to tractate *Yoma* and in Maimonides's *Laws of the Temple Vessels*:[49] those napkins were present in all thirteen places.

Know also that when the water is squeezed out from the "mists" into the Female, this constitutes a kind of "eating." For the "mists" have done the work of preparation; and for her it is through a process of eating, requiring chewing and digestion of every kind, that she absorbs new souls and intelligences. As it was upon the [Temple] altar, where the Bible uses the language of "eating" for the altar-fire's consumption and purification [of the sacrificial offerings]—*that which the fire shall eat*,[50] and so forth—so it is with the Shechinah.

Now, when she removes the napkin from her nether "face" and the God of Israel goes down into the *Tehiru*, he couples with her and thereby he too absorbs and "eats."[51] These are the souls fit for him in their shining clarity, which ascend [with him] to lofty heights; whereas the Insolent Waters cannot make the ascent by clinging to him because that *Vilon*-curtain is present, receiving whatever is worthy of reception, repelling the rest and blocking their ascent. This is why *a scholar enwraps himself in his cloak*, so that nothing may attach itself to him that does not share in the nature of the *hashmal* of which we have spoken—i.e., of light, a "cloak" that he peels back in secret from the place [of his genital].[52]

1:15—she wiping herself after each one. The Talmud gives no Biblical evidence for this claim, to which our author gives a typically grotesque twist: the Shechinah's thirteen ruptures function as vulva equivalents, each requiring its own "napkin." The use of Bathsheba to represent the Shechinah goes back to the classical Kabbalah (Zohar, III, 37a, 38b). But in the present context, the Shechinah's representation by a once adulterous (2 Sam 11:2–5), now sexually hyperactive woman strangely echoes the "blasphemer's" supposedly slanderous claims about her (above, section 1).

49. Talmud, b. Yoma 54a; Maimonides, *Mishneh Torah, Hilkhot Kelei ha-Miqdash* 7:17.

50. Lev 6:3.

51. Much as he, the God of Israel (as represented by Adam), shared in the forbidden "eating" with his Female (above, chapter 6, section 6).

52. See above, chapter 6, section 8. The quotation is from the Talmud, b. Shabb. 86a: although Jews normally avoid daylight sex in the interest of modesty, "a scholar enwraps himself in his cloak, and it is permitted." The God of Israel, of whom the "scholar" is an earthly representation, makes love enwrapped and protected in his "cloak" of light, which is peeled back "in secret"—alluding to the derivation of the first syllable of *hashmal* from *hashai*, "secret"; above, chapter 6, note 207—in the one spot essential for copulation. The avoidance of daytime sex perhaps alludes back to chapter 6, section 6, where the God of Israel is prohibited from coupling with the Lower Shechinah by day ("in the day wherein you eat of it") but not by night.

This is the significance of the Jerusalemite practice set forth in the *Midrash on Lamentations* to the verse *The noble sons of Zion*: whenever the napkin was spread out at mealtimes, guests might enter; the napkin removed, no guest had permission to come in.[53] The "guest" is known to symbolize *Yesod* [the penis], as the Bible says, *The guest, the Righteous, is as shining light*.[54] (See the Zohar on the Torah portion *Pinhas*, in the *Ra'ya Mehemna*: "GUEST" IS THE [sefirotic] RANK OF JOSEPH, and thus one may understand, *The guest says the blessing*.)[55] [p. 125] As long as the napkin or *handkerchief*,[56] symbolic of that *Vilon, was spread* to absorb the *Tehiru*-water and keep it from passing through, permission is granted [to the penis-"guest"] to come in and receive the female juices as though "eating." When the napkin is removed, however, the process of purifying the female juices and the mending of "eating" no longer takes place, and *guests might no longer enter*. Understand this.

5. Lest the Abyss Rise Up ...

[It is not only the Shechinah who is vulnerable to invasion through her sex organs. So is the God of Israel. The Insolent Waters are nourished by waste matter urinated into them by the divinities; why should they not use the same channels in reverse, rise up through them and flood the divine structures? The fragments of the Shattered vessels, represented as potsherds, must serve as barriers to keep them out.]

You must realize that the *Tehiru*, if it is to survive, is obliged to draw nourishment from the Shechinah and from the God of Israel. It is, moreover, the place to which are expelled the residual fluids, the waste

---

53. *Midrash Lamentations Rabbah* 4:4, expounding Lam 4:2: "This was a great custom in Jerusalem, that people would spread a handkerchief over their doorways. As long as the handkerchief was spread, guests were at liberty to enter. But if the handkerchief were taken away, guests might no longer enter beyond three paces." The midrashic text does not speak of mealtimes; that is the author's supposition.

54. Prov 4:18, understanding *orah*, "way," as *oreah*, "guest," and ignoring that "the righteous" is plural in the Biblical text. "The Righteous One" is standard Kabbalistic code for the phallic *sefirah Yesod*.

55. Free but essentially faithful quotation of Zohar, III, 244b (*Ra'ya Mehemna*), which gives a Kabbalistic interpretation of the Talmudic dictum that, at a shared meal, "the host breaks the bread and the guest says the blessing" (b. Ber. 46a). "The rank of Joseph" is *Yesod*. This sentence is found only in ms. Jerusalem 2491 (in parentheses), and may be a gloss.

56. *Mitpahat*, the word used in the midrash; versus the author's *mappah*, "napkin."

matter, the power of Judgment that they discharge—the urine, as it were, of the God of Israel and his Shechinah, which they excrete there, all that is waste and worthless, while retaining the choice matter within themselves. These are excreted through this urinary opening from the point of contact [between *Yesod* and *Malkhut*] indicated on the diagram above—to the side, however, into the *Tehiru*-waters, where they are absorbed by the Insolent Waters of which we have spoken.[57]

Now, the urinary aperture is exceedingly close to the seminal apertures, with only the smallest separation between them, as hinted at by *leavened bread* (symbolic of the urine) *and the unleavened* (symbolic of the seminal apertures) being *only the tiniest bit separated*, for it is only that *tiniest bit* that sets them apart.[58] And given that it sometimes happens that some trace of semen, the "interrupted flow"[59] that is the semen's barren refuse, flows out with the urine, this will reach [the Insolent Waters] mingled with the urine; and it is from this that they are nourished.

This was the symbolism of the *shitin* in the Temple.[60] Water and wine, the latter representing the holy semen—the *preserved wine*, and Judgment as well[61]—were poured into two apertures, there mingling

---

57. The "diagram above" is in chapter 7, section 2, the "point of contact" discussed at the end of section 2 and the beginning of section 3. The divine phallus is conduit both for the precious semen, ejaculated directly into *Malkhut*, and the worthless urine, eliminated "to the side" into the *Tehiru*. As we shall see in a moment, however, semen is sometimes released into the *Tehiru* along with the urine.

58. Horowitz, *Shnei Luhot ha-Berit, Massekhet Pesahim*, Third Homily, section 17, vol. 2, 252–53): leavened and unleavened bread are "only the tiniest bit separated," in that the only distinction between the Hebrew words for leavened bread (*hametz*, חמץ) and unleavened (*matzah*, מצה) is the almost imperceptible difference between the letters *hei* and *het*. (The two words are anagrams otherwise.) I do not know whether this observation is original with Isaiah Horowitz (1558–1628) or taken from some earlier source, from which our author may have drawn it.

59. An expression drawn from the Mishnah, m. Miqv. 8:2, which speaks of a drop-by-drop ("interrupted") flow of semen-like fluid from the penis, observed during urination, as being only doubtfully a seminal emission.

60. Spoken of in the Talmud as some sort of cavity or tunnel located beneath the altar in the Jerusalem Temple, variously said to be a natural formation (b. Sukkah 49a–b) or dug out by King David (53a–b), through which the water and wine libations poured into funnel-like openings in the altar were conveyed, according to some authorities, all the way down to the abyss. The name *shitin* is plural, although the context seems to require a single entity, and the singular form occurs in the parallels in the Tosefta (t. Sukkah 3:15) and the Palestinian Talmud (y. Sukkah 4:6). Our author interprets the name *shitin* by linking it to *sheten*, "urine" (below).

61. Alluding to the "wine preserved in its grapes from the Six Days of Creation," said in the Talmud (b. Ber. 34b and Sanh. 99a, expounding Isa 64:3) to be reserved as a future reward for the pious. Wine is a standard Kabbalistic symbol for the divine

with one another and flowing out into the abyss, namely the place of the *Tehiru*, going to that place of "formlessness" called "abyss."[62] The Bible hints at this when it says of the *shitin*, *The concealments of your thighs are like things hollowed out*,[63] locating it in that spot that is *the concealments of the thighs*.[64]

Understand this; [p. 126] and know that when this [element of semen] reaches the *Tehiru*, it brings [the waters] to life and they surge mightily upward, as the Gemara tells us: *One abyss calls out to another, Spurt forth your waters!*[65] They try to gain entry to that spot[66] via the urinary apertures, which are open—versus the seminal apertures, which are sealed up in the virginal state of which we have spoken[67]—and through them [the waters] attempt to penetrate and attach themselves to the Shechinah.

But this also you must know:

When [fol. 28b] the vessels were Shattered and the Cain-born vessels remained below, as we have seen[68]—so hinted in the verse *I will set enmity between the woman's seed and yours*[69]—the God of Israel ar-

---

attribute of Judgment.

62. *Tohu* and *tehom*, respectively; see the end of chapter 3, section 5, above. The author's language closely follows b. Sukkah 49a.

63. Song 7:2, applied to the *shitin* in b. Sukkah 49a; translated in accord with Rashi's interpretation of the Biblical and Talmudic passages.

64. I.e., the genital area. The *shitin*, though grammatically plural, is appropriately spoken of as singular: the semen/wine and urine/water are mixed together in a single channel.

65. Paraphrased from the Talmud, b. Ta'an. 25b, which expounds Ps 42:8—"one abyss calls out to another at the sound of your conduits"—as describing the "abysses'" response to the water and wine libations poured down on them through the "conduits" (the *shitin*, though the word is not used).

66. Presumably the divine genitalia, as in the preceding paragraph. The passage is somewhat garbled, and the mss. differ substantially among themselves.

67. Is the God of Israel here thought of as being virginal, no less than the Shechinah? (Whose virginity we have seen to be less than absolute.) So it would seem from the sequel.

68. Above, chapter 6, section 4: "All the *sefirot* ascended [for mending] only as intelligences, that is to say, in their 'Abel' aspect. Their vessels, generated by Cain, and all the more so their garment of *Ma'aseh Bereshit*, remained below." On the distinction between "vessels" and "intelligences," see chapter 4, section 2.

69. Loose quotation of Gen 3:15, addressing the serpent; above, chapter 6, section 6. The "serpent" and "Cain" are both symbolic of Creation-Human, the vessels that were Shattered; they are therefore interchangeable. The author's earlier exposition of Gen 3 had represented the God of Israel as the passive recipient of the Root's commands and punishments; here he seems to take a more active role.

THE VIRGIN OF GOD

ranged that they should partake of the quality of Judgment. This was especially true of the "Midianites," whose essence was that of *Gevurah*,[70] and of "Balaam," who, symbolic of the *sefirah Da'at* of the Shattered vessels, enclothed himself in *Gevurah*'s Judgment as *qosem* = *someq*, "redness" (as we have fully discussed above).[71] Thus he took on the quality of a fiery oven, blazing hot, and came to be called *Balaam son of Beor*, like that *day blazing like an oven*, and so forth.[72]

They were Shattered, as we have said; and this is the inner meaning of King David's prayer for the fall of the enemies and demonic powers,[73] that they be Shattered and destroyed as those vessels were. That was why he prayed to *make them like a fiery oven*, that the enemies be like that "oven" that was swallowed up and destroyed in fire[74]—i.e., the ones that fell below and were Shattered, and which the God of Israel gathered as potsherds, oven fragments, and fixed them in that place underneath the Shechinah where the urinary apertures are. There do they stand, blocking the *Tehiru*-waters from passing through those apertures.

This is the inner meaning of the verse *He has a flame in Zion, an oven in Jerusalem*: that "oven" is in "Jerusalem," keeping the Insolent Waters from rising upward.[75] [p. 127] It is the symbolism of the potsherd, the *haspa* with

---

70. The *sefirah* of strict Judgment.

71. Chapter 4, sections 6–7. Josh 13:22 calls Balaam "the sorcerer," *qosem*, which in Hebrew is an anagram for *someq*, "redness"—an attribute of the *sefirah Gevurah*. A similar but not quite identical bit of exegesis is proposed near the end of chapter 4, section 6.

72. Mal 3:19: "Behold the day comes, blazing [*bo'er*, with the same consonants as *be'or*, the name of Balaam's father] like an oven, and all the insolent ones [*zedim*, from the same root as *zedonim*, the "Insolent" Waters] and all evildoers shall be straw, and the coming day shall burn them up." With his "and so forth," the author suggests that his allusion is to the entire verse and what is to be done to the Insolent Waters: they are to be "burned up," dried by the Shechinah's fire, and thereby redeemed. (The opposite of the destruction promised by the Biblical verse!) In any case, the Beor = *bo'er* equation serves to link the fragments of the Shattered vessels to the "oven" and its range of Biblical and Talmudic associations.—Two mss. (Oxford 955, Jerusalem 3100) add here a note: "Cf. the divine epithets in *Me'orot Natan*." This presumably refers to the entry *tannur* ("oven") in Meir Poppers's alphabetical dictionary of divine epithets in the Lurianic writings (Frankfurt, 1709, 77a), which associates Malachi's "blazing oven" with the name Beor (in Gen 36:32).

73. *Qelippot*, a term very common in Kabbalah in general, very rare in this text.

74. Ps 21:10, which goes on to pray that the "enemies"—originally, of the king; here, of the divine order—be "swallowed up" in God's wrath, consumed in fire. The Hebrew for "swallow them up" is *yevalle'em*, which our author may have read as an allusion to "Balaam."

75. Isa 31:9, understanding "Jerusalem" as a representation of the Shechinah.

which King David sealed off the abyss *when David carved out the* shitin *and it tried to surge upward and flood the world.*⁷⁶ This speaks of what we have just described, that the Insolent Waters tried to rise up through the urinary apertures⁷⁷ and flood the whole structure of the Merkavah, and it was these pottery fragments that blocked their way.

It is well known that either the male's genitalia or the female's may be represented as "stars." Accordingly, when the Bible says, *He speaks to the potsherd that there be no rising and he seals off the stars,*⁷⁸ this means that the potsherd of which we have spoken prevents the Insolent Waters from "rising" upon the Merkavah, and they⁷⁹ seal off the "stars"—the two genital organs of which we have spoken⁸⁰—so that the Insolent Waters cannot enter them, and they remain in the state of *sealed fountain.*⁸¹ This is what is done with the potsherd: when the Judgments and the Insolent Waters well up and try to ascend, the God of Israel grasps that potsherd and gives it the strength to resist them.⁸²

This is the symbolism of what was done by Job, who, as I have written earlier, stands for the God of Israel.⁸³ He saw the swelling power of the Judgments; he feared lest the Insolent Waters burst through. Consequently, as the Bible says, *he took a potsherd to fence himself in with it*—to build a fence, that is, to block [the waters] lest they penetrate and lift themselves up on high.⁸⁴

---

76. Free quotation of Talmud, b. Sukkah 53a–b: "When David carved out the *shitin*, the abyss surged upward and tried to flood the world." David—whom our author understands as a representation of the God of Israel—forces it back down by the expedient of writing the Divine Name on a potsherd (Aramaic *haspa*) and throwing it into the water, whereupon "the abyss went down 16,000 cubits." The discussion of the previous three paragraphs, we now perceive, has been directed toward explaining how that potsherd got its power.

77. Interpreting *shitin* = *sheten*, "urine."

78. Job 9:11. *Heres*, in its Biblical context, certainly means not "potsherd" but "sun."

79. The author apparently shifts into thinking of the fragments of the Shattered vessels as a plural.

80. Of the God of Israel and of the Shechinah.

81. Song 4:12; see above, note 2.

82. We see here the author's ambivalence about the "Judgments." They are the powers that hold the forces of chaos in check, but they can themselves contribute to those forces.

83. Above, chapter 6, note 213.

84. Job 2:8, reading *le-hitgared* (להתגרד), "to scratch himself," as though it were its (graphically almost identical) anagram *le-hitgadder* (להתגדר), "to fence himself in."

For the serpents and dragons of the abyss surround him, seeking to eliminate him and make their way over him.⁸⁵ This is the significance of the oven *cut into segments*—shattered, that is, into *segments* and rendered into potsherds—*namely the serpent-oven, which they surrounded like serpents.*⁸⁶ The serpents surround it, as we have just said—and shall the oven align itself with the Insolent Waters and adhere to them (as in the verse that calls *all of you adulterers like the oven*),⁸⁷ such that they receive effluence from it and cling to it? Or shall it keep faith? This was the issue that divided Rabbi Eliezer and the sages, over whether or not it receives impurity; and you must understand.⁸⁸

The oven has the character of *huliyot*, "segments," and is therefore called *hol*, "sand."⁸⁹ Hence, *I appointed sand to be the sea's boundary, which it might not cross*;⁹⁰ i.e., the "segments" of that oven.

6. The Messiah in the Abyss

> [But it is not only his wastes that the God of Israel urinates into the Insolent Waters. From time to time, he will let pass there some particularly holy soul—Abraham's, or the Messiah's—to

---

85. Over God/Job's dead body, as it were. Our author normally holds back from personifying the forces of the Insolent Waters as dragons or serpents. Here he draws the image from Nathan of Gaza's *Treatise of the Dragons*, where the Messiah Sabbatai Zevi, of whom the suffering Job is a "type," "fell into the depth of the Great Abyss, and there the serpents would seduce him, saying to him . . . 'Where is thy God?'" (Scholem, *Sabbatai Ṣevi*, 310). It is no accident that Nathan's Messiah-in-the-abyss theme is about to make its appearance.

86. Slightly misquoting the story in the Talmud, b. B. Mesi'a 59a–b (a subtle and profound exploration of the locus of religious authority), in which Rabbi Eliezer disputes with "the sages" over whether or not something called a "serpent-oven" (*tannur shel 'akhnai*) is susceptible to impurity. The Talmud derives the oven's strange name from the disputants' having "surrounded it with arguments like [the coils of] a snake," to which our author gives his own peculiar twist; and the question of the oven's purity or impurity, which in the Talmud is a purely legal issue, is here given a mythic dimension.

87. Hos 7:4, which the author understands as offering the "oven" as the prime example of an adulterer, betraying its commitment to guard the Merkavah against the flooding of the Insolent Waters.

88. That "receiving impurity" has the volitional sense of welcoming impurity, yielding to the blandishments of the impure and allying with them—and not just, as the Talmudic story certainly intended, having the capacity to be rendered ritually impure.

89. Following the Talmudic passage: "If one cut an [oven] into segments and put sand between one segment and the next . . ."

90. Free quotation of Jer 5:22, understanding Jeremiah's "sea" to be the Insolent Waters.

gather and redeem the "sparks" trapped among them. (This idea goes back to theories proposed by earlier Sabbatian writers to explain and justify the Messiah's entering the realms of Gentiledom.) In this darkness the Messiah must dwell, until he can enter the Shechinah's womb to be reborn.

Both male and female genitalia, we saw in the preceding section, can be represented as "stars." Consequently, the Messiah can be called "son of the star," as was the second-century (CE) messianic pretender Bar Kokhba. But he was the wrong kind of "son of the star," come as semen from the divine organ and not as urine. This is why, hypervirile warrior though he was, Bar Kokhba's messiahship was an ineffectual failure. Rather, it is the mostly impotent Sabbatai Zevi, fallen as urine from a limp organ, who is the true star-Messiah.]

[p. 128] Know this: In order to raise from the *Tehiru* souls and intelligences that could not be raised with the *Vilon*-curtain of which we have spoken,[91] or to work destruction and the like in the *Tehiru*—especially so that the Externals should not become aware of what is going on and denounce it—it happens from time to time that the God of Israel will pass, through the urinary aperture, some exceptionally holy soul into the waters of the *Tehiru*. It will destroy and devastate them, gathering all the souls which it will complete and mend there until it be the God of Israel's will to raise that soul. Then it will rise, entering once more into the female juices, becoming a fetus through the confluence of male and female juices, its mending now complete.

This is the hidden significance of Abraham and our other righteous ancestors having entered into the "aperture of the Great Abyss"[92]—the God of Israel, in other words, having passed them through the urinary

---

91. In section 2, above.

92. *Nuqba di-tehoma rabbah*, a Zoharic phrase which Matt, trans., *Zohar*, translates "chasm of the immense abyss" or "hollow of the great abyss." The Zohar uses it to refer to the proper dwelling place of the demons, to which they are confined during the Sabbath (I, 14b, 48a). Our author gives the phrase a fresh meaning, understanding Aramaic *nuqba* as equivalent to Hebrew *neqev*, which he has used throughout this discussion for the urinary "aperture": not a characteristic of the abyss, but the entrance to it. The next few sentences are difficult—the mss. differ considerably among themselves, and all seem corrupt—but the overall thrust of the paragraph is clear. It rests on a midrashic interpretation of Gen 12:5, *the souls they had made in Haran*—an impossibility if taken literally; how does one "make" a soul?—as referring to the converts Abraham and Sarah had made during their sojourn in the city of Haran (*Midrash Genesis Rabbah* 39:14). Our author takes this a huge step further, allegorizing the Biblical account of Abraham's peregrinations as his descent into the Insolent Waters to "mend" and redeem them, and his subsequent ascent to his proper *sefirah* (*Hesed*, "Grace").

THE VIRGIN OF GOD

aperture so that they entered there—and the significance of Abraham and Sarai having entered Haran, i.e., through the urinary aperture and "hole."[93] (Hence the Zohar's "aperture of the Great Abyss": the Great Abyss is reached through an aperture.) While [Abraham] was there, he gathered all the sparks[94] that could be gathered and mended; and when this was finished, the God of Israel commanded him to *get yourself out from your land* to the Shechinah, where he became a fetus and rose, *ever progressing, toward the South*—as is well known.[95] *And he took with him* [fol. 29a] *the souls they had made in Haran*, that is to say, that which they had mended there and restored to being "souls"—an act represented by Abraham's having "made converts."

Similarly, the soul of the True Messiah[96] was expelled by the God of Israel through the urinary aperture and for that reason was called "Seth," as we find in a number of places in the midrash. Of Seth the Bible says, *God has placed for me another seed*, i.e., *seed coming from another place*, namely the soul of the Messiah, who was born from *another place*, not the seminal aperture but the urinary.[97] This is *the spirit of God hovering over the face of the waters* while *darkness was upon the face of the abyss*, which [spirit] the midrash identifies as *the spirit of the Messiah*.[98] For he falls there to stand in the breach, to gather up all things, and to destroy and shatter them—those Insolent Waters, that abyss-darkness that is the place of the *Tehiru*. This is the place his soul covers over, and where it has its dwelling.[99]

93. *Hor*, playing on the name "Haran" and referring to the hole at the tip of God's penis.

94. *Nitzotzin*, a word drawn from the conventional Sabbatian theology of Sabbatai's descent into the demonic realms (i.e., his conversion to Islam) to gather up the "sparks" imprisoned there.

95. Gen 12:1, 9. The author presupposes his readers' familiarity with the Zohar's exposition of the latter verse: "Then Abraham was crowned from rung to rung, until he ascended to his rung [i.e., his *sefirah*] . . . the South, share of Abraham . . . where he was fittingly bound, ascending to his rung: the South" (I, 80a, Matt, trans., *Zohar*). "South" is familiar Kabbalistic code for the *sefirah Hesed*.

96. *Mashiah ha-amitti*, regularly used in the Sabbatian literature for Sabbatai Zevi.

97. Gen 4:25, interpreted in *Midrash Genesis Rabbah* 23:5, *Ruth Rabbah* 8:1: "*Another seed*—seed coming [or "arising"] from another place. Who is that? King Messiah." The midrash seems to have intended the "other place" in a far more mundane sense: David, and therefore the Messiah, arose from a place "other" than Israel, namely the womb of Ruth the Moabitess. But the author feels free to read it in accordance with his cosmogony.

98. *Midrash Genesis Rabbah* 2:4, expounding Gen 1:2.

99. "Covers over" (*hofef*) interpreting the Biblical *merahefet*, "hovering." Note how

I CAME THIS DAY TO THE SPRING

This is *the gate of Rome*, which is the opening to the aperture of the Great Abyss; and there he *suffers illnesses*, as is well known—[p. 129] and how understandable, for one sitting in a place of such darkness and gloom![100] Thus *he made me sit in dark places, like the world's dead*:[101] like the fragments of the Shattered vessels, which are *the world's dead*, he forced me to sit in the dark places that are *Babel*. For we have earlier said that the *Tehiru* waters are called Babel in that they are a jumbled mixture[102] of Mindful and Mindless Lights; review our exposition of the Babel story, and you will understand.[103]

And this is how the Zohar expounds the verse *When a man digs a pit and an ox or a donkey falls into it*, to speak of how the two Messiahs fell there; see the extended discussion in that passage.[104] That is why [the Messiah] is *poor* and naked, without Torah or commandments[105] as that

---

the author has shifted into the present tense—natural enough, if it is Sabbatai Zevi he is thinking of.

100. Following the legend in the Talmud, b. Sanh. 98a, that the Messiah sits "at the entrance of Rome" amid "the poor, suffering from illnesses." By "illnesses," the Talmud surely intended leprosy, as Rashi says in his comment on the passage. But our author is surely thinking of the periodic depressions that afflicted Sabbatai Zevi, which he explains as wholly natural in someone whose soul dwells in such bleak surroundings. A mysterious visit to Rome by Nathan of Gaza in 1668 seems to be connected to this Talmudic tradition, and the Sabbatian believers' application of it to their Messiah; Scholem, *Sabbatai Ṣevi*, 771–74.

101. Lam 3:6; cf. Ps 143:3.

102. *Belulim*; from *balal*, "confuse," used to explain the name Babel in Gen 11:9.

103. Referring back to chapter 3, section 4—which, however, interprets Gen 11:1–9 to describe the separation of the Mindful from the Mindless Light, not their mixing. The introduction at this point of Babel—the Hebrew can mean "Babylon" or "Babylonia"—is presumably, as Maciejko points out, based on the Talmud, b. Sanh. 24a, which disparages Babylonian scholarship by calling it *belulah*, "confused," and by quoting Lam 3:6 with respect to it. But what the author wants to convey with it remains unclear.

104. Zohar, III, 279a (*Ra'ya Mehemna*), expounding Exod 21:33. The Zoharic passage speaks of an "aperture" (*nuqba*) that penetrates down to "the Great Abyss." "When that aperture is opened, whoever falls into it does not rise. Messiah ben David fell there, along with Messiah ben Joseph; for the one is *poor, riding on an ass* [Zech 9:9], and the other is *his firstborn ox* [Deut 33:17]. This is the meaning of *when a man digs a pit and does not cover it, and an ox or a donkey falls into it*, and it is why the Messiah is called *son of the fallen ones* [Talmud, b. Sanh. 96b]." This fills out the author's picture of the Messiah falling (or being excreted) through the urinary tract (= Talmudic *shitin*) into the *Tehiru*. His application of it to Sabbatai Zevi's salvific "fall" into the realms of Gentiledom has deep roots in Sabbatian tradition; see Scholem, *Sabbatai Ṣevi*, 819 (who, however, misattributes the treatise he is discussing to Abraham Cardozo; its real author was Nathan of Gaza's disciple Abraham Perez).

105. "Poor" (*'ani*), alluding to Zech 9:9 (previous note) and to the Talmud, b. Sanh. 98a. The idea that one is "naked" when bereft of the Torah's commandments—as

Zoharic passage says, and the *Tiqqunim* as well[106]: that in that place [the abyss] there is no light of Torah (and the blind therefore exempt from the commandments).[107] And the "light of Torah" can be nothing other than the structure of the Merkavah.

We now have the clue to what Nachmanides wrote in his Torah commentary, and Luria bore witness to its utter profundity: namely, that the Torah is in its essence irrelevant outside the Land of Israel, its binding force essentially restricted to the Land of Israel.[108] He was alluding to what we have just discussed, for "outside the Land of Israel" corresponds to the *Tehiru* and the Insolent Waters, where the Torah is of no relevance. "The Land of Israel," by contrast, corresponds to the structure of the Merkavah, where the Torah and commandments are obligatory. Understand this.

At the time of the Messiah's coming, however, he will rise up on high, into the Female.[109] This is what is represented by his entering the "Bird's Nest," i.e., the womb of the Shechinah, who is called Zipporah and has a "nest" of lights, as is well known.[110] There she will receive him, be-

---

Sabbatai Zevi was, after his conversion to Islam—goes back to the midrash: *Genesis Rabbah* 19:6, on Gen 3:7.

106. I do not know what passage in the *Tiqqunei Zohar* the author is referring to. Maciejko *ad loc.* cites the tenth of the additional *Tiqqunim* (ed. Zhitomir, p. 147a-b), which speaks of the two Messiahs in connection with the "ox" and the "donkey" and quotes Zech 9:9 (though not with reference to the Messiah), but its relevance to the author's thought here is at best remote.

107. Through a string of Biblical associations, the Zohar equates the "pit" of Exod 21:33 with the pit into which Joseph was thrown (Gen 37:24), which was "empty, no water in it"—or, as the Zohar expounds that verse (following the lead of *Midrash Genesis Rabbah* 84:16), "without Torah, but with serpents and scorpions inside it"—and thus we are carried back to the "serpents and dragons of the abyss." The Messiah, forced to dwell in this darkness, is thus exempt from obeying the commandments just as a blind person is (Talmud, b. Qidd. 31a and B. Qam. 87a), since the Torah is light which the blind cannot see.

108. Nachmanides on Lev 18:25: properly speaking, the force of the Torah's commandments is limited to the Holy Land, although the Jews must continue to practice them even in exile so they will not be strangers to them when, in messianic times, they are allowed to return. I do not know where Luria "bears witness" to the profundity of this radical, even shocking assertion.

109. As described at the beginning of this section. By the Messiah's "coming," the author surely intends Sabbatai Zevi's return from the abyss into which he plunged with his conversion to Islam. But it is also susceptible to a non-Sabbatian reading, in which the Messiah's soul has sojourned in the *Tehiru*—from the beginning of time, presumably—and emerges only at the eschaton.

110. The "Bird's Nest" (*qan tzippor*), taken originally from Deut 22:6-7, plays a central role in the long eschatological prophecy of Zohar, II, 7b-9a: "On that day King

I CAME THIS DAY TO THE SPRING

come impregnated with him, that he may be built up of male and female; and afterward he will redeem his people.

This is why the Bible says of the Messiah, *by way of a star from Jacob*.[111] This means, as we have said, that the "star" of which we have spoken is his path and it is this [star] that will fight the war.[112] Hence, *he will smash the head of Moab and bring cooling to all the children of Seth*,[113] such that they go down from the place of the urine—for he is named [Seth] from, *God has placed for me another seed*, as we have seen—[p. 130] and he cools [his children] from their boiling heat to keep them from rising up on high.

It was on the basis of Ben Koziba's name that Rabbi Akiba went astray, believing him to be the Messiah: he was called "Ben Kokhba," "son of the star," as though it were that star of which we have spoken that had

---

Messiah will arouse, emerging from the Garden of Eden, from the place called Bird's Nest, and . . . the whole world will tremble . . . when he rises and reveals himself in the land of Galilee" (Matt, trans., *Zohar*, 4:25–26). Our author explains what this "Bird's Nest" is, and how the Messiah comes to be "concealed" there until he goes forth to do his saving work. The Biblical name Zipporah is from *tzippor*, "bird"; and her "nest of lights" is taken from the end of Zohar, II, 8b, where the Messiah "will reveal himself from the radiance of the Bird's Nest" (Matt, trans., *Zohar*, 4:32).

111. Reading Num 24:17, *darakh kokhav mi-ya'aqov* ("a star has marched forth from Jacob") as if it were *derekh kokhav*. The author apparently reads the phrase in context as: "*by way of a star* from Jacob, and from Israel, a rod shall arise . . . " For him, as we have seen (above, section 5), "star" can be a designation for the female genital, through which the Messiah enters and subsequently emerges from the Shechinah's womb.

112. The subject of "this" might also be the Messiah. But it seems more probable that it is an allusion to the messianic warrior star in Zohar, II, 7b: ". . . a single star will rise from the side of the east, flaming in all colors—and seven other stars surrounding that star, waging war with it on all sides. . . . That star will battle them with flaming missiles . . . when they wage war before the eyes of the whole world" (Matt, trans., *Zohar*, 4:26–27). The star is not quite equivalent to the Messiah, but the two parallel each other: the Messiah, like the star, must battle a confederacy of "all kings of the world . . . waging war against him" (Matt, trans., *Zohar*, 4:27).

113. The continuation of Num 24:17, vocalizing *ve-qarqar* as a verb, *ve-qirqer*, and understanding it as a causative form from the root *qrr*, "to be cold." The Insolent Waters are apparently treated as the "children" of the Seth-Messiah (on which equation, and the invocation of Gen 4:25, see note 97 above), which he "cools" to keep them from boiling up through the urinary aperture, as one turns down the heat from a pot on the stove to keep it from boiling over. I am not sure how the author understands the preceding "smash the head of Moab."

THE VIRGIN OF GOD

begotten him.[114] But [Ben Koziba] came as semen, as erection,[115] which demands the whole body's arousal. Whereas it must be *as urine*—which requires no erection, which involves only that one single organ, and which takes place solely through falling[116]—that [the Messiah] comes to be named for that star.[117] (And so the prophet laments over him: *How are you fallen from heaven, O Helel son of Dawn!*[118] For he stands for the God of Israel who is called "Helel"—as Rashi and the Tosafot say of Hillel's dictum, *If I am here, all is here*[119]—"son of Dawn," i.e., the Root, as has earlier been said.[120])

114. "Ben Koziba," as the rabbinic literature calls him, is the second-century CE Jewish rebel leader usually known to history as "Bar Kokhba," Aramaic for "son of the star." (Hebrew "Ben" = Aramaic "Bar.") *Midrash Lamentations Rabbah* 2:9 represents Rabbi Akiba as proclaiming him Messiah, on the basis of Num 24:17: "When Rabbi Akiba saw Ben Koziba he would say, '*A star has marched forth from Jacob*, Kokhba has marched forth from Jacob. This is King Messiah!'"

115. Referring to the hyperpotency attributed by the rabbinic sources to the mighty Ben Koziba.

116. Through the urinary tract, as described at the beginning of this section, and as opposed to the semen ejaculated from an erect penis.

117. Since, to be truly "son of the star," he must be linked to the genital organ alone—recall that the "star of which we have spoken" is the genital, male or female—whereas Ben Koziba must be "son" of the entire aroused male body. The paradoxical outcome is that the star-warrior prophesied in the Zohar was not the hypervirile Bar Kokhba, but the mostly impotent Sabbatai Zevi.

118. Isa 14:12, the start of a taunt-song over the fallen "Lucifer" (as the Latin Vulgate, followed by the King James Bible, translates the name Helel). This Biblical passage was a lifelong favorite of Sabbatai Zevi's, which he applied to himself. As a young man in Izmir, he would recite verse 14 ("I will ascend upon the heights of the clouds, I will be like the Most High") with such emphasis that he imagined himself levitating; and in a letter written a few months before his death, he signed himself "the man raised up on high, above the heights of the Father"—substituting *av*, "father," for the almost identical sounding *'av*, "clouds." (See Halperin, *Sabbatai Zevi*, 4, 87.) While in the Biblical context Isaiah's "lament" is ironic, mocking, our author takes it as a serious expression of grief over the "fallen" Savior.

119. Talmud, b. Sukkah 53a: "They said of Hillel the Elder, when he was rejoicing in the Joy of the Water-drawing [in the Jerusalem Temple], that he would say thus: 'If I am here, all is here; and if I am not here, who is here?'" Rashi explains that ancient sage Hillel—whom our author equates with Isaiah's Helel—was speaking in the person of God, a suggestion modified by the Tosafot *ad loc*.

120. On the representation of the Root as "dawn," see above, chapter 5, section 3. The Messiah Helel has fallen from "heaven," a word used frequently in this text to indicate the God of Israel and the *sefirah Tif'eret* in which he has taken up residence (e.g., the beginning of the next section). Yet the author here blurs the distinction between the Messiah and the God who has passed him through his urinary tract: the Messiah is a symbolic representation of the God of Israel (*be-sod elohei yisra'el*), but also perhaps God's embodiment. The doctrine that Sabbatai Zevi was elevated after his death to the

This is why, as we are told in the *Midrash on Lamentations*,[121] the Messiah was born at the very instant of destruction when the Temple was set on fire, when the Judgments and the *Tehiru* waters welled up and sought to overflow and destroy the Merkavah, passing via the aperture of which we have spoken.[122] *As urine*, he served as lofty wall, as shield and buckler,[123] to keep them from drawing near the holy place.

7. Two Lower Shechinahs: "Leah," "Rachel"

[We have wandered rather far from the subject of the virgin Shechinah. Now we are brought back to her, through a contrast between her and her nonvirginal sister who shares the sefirotic vessel with *Yesod*. The two are represented in the book of Genesis by Jacob's two wives, Leah and Rachel.

Both of these can serve as Enclothements for the Higher Shechinah. As we have seen, she has decided to establish her dwelling within "Leah," "Rachel" being too distant from the God of Israel; she has not yet been banished, as she shortly will be, to "Rachel." And here there is a source of jealousy: "Jacob," Enclothement for the God of Israel, lusts only for "Rachel." Sexual jealousy among the Shechinahs will, accordingly, be the theme of the coming sections.]

Let us return now to our earlier subject, and speak of the second female: the one represented by Miriam, who dwells within *Yesod*, and within whom the Higher Shechinah—Mother of All Living,[124] Tree of Life, Shechinah of the God of Israel—has established her presence. The God of Israel, meanwhile, is enclothed within the external *Tif'eret*, represented by Jacob, as we well know.[125]

---

rank of God—the traditional God having vanished into the empyrean—was held by the most radical among his followers.

121. *Midrash Lamentations Rabbah* 1:51: the Messiah is born immediately after the destruction of the Temple. Sabbatai Zevi was famously born on the Ninth of Av, the fast day commemorating the Temple's destruction.

122. The urinary aperture.

123. A Biblical phrase (e.g., Jer 46:3, Ps 35:2) indicating two different kinds of shield. The author perhaps derives the second word, *tzinnah*, from the root *tznn*, "to be cold," and understands it as a cooling agent: to cool down, and thereby restrain, the boiling waters.

124. *Em kol hai*, used in Gen 3:20 to explain the name "Eve."

125. See above, chapter 6, section 6.

THE VIRGIN OF GOD

Know this: that we have earlier said that the *Malkhut* of Emanation was always and still remains virginal, for the reason we have explained;[126] while the Higher Shechinah and "Miriam" are both sexually open, as we have said. She [the "Miriam" Shechinah] is represented by "Leah," and the Lower Shechinah (as we have said) by "Rachel."[127]

Rachel was barren, and so forth,[128] receiving from the two of them, the God of Israel and his Shechinah, both of them dwelling in the shape of *Tif'eret* and its points, while *Malkhut* was below them both.[129] The two of them would thus pour out their effluence to her, as we have said vis-à-vis the Tree of Life and the Tree of Knowledge.[130] Thus it was that *God created the two great lights*, namely the God of Israel and his Shechinah, *and placed them in the firmament of heaven*, the two of them dwelling in the shape of *Tif'eret* that is called "heaven," *to shine light upon the earth*, namely the *Malkhut* of Emanation, which is known to be represented by "earth."[131]

[p. 131] Know also that the God of Israel, enclothed within Jacob, lusts only for Rachel, she being a virgin with a narrow vagina. For when the God of Israel enclothes himself in Jacob, [fol. 29b] Judgment and arousal are his nature; while Rachel is like the doe, whose vagina is narrow and thus appeals to her husband.[132]—Understand! for we have

---

126. That the Insolent Waters, amid which she walks, have no entry to her; above, section 1.

127. Above, chapter 6, section 4.

128. Gen 29:31. The following verses, which recount Leah's string of pregnancies, seem to suggest to our author that "Rachel" could bear no fruit, but only receive from others.

129. *Tif'eret*'s "points" are the satellite *sefirot* of *Hesed, Gevurah, Netzah, Hod*, and *Yesod*, which are included with *Tif'eret* in the "shape" of Little-face (a.k.a. "the Six Points"; cf. above, chapter 5, section 5). The Miriam/Leah Shechinah does not reside within *Tif'eret* strictly speaking, but within *Yesod*, which is however a part of "greater *Tif'eret*."

130. Cf. above, chapter 6, section 6.

131. Gen 1:16–17, freely quoted. As in his exegesis of Gen 3 (above, chapter 6, section 6), the author presumably understands "God" here to be the Root, originator of both the God of Israel and his Shechinah.

132. Mss. Jerusalem 2491 and 3100, which are fuller and more pleonastic than Oxford 955, add: "as it says in the Zohar." The reference is to the Zoharic myth of the *ayalta*—II, 52b, 219b, and most fully III, 249a–b—which represents the female *sefirah* *Malkhut* as a doe in the agonies of birth (cf. Berger, "Ayalta"). The attribution of the doe's sex appeal to her narrow vagina, however, is not from the Zohar but the Talmud, b. 'Erub. 54b, Yoma 29a, cf. B. Bat. 16b.

permission to speak; *from my flesh do I perceive God.*[133]—Leah is by contrast sexually open, her vagina wide, and therefore less appealing to her husband than Rachel.

This is why the Bible says that *Leah's eyes*—her nether "eyes," that is—*were soft*; which word *rakkot*, "soft," the Gemara interprets to mean *arukkot*, "enlarged."[134] For she was sexually opened, and they were "soft" and enlarged; her husband was therefore not so very fond of her. Rather, all his lusting was for Rachel.[135]

But the Root—standing for *Ein Sof* and symbolized by Laban, as Luria has written in his treatise on the World of the Bonded and the Points—would not allow this.[136] He therefore himself coupled with [the

---

133. Job 19:26; see above, chapter 1, note 13. The author clearly has the sense that his attribution of sex to the divinity is a bit over the top, and needs to invoke his standard Biblical warrant for its appropriateness.

134. Gen 29:17, interpreted in Talmud, b. B. Bat. 123a. *Arukkot* would normally mean "long"; but Rashbam's commentary on the Gemara (printed in place of Rashi's for most of Bava Batra), glosses it as "large," and the author's use of the Talmudic passage best makes sense if we assume he follows this.

135. Ms. Jerusalem 2491 inserts here a long passage, omitted from Oxford 955 and Jerusalem 3100, which interrupts the flow of the author's argument, partly repeats what has earlier been said, and is best regarded as an interpolation. "Now, when I say that the God of Israel desires the Lower Shechinah who is represented as *Malkhut*—comprised of a Cainite vessel and an internality that is Abel's female, generated through the Shechinah as we have seen—you must realize that this is because he has enclothed himself within the external *Tif'eret* like the soul within the body, and he employs this [body,] and the Enclothement to which he is tightly bound, for the purpose of copulation. He then partakes of arousal and Judgment—*from my flesh do I perceive God*—the body compelling the soul to gratify its powerful lust; and it is she of the narrow vagina for whom he most hankers. Further, he perceives the Higher Shechinah [who would properly be his sex partner] as his mother; he is repelled by the idea of sex with his mother, and therefore has no urge to couple with her. Rather, he wants the Lower Shechinah, who is his wife. But when he extends himself and rises above his self-extension, he does not couple with his Shechinah; understand this." It is far from clear what is intended by this last sentence; perhaps a reference to the God of Israel's ascending "to the Root, to the place of extension," for a homosexual encounter with the superior entity (above, chapter 2, section 2), akin to what is described in the following? During that interval, he will not engage in sex with any of his female Shechinahs.

136. To allow "Jacob" to couple with "Rachel." The Lurianic reference is to Vital, *Etz Hayyim*, I.vi.1, 74–75, where the Biblical figure of Jacob's father-in-law, Laban, is said to "symbolize the Supernal Whiteness [*loven ha-'elyon*, playing on the name *lavan*, "Laban"] that was prior to all this Emanation, and that generated all the entities . . . needed for the Emanation . . . which is called by the name Jacob." What follows is a reasonable summary of the story of Jacob's marital misadventures in Gen 29:15–30— barring, of course, the homosexual coupling with "Laban," on which see above, chapter 2, sections 2–3; chapter 5, section 1; chapter 6, section 8. "Laban's" refusal to permit this coupling, and "God's" command to "Adam" not to "eat" of the "Tree of Knowledge"

God of Israel], performing that copulation, as we have earlier said, in a state of Deep Sleep.[137] It was in this state that [the God of Israel] had sex with Leah, unawares,[138] for he was in Deep Sleep and she had provided him tokens—the lower token, that is, which you must understand on your own, for it is not permitted to say any more about this in writing.[139]

So he copulated with Leah; *and in the morning*—that is, once the dawn that represents the Root[140] had passed, and it was *in the morning* that represents the Distant One who endows the heart with thought—who is the heart's knowledge, the "God" indicated in the phrase *God of the Lord's knowledge*,[141] meaning that he is his knowledge and his thought—it was then that he thereby recognized that *she was Leah*.[142]

[p. 132] You must realize that the God of Israel, while coupling with the Root in a state of Deep Sleep and dream, experiences the massive outpouring of light as do the prophets while the prophetic spirit rests upon them: in a state of Deep Sleep on account of the light's profusion, one's spirit as it were truly separated from him and clinging there.[143] So it is with the God of Israel. The Shechinah,[144] however, is at

---

(above, chapter 6, section 6), have the same meaning: the God of Israel must not couple with the Lower Shechinah.

137. *Tardemah*, the state in which the God of Israel is anally penetrated by the Root. See above, chapter 2, sections 2–3 and chapter 5, section 1.

138. *Ve-lo yada'*, perhaps following Gen 19:33, 35, where Lot is too drunk to know he has just had sex with his daughters; i.e., he was in a state of unconsciousness, whose passing is described in the next paragraph.

139. Following the Talmud, b. Meg. 13b, where Jacob provides Rachel with "tokens" (*simanim*) by which he can recognize her. On the wedding night, however, Rachel gives these "tokens" to Leah, who presumably offers them to Jacob as proof that she is Rachel. Our author explains the Talmud's unspecified "tokens" as "the lower token" (*siman ha-tahton*), which presumably has something to do with her (or his?) genitalia. But we cannot be sure, for the author refuses to explain.

140. Who has "Jacob" in a state of Deep Sleep.

141. 1 Sam 2:3, *el de'ot YHVH*, normally translated "a God of knowledge is the Lord." Our author treats the three words as being in construct with one another, *de'ot YHVH* as "the Lord's knowledge" or "the Lord's awareness," and *el* as the higher deity who possesses and can grant this awareness. "Heart" in this passage is the God of Israel, as in chapter 2, section 1.

142. Gen 29:25: "In the morning, behold, she was Leah." The symbolism of dawn = the Root, morning = the Distant One, has been set forth in chapter 5, section 3.

143. To the source of the light, presumably. Chapter 2, section 3 speaks similarly of the intense illumination that accompanies a sexual encounter with the Root.

144. So ms. Jerusalem 2941. "*Malkhut*," the reading of Oxford 955 and Jerusalem 3100, is difficult to square with the context, which speaks of an entity dwelling in the same body as the God of Israel—whether the "Leah" Shechinah or the Higher

a level lower than his, even though she is in the same body as he and, being lower, is in a state of wakefulness, like one aroused from sleep. She stands behind him, as it were, and through him receives illumination—and therefore comprehends more than he does, since her light is less intense. Hence *greater understanding has been granted to woman than to man*.[145] Understand this.

In this same way Pharaoh, symbolic of the God of Israel,[146] was in the dreamer's role, while Joseph, symbolizing, as we have seen, the Shechinah who dwells in *Yesod*,[147] would stand behind him, understanding more fully, functioning as the interpreter and the one with *greater understanding*. Thus Pharaoh says to Joseph, *Behind me, God has made known to you all this*;[148] and the Zohar interprets: YOU WERE BEHIND ME—AT THE TIME I DREAMED THE DREAM, YOU WERE PRESENT THERE.[149] This is as we have said: he stood[150] behind him at the time of his dreaming and, through him, received the effluence as well.

That is why the Bible makes use of what is recognized to be the language of copulation, saying *God has made known*[151]—she [the Shechinah] having been behind him [the God of Israel], for it was through him that she received the effluence. Consequently, *there is no one understanding and wise like yourself*, you having been *granted greater*

Shechinah who dwells within her—and at a higher level than *Malkhut*. Which of these two Shechinahs the author has in mind is unclear; the subsequent identification of Joseph with "the Shechinah who dwells in *Yesod*" would point to the former. There is perhaps an exegetical agenda here: to explain how it was that Leah, unlike Jacob, seems to have known full well what was happening on their wedding night.

145. Talmud, b. Nid. 45b. A paradox: the female sees more than the male, being less blinded by the light.

146. See above, chapter 6, section 3.

147. This is not quite accurate. In chapter 6, section 3, the Biblical "essences of Joseph" (*'atzmot yosef*, more naturally translated "bones of Joseph") is equated with the female dwelling with *Yesod*, while the *sefirah Yesod* itself is, as in the traditional Kabbalah, represented by Joseph.

148. Gen 41:39—reading, as our author does (following the Zohar), *aharai*, "behind me," in place of *aharei*, "after."

149. Zohar, I, 196a, implying that Joseph co-experienced the dream with Pharaoh. To which our author adds: but Joseph was less caught up in the dream experience, therefore was able to understand it in a way Pharaoh could not.

150. So mss Oxford 955 and Jerusalem 3100. Ms. Jerusalem 2491 uses here a feminine verb (for the Shechinah, anticipating the next paragraph), but reverts to masculine (Joseph) later in the sentence.

151. Which is "the language of copulation," in that the Bible uses "knowing" to mean sex.

understanding, and *you shall be over my house*.¹⁵² That is to say, you shall be higher than Emanation, which is called [the God of Israel's] house, *and by your word shall all my people be nourished*.¹⁵³

Hence, *you must obey all that Sarah tells you*, from which the midrash infers that *Abraham was Sarah's inferior in prophecy*.¹⁵⁴ And this is just as we have said—that in the magnitude of his illumination he [the God of Israel] did not have the capacity to distinguish as did the Shechinah, which was at the time represented by Sarai.¹⁵⁵

8. Jealousy Among the Shechinahs

[The God of Israel's hankering for the Rachel-Shechinah—a virgin, but as we shall see only technically so—arouses the jealousy of the Higher Shechinah. A Talmudic story describes, in heavy disguise, her complaint to the Root about the inequity of their current sexual arrangements, and her consequent banishment to dwell within "Rachel"—a banishment demanded by the God of Israel, who afterward must atone for having wronged the Higher Shechinah and disrespected the authority of the Root. Meanwhile a parallel drama plays itself out in Enclothement, as reflected in the twelfth chapter of Numbers; and the Bible's seemingly irrelevant remark that "the man Moses [= the God of Israel in his Enclothement] was very humble, more than anyone on the face of the earth" leads into an excursus on the humility of God.]

All the sexual desire of the God of Israel being for Rachel, as the Zohar explains in multiple places,¹⁵⁶ the Higher Shechinah grew jealous of *Malkhut*'s receiving effluence both from him who is the God of Israel and from herself. She demanded that [p. 133] the customary procedure of the supernal worlds be followed, that she receive all the God of Israel's

---

152. Weaving together Gen 41:39–40 and the Talmudic maxim quoted above.

153. Gen 41:40, as understood by Rashi. Ms. Jerusalem 2491 reads, in place of "Emanation," "the *Malkhut* of Emanation," evidently taking this to express the superiority of the "Leah" over the "Rachel"-Shechinah.

154. *Midrash Exodus Rabbah* 1:1, expounding Gen 21:12 (addressed by the Lord to Abraham); cf. Talmud, b. Meg. 14a.

155. I do not know why the author uses here the original form of Sarah's name (Gen 17:15).

156. This has already been asserted in the previous section, but without reference to the Zohar. I do not know what Zoharic passages the author has in mind.

effluence and that he not pour it into the *Malkhut* of Emanation. Rather, only she herself was to pour it into Emanation's *Malkhut*.

This was the complaint of the "moon" [= Higher Shechinah] when *she spoke before the Blessed Holy One* (in the Zohar, *qammei qudsha berikh hu*)—"before": as in the previously quoted *before there reigned any king*, and so forth, meaning that she made her complaint to the Root.[157] *Two monarchs, said she*, meaning herself and the God of Israel, *cannot make use of a single crown*. For *Malkhut* is represented as a crown (as in *a worthy woman is the crown of her husband*),[158] and both he and she were using her for sex.

Now, Zohar Hadash on the Song of Songs represents her as saying, *One monarch cannot make use of two crowns*.[159] This seems at first sight unintelligible, and in apparent contradiction [to the Talmud]. Yet, taken in accordance with what I have written, it makes perfect sense. It speaks of the God of Israel who has two females, i.e., two "crowns"; and of this [the Higher Shechinah] complained that he *cannot make* [sexual] *use of two crowns*. Rather, he should be having sex with her, and she have sex with *Malkhut*—this complaint she lodged with the Root, who was *before the Blessed Holy One*.[160]

But the God of Israel, in the intensity of his lust for *Malkhut*, did not wait for the Root to tell him what he might do with her. Before the Root could speak, he himself said, *Go and diminish yourself*. That is, she was to descend from the place where she had hitherto dwelt, in *Yesod* of Emanation, and go down [fol. 30a] into *Malkhut* of Emanation to reside

---

157. Drawing on the legend in the Talmud, b. Hul. 60b, that the sun and the moon were originally of equal magnitude (Gen 1:15) until the moon impudently demanded her own aggrandizement and was punished by being herself diminished. (She argued that "two kings cannot make use of a single crown," i.e., share the same rank—to which God responded, "Go and diminish yourself.") The Zohar (II, 144b) briefly alludes to this legend. I am not sure why the author makes a point of quoting the Zohar's Aramaic recasting of it, since the equivalent Hebrew of the Talmud (*lifnei ha-qadosh barukh hu*) will serve his purpose more effectively: *lifnei* is used in Gen 36:31 with a temporal meaning ("prior to"); just so here, the "moon" lodged her complaint with an entity "prior to" the Blessed Holy One (= God of Israel), i.e., the Root.

158. Prov 12:4, regularly applied by the Kabbalists to the *sefirah Malkhut*. It only slightly blemishes the author's argument that the word used for "crown" in the Biblical verse (*'atarah*) is not the same as the one used in the Talmudic passage (*keter*).

159. *Sefer Zohar Hadash*, 18b-c; Ashlag, *Sefer ha-Zohar*, 19:150–53. The full citation of "*Zohar Hadash* on the Song of Songs" occurs only in ms. Jerusalem 3100; Oxford 955 cites just "*Zohar Hadash*," Jerusalem 2491 "the *Tiqqunim*."

160. Chronologically prior to the God of Israel.

THE VIRGIN OF GOD

there, so she could couple with *Malkhut* by herself.[161] *Go* meant that she should depart from her place, *and diminish yourself*, that his Shechinah must squeeze herself into the vessel of *Malkhut*; and the text is careful to say that it was the Blessed Holy One who told her to *go*. She spoke *before* the Blessed Holy One,[162] while it was the Blessed Holy One who gave her the reply *Go and diminish yourself*.

That which is told in *Midrash Rabbah*—why is she called *lesser light? because she entered another's domain*[163]—makes perfect sense in accordance with what I have said. She entered into *Malkhut* of Emanation to reside there, and this was *another's domain*, and thus did she herself come to be *the lesser light*, as was *Malkhut* of Emanation.

[p. 134] [The "moon"] goes on to say:[164] *Because I spoke before you an honest word*—making precise use of *before you*, to indicate that [she said this] to the Root—*must I be diminished? And the Blessed Holy One said, Bring on my behalf an atonement-sacrifice*, because he had offended against the Root's dignity by not waiting for its answer, but at once pronouncing her judgment on his own. The words *your desire is for your husband*[165] apply to what we have said, that [the Higher Shechinah] complained against *Malkhut* of Emanation; *and he shall rule over you* means that [your "husband," the God of Israel] can sentence you to go down to a lower level. Yet *a sin-offering* is prescribed *for YHVH*,[166] inasmuch as [by doing so] he offended against the Root's dignity.

Now, the Enclothement of the God of Israel's Shechinah, which we have seen to be represented as Miriam,[167] also launched a complaint just as her Interiority did. This is the inner meaning of *Miriam and*

---

161. Presumably, by the very act of indwelling.

162. Not "to" the Blessed Holy One, but to an entity that was "prior to" the Blessed Holy One.

163. Free quotation of *Midrash Genesis Rabbah* 6:3, expounding Gen 1:16.

164. This is the continuation of the story in b. Hul. 60b, explaining why (according to a hyperliteral reading of Num 28:15) a sin-offering must be made each new moon on God's behalf: by diminishing the moon, he committed a sin. But what exactly was that sin? The Talmudic story implies that it was entirely a matter of the moon's hurt feelings; our author offers a more compelling explanation.

165. Gen 3:16, spoken by God (= the Root) to Eve (= the Higher Shechinah), and understood by our author as supplying a motivation for the Higher Shechinah's complaint, namely, sexual jealousy.

166. Num 28:15.

167. Above, chapter 6, sections 3 and 6.

Aaron—representing that first female who dwells in *Yesod*, whom we have seen to be the "essences of Joseph"[168]—*spoke against Moses*, i.e. the God of Israel, *on account of the Ethiopian woman he had taken*,[169] that is, his coupling with *Malkhut* of Emanation, who is represented as an Ethiopian woman, calling herself *black and beautiful*.[170] *They said: Has not the Lord also spoken with us?* referring to their having stood behind [the God of Israel], receiving effluence, at the time of his coupling with the Root, as described above.[171] They consequently raged against his desiring the Shechinah who was like an *Ethiopian woman* compared to them, having nothing of her own.[172]

The passage goes on to say that *the man Moses was very humble*. To understand this, you must realize that the God of Israel's Enclothement is *Tif'eret* of Emanation with its Six Points, to which the Zohar gives the name Little-face. This in spite of its receiving more of the rain's overflow than all the worlds, and being better structured than them all.[173]

This is the significance of *Hebron was built seven years* and so forth.[174] "Hebron" represents *Tif'eret* of Emanation, where the band of Patriarchs are buried and concealed[175] and where the Root shines as Dawn, as in,

168. Above, chapter 6, section 3.

169. Num 12:1. The author focuses on Miriam, ignoring for the time being the presence of Aaron (= the male *Yesod*; chapter 6, section 3). He has some warrant for this in the language of the Biblical verse, which uses feminine singular for the verb "spoke," even though its subject is both Miriam and Aaron.

170. Song 1:5, regularly applied in the traditional Kabbalah (e.g., Zohar, I, 49a–b, II, 14a) to the *sefirah Malkhut*, her "blackness" understood as the absence of any self-illumination.

171. Above, section 7, the Miriam-Shechinah sharing in the experience of the Higher Shechinah who dwells within her.

172. That is, no illumination; said in the Zohar of *Malkhut*, represented as the moon who has no light of her own but only that which she reflects from the sun. Bizarre as this interpretation of the seemingly straightforward story in Num 12 may seem, it answers the otherwise puzzling question of what relevance Miriam and Aaron's protest in verse 2 has to Moses's Ethiopian wife.

173. On the terminology of this paragraph, and the symbolism of the "rain," see above, chapter 5, sections 5 and 7. Here and in the coming paragraphs the author dwells on the incongruity of the God of Israel's Enclothement being called Little-face in spite of its evident superiority, and correlates this with Moses's "humility" in Num 12:3.

174. Num 13:22, quoted to demonstrate the truth of the author's last assertion, that Little-face is more thoroughly built up than the rest of Emanation.

175. In Kabbalistic thought, three of the Six Points, the *sefirot Hesed, Gevurah*, and *Tif'eret*, are symbolized by Abraham, Isaac, and Jacob, all of whom are buried in Hebron. "Hebron" can therefore be equated with "Greater *Tif'eret*" (the "Six Points") as the location of this Patriarchal "band." (The word *havurah*, "band," is from the same root

Does the eastern sky shine as far as Hebron?[176] *It was built seven years before Zoan of Egypt*: the other worlds are called "Zoan of Egypt" because they came from the Shechinah, which in her condition as placenta is called "Egypt," *Mitzrayim—metzar yam*, "the straits of the sea"—as discussed above in connection with the verse *A people come forth from Egypt*.[177] [p. 135] And they are called *Zoan* in that they were relocated from their original place and suspended, with the Balance, in a place they had not previously been, as we have seen;[178] hence *Zoan*, implying "relocation," as in *a tent that shall not experience relocation*.[179]

[The Talmud,] expounding this verse, asks, *what is meant by "built"? If you say*, and so forth, *would a man ever build*, and so forth—treating the one [Hebron] as symbolic of Little-face, the other [Zoan] as symbolic of Long-face[180]—*but rather that it was structured*, and so forth,[181] many times better than the higher worlds that are called "Zoan of Egypt." The God of Israel, moreover, dwells there openly, which cannot be said of any of the higher worlds. Yet he is called Little-face, for a reason indeed to be presently discussed, but also because he is humble and makes himself little with respect to the higher worlds, entering into Mother's womb to experience Nursing and Maturity, as Luria has described in detail.[182]

---

as *hevron*, "Hebron.")

176. Mishnah, m. Yoma 3:1, Tamid 3:2, where the question interrogates whether the dawn has broken. Our author takes it as referring to the intense illumination that occurs when the Root (= Dawn; above, chapter 5, section 3) copulates with the God of Israel (= Hebron). This is of course in total disregard of the context, but it responds to a legitimate exegetical question: why does the Mishnah single out Hebron?

177. Num 22:5, expounded above, chapter 4, section 6. On the Higher Shechinah as placenta, see above, chapter 3, section 1.

178. Referring back to chapter 5, section 9, expounding the opening of the Book of Concealment (Zohar, II, 176b), where the Balance is said to have been "suspended in a place where it was not."

179. Isa 33:20, where the verb *yitz'an*, "experience relocation," is from the same root as "Zoan" and thus can serve as lexical evidence for the meaning of the place-name.

180. *Arikh Anpin*, the sefirotic "Enclothement" of the Holy Distant One (above, chapter 5, sections 5 and 7).

181. Elliptical quotation of Talmud, b. Ketub. 112a: "What is meant by 'built'? If you say, 'built' is to be taken literally [i.e., that Hebron was built seven years before Zoan], would a man ever build a house for his younger son before building one for his older son [alluding to Gen 10:6, where Mitzrayim/Egypt is Ham's second son, Canaan his fourth]? ... But rather, [it means] that [Hebron] was structured seven times better than Zoan [and therefore yielded more produce]." This Talmudic midrash completes our author's argument for the superiority of Little-face's structure over those of the higher manifestations of Divinity.

182. See above, chapter 5, section 5. For "Mother's womb," mss. Oxford 955 and

9. Excursus: the concealment of God

[The God of Israel, in his great humility, conceals and abases himself so none can recognize his true grandeur; he is rewarded by being exalted by the Root. So Paul says of Jesus Christ in the Epistle to the Philippians; and some influence of the Christian doctrine of the *kenosis*, the "self-emptying" that enabled Christ's ignominious death on the cross, seems probable.]

The God of Israel goes into concealment, to such a degree that Father and Mother and all the higher worlds fall into error with regard to him.[183] They do not know the secret of the God of Israel dwelling among them, or *where is the place of his glory?*[184] for they cannot grasp the place of his encampment. He then has the quality of a persecuted fugitive, of one *abandoned by my father and my mother*,[185] and when the Root sees the magnitude of his humility, he desires him and couples with him, as the Scripture says, *God seeks out the persecuted*.[186]

He is persecuted, he is abandoned—and for that reason [the Root] *seeks him out* and magnifies him exceedingly. In consequence, the Shechinah also experiences great illumination.[187] This is the meaning of what was said by David: *I will be yet more despised than this*, and so forth, *with*

Jerusalem 3100 have "the womb of Father and Mother," which at first seems incongruous, but makes sense against the background of the earlier passage.

183. This can be reconciled with the author's assertion in the preceding section, that the God of Israel "dwells openly" within Little-face, by supposing that, as the sequel suggests, it speaks of a transitory occultation.

184. Spoken by the angels in the *Qedushah* prayer, on the basic of the Talmudic exegesis of Ezek 3:12 (b. Hag. 13b).

185. Ps 27:10, understood by our author as referring to the sefirotic entities "Father" and "Mother." Ms. Jerusalem 2491 adds, "and so forth," referring to the rest of the Biblical verse "YHVH will gather me in"—which transitions smoothly into what follows.

186. Eccl 3:15. At the time these words were written, Sabbatai Zevi's followers had been a persecuted, abandoned minority within the Jewish people for over half a century, the truth they proclaimed mocked and unrecognized.

187. At the time of the Root's coupling with the God of Israel; above, end of section 7. The link between the prophetic competence of "Aaron" and "Miriam" in Num 12:2, and the humility of "Moses" in verse 3, is thereby accounted for.

them shall I be honored[188]—all things being, in other words, *proportional to the magnitude of one's humility.*[189]

There is another reason for this as well:[190] to protect the Jewish people in their failure to recognize their Father in heaven, who is the God of Israel.[191]

All the [Kabbalistic] worlds, inasmuch as they are Enclothement and no more, have the quality of the female, of Judgment, and they act as denouncers of the Jewish people.[192] [p. 136] Therefore [the God of Israel] reduces and conceals himself to such an extent that they cannot recognize him at all; and afterwards, when he rises and couples with the Root and they see his greatness, they cannot denounce the Jews, for they also had refused to recognize him. Hence *your humility makes me great*, for it is he who magnifies him;[193] and *he descended from occasioning the sin.*[194] That is to say, he diminished himself as a sort of descent, a smallness, so that all the worlds should commit the sin of failing to recognize him.[195]

---

188. 2 Sam 6:22, David's words to his wife Michal: "I will be yet more despised than this, debased in my own sight; and as for the maidservants of whom you speak, with them shall I be honored." The author infers that the more one allows oneself to be despised, the more one is honored.

189. Mishnah, m. Pe'ah 1:2, a difficult passage which the author employs in total disregard for its context.

190. For the God of Israel's concealment, apart from his modesty.

191. It is a familiar trope of the Sabbatian literature that the Jews fail to recognize the true God, in fulfillment of the prophecy of 2 Chr 15:3: "Israel shall abide many days without a true God, without a teaching priest, without Torah." See, e.g., Halperin, *Abraham Miguel Cardozo*, 184–201; and below, chapter 9, section 4.

192. Enclothement is "female," in that it is a container for something else; and female = Judgment is a traditional Kabbalistic equation.

193. Ps 18:36. In the author's gloss on the verse, "he" would seem to be the Root, "him" the God of Israel; but this does not square very well with the Biblical text, where one individual's humility—in its present context, this would have to be the God of Israel—makes another individual "great." Perhaps, following the Bible but contrary to the grammar of the gloss, take humility as the subject of "magnifies"? Or, against the context, take the Jewish people as the object of the verb? (This is perhaps suggested by ms. Oxford 955, which reads "them" in place of "him.") Neither suggestion is very satisfactory.

194. Lev 9:22, which, in its Biblical context, certainly means that Aaron "came down from making the sin-offering, the whole-offering, and the peace-offerings." The author, however, wants to understand *hattat*, *'olah*, and *shelamim* as "sin," "ascent," and "peacemakings," and—only here, it seems—to take "Aaron" as symbolic of the God of Israel. I translate accordingly.

195. The language of this passage, and its use to illustrate the virtue of humility, is very suggestive of Paul's words in Phil 2:3-11. "Do nothing from selfishness or conceit, but in humility count others better than yourselves. . . . Have this in mind among

The Bible goes on to explain why he did this: *and the ascent*, meaning that afterward he shall rise to lofty heights as we have said[196]—as expressed in *God seeks out the persecuted*—and then *the peacemakings*, in order to make peace between the Jewish people and their Father in heaven, so that no accusation might be launched against them.

When the Bible says, *Above this I did choose on account of poverty*,[197] it means that the Root chose the Shechinah who is called *Above* (as we know from *above the Lord*[198]); and *I did choose* the God of Israel, who is called *This*.[199] Why were they chosen? *On account of poverty*, i.e., humility—meaning, as we have said, that they [fol. 30b] reduced themselves. Thus it was that *the man Moses was very humble, more than anyone on the face of the earth*:[200] i.e., more than all the worlds that draw their nourishment from *Malkhut*, who is called "earth" as we have said, and who is *your Malkhut, Malkhut of all the worlds*.[201]

---

ourselves, which you have in Christ Jesus, who, though he was in the form of God, did not count equality with God a thing to be grasped, but emptied himself, taking the form of a servant, being born in the likeness of men. And being found in human form he humbled himself and became obedient unto death, even death on a cross. Therefore God has highly exalted him and bestowed on him the name which is above every name ... " (RSV). Some influence of the Christian doctrine of the divine *kenosis* ("emptying")—a core teaching of the eighteenth-century Moravians, as I am informed by Moravian historian Craig D. Atwood—seems very likely.

196. For the abbreviation כנ"ל (ms. Jerusalem 2491), the other mss. have ביוה"כ (Oxford 955) or ביה"כ (Jerusalem 3100), *be-yom ha-kippurim*, "on Yom Kippur." This reading makes no sense in context, but may allude to Sabbatai Zevi's death on Yom Kippur 1676, and the belief that after his death he was elevated to the rank of divinity.

197. Job 36:21, altering—arbitrarily and gratuitously, it would seem—the Bible's *baharta*, "you chose," to *baharti*, "I chose." The author returns to the point he made at the beginning of this section, that it was the God of Israel's humility that inspired the Root's affection for him. He reads the two words *'al zeh* ("above this") hyperliterally, identifying the first with the Shechinah and the second with the God of Israel; see the following two notes.

198. Isa 58:14 (reading על ה', in place of the mss. עלה), which the Zohar understands hyperliterally to mean that "you shall rejoice *above the Lord*"—i.e., in a realm superior to "the Lord" (= *Tif'eret*), often identified as the female *sefirah Binah* (e.g., I, 216a; see Matt, trans., *Zohar*, 3:302). Our author builds on this interpretation, but takes "above the Lord" to be a yet higher female, the Higher Shechinah.

199. The identification of "this" (*zeh*) with the masculine element of divinity goes back to the Zohar, II, 37b, which also links it (following Exod 32:1) to Moses.

200. Thus returning to Num 12:3.

201. Ps 145:13; see above, chapter 5, section 6. The equation of "earth" with the *sefirah Malkhut* is a staple of Kabbalah.

10. Banishment

[The exposition of Num 12 resumes, with the banishment of "Miriam"—another name for the "Leah" Shechinah—and the Higher Shechinah within her into the lower "Rachel" Shechinah. This demotion, comparable to a death, may be contrasted with the exaltation of the God of Israel described in the previous section.]

The Root grew angry. So did the God of Israel; and he commanded them to go out to the entrance to the Tent of Meeting, i.e., *Malkhut*.[202] There he explained to them the distinction:[203] that they achieve their awareness via the dream that comes to the God of Israel, whereas the God of Israel himself, represented in Enclothement by Moses, speaks with the Root *mouth to mouth*.[204] Like Deep Sleep, therefore, [the Root] is upon him—not so they! For they achieve their awareness from behind him, as though by hearing. So we have said: YOU WERE BEHIND ME AT THE TIME I DREAMED.[205]

As in Interiority, so in Enclothement. The external *Tif'eret* achieves awareness of the God of Israel *mouth to mouth*. Not so Miriam, who is the first female and the Enclothement of the Higher Shechinah,[206] and whose awareness of the God of Israel comes only through dream. [p. 137] The distinction between the Shechinah and the God of Israel vis-à-vis their awareness of the Root has its parallel, in Enclothement, in that between the external *Tif'eret* (i.e., Moses) and the Shechinah's Enclothement

---

202. Cf. Num 12:4, where God issues this command to Moses, Aaron, and Miriam; our author anticipates verse 5, where Aaron and Miriam are singled out. The subject of the verbs is unclear; one would assume it has to be the Root (= God) who gives the command. But, confusingly, the author seems to represent it as having been the God of Israel, who has hitherto = Moses but now shifts to = the Biblical God, taking the Root's place in the author's exegesis of the Bible story as its emphasis shifts from Interiority to Enclothement (below). The equation of *Malkhut* with the Tent of Meeting or its entrance is familiar from the Zohar; mss. Jerusalem 2491 and 3100 add, "as mentioned above," but this seems to be the first time the author has used it. Perhaps we should emend בנ״ל to בנו׳, "as is well known."

203. Between their awareness of the higher divinity and "Moses's."

204. Num 12:8. The previous verses have described how God speaks with prophets other than Moses "in a dream," which the author is forced to interpret, in accord with section 7 above, as the dream of the God of Israel to which the Shechinah is witness.

205. Zohar, I, 196a, quoted above, section 7.

206. On the symbolism of Miriam, see above, chapter 6, section 3; on the language of "first" and "second" female, the beginning of chapter 6, section 6. The author is not entirely consistent with his terminology: in section 7 above, Miriam is the "second female."

(i.e., Miriam) vis-à-vis their awareness of the God of Israel. All this we have discussed at length in connection with THROUGH HIS SIGNS HE IS KNOWN;[207] refer back to that passage, and you will understand.

He[208] therefore expelled [Miriam] from within *Yesod*, and she remained outside. So we read, *YHVH's anger was kindled against them and he departed*—removed himself from them, went forth and went his way. *The cloud*, representing *Yesod, turned away from over the Tent*, representing the Shechinah, *and Miriam was leprous as snow.*[209] This was, as we well know, because the Judgments had gotten power within her and the illumination of the God of Israel had removed itself from her. "Leprous" has the sense of "uncovered," as the Targum renders [the "uncovering"] of the leper, and the meaning is that she had been driven outside.[210]

Thereupon Aaron, who, as I have written, was the male *Yesod* and bound up with Miriam,[211] cried out, *Please, let her not be like a dead person*,[212] i.e., suffer Shattering, demotion in rank being a kind of death.[213] She was half his body, he says, dwelling with him inside a single shape;[214] and when he speaks of [the dead person's] *going forth from its mother's womb*, this refers to the time when the Higher Shechinah gave birth to her in the process of building the structure of Emanation,[215] and she was half his body, half the shape. (Hence: *its flesh half eaten away.*)

---

207. Variant text of Zohar, III, 128b (*Idra Rabbah*); see the author's extended discussion of the *Idra* passage and of Enclothement versus Interiority in chapter 5, sections 8–9.

208. Apparently now the God of Israel.

209. Num 12:9–10.

210. The author draws on Lev 13:45, where the leper goes about with head uncovered (according to the view of Rabbi Akiba in the Talmud, b. Mo'ed Qat. 15a), to show that Miriam's "leprosy" consisted of her being "uncovered," driven from the shelter of the *sefirah Yesod*. (He is perhaps inspired by the reverse equation in *Midrash Numbers Rabbah* 7:1.) I am not sure why he invokes the Targum in support of his view; it translates Hebrew *parua'* with the Aramaic equivalent *peria'* but does nothing to clarify its meaning.

211. Above, chapter 6, section 3.

212. Num 12:12, Aaron's appeal to Moses on Miriam's behalf, referring in its Biblical context to a stillborn infant.

213. Zohar, III, 135b (*Idra Rabbah*), applied in chapter 5, section 9, to the "Shattering" of the *sefirah Yesod*. For the "Miriam" Shechinah to descend from *Yesod* into *Malkhut* is a demotion, therefore a "death."

214. I.e., the structure of *Yesod*. Aaron is simultaneously *Yesod* itself and, like Miriam, a dweller within it.

215. As described in chapter 5, section 5, above.

THE VIRGIN OF GOD

So Moses made his plea:[216] *O God—El*, who is the Distant One, and also the Root who is called *El*, as we have said. *Na*, he said—*nun-aleph*, the letter *aleph* representing the Root, as is well known, and the Distant One represented by *Mi*, the Fifty Gates of Understanding, and thus called *Na*. When [Moses] said, *El Na, heal her please*, and God replied, *If her father had spit in her face*—which Rashi glosses as "he showed her angry faces," i.e., [those of] the God of Israel and the Root[217]—she was sentenced to *go and diminish yourself*, i.e., descend into the Shechinah that is the *Malkhut* of Emanation, there to have her dwelling and resting place. Hence, *she shall be contained within Seven-Days*,[218] meaning that *Malkhut*, represented as "Seven-Days," shall contain her (as in the phrase *too small to contain*[219]). There she shall be incorporated, and there shall she dwell.

And so it was. *Miriam was enclosed within Seven-Days*[220]—the Lower Shechinah, which is *Malkhut*—that is, she was enclosed there, dwelt there. [p. 138] And so, to sum up:

1. The Shechinah of the God of Israel, a.k.a. "Higher Shechinah"; and

---

216. Num 12:13: *el na refa na lah*, "God, please, heal her please." The author understands the plea as addressed by the God of Israel (= Moses) to the higher divinities, the Root and the Distant One. The equation of *El* with both of these is set forth in chapter 5, section 1. The interpretation of *Na* is rather more convoluted. The word's first letter, *nun*, has the numerical value of 50, and is therefore equated with the interrogative *Mi*, "who?" which in the Kabbalah can be taken as a divine epithet, normally applied to the *sefirah Binah*, "Understanding." Our author has earlier applied it to the Root (= the Will of Ein Sof; chapter 1, section 5) and then, without explanation for the shift, used it for the Distant One (chapter 5, section 7 end). In the traditional Kabbalah, the letter *aleph* represents the highest *sefirah*, *Keter*, which is on the boundary with Ein Sof; or, *Keter* + the next two *sefirot*, *Hokhmah* and *Binah*—this is how our author explains it, in chapter 1, section 2—or, the totality of the sefirotic system (Zohar, I, 21a; Matt, trans., Zohar, 1:161). I assume our author has some precedent for here identifying it with a super-sefirotic entity, but I cannot point to any specific source. The outcome is that, like *El*, the next word, *Na*, combines the Root and the Distant One.

217. Num 12:14. Rashi's gloss, in its original context, means simply, "he scowled at her." Our author takes it hyperliterally as implying that Miriam was shown more than one "angry face," and proceeds to identify these "faces" as those of the Root and the God of Israel, both of whom may correspond to the "God" of the Bible story. "Go and diminish yourself" harks back to the Talmudic story of the moon's diminution, discussed in section 8 above.

218. Num 12:14, *tikkalem shiv'at yamim*, "she shall be ashamed for seven days." The author, ignoring the final *mem* of *tikkalem*, derives it from the root meaning "contain, incorporate."

219. 1 Kgs 8:64.

220. Num 12:15.

2. her Enclothement, who is symbolically represented as "Miriam" and as the "essences of Joseph";[221] all dwelt inside

3. the Lower Shechinah, who is *Malkhut* of Emanation and is called "Seven-Days" or "Daughter-of-Seven," Bathsheba.[222]

This is the significance of Jacob's marrying Leah, who was the equivalent of his mother, as the Zohar explains: LEAH WAS HATED, FROM WHICH WE LEARN THAT A MAN IS REPELLED BY SEX WITH HIS MOTHER.[223] This makes perfect sense in accordance with what we have said: that the God of Israel's Shechinah gave birth to Jacob (who is the external *Tif'eret*), and now she is enclothed within Rachel (the Lower Shechinah),[224] while the God of Israel is enclothed within Jacob. When they make love, therefore, Jacob has sex with his mother, who is the Higher Shechinah. (See the discussion above, of the Shechinah's being called "mother" of the God of Israel in her role as *mother of all living*.[225])

11. The Imagery of Enclothement

[What does it mean for one Shechinah to be "enclothed" in another? The author undertakes to clarify this through a symbolization—begun here, continued through sections 13–15—of the Jerusalem Temple and its most sacred apparatus as representations of the Shechinahs. The tablets of the Ten Commandments represent the Higher Shechinah, the ark in which they are deposited the Lower "Miriam" Shechinah. (The "Rachel" Shechinah can also be an ark; hence the two arks that

---

221. Above, chapter 6, section 3.

222. The use of "Bathsheba" (*bat sheva'*, "daughter of seven") as code for *Malkhut* is familiar from the traditional Kabbalah. The author seems to use this to support his far more dubious equation—essential to his exegesis of Num 12—of "seven days" with *Malkhut*. Ms. Jerusalem 2491 adds here ובה׳ הזווג, "and in her is the coupling"—or possibly, "the coupling is with the Lord"?—the "coupling" presumably being that of the God of Israel with his multiple Shechinahs. But it is very awkward,

223. Gen 29:31, interpreted in Zohar, I, 154b. Mss. Oxford 955 and Jerusalem 3100 add that this occurs "in several places" in the Zohar, but I am aware only of this one.

224. So all the mss., but it would make more sense to read "Leah."

225. This parenthetical note seems to contradict the exposition of Gen 3:20 in chapter 2, section 3, where the Higher Shechinah emerges from the God of Israel and is hardly his "mother." It also seems to miss the point of what has just been said, where it is not the God of Israel but his "Enclothement" *Tif'eret* who has sex with the Mother. Though found in all mss., always marked off by parentheses or the equivalent, it seems likely to be an interpolation.

accompanied the Israelites in the wilderness.) And the God of Israel? He is the writing engraved on the tablets, inscribed within the Higher Shechinah.]

Our next task must be to clarify the precise nature of this "Enclothement" of one entity within another.

You must recognize that the Higher Shechinah, which is "the Shechinah of the God of Israel," is symbolically represented by the *tablets* that are *the work of God*,[226] namely the Root; for it is he who (as we have seen) couples with the God of Israel, as implied by *my sister, daughter of my Father*.[227] This is why they are called *tablets of Stone*:[228] [the Shechinah] is that "Foundation Stone" from which the world was established, as we have explained at some length.[229] The "essences of Joseph," a.k.a. "Miriam," are represented as the "Ark of the Lord" (as we have said), [Joseph having been] *put into the Ark*,[230] which was where the tablets were placed.[231] And the God of Israel is symbolically equivalent to the Torah—all inside the Female, his mark there inscribed, as the Zohar explains. Consequently the Ten Commandments, which had the quality of the God of Israel's shape, were *engraved upon the tablets*,[232] HIS MARK WHICH HE INSCRIBED WITHIN HER.[233]

Now, prior to the Shechinah's descent into *Malkhut*,[234] *Malkhut* also had the quality of an "ark." Within her was the inscription of the God of Israel, of the fragments of the Shattered vessels that remained

---

226. Exod 32:16, describing Moses's descent from Sinai with the two tablets of the Ten Commandments.

227. Gen 20:12, as interpreted above, chapter 2, section 3: the Higher Shechinah emerges from the homosexual coupling of the Root with the God of Israel, an event represented in the Bible as Eve's emergence from Adam's state of "Deep Sleep."

228. Exod 31:18.

229. Above, chapter 1, section 2.

230. Gen 50:26, where Joseph is embalmed and "put into the coffin"; the Hebrew word *aron* can mean both "ark" and "coffin."

231. Deut 10:1-5, 1 Kgs 8:9. On the symbolism of the Ark, cf. above, chapter 6, section 3—where, however, it is Aaron and not Miriam who is identified with it.

232. Exod 32:16.

233. These last words are in Aramaic, evidently a quote from the Zohar passage to which the author has just alluded. I have not been able to locate the passage.

234. As described in the preceding sections.

inside her.²³⁵ This is the significance of *the two arks*,²³⁶ one of which goes forth to war—namely, *Malkhut* of Emanation, who enters the *Tehiru* by night to take a captivity captive and seize the spoils;²³⁷ and this is the *ark of the Shechinah*.²³⁸ The second "ark" is the one represented by Miriam, as described above, which cannot go into battle because she is in the condition of having been sexually penetrated. [p. 139] Hence *the two arks that traveled with Israel in the desert*,²³⁹ one *of Joseph*—representing Miriam and the "essences of Joseph," as we have said—and the other *of the Shechinah*, i.e., the *Malkhut* of Emanation.

Subsequently, in David's time, the Shechinah dwelt below, within *Malkhut* of Emanation. This is what is meant by *the essences of Joseph did they bury in Shechem*,²⁴⁰ which, as is well known, signifies *Malkhut* (as in, *I gave you one shekhem over your brothers*, and so forth).²⁴¹ Understand this.

235. Presumably, those gathered by *Malkhut* during her nightly descent into the *Tehiru* (above, chapter 6, section 6), the "spoils" to which the author will presently allude. Their relation to "the inscription of the God of Israel"—for which ms. Jerusalem 2491 has "the lights inscribed by the God of Israel"—is not clear.

236. Which, according to the Talmud (b. Sotah 13a–b) and its midrashic parallels (below), traveled with the Israelites in the desert: the Ark of the Covenant and the "ark" (*aron*) containing Joseph's remains.

237. The language is plainly modeled after Ps 68:19, "You ascended to the heights, you took a captivity captive, you took gifts for humans"—a verse applied in the rabbinic midrash to Moses's ascent to heaven, his battle with the angels, and his seizing the Torah from them for the benefit of humankind (Halperin, *Faces*, 292–307). But unlike Moses, *Malkhut* makes a *descent*—into the *Tehiru*, her purpose closely akin to that of Christ's "harrowing of hell." It seems to me likely that our author views this passage through the prism of its exegesis in the New Testament, Eph 4:8-10, RSV ("In saying, 'He ascended,' what does it mean but that he had also descended into the lower parts of the earth?") and its subsequent Christian elaborations, which he had perhaps learned from the Moravians. The "human gifts" of the psalm thus become the souls "mended," purified, and raised by *Malkhut*'s invasion.

238. Of which the Talmudic passage speaks; reading 'שכ, "Shechinah," for ש"ב, *shivrei kelim*, "fragments of the vessels." It is thinkable that the author intended to combine the two meanings, both of which will suit his argument.

239. Following the language of the midrash Pesiqta de-Rav Kahana 11:12.

240. Josh 24:32. The relevance of the seemingly gratuitous reference to David will become clear in the following discussion.

241. Gen 48:22. *Shekhem*, spelled in Hebrew the same as the name of the city, normally means "shoulder"; here it seems to have the sense of "portion." Its identification with *Malkhut* rests on Zohar, I, 80a (*Sitrei Torah*), which in turn rests on a traditional understanding of *beharbi u-veqashti* in the rest of the verse ("which I took from the Amorite *with my sword and my bow*") as "with my prayers": it is the divine presence, the Shechinah, that can be "taken" with prayer.

12. David and Bathsheba

[A digression, it would seem. Yet "David" foreshadows some of the themes to be taken up in connection with the Temple, as well as the messianic denouement of chapter 9. We are given a revelation as surprising in its way as the equation of the Biblical Pharaoh with the God of Israel: that David, so thoroughly masculine in the Bible's portrayal of him, is essentially female, a representation of the Higher Shechinah. His dalliance with Bathsheba, who represents the Lower ("Rachel") Shechinah, is a lesbian amour exactly parallel to Eve's (= Higher Shechinah) eating from the Tree of Knowledge (= Lower Shechinah); and it is no accident that the Talmud uses the language of "eating" in connection with it. The Talmud's calling the Messiah "son of the fallen ones" now also makes sense, for he is the "son" of the Higher Shechinah who fell from her place into the "Rachel" Shechinah, and also the Higher Shechinah herself. We are now better prepared to find, as we will in chapter 9, the Messiah Sabbatai Zevi ("David") taking on the female role vis-à-vis the Distant One.]

You must recognize that "David" represents the Higher Shechinah, and that the God of Israel and the Shechinah are represented as "Davids," lovers,[242] as is well known. That is why [fol. 31a] he is called "David"— because he is a lover.[243]

Bathsheba represents the Lower Shechinah, *Malkhut* of Emanation; that is why she is named Bathsheba.[244] We have earlier said that the Higher Shechinah is represented by the Tree of Life, and that Adam's wife caused damage by not postponing her sex with the Shechinah that is *Malkhut* of Emanation until the nighttime, when the power of fire would be dominant and the *Tehiru* waters would have no hold upon them.[245]

---

242. *Dodim*, which can be read as plural of "David" but also of *dod*, the designation of the lover in the Song of Songs (e.g., 5:9). Ms. Jerusalem 2491 illustrates the point by quoting Song 1:2—where, however, "your *dodim*" seems to refer to lovemaking rather than "lovers."

243. The discussion that follows is apt to be confusing unless one remembers that David, although historically male, here represents a *female* entity, the Higher Shechinah. (There is precedent for this in the traditional Kabbalah, where David is the embodiment of the female *sefirah Malkhut*; but cf. Wolfson's reservations: Wolfson, "*Malkhut Ein Sof*," 53.) His/her sex with Bathsheba is therefore a lesbian act, exactly parallel to "Eve's" "eating" from the "Tree of Knowledge," as the author goes on to point out. The implications for his perceptions of the new "David," Sabbatai Zevi, are substantial.

244. "Daughter of seven," so called because *Malkhut* is constituted of six higher *sefirot* plus herself (Zohar, III, 37a).

245. As described in chapter 6, section 6. The author perhaps reminds us that

But [*Malkhut*] was made to engage in sex before her proper time, during the day, and the *Tehiru* waters were able to take hold of them; and this was David's sin as well. He had sex with Bathsheba at a time when the *Tehiru* waters were still able to get hold of her.

[These waters] are the mark left by the Mindless Light, as we have said, made (as we have said) by the process of Self-folding and represented by *Heth*.[246] Hence [Bathsheba] is *the woman of Uri-Yah the Hethite*:[247] the mark left by the God of Israel in his Self-folding is called *Yah* and partakes of the quality of *Heth* [= the *Tehiru*], and daylight [*or*] still had a grip on them that could not be remedied, for night had not yet fallen. That was his sin; and it was said of it that *he ate her unripe*—before her proper time, that is—and that David *treated the daytime as though it were night*, meaning that he made love during the day when he should have waited for nightfall.[248]

This is the meaning of the formula *David king of Israel lives and endures*:[249] that he represents the Tree of Life,[250] entirely unaffected by death. [p. 140] But after the sinful complaint of which we have spoken,[251] he was expelled from his proper dwelling and became as an aborted fetus, inasmuch as he had "fallen" from his place.[252] Adam, representing

---

the Higher Shechinah is the Tree of Life in anticipation of what he will say two paragraphs on.

246. An imprecise summary of what is described in chapter 3, sections 1–2, 5. The term "Self-folding" (*hitqappelut*) is used there both for the male Shape's folding himself to enter the Female's womb, and the Mindful Light's doing the same to enter its allotted half-square (represented by the Hebrew letter *het*); here the author seems to make use of both meanings. On the symbolism of the Biblical name *Heth* (= *het*), see chapter 6, section 4—where the "daughters of Heth" (Gen 27:46) are "spirits that were left wholly unfinished, unmended"—and section 6, where "Heth" = the *Tehiru*.

247. 2 Sam 11:3: "the wife of Uriah the Hittite." Our author breaks "Uriah" into *Uri* (= *or*, "light") and *Yah*, an abbreviated form of the name YHVH. The effect is to turn "Uriah the Hittite" from Bathsheba's husband into a symbolic description of the metaphysical consequences of her ill-considered encounter with "David."

248. Both quotations, the second very free, from the Talmud, b. Sanh. 107a. The Talmudic description of David's sin as the eating of an unripe fruit—in its original context, meaning that David should have waited for Bathsheba to become his legitimate wife—helps our author equate his transgression with "Eve's."

249. Talmud, b. Rosh Hash. 25a, used to announce the appearance of a new moon—"David," as Rashi says, representing the moon.

250. Both being symbols of the Higher Shechinah.

251. Referring to the Talmudic story of the "moon's" (= Higher Shechinah's) complaint; above, section 8. Since the current context speaks of David, the author continues to use masculine pronouns for this female entity.

252. *Nefel*, an aborted fetus, is from the root *nafal*, "to fall."

the God of Israel, took pity on him and granted him seventy of his own years: i.e., the Lower Shechinah, who, as is well known, is represented as "seven days" or "seven years."[253] There he dwelt; and she consequently received the name "*Malkhut*, David's house,"[254] for she was his house and he had settled within her.

This is why the Messiah is called Bar Naflei, "son of the fallen ones," for he is a representation of the Higher Shechinah, who fell from her place.[255] And, in truth, it was the will of the God of Israel that she fall, for it is perfectly true that *two monarchs cannot make use of a single crown*, nor can *any dominion encroach upon another, even in the smallest degree*.[256] That was why he commanded her to go down.

It is also the inner meaning of what Saul (who represents *Yesod*,[257] as we know from Luria's writings) said to Jonathan (who represents Moses and *Tif'eret*, as is well known):[258] *So long as Jesse's son is alive over the ground*, meaning that he is above *Malkhut* and not contained within her, *you and your Malkhut cannot be secure*.[259] For, as the "moon" protested, *two monarchs cannot make use of a single crown*.

---

253. Inspired by *Midrash Genesis Rabbah* 19:8, in which Adam is allotted a thousand-year lifespan after his sin, but breaks off seventy of those years and gives them to his descendants (Ps 90:10; hence he dies at age 930, Gen 5:5). David, as author of the Psalms, is evidently considered the foremost of those descendants. Our author seems to use *Malkhut*'s name "Bathsheba" (*bat sheva'*, "daughter of seven") to support his dubious equation with "seven days" (cf. note 222, above) and now also "seven years," further equated with "seventy years." We shall see more of those "seven years" below. (Despite the masculine pronouns, the essential subject is still the "dwelling" of the Higher Shechinah within the *sefirah Malkhut*.)

254. *Malkhut bet david*, a Talmudic phrase more usually understood as "the kingdom of the house of David."

255. Talmud, b. Sanh. 96b–97a: "Rav Nachman said to Rabbi Isaac, 'Have you heard when Bar Naflei will come?' He said to him, 'Who is Bar Naflei?' He said, 'The Messiah.' 'And you call the Messiah Bar Naflei?' He said to him, 'Yes, as it is written, "On that day I will raise up the fallen [*nofelet*] hut of David" [Amos 9:11].'" The fall of the Higher Shechinah has been described in section 8, above.

256. A catchphrase used in the Talmud (e.g., b. Ber. 48b) to convey that successive monarchies cannot in any measure overlap.

257. So ms Jerusalem 2491. Ms. Oxford 955 has "*Tif'eret*," Jerusalem 3100 "the Root." Vital's *'Etz Hayyim*, viii.4, 38d, which identifies the Edomite king "Shaul [= Saul] of Rehoboth by the River" (Gen 36:37) with the *sefirah Yesod* and extends this identification to the more familiar King Saul, practically guarantees the reading *Yesod*. But I do not know how the variants might have originated.

258. I do not know the author's basis for this identification, which seems out of step with his argument: to be entirely consistent, "Jonathan" ought to = the God of Israel.

259. 1 Sam 20:31. *Malkhut* here would normally be translated "kingship." For our

Understand this, and with it you will see why it was that David dwelt for seven years in Hebron—that is, inside the shape of *Tif'eret*, which we have already seen to be represented by Hebron—afterward dwelling in Jerusalem, which stands for *Malkhut* of Emanation.[260] And this is the significance of David's saying, *The jealousy of your house ate me up*.[261] He was jealous over *Malkhut*, which is *your house*; and that was what *ate me up* and brought about my descent.[262]

13. The Temple and Its Symbolism

> [The Temple represents the "Rachel" Shechinah, its structure parallel to that of the female reproductive organs, with the Holy of Holies as its "womb" equivalent. There the ark containing the Higher Shechinah was brought to dwell, by "Solomon," who stands for the God of Israel. This was a "death" for the "Miriam" Shechinah, who was the Eighth King of chapter 4; and that solves the old problem of why the Eighth King, who the book of Genesis implies survived the Shattering, had "died" by the time the book of Chronicles was written.]

If we are to convey the nature of the place in which the Tablets and the Ark, symbolizing the Higher Shechinah with its vessel,[263] took up their dwelling, you must realize that the Lower Shechinah is represented by the Temple. This is as we have said, that she descends into the *Tehiru* where she offers sacrifices, the fire arranged upon the altar, and so forth. (See our extended discussion, above.)[264]

---

author, however, it is the *sefirah Malkhut*—regularly represented in Kabbalistic symbolism by "ground" or "earth"—that is intended: as long as the Higher Shechinah is distinct from and superior to *Malkhut*, able to compete with the God of Israel for *Malkhut*'s favors, the God of Israel's sexual control of *Malkhut* will not be secure. (In this and the next paragraph, "David" is treated as masculine, even though the referent is the female Shechinah.)

260. 2 Sam 5:5. On the symbolism of Hebron, see above, section 8; the number seven, earlier associated with *Malkhut*, does not seem to be given symbolic meaning here. "David" formerly dwelt in *Tif'eret*, in that *Yesod* is the locus of the "Miriam" Shechinah, and it is also part of "Greater Tif'eret," the Six Points.

261. Ps 69:10, understanding the speaker as the Higher Shechinah and the one addressed as the God of Israel.

262. And so, from being the "eater" (above), David becomes the "eaten."

263. I.e., the "Miriam" Shechinah (reading singular *keli*, with ms. Jerusalem 2491); see above, end of section 10 and beginning of section 11.

264. Chapter 4, section 3. The "sacrifices" are the Shechinah's offerings of purified souls, the "fire" her instrument for their purification.

THE VIRGIN OF GOD

Know also that the female womb is comprised of three compartments: [1] the *heder*, "room," which is the source of the womb; [2] the *prozdor*, "corridor," which is the external structure;²⁶⁵ and [3] the *'aliyah*, "upper chamber," with an open passageway leading from the *'aliyah* to the *heder*.²⁶⁶ It is well known, likewise, that the male organ penetrates from the *prozdor* to the *'aliyah* but does not enter the womb proper, [p. 141] and the semen descends from there into the *heder* because that passageway is open to it.

You must understand, now, that the Temple is symbolically equivalent to the *prozdor*, the external structure, while the *heder* is equivalent to the Holy of Holies. There the male organ does not penetrate—as hinted in the words *No man shall come into it*,²⁶⁷ meaning that no sexual activity takes place there, but only in the *'aliyah* of the Holy of Holies. This is the symbolic meaning of the *passageway that was open from the 'aliyah of the Holy of Holies, through which they would lower the artisans in chests*²⁶⁸— referring to the effluence that goes down into the female, called "artisan" because it is the one that builds and designs everything. (It descends into the womb in the form of letters, its essence in Interiority being letters.²⁶⁹) *In chests—in order that they not feast their eyes*,²⁷⁰ it being forbidden to look upon the genitals while having sex, as we well know.

---

265. Or, "the outer Temple," as opposed to the Holy of Holies. This equation is stated explicitly below.

266. The tripartite division is taken from the Mishnah, m. Nid. 2:5, while the "open passageway" (*lul patuah*) is added from the Talmud's discussion of the Mishnah passage (b. Nid. 17b). In modern terminology, the *heder* is normally taken to be the uterus, and the *prozdor* the vaginal canal, while the anatomical referent of the *'aliyah* remains disputed. Brown, "Niddah 17b," quotes Preuss's view (*Biblisch-talmudische Medizin*, 130–35) that the *prozdor* is the vulva and the *'aliyah* the vagina, but dismisses it as not fitting in with the text of the Mishnah. It would, however, fit very well what our author says in this and the next sentence. Perhaps our author anticipated Preuss's identifications, mistaken as they may be.

267. Ezek 44:2, understood in traditional Christian exegesis to refer to the Virgin Mary.

268. Slightly free quotation of Mishnah, m. Mid. 4:5. No one may enter the Holy of Holies except the high priest on the Day of Atonement; yet handymen must also get in somehow to perform whatever repairs may be needed. The solution is to lower them in chests, suspended from ropes, through openings (plural in the Mishnah text, singular in this quotation) in the ceiling from the "upper chamber" above the Holy of Holies.

269. Of the Ten Commandments (= the male God of Israel), engraved upon the "tablets" that are the Higher Shechinah. See the beginning of section 11, above.

270. The continuation of the Mishnah passage, its final words "on the Holy of Holies" omitted, presumably because they do not suit the author's interpretation of the forbidden sight as the genitalia.

The Higher Shechinah, represented by the Ark and the tablets, was placed inside the Holy of Holies. The seed and the effluence do not come to her at once, but only after a purification process in the *'aliyah* of the Holy of Holies has brought them into a state of extreme luminescence and purity, whereupon they descend through the passageway into the Holy of Holies. This is why the *'aliyah* is also represented symbolically by the Woodshed Chamber, for it is well known that all the effluence is represented as wood—the Tree of Life, the Tree of Knowledge[271]—and there the superior wood that was fit to be burned on the altar was separated out from the rest.[272] And [that place] is called *dar*, meaning "dweller,"[273] for it is the place where the male organ is active.

This is why in David's time there were no longer two arks, as there had been in the days of Moses: one of them had been incorporated into the other, as we have shown.[274] It was the God of Israel, represented as Solomon, who brought the "Ark" into the "Holy of Holies"; and this is what is meant by *remember David your servant*,[275] inasmuch as he is a representation of the Ark of the Lord, as we have said.

It is the meaning also of what is said in the Zohar on the Torah portion *Bereshit*: YOU SHALL KEEP MY SABBATHS—THIS IS A SQUARE INSIDE A CIRCLE,[276] namely the Higher Shechinah, which has the quality

---

271. The same word, *'etz*, is used in Biblical Hebrew to mean "tree" and in rabbinic Hebrew to mean "wood."

272. The Woodshed Chamber (*lishkat dir ha-'etzim*) was an unroofed chamber at the northeast corner of the Women's Court of the Temple where the wood for the altar was stored, and where any worm-infested wood, unfit for use on the altar, was sorted out and eliminated (Talmud, b. Yoma 16a; also Mishnah, m. Mid. 2:5). Popular tradition held that the Ark was concealed beneath its floor (b. Yoma 54a, cf. m. Sheqal. 6:1). It could therefore be functionally and symbolically equated with the *'aliyah* over the Holy of Holies, even though the two were at some physical distance from one another.

273. Following ms. Oxford 955, which vocalizes the Mishnah's *dir*, "shed," as *dar*, "dweller," and (with the other mss.) goes on to explain that "this is the language of dwelling." The penis, being active within the *'aliyah*-vagina, is a "dweller" there.

274. At the end of section 11: the "Miriam" Shechinah, with the Upper Shechinah dwelling inside it, has been collapsed into the Lower ("Rachel") Shechinah, which is the Ark of the Covenant and also the Holy of Holies. Solomon's bringing the Ark into the Holy of Holies is therefore symbolic of the God of Israel decreeing that the Higher Shechinah descend to dwell within *Malkhut*. The author is less than consistent in his identifications of the Ark with one Shechinah or another.

275. Slightly altered version of 2 Chr 6:42, the conclusion of Solomon's prayer at the dedication of the Temple. David is the Higher Shechinah (beginning of section 12, above), and therefore the Ark that Solomon has installed in the Holy of Holies.

276. Free quotation of Zohar, I, 5b, which expounds the plural "Sabbaths" of Lev 19:30 to refer to the various sefirotic aspects of the Sabbath.

of a square, inasmuch as it was represented by the Tablets that were as long as they were wide.²⁷⁷ But the Lower Shechinah, *qua* womb, is circular, as set forth in Zohar and Tiqqunei Zohar: LIKE [fol. 31b] A SQUARE IN FORMLESSNESS, FIXED INSIDE A RING which represents the womb.²⁷⁸ Understand.

[p. 142] This is set forth in the Zohar at the end of the *Idra Zuta*, which speaks of how IN THIS YESOD-PHALLUS, [the Male's desire] ENTERS THE FEMALE UNTO THAT PLACE CALLED ZION AND JERUSALEM, WHICH IS THE PLACE OF COVERING FOR THE FEMALE, LIKE THE WOMB FOR A WOMAN²⁷⁹—i.e., a mere "covering," Enclothement, for the Higher Shechinah. Study that passage, keeping in mind what we have just said, and you will understand it well.

Know that the Higher Shechinah is called "lion." This is why Judah is *a lion's cub*,²⁸⁰ he being entirely a representation of the Higher Shechinah. The Lower Shechinah, meanwhile, is represented as a dog, which is known to be the Name of Fifty-two.²⁸¹ The dog is "all heart";²⁸² the Shechinah is called HEART OF ALL HEARTS, and therefore can be represented by the dog. So we find in the Zohar: HE WAS GRIEVED UNTO HIS HEART—THE HEART OF ALL HEARTS.²⁸³ When the sin was committed, in

---

277. According to the Talmud, b. Ned. 38a, B. Bat. 14a.

278. *Qutra be-gulma na'itz be-'izqa*; from the description of creation with which the Zohar proper begins (I, 15a; quoted in *Tiqqunei Zohar* 4, 19a). Matt, trans., *Zohar* 1:108 translates "a cluster of vapor forming in formlessness, thrust in a ring." He remarks: "*Qutra* means both 'knot' and 'smoke' in the *Zohar*," and adds that some commentators suggest we take it here as "form" ("a form in formlessness"). Our author's citation of the passage in this context will best make sense if we suppose that he vocalized *quatra*, and understood it in the light of the Romance-language words for "four" or "square."

279. Zohar, III, 296a, adding "and Jerusalem" on the basis of 296b.

280. Gen 49:9.

281. "The Name of Fifty-two" is one of the four possible numerical values of the full spelling of the Tetragrammaton, each of which is traditionally associated with a different level of the sefirotic hierarchy; the Name of Fifty-two is connected with *Malkhut*. The Hebrew word for dog, *kelev*, has the numerical value of 52, a coincidence that serves the author as the first of two strained arguments for his Lower Shechinah = dog equation.

282. *Kelev* derived from *kullo lev*, "he is all heart," an etymology found, as Maciejko *ad loc.* points out, in the commentary of Samuel Edels (Mahrsha) on the Talmud, b. Sanh. 97a (who takes it to refer to the dog's fidelity to its master). It also occurs in Judah Loew of Prague's *Hiddushei Aggadot* on b. Hor. 13a. Our author might have taken it from either, or from a popular tradition that both drew upon. (Ms. Jerusalem 2491 attributes it to "our rabbis of blessed memory," i.e., the sages of the Mishnah and Talmud, but it seems to have no ancient source.)

283. Elliptical quotation of Zohar, III, 144a (*Idra Rabbah*), expounding Gen 6:6.

other words, [God] grieved the Shechinah for having taken the initiative with him, as we have shown at length from the Zohar's treatment of the verse *A thought-begotten son is his mother's grief*.[284] Understand.

This will explain why the Davidic kingship is likened to a lion, and similarly why the Temple is called *Ariel*, "lion of God": it is on account of the Higher Shechinah, for whom both David and the lion function as symbols. Hence, *Ariel, Ariel, city where David encamped*, meaning that it was there that David made encampment.[285]

It is likewise the sense of what the Bible tells us of Benaiah the son of Jehoiada—who represents the God of Israel, as the Zohar explains in its introduction to the Torah portion *Bereshit*[286]—that *he it was who descended and smote the lion*, which is to say, the Higher Shechinah, *in the pit*.[287] We are to read the word *bor*, "pit," as *be'er*, "spring" of living waters, meaning, [he went down? or he caused her to go down?] into the female's *heder* [womb] which is both "fountain" and "pit."[288] This

---

The author's Zohar exegesis is exceedingly strained and farfetched. The Zohar, reasonably, understands the Bible's *va-yit'atzev* as reflexive ("he grieved himself"), and God *displays* his grief to "the heart of all hearts," the higher divinity inside him. But the author is set upon using this passage to show that the Shechinah is the "heart of all hearts," and therefore the dog. Contrast the Zohar, I, 6b, where—in accordance with the overwhelmingly negative valence of the dog in traditional Jewish thought—the "dog" is a demonic entity who eats the sacrifices in place of the divine lion. As in his rehabilitation of Cain and Pharaoh, the author works a dramatic reversal of the image's conventional valuation.

284. Prov 10:1, quoted in Zohar, I, 22a-b; above, chapter 3, sections 6-7, describing the emergence of "Creation-Human" (represented in the Bible by Cain and the serpent). "The sin" is that of "Adam" and "Eve" (= the God of Israel and the Higher Shechinah), described in chapter 6, section 6. The author seems to have forgotten that the Shechinah whose ill-considered initiative called forth Creation-Human was the Higher Shechinah, not the Lower.

285. Isa 29:1, interpreted to mean that "David" (= Higher Shechinah) "encamped" in Ariel, the Temple (= Lower Shechinah).

286. Zohar, I, 6a-b, where Benaiah is equated with "the Lord of hosts," by which the Zohar evidently intends the *sefirah Yesod*, but which our author takes as equivalent to the God of Israel. The Zohar goes on to expound the Samuel and Chronicles passages (below) in a manner that differs considerably from our author's.

287. 1 Chr 11:22-23; parallel in 2 Sam 23:20-21.

288. The consonantal text of Samuel does in fact read *be'er*, "spring," but vocalizes it as *bor*, "pit," as in Chronicles. The phrase *be'er mayim hayyim*, "spring of living waters," occurs in Song of Song 4:15 with a plainly sexual meaning. On the *heder*, "womb" = the Holy of Holies, see the beginning of this section. If Benaiah himself goes down into that womb, as the Biblical passage would seem to require, his "smiting" of the Higher Shechinah there would seem to be a sex act. But it is also possible that the author takes his "descending" as transitive, "he caused to descend," and that

took place *on a day of snow*, when the Judgments that are harsh as snow had gained mastery over the Shechinah, as we have seen with Miriam's being *leprous as snow*.[289]

[p. 143] The text proceeds to explain that *he smote an Egyptian man, a man of appearance*.[290] This means that, as we have said earlier, he enclothed himself within Moses and descended into the midst of the *Tehiru*, where he rescued the Shechinah from the hand of the Egyptian, as it is written, *And he smote the Egyptian*.[291] When it calls him *a man of appearance*, that means he was husband to the Shechinah, as is well known.[292]

Now, the book of Chronicles was composed after the Mending, after the Higher Shechinah had descended into the Holy of Holies, and consequently can describe how *they brought the Ark of God to the inner chamber*, and so forth.[293] That is why it is written in the book of Chronicles that King Hadar died:[294] any demotion in rank, as we know, qualifies as a "death," and [the "Miriam"-Shechinah] had gone down from the rank of *Yesod* to that of *Malkhut*, and there taken up residence. "Death" therefore may be said of her, and thus *King Hadar died*, calling him "dead" in that he had gone down in rank. In the Torah of Moses, by contrast—while she was still "alive," prior to her descent—no mention of [Hadar's] death is made.

---

the God of Israel "smites" the Higher Shechinah by demoting her in rank. The sequel will support both options.

289. Num 12:10; above, section 10.

290. 2 Sam 23:21.

291. Exod 2:12, where Moses kills an Egyptian taskmaster and rescues the Israelite victim of his abuse. This Biblical action is applied to the God of Israel's rescue of the Rachel-Shechinah in chapter 6, section 4. The phrase "from the hand of the Egyptian" is taken from 2 Sam 23:21.

292. From the Zohar, I, 6b, where Moses, the "Egyptian man" (Exod 2:19) who is the Shechinah's human husband, is the object of "Benaiah's" (= *Yesod*'s) attack. How the identification will work in this context, where Benaiah = Moses = the attacker, is unclear.

293. A slightly free quotation of 2 Chr 5:7, which goes on to equate "the inner chamber of the house" with the Holy of Holies. For "the Higher Shechinah," ms. Jerusalem 2491 reads "Shechinah and Ark," seemingly restricting the "Ark" to the "Miriam"-Shechinah in which the Higher Shechinah has taken up her dwelling. This reading makes sense, for it is the "Miriam"-Shechinah whose "death" in 1 Chr the author feels compelled to explain.

294. 1 Chr 1:51; versus Gen 36:39, where Hadar's death goes unmentioned. ("Hadar," the king's name in Genesis, is normally used in this passage, as against Chronicles' "Hadad.") The contradiction is posed as a problem in chapter 4, section 1, its solution promised in chapter 6, section 8. Now the author fulfills his promise.

From this you will understand why, throughout the book of Chronicles, David's name is spelled with a *yod*.²⁹⁵ He had become incorporated within the Lower Shechinah, who is represented by the tiny point that is the letter *yod* [י] and by *black am I and beautiful*—see the Zohar Hadash on the Song of Songs.²⁹⁶ That is why "David" is given that *yod*; and you must understand.

You must realize also that this is why it is written in the Zohar that the Davidic Messiah is represented by the lion.²⁹⁷

14. First and Second Temples—Concealment of the Ark

[Against this background, historical differences between the First and Second Temples become intelligible. The Temple, as Lower Shechinah, shares in and is dominated by the numinosity of the Higher Shechinah, who dwells in her womb (= Holy of Holies). So matters remain until the God of Israel, reacting to human sin, parts from his Shechinah(s). He then hides the Higher Shechinah away, protected by a wall of fire from the incursions of the Insolent Waters. (Recall that the Lower Shechinah descends nightly into these waters, and unlike her the Higher Shechinah does not have her virginity to shield her.) This is why the ark, which has come to represent the Higher Shechinah, could not be visibly present in the Second Temple. It is why during Second Temple times there was no Davidic kingship—"David" being the Higher Shechinah, as we saw in section 12—and why the Messiah, who also represents the Higher Shechinah, is destined to restore both kingship and ark. It also explains why, according to rabbinic tradition, the fire that

---

295. Throughout the Bible, "David" is normally, though not exclusively, written *dalet-vav-dalet*, דוד. Chronicles, however, invariably inserts a *yod* after the *vav* (דויד).

296. Song 1:5, expounded in *Sefer Zohar Hadash*, 16c–17a; cf. the commentary in Ashlag, *Sefer ha-Zohar*, 19:133–39: The letter *yod* is solid black, unlike most Hebrew letters, which combine their blackness with the white of the space they encompass; it is therefore an appropriate representation of the "black and beautiful" lady of the Song passage, who is agreed to be the *sefirah Malkhut* (above, note 170). It would be more convenient for the author if, like the *yod*, *Malkhut* were enclosed within "David" and not the other way around; but he must make do with what he has.

297. Zohar, II, 119b–20b. Of course the link is far more straightforward and less complex than our author's discussion: the Davidic Messiah is from the tribe of Judah, which is a lion cub (Gen 49:9). But our author has filled in the depths that lie beneath it—and, consequently, beneath Sabbatai Zevi's self-designation as "exalted Lion," (*arya de-vei ʿillaʾei*, drawn from the Talmud, b. Hul. 59b): Scholem, *Sabbatai Ṣevi*, 914–16; cf. Scholem, *Sabbatai Ṣevi*, 274; Halperin, *Sabbatai Zevi*, 86–87.

THE VIRGIN OF GOD

consumed the sacrifices on the altar took the shape of a lion in the First Temple, a dog in the Second. These animals, as we saw in the previous section, represent the Higher and Lower Shechinahs respectively.]

The First Temple, built by Solomon, who represents the God of Israel, partook of the quality of the Concealed World, as the Zohar tells us.[298] The altar-fire, accordingly, *crouched like a lion*,[299] inasmuch as this was the source of its energy. But in the Second Temple, which represented the Lower Shechinah, it *crouched like a dog*, namely the Lower Shechinah, which is represented by the dog, as we have said.[300] [p. 144] (And this was the significance of Caleb's saying, *I brought back word in accordance with my heart*; for as we have said, he is "all heart.")[301]

[The Higher Shechinah] dwells within the womb, the "fountain,"[302] of the [Lower] Shechinah; and that Lower Shechinah is, as we have said, in the quality of a virgin, fit to go down into battle.[303] It is in this connection that the Bible commands the high priest, who stands for the God of Israel: *He shall take a woman in her virginity*, meaning that he must take a woman who is sealed up within her virginity, encompassed by virginity.[304]

298. Zohar, I, 18a, uses the phrase "concealed world" (*'alma de-itkasya*) for the higher, more hidden *sefirot*, as opposed to the "revealed" *Malkhut*; it does not, however, make a connection with the First Temple. Our author seems to apply the term to the sphere of Interiority, as opposed to Enclothement.

299. Talmud, b. Yoma 21b, describing the fire that consumed the sacrifices on the altar. The Zohar (I, 6b) expands this tradition—"the shape of a lion would descend from above and the people would see it upon the altar, crouching over its prey and eating the sacrifices like a mighty man"—and goes on to identify this lion with the angel Uriel, "whose face is that of a lion" (*aryeh*). For our author, the lion is a manifestation of the Higher Shechinah (above), who is the grantor of energy (*mashpia'*) to Solomon's Temple.

300. b. Yoma 21b: "Rabbi Hanina prefect of the priests said, I saw it crouching like a dog"; and the Gemara goes on to explsain that this was in the time of the Second Temple, versus the leonine fire of the First Temple. The Zohar (I, 6b) tells how, after "Benaiah" killed the "lion," the demonic forces ("dogs") were emboldened to send a dog to eat the sacrifices. This presumably refers to Second Temple times.

301. Reprising the etymology of *kelev*, "dog," as *kullo lev*, "he is all heart," and transferring it to the Biblical Caleb—the speaker in Josh 14:7—whose name *kalev* is the equivalent of *kelev*. The point of this parenthetical note is not altogether clear. Perhaps it is intended to bolster the dog = heart equation and thereby to support the author's positive transvaluation of the dog.

302. See above, note 288.

303. In the *Tehiru*.

304. Taking *bi-vetuleha*, "in her virginity" (Lev 21:13) hyperliterally: the God of

True enough, we sometimes find that the God of Israel takes the Shechinah out from the womb to the heights and has sex with her there—sometimes, indeed, she ascends with him to the Curtain and beyond—while at other times he leaves her inside the [Lower Shechinah's] womb for their sex. This is the significance of Ahasuerus's having *experienced* [Esther] *as virginal when he was in the mood for that, or as sexually open when that was his fancy;*[305] and it is known that Ahasuerus is a representation of the God of Israel.[306] But the high priest is bidden to *take a woman in her virginity*, not removing her from her proper location, as the Zohar interprets *a woman in her virginity* to mean that SHE MUST NEVER GO OUT FROM THE GATE OF HER COURTYARD;[307] and you must understand. The result was that she remained within the womb of the [Lower] Shechinah (symbolized by the Holy of Holies) until the time came for the Temple to be destroyed, whereupon the Ark was hidden away.[308]

With regard to that concealment, this is what you must know:

The difficulty inherent in the Gemara's assertion, that *when the Gentiles entered the Temple they found the cherubim entwined together*,[309] has long been noted; for is it not the case that *when the Jews are disobedient to God's will*, [the cherubim's] *faces are turned toward the Temple?*[310] Some of our contemporaries, indeed [fol. 32a], have tried to resolve the contradiction though a man's *obligation, when he sets forth on a journey, to make love to his wife.*[311] At that time of exile, the God of Israel was de-

---

Israel must have sex with the Higher Shechinah when she is enclosed within the virginal womb of the Lower Shechinah.

305. Talmud, b. Meg. 13a.

306. An identification made above, chapter 6, section 4. I am not aware of any earlier antecedents for it.

307. Zohar, III, 90a.

308. The author does not explicitly resolve the contradiction that the God of Israel, *qua* Ahasuerus, is privileged to do what is forbidden to him *qua* high priest. We must suppose that the Higher Shechinah, though prohibited from leaving the "womb" of the Lower in any regular way, is nevertheless allowed to slip out for occasional trysts.

309. In sexual embrace; b. Yoma 54b. For the Talmud, the male and female cherubim are sculpted figures, but for our author they are living divine entities: the God of Israel and the Shechinah.

310. They do not face each other, as they would during sex; Talmud, b. B. Bat. 99a. And clearly the Jews *were* disobedient to God's will; otherwise why would the Temple be destroyed?

311. *Lifqod et ishto*; Talmud, b. Yebam. 62b. We shall presently see that the verb *paqad*, which in its Talmudic context certainly means "to make love," can be given a very different meaning.

THE VIRGIN OF GOD

parting for the heights—as it is written, *My man is gone, taking with him the bundle of silver*,[312] i.e., the effluence for which all beings yearn—and was therefore obliged to couple with her.[313]

All well and good! [p. 145] But you must probe more deeply, and ask: why, indeed, should a man departing on a journey be required to make love to his wife? What could be the reason for this commandment? It remains problematic, moreover, that whatever the reason for this coupling may have been, it must have involved the joining of the *hei* to the *vav*.[314] And if *hei* were joined to *vav*, how could the Externals have gained control over God's Temple? Is this not precisely what brings about their downfall, the joining of the *hei* to the *vav*?—and all the unifications, all the commandments of the Torah are directed toward this end, as we shall explain when we come to discuss the subject of unification.[315]

This, however, is what you must know: Inasmuch as the Higher Shechinah, in its manifestation as the Ark, was in the Temple, within that which was represented by the Holy of Holies—and inasmuch as the Externals were granted free rein over the Temple (a representation of *Malkhut*) at the God of Israel's departure, and the Insolent Waters flooded it entirely—the God of Israel was concerned lest they do damage to the Higher Shechinah. She was sexually open, after all, and there was legitimate concern that she be damaged through the Insolent Waters finding their way inside her, she being different in this respect from *Malkhut* of Emanation, who remains virginal, as we have seen.[316]

What, then, did the God of Israel do? He hid her away. How did he hide her? By pouring out upon her a fierce blaze of fire, which rose up all around her like a wall, like a sheltering hut, to keep the Externals from drawing near, from coming to approach her; and this fire surrounded and concealed her so that no External could get close.

---

312. Slightly abbreviated quotation of Prov 7:19-20. (Cf. the use of this passage in the Talmud, b. Sanh. 96b, where the "man" is similarly understood to be the departed God.) The Hebrew word *kesef*, "silver," suggests to our author the Aramaic *kesifin*, "yearning."

313. And therefore the cherubim would face each other in spite of the people's disobedience, for this one parting act of love. I do not know who the author has in mind for the proponents of this difficulty, or its ingenious resolution.

314. The final *hei* of the Tetragrammaton symbolizes *Malkhut*, the Shechinah, while the phallic *vav* stands for *Tif'eret*, the embodiment of the male divinity.

315. Cf. below, chapter 9, section 1.

316. And therefore can enter to do battle amid the Insolent Waters.

And this was that coupling,[317] in a blaze of fire, which is hinted at in *from heaven*, i.e., the God of Israel, *he sent fire into my essences*, namely the Joseph-essences that are Miriam,[318] *and it mastered her*, meaning that it surrounded so tightly one could not turn right or left.[319] It is what is written of Job, *qua* representation of the God of Israel, that *he pours to the earth his bile*,[320] namely the blazing power of Judgment which is known to be represented as bile, poured to the "earth"[321] to encompass her.

This is the symbolism of the "man setting forth on a journey." While he is present here, he can protect [his wife]—*a woman's husband will protect her*[322]—but when he departs he must hide her away. This is the real meaning of *lifqod*,[323] i.e., [to make his wife] a *piqqadon*, a "thing entrusted,"[324] which he must hide away so others cannot come near her. Hence this usage, unparalleled in the Talmud, of the verb *paqad*:[325] it indicates something "entrusted," hidden away, [p. 146] and refers to the Ark's having been *concealed in its place*.[326]

Now in Second Temple times, even though the Temple structure had been built, the wall of fire of which we have spoken remained in place and the "Ark" of which we have spoken[327] remained in a state of concealment. That is why there was no Ark in the Second Temple, and why all its effluence was that of the Lower Shechinah. So we find in the Zohar and the *Tiqqunim*: THE SECOND TEMPLE PARTOOK OF THE LOWER SHECHINAH,

---

317. That the Gentiles saw when they stormed into the Temple.

318. I.e., the Shechinah that is the "Enclothement" of the Higher Shechinah, and that enters with it into the Lower. In its Biblical context, of course, *'atzmotai* means "my bones"; "my essences" is the author's highly distinctive interpretation.

319. Lam 1:13, describing the destruction of Jerusalem.

320. Job 16:13, altering "my bile" (*mererati*) to "his bile" (*mererato*).

321. Kabbalistic code for *Malkhut*.

322. Misquotation of the Talmudic saying "a woman's husband will bring her joy" (b. Rosh Hash. 6b, Qidd. 34b), which differs from our author's quotation by only one Hebrew letter.

323. Which we earlier took to mean, "make love."

324. Or "deposited," for protection and guarding.

325. Indeed, there seems no example of *paqad* used for sexual intercourse other than this and a neighboring passage in b. Yebam. 62b, both drawing on the use of the verb in Job 5:24.

326. Talmud, b. Yoma 53b–54a.

327. That is, the Higher Shechinah.

THE ONE REVEALED.[328] Therefore the fire *crouched like a dog*, as we have seen, in the character of the Name of Fifty-two.[329]

And thus it was that during the time of the Second Temple, the Davidic kingship was altogether absent. For the Davidic line represents the Higher Shechinah, as we have said. Since the latter was hidden away, the Davidic kingship was also lacking, the one being dependent on the other—until the coming of our true Messiah, at which time the Ark shall be revealed. Hence *I myself will be for her, says YHVH, a wall of fire*,[330] meaning that in place of that protective "wall of fire" of which we have spoken, *I myself will be* there *for her*, guarding her as a husband should.[331] He will then restore the kingship to the Davidic line.

Know, however, that inasmuch as the Davidic Messiah represents both the Higher Shechinah and the Ark, which *cannot be seen from the outside*[332] but concealed within *Malkhut*, the Davidic Messiah must correspondingly be concealed, enclothed within a merchant's body,[333] which serves him as a vehicle to dwell within. This is the significance of Moses's mask;[334] but here is not the place to enter into the details. Why

---

328. Conflating Zohar, I, 26a with III, 221a. The former passage associates the First Temple with the "Higher Shechinah" and the Second with the "Lower"—probably intended as the *sefirot Binah* and *Malkhut*, respectively—while the latter passage predicts the descent of the two Temples from heaven: the First "in a state of concealment," the Second "in a revealed state." I am not aware of anything similar in *Tiqqunei Zohar*.

329. I.e., as *Malkhut*.

330. Zech 2:9.

331. The speaker is the God of Israel, husband to the Higher Shechinah.

332. 1 Kgs 8:8, referring to the poles of the Ark; expounded in the Talmud, b. Yoma 54a, to mean that "they could be seen yet not seen . . . pressing against the curtain [separating the outer Temple from the Holy of Holies] and standing out from it like a woman's nipples." The Talmud's sexualization of the Ark has inspired our author.

333. The words "within a merchant's body" (*be-guf soher*) are found only in ms. Jerusalem 2491. It seems they must be retained, for otherwise the following reference to the Messiah's "vehicle"—the text uses the significant term *merkavah*—is without any antecedent. But I cannot imagine why the Messiah, whether Sabbatai Zevi or anyone else, should be called a "merchant." (A Hebrew document from 1666 speaks of Sabbatai as "merchandise" purchased by the collectivity of the Jewish people; Halperin, *Sabbatai Zevi*, 44–46. But it is hard to see how this might be relevant.) Is it thinkable that the reading was originally *tugar* (תוגר), "Turk," and it was either corrupted directly into *soher* (סוחר), or else written as *taggar* (תגר), a less common word for "merchant," which was afterward altered to the more familiar *soher*? The reference will then be to Sabbatai's "enclothement" in a Turkish, Muslim body.

334. Exod 34:33–35.

discuss how matters are to be ordered in the Messiah's days?[335] When he comes, we shall be waiting.

With regard to the place of [the Ark's] concealment, there are two opinions.[336] One holds that *it was hidden away in its place*, that is to say the Holy of Holies, the "womb" of which we have spoken, and from there does it receive.[337] The other view is that it was in the Woodshed Chamber, which the Talmudic sages represented as an upper chamber [*'aliyah*], a manner of "woodshed" where the semen is purified, its choicest and purest elements to be absorbed by the Shechinah through the open passageway.[338] In her Exile-state, however, she must accept not the choice but the refuse, as the Zohar makes clear; hence she sits there in the upper chamber.[339]

This is what is meant by the Ark being *hidden away in the Woodshed Chamber*,[340] and a rupture had to be made to bring [it/her] out from the Holy of Holies to the Woodshed Chamber. And this is why, when people performed their prostrations in the Temple toward the thirteen ruptures of which we have spoken,[341] they added one prostration more, toward the Woodshed Chamber, for *they knew quite certainly that the Ark was hidden away there*.[342] [p. 147] Besides, [the Woodshed Chamber] was then a sort of rupture—as in, *how have you made a rupture for yourself!*[343]—and consequently required [fol. 32b] a prostration to fortify it like the others.

---

335. *Hilkheta li-meshiha*; a phrase from the Talmud, b. Sanh. 51b, Zebah. 45a.

336. Set forth in the Talmud, b. Yoma 53b–54a. Predictably, the author ignores the third option offered in the Talmudic passage, that the Ark was not "concealed" at all, but taken with the Jews into Babylonian exile.

337. The "semen" described at the beginning of section 13, of which we shall presently hear more.

338. See above, note 272 on the Woodshed Chamber, and, on the "open passageway," note 268. The author weaves the Talmudic source together with his distinctive interpretation of it, conflating the features of the Temple with those of the female body, the wood for the altar—which requires a "purification" by sorting—with the semen infused into that body.

339. As opposed, in this alternative rabbinic view, to waiting for the choicest of the "semen" to trickle down to her through the passageway. I do not know what Zoharic passage the author refers to.

340. Talmud, b. Yoma 54a.

341. Represented by the thirteen gates of the Temple Mount; above, chapter 6, section 4.

342. Mishnah, m. Sheqal. 6:1–2, on the fourteenth prostration.

343. Gen 38:29, spoken by the midwife to the infant Perez at his birth and that of his twin brother. The verse's relevance to the present context is unclear.

15. Shechinah: Nourisher and Nourished

[As a coda to his exposition of the Temple symbolism, the author draws on Ezekiel's vision (47:1–12) of a life-giving stream issuing forth from the Temple, healing the waters into which it flows. This is the nourishment urinated into the *Tehiru* jointly by the Lower Shechinah and the Higher Shechinah inside her; and these are in turn nourished by the *Tehiru*'s "choice elements," which they share with their lover, the God of Israel.]

Know this: that a fountain goes forth from the Holy of Holies,[344] and this is also an aspect of the Female, namely her urinary aperture.[345] These flow into *Malkhut* and descend from there until they reach the *Tehiru*, and from them the vessels of Cain and his offspring—i.e., those vessels for Abel that remained below—receive their nourishment.[346] The Shechinah receives the *Tehiru* waters as though eating them, picking out the most exceedingly choice and pure. The Higher Shechinah receives those choice elements and conveys them to the upper worlds. So says the Bible: *"Sevenfold" shall Cain be maintained*, meaning that the upper worlds, all of which partake of the nature of "Cain," depend for their continued existence on "Sevenfold," namely the Higher Shechinah.[347] *But Lamech*, who represents the fragments of the Shattered vessels that are in the *Tehiru*, [is maintained by] *"Seventy"* (i.e., the Higher Shechinah) *and "Seven"* (i.e., the Lower Shechinah). For he requires the assistance of them both.

In receiving those choice elements, [the Higher Shechinah] takes into herself nothing whatsoever of the *Tehiru*-waters, for IN THE WORLD TO COME THERE IS NEITHER EATING NOR DRINKING.[348] Yet inasmuch as

---

344. Following the language of Joel 4:18: "On that day . . . a fountain shall go forth from the house of the Lord." But the phenomenon, of a mighty stream flowing from the sanctuary, is more fully described in Ezek 47:1–12.

345. On this entire section, cf. section 5 above.

346. The language here is somewhat confusing. Earlier in the treatise (chapter 4, section 2 and chapter 6, sections 3–4), the author has distinguished the inner aspects ("intelligences") of the primordial *sefirot*, which he calls "Abel," from their "Cainite" vessels, which remained below in the *Tehiru* when the inner "intelligences" were raised from it. This seems to be his intent when he calls the latter "vessels for Abel."

347. Gen 4:24; see above, chapter 6, section 2, on the restoration of "Primordial Human" (= Cain), which seems to be what the author means here by the "upper worlds."

348. Zohar, II, 153b, III, 241b (see below); based on the Talmud, b. Ber. 17a. In Kabbalistic symbolism, "the World to Come" (Hebrew *ha-'olam ha-ba*, Aramaic *'alma de-atei*) is code for the *sefirah Binah*, which is sometimes called "the Higher Shechinah." Hence our author's interpretation of the Zoharic dictum to mean that the Higher

she dwells within the Lower Shechinah, out of respect for her, she ingests the choice elements in the same way, as a form of eating. We learn this from the Zohar,[349] where the prophet Elijah asks Rabbi Shimon ben Yohai how the Bible can say, *I have come into my garden, my sister, my bride* (i.e., the Lower Shechinah) and so forth, *eat, friends, drink and become intoxicated, lovers*—speaking of the God of Israel and his Shechinah, as we saw vis-à-vis the name "David"—in spite of there being NEITHER EATING NOR DRINKING IN THE WORLD TO COME. To which Rabbi Shimon ben Yohai replies that one alters one's habits out of respect for one's host—in this case the Lower Shechinah, who is known to be, as it were, the "lady of the house" and the host, as we have just said.[350]

16. Shechinah: The Sex Life of a Virgin

[From its beginning, this chapter has insisted on the virginity of the "Rachel" Shechinah, declaring it a blasphemy deserving of death to cast aspersions on that virginity. Yet it has also hinted at a fair amount of sexual activity on the part of that "virgin." We are now shown how this can be.

The God of Israel, to begin with, knows two techniques— one with the penis stiffly erect, the other with it undulating like a serpent—for having sex with a female while leaving her a virgin. Both of these were shown to Moses, who, acting as the God of Israel's "Enclothement," had sex on his behalf with the virgin Shechinah, manifested as a rock in the desert. At times, also, the Shechinah makes herself into a little girl, whose virginity—according to a rabbinic formulation that is bound to

---

Shechinah (as opposed to the Lower; see Zohar, II, 153b) neither eats nor drinks.

349. III, 241b–42a, quoting Song 5:1. The focus of Elijah's question, as the Zohar makes clear, is on the words that our author skips over with "and so forth" ("I have eaten my honeycomb with my honey, I have drunk my wine with my milk"), which seem to contradict the dictum that there is no eating or drinking in "the World to Come." Rabbi Shimon's response, in the Zohar, is that although the "bridegroom" (*Tif'eret*) would normally neither eat nor drink, on his visits to his "bride" (*Malkhut*) he does both for her sake. Our author, for whom neither of the romantic partners would eat or drink, recasts Shimon's reply to introduce a third party: the Lower Shechinah, who serves as "hostess" for the superior entities. On the God of Israel and the Higher Shechinah as "lovers" (= "Davids"), see the beginning of section 12, above.

350. I suspect that the author's gloss on Song 5:1, "i.e., the Lower Shechinah," refers not to the sister/bride of the Bible verse (who is the Higher Shechinah), but to the "garden" where the lovers' rendezvous takes place. ("Garden" is a standard Kabbalistic symbol for the *sefirah Malkhut*.) They enjoy the Lower Shechinah's hospitality for their tryst; therefore courtesy obliges them to follow her practice of eating and drinking.

THE VIRGIN OF GOD

disgust the modern reader—automatically renews itself each time it is taken. And the God of Israel will at times masturbate the Shechinah with his finger. In all these ways, her virginity remains intact—until messianic times when, as we will see in the next chapter, she will be permanently relieved of it.]

If you are to understand the nature of the Shechinah's sexual activity, given that she is in a state of virginity, you must grasp that what the Gemara says about Samuel's being *expert at inclination* is a known fact, namely that if one inclines to the "north" side while having sex, [p. 148] the woman will remain a virgin.[351] And so it is when the God of Israel wants to couple with the Shechinah: he inclines himself, as it were, to the "north" side and thus can have sex any number of times, while she remains a virgin. So the Bible says, *He inclined the heaven and went down*, meaning that he *inclined* to the side and then *went down* to copulate.[352]

Now you can understand why the *sefirah Yesod* is represented as a rod, *matteh*.[353] It is because when the God of Israel comes to have sex, he inclines [*matteh*] himself in order to perform the act; and, while he inclines himself, his penis [*yesod*] stiffens like a rod.[354]

Be aware, though, that this is the case only when the Judgments do not predominate in the lower regions. When they do predominate, it is

---

351. The Talmud (b. Hag. 14b–15a), confronted with the question of whether a woman who is a virgin may nonetheless become pregnant, quotes Samuel's boast that "I can copulate any number of times without blood." ("Samuel" is not the Biblical prophet, but a Babylonian rabbi of the early third century CE.) Rashi explains that Samuel was "expert at inclination" (*baqi be-hatayah*)—a phrase taken from the Talmud, b. Ketub. 6b, and used there evidently to refer to some mode of intercourse that leaves the hymen intact. (Our author seems to visualize this technique better than I can; and on the entire passage, with its alternating "rod" and "serpent" modes of the phallus, see Lefler, "When They Came," 231–35.) By the "north" side, the author apparently means the left, as indicated in the sequel. I am not aware of *tzafon* elsewhere having the meaning "left"; but the association of "left" and "north" is embedded deep in the Hebrew language—*semol*, the usual word for "left," can also mean "north"—and is familiar from the Zohar (II, 24a, quoted in chapter 7, section 2; III, 118b). He presumably chooses to speak here of the "north" because of its layers of Kabbalistic association, which he will draw upon in the next paragraph.

352. 2 Sam 22:10 = Ps 18:10. "Heaven" is a standard Kabbalistic code word for the male divinity (as opposed to the female "earth"), which in our author's theology would function as "body" for the God of Israel.

353. The Hebrew word is both a noun meaning "rod" and a verb participle meaning "to incline (oneself)."

354. And thus is straight while the body is "inclined," as opposed to the sort of lovemaking described below.

not possible for the God of Israel to incline himself toward the north,[355] for if he were to do so, the Judgments would grow yet more powerful, resulting in destruction and division throughout the Merkavah. How, then, do they copulate?

He remains in his place, facing her directly,[356] without inclining toward any side whatever. His penis, however, bends itself in a twisting, crooked fashion until it lies at a diagonal, and in the direction of its bending he couples with the Shechinah. It partakes then of a serpent's nature.

Now you will understand the Bible verse that speaks of *the way of a man with a maiden*,[357] referring to the quality of *a man*, which is to say virility;[358] that is his *way with a maiden*, who is a virgin.[359] But when he does not have that quality of virility, then his is *the way of a serpent*: his penis bends itself like a serpent, as we have said, and enters into the *rock* that is the virgin (who is called *the rock of testimony* that *you must seal up*, referring to her virginity).[360] You will also understand why the penis[361] is called both *rod* and *serpent*, in accordance with the two modes, the two aspects that we have just observed.

You can comprehend as well, on this basis, what Moses meant by saying, *They will not believe me, for they will say, YHVH has not appeared*

---

355. The domain of Judgment, in Kabbalistic symbolism, corresponding to the left side of the sefirotic tree.

356. Literally, "in the place of straightness," alluding to the straight vertical line that connects *Tif'eret* with *Malkhut* in the sefirotic diagrams.

357. Prov 30:19, where the speaker confesses himself baffled by "the way of a serpent on a rock" and "the way of a man with a maiden."

358. *Gevurah*, from the same root as *gever*, a man. The word is also the name of the *sefirah* of strict Judgment; the context would suggest that the more general meaning is intended here, referring to the penis stiffly erect like a rod.

359. The apparent equation of *'almah*, "maiden," with *betulah*, "virgin," has obvious implications for the interpretation of Isa 7:14, "the maiden shall conceive," and therefore for the Jewish-Christian debate. I do not know how conscious our author is of this.

360. The words in parentheses, found only in ms. Jerusalem 2491, quote Isa 8:16, normally translated "bind up the testimony, seal up (the teaching)." The imperative *tzor*, "bind up," is read as *tzur*, "rock," and taken as the object of the following imperative "seal up" (*hatom*), as a virgin is sealed (*hatum*, Song 4:12). This would seem to be an interpolation: it is altogether missing from ms. Oxford 955; and ms. Jerusalem 3100, which normally agrees with Oxford, includes the parenthesis but replaces the Isaiah quote with the words צור תרים מעמה. I do not know where these words are taken from, or what they are supposed to mean ("she removes the rock from being with her"?).

361. Or, the *sefirah Yesod*, which would better fit the present context. But I am not aware of either term being actually applied to *Yesod* in the traditional Kabbalah.

to you.[362] His point was that, the Shechinah being in exile[363] and in a virginal state, there could be no coupling of male and female; and it is known that all prophetic vision must come via the Shechinah.[364] That was why he argued that the Israelites would deny him, insisting that he could not possibly have seen a prophetic vision, given that the exiled, virginal Shechinah could not have had sexual intercourse.

[p. 149] In reply, [God] demonstrated for him two modes of coupling. First, *"What is that in your hand?" "A rod,"* i.e., the penis. *"Throw it to the earth!" And he threw it to the earth*—i.e., to the Shechinah,[365] thereby having sex with her—*and it became a serpent*, and so forth, so that sex could happen even though the Shechinah was not opened for it, still being a virgin. When Moses saw their sex act, he fled from before it,[366] for it is forbidden to watch lovemaking lest one derive voyeuristic pleasure from it. Hence, *Moses hid his face.*[367]

And again [God] showed him a mode of intercourse: sex on the left side, after Samuel's manner of "inclination." Hence he said to him, *Extend your hand*,[368] alluding to the well-known fact that whenever the Scriptures speak of *your hand* it is the left, being the weaker hand, that is intended. (Thus it is written of the phylactery, *it shall be a sign upon your hand*.[369]) *Extend your hand*—that is to say, to the left, as did Samuel—*and seize its tail. And it became a rod in his hand*, meaning that it would turn itself from a serpent back into a rod, like a staff inclined leftward[370]—and so he displayed for him two modes of sexual intercourse.

This is the meaning of the penis's [fol. 33a] TURNING FROM A ROD INTO A SNAKE AND FROM A SNAKE INTO A ROD.[371] It applies to the time

---

362. Exod 4:1. The author undertakes to explain, what is not clear from the Bible story, why Moses expected that the Israelites would doubt his mission, and precisely how the signs God showed him were relevant to their doubts.

363. Since the Israelites were enslaved in Egypt. The association between exile and the Shechinah's virginity is here introduced for the first time.

364. Cf. above, section 7, on the Shechinah's role in prophetic vision.

365. Represented as "earth" in standard Kabbalistic symbolism.

366. And not, as one would imagine from reading Exod 4:3, from the snake.

367. Exod 3:6: "Moses hid his face, because he was afraid to look at God." Does the author hint that God = sex?

368. Exod 4:4.

369. Exod 13:16, as interpreted in the Talmud, b. Menah. 36b–37a. The phylactery is in fact worn on the left arm.

370. Ms. Jerusalem reads "northward."

371. Zohar, III, 255a, 277a (*Ra'ya Mehemna*), *Tiqqunei Zohar* 60 (93b), 69 (108b).

before the revelation of the Torah, when sin had no existence, and there was no opportunity for the Judgments to gain dominance.³⁷² Sex in the "inclination" mode was therefore possible, as we have said.

That is why God spoke [to Moses] of *your rod with which you struck the Nile*,³⁷³ referring to the penis that performs the sex, which is represented by *your having struck*, as one says, *until the blow be healed*.³⁷⁴ *Take it in your hand*: not in the form of a serpent, but *in your hand*, meaning the left hand; *and I stand upon the rock* that is the Virgin of Israel, as we have seen in connection with *the way of a serpent on a rock*.³⁷⁵ *And you shall strike the rock*, coupling and having sex with it; and this he did in the presence of *the elders of Israel*, who, as THE LADY'S WEDDING ATTENDANTS,³⁷⁶ were permitted to watch the lovemaking. The rest of the Israelites, however, were not present, for watching was forbidden to them—as we have said.³⁷⁷

Now indeed, after Miriam had died and the Judgments grown powerful, the God of Israel did not wish to copulate in the "inclination" mode, lest the Judgments overwhelm.³⁷⁸ He therefore said to *take the rod* but not to take it *in your hand*,³⁷⁹ because "inclination" was not then possible, on

---

It is possible that, by *yesod*, the author intends the *sefirah Yesod*; but in none of these passages from the later strata of the Zohar are the transformations applied to the *sefirah Yesod*.

372. A remarkably Pauline sentiment!

373. Exod 17:5, from the first of the Pentateuch's two stories of Moses's striking a rock and producing water from it.

374. Mishnah, m. Nid. 10:1, referring to the "blow" inflicted on an underage bride by her first intercourse. *Makkah*, "blow," is from the same root as *hikkita*, the verb used in Exod 17:5 for Moses's having "struck" the Nile, and confirms that that "striking" was a sexual act.

375. Prov 30:19 (see above), the same word *tzur* being used for "rock" both here and in Exod 17:6.

376. A Zoharic phrase, applied to Aaron (III, 53b) or to his descendants the priests (II, 49b).

377. And thus does the author explain the peculiarity that Moses struck the rock in the sight of the elders alone, and not the entire Israelite people (Exod 17:6; versus Num 20:8, 10)—even though all were in need of the water produced thereby. The relationship between God and Moses here becomes more intelligible when we recall that Moses = the *sefirah Tif'eret*, which functions as the "body" of the God of Israel, enacting his sex with the Shechinah/rock.

378. The second Pentateuchal story of Moses striking the rock begins with the seemingly irrelevant detail of Miriam's death; Num 20:1. The author sets himself to explain why the act that was so successful in the first story (Exod 17:1–7) has become a grave sin in the second.

379. Num 20:8, versus Exod 17:5.

account of the Judgments. He commanded him to perform, not a full sex act, but something in the way of kissing; hence, *you shall speak to the rock*, he said, for kissing is a connection of souls with one another.[380] [p. 150] That was why he commanded him to assemble all the congregation—inasmuch as this was not the hour of sex, everyone was permitted to watch—and why Aaron, as representation of Grace, went with them.[381]

But Moses performed the sex act: *he lifted his hand and struck the rock with his rod*, meaning that he coupled with it.[382] He did this twice, for *a woman will not conceive from her first intercourse*.[383] Moses aimed, moreover, at strengthening the Graces, and therefore "struck" twice, for *he who wants his children to be male*—that is, having the nature of the Graces—*should make love and then do it again*.[384] Yet Moses's act was injurious, in two ways. First, he engaged in coupling at an inappropriate time, and it was the Judgments that were greatly empowered. (This was the *Rock of the Dispute* and *Desertward Rock*, discussed in the Zohar and by all the Kabbalists, where Judgment was stirred up.[385]) He caused further injury by doing the coupling in full view of all the Israelites, as the text says, *Because you did not believe in me, enacting betrothal for me*

---

380. Communicated through the mouth, like speech. For the author's view of kissing, see above, chapter 5, section 7.

381. Num 20:8, vs. Exod 17:1-7, which leaves Aaron unmentioned. The identification of Aaron with the *sefirah Hesed* ("Grace") is a Kabbalistic staple; the author perhaps presupposes the equation of kissing with the dew, and the latter with the realm of the Distant One, where "all is pure Mercy" (above, chapter 5, section 7).

382. Num 20:11. That Moses's "sin" in striking the rock involved a sex act was proposed in 1913 by psychoanalyst Hanns Sachs (incorporated into the 1919 edition of Freud's *Interpretation of Dreams*; Freud, *Interpretation*, 412–16); I develop Sachs's interpretation in Halperin, "Hidden Made Manifest." The sexual association of Moses's act is presupposed in the Zohar's "myth of the hind" (III, 249a-b, in Tishby, *Wisdom*, 1:393–96). But I am not aware of any earlier source that develops it as explicitly as does our author.

383. Talmud, b. Yebam. 34a-b; *Midrash Genesis Rabbah* 45:4, 51:9.

384. Talmud, b. 'Erub. 100b, Nid. 31b. In Kabbalistic thought—counterintuitively, to our way of thinking—"Grace" is associated with the masculine, "Judgment" with the feminine.

385. The phrase "Rock of the Dispute" is from 1 Sam 23:28, with the plural of the Biblical text changed to singular, perhaps foreshadowing the intra-rabbinic "dispute" (Hebrew *mahloqet*, Aramaic *pelugta*) about to be discussed. The author seems to identify it with the "Desertward Rock" of Isa 16:1. (The word used for "rock" in both these passages is *sela'*, as throughout Num 20; versus *tzur* in Exod 17.) I do not know what Kabbalistic "discussions" of these phrases he has in mind.

before the eyes of the children of Israel—effecting betrothal through an act of sexual intercourse, in the sight of all Israel.[386] Understand.

This is the significance of the dispute between the schools of Shammai and Hillel.[387] At evening time, as we know, the sun inclines toward the west, as though for sex; and the school of Shammai—representing Judgment, as the Zohar and Luria make plain[388]—therefore ruled that in the evening one should *incline and recite*; i.e., have sex in the "inclination" mode of which we have spoken. The Hillelite school, representing the Mercies, refused to agree, pointing out that by "inclining" the Judgments would be empowered. Rather, said they, *he should recite in his way*, not "inclining" at all but in the manner we have seen to be that of the serpent.[389]

This was the point of Rabbi Tarfon's narrative. It is known that Rabbi Tarfon is symbolically equivalent to Solomon—as Luria says, that he betrothed one thousand women during a drought year because he was Solomon's reincarnation, thus mending his sin of multiplying wives up to one thousand—who was a representation of the God of Israel.[390]

---

386. Num 20:12, normally translated: "The Lord said to Moses and Aaron, 'Because you did not believe in me, to sanctify me before the eyes of the children of Israel . . .'" The author understands *le-haqdisheni*, "to sanctify me," as though it were *le-qaddesheni*, from the same root: "to perform an act of *qiddushin*, betrothal, for me." The Mishnah, m. Qidd. 1:1, lists sexual intercourse as one of the three methods by which a man can betroth a woman. Moses, according to our author's reading of the Biblical text, used that method, improperly, in full public view.

387. Over the position in which one should recite the evening Shema; Mishnah, m. Ber. 1:3: "The school of Shammai says, In the evening everyone should incline [on one's side, as though lying down] and recite it, and in the morning stand erect, as it is written, 'When you lie down and when you rise up' [Deut 6:7]. The school of Hillel says, Everyone should recite in his [own] way, as it is written, 'As you go in the way' . . . Rabbi Tarfon said, I was on a journey [literally, "coming in the way"], and I inclined to recite in accordance with the school of Shammai, and thereby I put myself in danger from bandits. They said to him, You brought this on yourself by violating the ruling of the school of Hillel." On Rabbi Tarfon and his encounter with the "bandits," see below.

388. In the early rabbinic debates over the application of Torah law, the Shammaite school consistently took the stricter position, the Hillelites the more lenient. The natural (Kabbalistic) inference, that Hillel manifests the Divine potential of Grace and Shammai that of Judgment, is drawn in Zohar, III, 245a (*Ra'ya Mehemna*), Vital, *Sha'ar ha-Gilgulim, haqdamah* 36, 122.

389. I.e., the "way" of the serpent upon the rock, the word "way" being the connecting link between the Hillelites' utterance and Prov 30:19.

390. See above, sections 13–14, and chapter 1, end of section 4. First Kings 11:3 tells how Solomon took a thousand wives—actually, seven hundred wives and three hundred concubines—in violation of Deut 17:17. Tosefta, t. Ketub. 5:1, tells how Rabbi Tarfon betrothed three hundred women in time of drought, in order to

Hence he said, *I was coming in the way*, i.e., to copulate, that *way of a man with a maiden* that we have earlier seen.³⁹¹ *And I inclined myself to recite*, in the leftward "inclination" mode, as we have seen, *and thereby I put myself in danger*—speaking precisely³⁹²—*from bandits*, i.e., the burgeoning power of the Judgments. Understand.

[p. 151] On this basis you will understand how it is that on Passover—that *night of protection from the demons*,³⁹³ when one need have no fear of "bandits" and Judgments—one inclines leftward, as though performing sexual intercourse.³⁹⁴

All this applies when the Shechinah is in a state of maturity. However, when her status is that of a child³⁹⁵—that is to say, when she does not reach *Tif'eret* but only *Netzah-Hod-Yesod*, and is then a child of three years less one day, the "three years" being *Netzah*, *Hod*, and *Yesod*, while *Tif'eret*, who is the God of Israel, is called "one day" (as the *Idra* expounds *one day for YHVH*)³⁹⁶—then her virginity automatically renews itself, and he can go ahead and have sex with her.

---

authorize the starving ladies to eat of his priestly tithes, but does not connect the number with Solomon's concubines, nor am I aware of anything in the Lurianic writings that makes such a link.

391. Prov 30:19, discussed above.

392. That is, Tarfon (= the God of Israel) makes clear that it was he who put himself into danger—as Tarfon's colleagues are not slow to point out to him in the Mishnah—and that he was not simply a victim of circumstance. The implication, that the God of Israel is both fallible and vulnerable, is to be noted.

393. Talmud, b. Pesah. 109b, expounding Exod 12:42.

394. According to the Mishnah (m. Pesah. 10:1), the ritual meal for the eve of Passover must be eaten while reclining, while the Talmud (b. Pesah. 108a) specifies that the reclining must be toward the left. Our author sees this as an enactment of the God of Israel's position in making love to the Shechinah—in the "inclination" mode, since on Passover eve one need have no fear of the power of the Judgments.

395. To understand what follows, the reader must recall that according to rabbinic theory, sexual intercourse with a girl under three years and one day old has no physiological consequences, and therefore no legal ones. In the Mishnah's singularly repellent formulation (m. Nid. 5:4), "it is as though one were to put a finger in her eye"; and Rashi comments: "just as the tear evoked by the finger is replaced by another, so the virginity of a girl less than [three years and one day] renews as another [virginity]" (on Talmud, b. Ketub. 11b). See Meacham, "Legal-Religious Status." Our author finds Kabbalistic symbolism in the girl's three years and one day; see the following note.

396. The image is drawn from the Lurianic tradition, where each of the five "shapes" is an anthropomorphic representation of a *sefirah*—or, in the case of *Ze'ir Anpin*, six *sefirot*—yet also has within it a full set of ten *sefirot*, arranged according to the structure of the human body. Of these latter *sefirot*, *Tif'eret* is the trunk of the body, *Netzah* and

Thus it is that the Shechinah will every so often make herself into a child so she can have sex; for then, as a child, her virginity renews itself. *My eye waters over with tears*,[397] for she is now, as it were, a child, and it is as our sages say in the Gemara: *He is like one who puts a finger in her eye—she sheds a tear and has more tears remaining.*[398]

When the Bible says, *YHVH gives command, and he will strike the big house into fragments* (as opposed to "cracks"), it speaks of when she is in her state of maturity, when her virginity will not renew itself. And when it says, *and the small house into cracks*, it intends full sexual intercourse, resulting in "cracks."[399] Understand.

You must realize that even though by using "inclination" one can penetrate even the virginal Female,[400] the *Tehiru*-waters are quite incapable of gaining entry into her. They are "Babylonians," inexpert in "inclination," as we have said in connection with the builders of the Tower of Babel, who are *those Babylonians unskilled at inclination*.[401]

You must be aware also that there are times when the God of Israel, instead of having sexual intercourse [with the Shechinah], masturbates her with his finger. This is because *a woman cannot be impregnated by a first intercourse*;[402] he will not [fol. 33b] waste even a single drop of ejaculate, and consequently uses his finger.[403] (So we find in *Pirqei*

Hod the two thighs, *Yesod* the genital. Thus, when *Ze'ir Anpin*'s Female (= the God of Israel's Shechinah) is in her "child" status, her head extends only up to his genitalia and thighs, not beyond them to his trunk—which is *Tif'eret*, the missing "one day." (The author misrepresents his rabbinic sources, which speak of three years *plus* one day.) The *Idra Rabbah*'s exposition of Zech 14:7, to which the author refers, is in Zohar, III, 134b; it speaks, however, not of the God of Israel or his counterpart in the traditional Kabbalah, but of an aspect of the higher divinity whom our author calls the Distant One.

397. Free quotation of Jer 13:17.

398. And thus her virginity renews itself. The Gemara quotation combines b. Ketub. 11b with Nid. 13a, 43a.

399. Amos 6:11, understood as follows: The "house" is the Shechinah, which can be "big" (in her state of maturity, "bigness") or "small" (in her child state). When the God of Israel has sex with ("strikes") the mature Shechinah, her virginity is destroyed "fragmented," unless he uses some device like "inclination." With the child-Shechinah, by contrast, full intercourse results only in "cracks," presumably self-healing. (On the "cracks" or "gashes" in the Shechinah, see above, chapter 6, section 4.)

400. The ever-virginal Lower Shechinah.

401. Alluded to in the Talmud, b. Ketub. 6b. The identification of the "Babelites" (= Babylonians) of Gen 11:1–9 with the waters of the *Tehiru* is developed above: in chapter 3, section 4, and in section 6 of this chapter.

402. Talmud, b. Yebam. 34a–b.

403. For the first intercourse, which would be barren in any case.

Rabbi Eliezer that Jacob manipulated with his finger; and so also the Tosafot have written.[404])

[p. 152] This is hinted at in the ruling that *the host*, i.e., the God of Israel, *breaks the bread* with his hand and therefore requires handwashing, that the Insolent Waters not seize upon him.[405] *And the guest blesses*, i.e., *Yesod*, the penis, which makes the sexual connection but cannot perform the finger-manipulation, and so the guest does not break the bread. When we hear that *a woman's eye is narrow for guests*,[406] the sense is that when she is with "guests," her lower "eye" is narrow—as befits a virgin.

---

404. Referring apparently to Pirqei Rabbi Eliezer, chapter 16, where Isaac removes Rebecca's hymen with his finger and shows it to Abraham in proof of her virginity, "and this became the Israelite practice, to remove the hymen with the finger." This is not quite the same as what our author describes. However, Vital's *Sha'ar ha-Kavvanot, Derushei ha-Lailah* 3, 1:345 (cited by Maciejko), conflates the practice described in Pirqei Rabbi Eliezer with the hand-manipulations of b. Yebam. 34a–b, apparently regarding them as the same, and our author seems to follow him on this point. (Odd, though, that he makes no appeal to Luria's authority, referring instead to the Tosafot, which seem to contain nothing of the kind.) The reference to Pirqei Rabbi Eliezer, which it seems from the foregoing must be original, is found only in ms. Jerusalem 2491. The other mss. give the source for the information about Jacob as "the legal authorities" (*poseq[im]*, 'פוסק; Jerusalem 3100) or פרסקום, which is plainly a corruption of *poseqim* (Oxford 955). It is hard to imagine the error that originated these readings.

405. Talmud, b. Ber. 46a. Our author takes the bread-breaking as symbolic of the male's stimulation of the female's genital. He must therefore take special care, lest the Insolent Waters take advantage of his hand to get past the barrier imposed by the female's (technical) virginity.

406. Talmud, b. B. Mesi'a 87a, where the phrase obviously means that a woman is less generous toward guests than her husband is. But for our author, "guest" is now a code term for penis.

9

The Salvation of God

1. **Passage of Effluence—The Ideal State**

    [We now can define the function of prayer, all things being as they ought. It is to join the unit of God of Israel + Shechinah, *in theory* indissolubly fused together, to the Root. The God of Israel himself becomes female during this coupling, while the inherently genderless Root performs it as a male. In this way, through the Female, the Root's effluence may be safely transmitted to the lower worlds. (All this is *in theory*. We will soon see how out of step with reality the theory is.)

    The Distant One, who has no Female, is excluded from the process of transmission. The disastrous results, when his Mercies come thundering down as uncontained ejaculate, were all too evident in the Shattering of the Vessels. The Torah's commandments, which apply solely to the God of Israel and those covenanted to him, are therefore a vital part of the process, as they would not be if the Distant One were the central actor.]

From all the foregoing, it will follow that we are to direct our prayers and intentions toward the God of Israel, who dwells in *Tif'eret*, inasmuch as he is the essential Director of the worlds and everything—all the Balance—depends upon him. The Shechinah couples with him; and in consequence, when we pray to him we bring down effluence from him into the Female via that Balance, and she proceeds to dispense it. The effluence is thus in balance, derived from the coupling of male and female, and can serve to maintain all the worlds.

When we pray to the Distant One or to the Root, by contrast, they send down pure Mercies. There is no coupling whatsoever with the Shechinah; it all comes forth in the form of uncontained ejaculate, and therefore devastates the worlds and brings about Shattering to the vessels. For the whole essence of the Shattering of the Vessels came from their taking their nourishment from the Distant One, as we have seen.[1]

No, it is to the God of Israel that we must pray—and such that our prayers and our intentions will be for the purpose of coupling him with the Root, so that effluence from it can reach him. When that effluence reaches him, the Shechinah receives it as well. For she is in perpetual adhesion to him—YOU WERE BEHIND ME and so forth, as we have seen[2]—and no blessing can possibly work an effect on him absent the conjunction of male and female.[3]

This is why we do not say,[4] *in order to bring about the unification of the Blessed Holy One with his Shechinah.* For this there would be no need![5] Rather, we say, *in order to bring about the unification of the Blessed Holy One and his Shechinah*—that is, to unify the Blessed Holy One *and* his Shechinah with the Root, in the sphere of the Infinite.

Similarly, when we recite the blessing formula *blessed are you, O Lord*, we direct our thought toward the name of the God of Israel, which is the name *YHVH*, while speaking the name *Adonai,* "Lord."[6] The intention thereby encompasses the God of Israel and the Shechinah as a unit, which we bless to couple with the Root, as hinted at in the words,

---

1. Above, chapter 3, section 9; chapter 4, section 5; chapter 5, section 6.

2. Zohar, I, 196a, quoted and interpreted in chapter 8, section 7.

3. It is not quite clear whether the "blessing" the author has in mind is the Root's effluence itself, or (as the sequel suggests) the human prayers that evoke that effluence. Either way, he is surely influenced by the Talmud, b. Yebam. 62b: "Anyone who has no wife dwells without joy, without blessing, without goodness."

4. In the formula of intent, developed by the sixteenth-century Kabbalists and spread throughout the Jewish world, that is to be said prior to the performance of one or another of Judaism's prescribed rituals. It is fairly clear, however, that the meaning our author refuses to give the formula is precisely the one that it properly bears; that is, to join the Blessed Holy One (*Tif'eret*) with his Shechinah (*Malkhut*). See Hallamish, *Kabbalah in Liturgy*, 45–70.

5. The two being already in perpetual connection, as we have just seen.

6. Since the Four-letter Name of God, YHVH, is too sacred to be pronounced, the worshiper speaks the name Adonai instead. The Kabbalists see in this the fusion of the male element of God (YHVH) with the female (Adonai)—a concept to which the author adds his distinctive twist. Cf. Verman, "Development."

Give power to God.⁷ *Who made us holy with his commandments*,⁸ referring to the commandments that the Root gave to [the God of Israel] and imposed upon him, whereupon *he made us holy* in that it was he [the God of Israel] who gave Israel the Torah and imposed all the commandments upon us; hence, *the Torah was given to Moses alone*.⁹

[p. 153] The same is true of the unification we perform when we recite the *Shema*:¹⁰ *YHVH our God*, i.e., the God of Israel, who is our God and whose servants we are,¹¹ *YHVH*, i.e., the Distant One, *is One*, speaking of the Root, who is One in perfect unity, without any trace whatsoever of male and female. (This "One"-ness is that of the "Brother" joined to the letter *dalet*, its significance that of the *karmela* discussed earlier.)¹² We then recite,¹³ *Blessed be the name of his glorious Malkhut*, effecting the coupling with *Malkhut*, which takes place in secret. Understand.

This is the implication of what is said in the Zohar, at the end of the Torah portion *Ha'azinu*: YHVH IS NEAR TO ALL WHO CALL UPON HIM, TO

---

7. Ps 68:35, evidently understood to mean that we must "empower" God (God of Israel + Shechinah) by "plugging it in" to the source of power which is the Root. I do not know whether this may be an allusion to the Kabbalistic treatise *'Oz Lelohim* ("Power to God," from this Psalms verse), published by the quasi-Sabbatean Nehemiah Hayon in 1713, some twelve years before the appearance of the present text.

8. The continuation of the blessing-formula.

9. Talmud, b. Ned. 38a: "The Torah was given only to Moses and his offspring ... but, as an act of generosity, Moses gave it to Israel." Our author takes this to mean that "Moses" (= the God of Israel) was the sole recipient of the commandments from a higher source (the Root), which he then transmitted to the Jewish people. On the Root's imposing the Torah's commandments on the God of Israel, see above, chapter 5, section 2, and cf. chapter 6, section 6.

10. Deut 6:4, the central credo of Judaism: "Hear O Israel, YHVH our God, YHVH is One."

11. Following Ps 100:3.

12. Following the traditional Kabbalah, the author splits the word *ehad* ("one"; אחד) into *ah* ("brother"; אח), referring to the *sefirah Tif'eret*, and the letter *dalet* (ד = *Malkhut*); God's "Oneness" is thus a fusion of male and female elements into a single body. See Cordovero, "Sha'ar 'Erkhei ha-Kinnuyim," s.v. *ah* and *ehad*. On *karmela* as the realm in which the male Graces and female Judgments are inextricably mixed together, see above, chapter 1, section 4. The author seems to intend to develop his point that our liturgical utterances bond the male + female unit to the genderless Root, but his interpretation of the Shema does not serve his purpose very well, and the sentence that follows distracts from it.

13. In a whisper, following the recitation of the Shema in a normal tone of voice. On the God of Israel's sex "in secret," see above, chapter 6, section 8 and chapter 8, section 4.

THE SALVATION OF GOD

ALL THOSE WHO CALL UPON HIM IN TRUTH. IS THERE ANYONE WHO CALLS UPON HIM IN FALSEHOOD? and so forth. *IN TRUTH: AS THE SEAL OF THE KING'S SIGNET-RING,* and so forth.[14] What it means is this:

It is known that the Root partakes of the nature of the Infinite, where no image of letter or vowel-point exists.[15] How, then, can we possibly speak of this imageless, formless entity as "coupling" with the Shape of the Path of Emanation?[16] But take heed: We normally use the word "seal," as is well known, to refer to the seal that one stamps upon paper or the like, whose letters protrude and which consequently is male in character. The seal upon a signet-ring, however, is incised; and this is THE SEAL OF THE KING'S SIGNET-RING, and its character is female. When the God of Israel is in the lower realms, his nature is male; he can be represented by the seal of the protuberant kind. But in the higher realms, over against the Root, he is female: an incised seal, SEAL OF THE SIGNET-RING.

In making use of seals, the practice is to take the signet-ring seal and press it against the wax. Or the reverse: you take the soft, smooth wax and stamp it upon the signet-ring seal, whereupon the letters will stand out upon the wax in proportion to the degree of pressure placed upon it, and it will thus take on the quality of maleness. But remove the wax, and it will remain without any vowel-point or shape of a letter.

So it is here. The Root has no "vowel" or "vowel-point" whatever. The Shape of the Path of Emanation,[17] however, is incised in the manner of that SEAL OF THE SIGNET-RING, and the Root, pushing against him, protrudes in proportion to the degree of that pressure and takes on the character of a male. Once the incised ["letters"][18] are removed, it is left without any colors or "letter" at all.

---

14. Much-abbreviated quotation of Zohar, III, 297a, expounding Ps 145:18. The Zohar finds it peculiar to speak of calling on God "in truth" (*emet*), because that implies there are those who call upon him in falsehood. It explains that "one who calls and does not know upon whom he calls" indeed calls in falsehood, and goes on to equate "truth" with "the seal of the king's signet-ring, which is the perfection of all." We shall presently see, however, that *emet* does not really mean "truth," and that with its image of the signet-ring the Zohar is revealing something profound about the God of Israel and his relation to the Root.

15. The use of the features of Hebrew script to illustrate the absence of differentiation within the Root seems odd, until we realize the author is anticipating the "seal" analogy he will presently make.

16. I.e., the God of Israel; above, chapter 2, sections 2–3.

17. Ms. Jerusalem 2491: "the God of Israel."

18. Reading *sheqa'* for the mss. *shefa'*, "effluence." The reference is to the "incised" God of Israel.

[p. 154] Now in the higher realms, when [the God of Israel] is concave and female in character, he is called *emet*,[19] as we speak of a "water *emet*" [channel] or a "building *emet*," and, in the Palestinian Talmud, of *emet* as *a brickwork structure*—that is, broad at the base and narrow on top, like a female who is broad below and narrow above, so as to hold the fetus. But when he is below, functioning as a male, he is not called [fol. 34a] *emet*. And hence: YHVH *is near to all who call upon him, to all those who call upon hei-vav*,[20] meaning, who couple the *hei* to the *vav*, specifically when he is engaged in copulation in the higher realms as a female; and this is what is meant by EMET, THE SEAL OF THE SIGNET-RING, for that SEAL is by nature female and receives effluence. Understand.

Thus, similarly, *The seal becomes like a homer*, meaning (as we have said earlier) that the *homer*, the "material," is pressed against the "seal" and clings to it (just as we have said); *standing erect like a garment*, i.e., the God of Israel *qua* female, enclothing [the Root].[21] And so the verse is well explained.

19. *Emet*, which we have assumed to mean "truth" in Ps 145:18 and its Zoharic exposition, now turns out to indicate something concave—incised, hollowed out—and therefore female, as is the God of Israel in the presence of the Root. The author goes on to buttress this (wildly implausible) exegesis with the alleged use of *emet* in the phrases *amat ha-mayim*, "water channel," and *amat ha-binyan*—normally used for a measure, "cubit" (e.g., Mishnah, m. Kelim 17:10), but also a physical object, apparently a stick of some sort (Talmud, b. Shabb. 31a). (*Amat* in these phrases is not the same word as *emet*, but the identical spelling allows the author to treat it as such.) The reference to the Palestinian Talmud is actually to the Babylonian Talmud, b. Shabb. 104a. In this passage, which the author strips of its context, Aramaic (מלבן לבוני/ה) seems to mean, "a level foundation" (Jastrow, comp., *Dictionary*, s.v. *levan*); I am obliged to conjecture his understanding of it from the use he goes on to make of it. He is plainly inspired by the Talmud, b. Ber. 61a, 'Erub. 18a–b: "The Blessed Holy One built Eve like a storehouse [*binyan otzar*]. Just as a storehouse is narrow above and broad below, in order to hold the produce, so a woman is narrow above and broad below, in order to hold the fetus."

20. Ps 145:18, retranslated in accordance with the author's understanding of it. Not only has he re-conceived the meaning of *emet*, but he has detached the suffix of *yiqre'uhu* ("call upon him"), consisting of the letters *hei-vav*, from the verb to which they are attached and given them Kabbalistic significance: *vav* and *hei*, the third and fourth letters of the Tetragrammaton, are standard symbols for the male *Tif'eret* and the female *Malkhut* respectively. Those "who call upon him" are those who fuse the two into a single unit, as above, and then couple that unit (which is now female, concave, *emet*) with the effluence-giving Root.

21. Job 38:14, interpreted quite differently in chapter 3, section 1. Here the raw, shapeless "material" (the Root) is given its male form through adhesion to the female "seal" (God of Israel); and the "garment" of the second part of the verse is no longer the Shechinah enclothing the embryonic God of Israel, as in chapter 3, but the God of Israel herself (!) enclothing the Root.

2. Passage of Effluence—The Ideal Interrupted

[But in this exile time, things are not as they ought to be. The God of Israel will sometimes make a conscious decision, reacting to the sinfulness of the time, not to ejaculate the effluence into his Female. Sometimes, unconscious in the domain of the Root, he may be impotent and incapable of ejaculation; or, in the yet loftier darkness of the Ein Sof's substrate, altogether sexless. Or, if he is not separated from his Shechinah, she may be separated from him, raised into the domain of the Root. He is to follow her, it would seem—"Das Ewig-Weibliche zieht uns hinan"[22]—both reverting to virginity in the process. It will only be in messianic times, as we will see, that she can be raised above him without arousing his jealousy, or doing any harm to him or their sexual connection.]

Know this:[23] during exile times, the Temple being destroyed, the "rain" that symbolizes the effluence of the God of Israel, and the semen that he ejaculates into the Female, can become stopped up.[24] This is conveyed by the verse *He shall stop up the heavens so there be no rain*, with the result that *the river shall be parched and dried*, as the Zohar explains.[25]

This can happen under a number of circumstances. One is when the God of Israel indwells in *Tif'eret*, and yet, due to the sinfulness of the generation, he closes up his spirit so as not to spill the effluence into *Malkhut*, his Female.[26] This is why he is called "King Solomon," *Shelomoh*, "to whom *shalom*, peace, belongs": he is able, as we have said, to stop up his spirit at will, and thus *shalom*—*Yesod*/penis, that is—"belongs to him," is under his control.[27]

---

22. "The Eternal-Feminine draws us upward"; from the end of Goethe's *Faust*.

23. Ms. Oxford 976 resumes at this point.

24. Symbolism of the "rain" developed above, chapter 5, section 7.

25. Deut 11:17; Job 14:11; the latter verse is regularly used in the Kabbalah to indicate the drying up of the flow of divine effluence (e.g., Zohar, I, 26a). I am not aware of any Zoharic passage that combines it with Deut 11:17. Perhaps the author is thinking of Zohar, II, 166b–67a, where the river's drying up takes place "in the time when the Jewish people is in exile."

26. Emphasizing that the God of Israel works through his *Tif'eret* "body," having sex with *Malkhut*, which is the "body" of his Female; through the closing up of his "spirit," he is able to control his "physical" penis *Yesod*. This explanation, which blames human sin for the "river's" drying up, is standard in the traditional Kabbalah. It is significant that the author presents it as only one of several options, the others being more to his taste and in better accord with his system.

27. On "Solomon" as a designation for the male God, and the etymology of the

It also happens that he ascends to a higher plane in a state of entrancement, during which time he is without consciousness ["knowledge"], as we have earlier seen.[28] *For YHVH is a God of knowledge;*[29] and yet when he removes himself to that higher plane, in a state of entrancement, he is in an unconscious condition. Without consciousness there can be no erection, and thus he is unable to couple with the Shechinah. This is the meaning of *by knowledge shall the rooms become filled:*[30] it is when he has "knowledge," consciousness, that the "rooms" that symbolize *Malkhut* can become filled. [p. 155] Without consciousness this cannot be; rather, he is in the state of Job, who *speaks without knowledge*[31] and cannot copulate.

There are yet other times when he ascends and hides himself within the substrate of Ein Sof.[32] He does not then couple with the Root, but remains within the "Darkness" and "Mother" that is Ein Sof's substrate—as suggested by *he makes darkness his concealment* and *I will garb the heaven in blackness*[33]—and he does not engage in sex. Hence the Zohar's query, WHEN DOES THE KING'S LOVEMAKING TAKE PLACE? and its reply, SHE IS INDEED MY SISTER, THE DAUGHTER OF MY FATHER BUT NOT OF MY MOTHER.[34] The Zohar goes on to explain that when he dwells and

---

name, see above, chapter 6, note 214. The equation of *shalom* with the phallic *sefirah Yesod* is a staple of the traditional Kabbalah.

28. On the state of "entrancement" (*dormita*), see above, chapter 2, section 2. *Da'at*, normally translated "knowledge" (as in Gen 2:17), here seems to mean something more like "consciousness." It is said in chapter 4, section 6, to be the essence of copulation. The tension between this passage and what the author has earlier said and will go on to say—that the God of Israel is fused with the Shechinah while coupling with the Root, and that "when he couples with the Root he couples with the Shechinah as well"—reflects the gap between the ideal theory and the sad reality of exile time.

29. 1 Sam 2:3, quoted and understood very differently, in reference to the Distant One, in chapter 8, section 7.

30. Prov 24:4.

31. Paraphrasing Job 35:16; cf. 38:2, 42:3. Job as representation of the God of Israel is by now familiar to us; see above, chapter 6, note 213.

32. This "substrate" is introduced in chapter 1, section 5; its association with the "Mother" is developed in chapter 3, section 7. The God of Israel's sexless banishment to that sphere is mentioned, though not described in any detail, in chapter 6, section 7.

33. Ps 18:12, quoted also in chapter 6, section 7; Isa 50:3. "Heaven" is standard Kabbalistic code for *Tif'eret*, extended by our author to the God of Israel.

34. Very free quotation of Zohar, III, 100b, in which Gen 20:12 is invoked to answer the question that has been posed. Unpacking this cryptic reply, the Zohar explains that *Tif'eret* couples with *Malkhut* "only when she is illumined from the Supernal Father" (the *sefirah Hokhmah*) and not from the Mother (*Binah*); i.e., when she is "the daughter of my father but not of my mother." Our author distorts this considerably, making the

unites himself with the Father, who is called "Holiness"—that is, when he couples with the Root—then he couples with the Shechinah as well. But when he dwells within the Mother, whose character is Mindless Light, as we have said, he makes love not at all.

And there is yet another circumstance, hinted at in the verse *To a mare in Pharaoh's chariotry have I compared you, my spouse.*[35]

The Shechinah has previously said to the God of Israel: *The king has brought me into his chambers; we will rejoice and be glad in you.*[36] There are times, in other words, when the Shechinah ascends higher than the God of Israel, all the way to the Root—which, however, does not couple with her, but only takes her on high in order to make her attractive to her husband. The Shechinah can then say to the God of Israel (as we read in *Zohar Hadash*):[37] "Do not say that I am pursuing you, begging you, for *the king has brought me into his chambers*—I have been higher than you, in the very domain of the Root. Yet I had no wish for sex; all my desire is for you"—this being the meaning of, *we will rejoice and be glad in you.* Consult *Zohar Hadash*, and you will understand.

It is to this that the God of Israel replies, *To a mare*, and so forth; meaning that, apart from the reason just stated—to make her attractive to her husband—yet another motive is involved. When the Root wants the God of Israel to turn his attention away from things below, and to ascend on high in the state of entrancement, he lifts the Shechinah up above him. And, given that THE MALE'S WHOLE DESIRE IS TO RUN AFTER THE FEMALE,[38] he too will depart for the heights in a state of entrancement.

Thus Pharaoh (i.e., the God of Israel) says to Joseph (i.e., the Shechinah, as we have seen): *Go up*, to the upper realms, *and bury your father.*[39] He is to be in a state of "burial," that is, entrancement. [p. 156]

---

male and not the female the determinative partner.

35. Song 1:9.

36. Song 1:4.

37. Paraphrasing *Sefer Zohar Hadash*, 9c; Ashlag, *Sefer ha-Zohar*, 19:68–70. The passage concludes: "I and my hosts 'will rejoice and be glad in you': our pleasure and desire is to be with you and not separated from you.... For a woman has no pleasure or desire except with her husband—not with her mother and her father. 'The king has brought me into his chambers,' and I have had pleasure and desire for none but you."

38. Paraphrasing Zohar, I, 245a.

39. Gen 50:6. The author's previously established identification of Pharaoh with the God of Israel (above, chapter 6, sections 1 and 3) here leads him into incoherence. For his exegesis to work, "Pharaoh" must represent the Root, and Joseph's "father" the God of Israel.

Similarly, Ezekiel is told to *bind your splendor up over you*, meaning that she is to be above, a "head" for him, leading him upward.⁴⁰ Why? The text goes on to explain: *Behold I am taking away from you the desire of your eyes*, namely his wife; specifically, *be-maggefah*, meaning "as a virgin" (as one speaks of the *megufah*, the "stopper," of a cask).⁴¹ When she makes her ascent, she too is in a state of virginity.

When, however, the Root wishes [fol. 34b] for him to turn his attention to matters below, he sends the Shechinah down and [the God of Israel's] attention will also turn downward. This was how Pharaoh handled his horses. When he wanted the stallions to run, he set the mares before them; when he wanted them to halt, he placed the mares behind.⁴² Hence the God of Israel's retort to the Shechinah, when she says she was above him—yes, in order that his attention be diverted there!⁴³ *You were just like a mare in Pharaoh's chariotry, dear spouse!* he says—as we have shown.

3. Passage of Effluence—Provisional Arrangements

> [Then what are the lower worlds (ours included) to do? They, and even the God of Israel himself, must subsist on the meager "dew" provided by the Distant One, conveyed not directly through Interiority, but through the channels of Enclothement. (More on this in the next section.) This "dew" is not destructive like the Distant One's ejaculate, but hardly enough to survive on.]

---

40. Ezek 24:17; *pe'er*, literally "splendor" (from the same root as *Tif'eret*), is normally understood as some form of headgear (verse 23, from which the author derives the association with the "head"). The author equates it with Ezekiel's wife, who is taken from him by the God who is the Root: as "Ewig-Weibliche," she draws him upward.

41. Verse 16. *Be-maggefah* is normally translated "at a stroke"; our author takes it to mean that the Shechinah is carried up on high "with a stopper" (e.g., Mishnah, m. Shabb. 22:3), her "cask" sealed. "She too" in the next sentence is slightly puzzling (unless it is "he too"; the verbs could be masculine as well as feminine). The author seems to imply that, in his unsexed state of "entrancement," the God of Israel reverts to his virginal condition, and the Shechinah does as well.

42. Inspired by rabbinic midrashim on Song 1:9, where God uses an illusory mare to draw Pharaoh's stallions into the Red Sea: Tanhuma *Shofetim* #14, *Pirqei de-Rabbi Eliezer* chapter 41.

43. And he the person of real interest (he says), she just the bait dangled before him. The petty narcissism of this lover's quarrel—between two of the highest divine entities!—is both comic and sad.

During all this time, then, that [the God of Israel] sends down no "rain"—on what does the world survive?

It is maintained entirely by the "dew" equivalent that descends from the Distant One, as we have described.[44] This "dew" is never stopped up, as the Gemara tells us,[45] and on it the world can sustain itself. True, it is not much. Yet it is not stopped up, and it bestows a certain limited measure of life, keeping the world's creatures from becoming entirely corpse-like. This is not the effluence of blessing, however, since it lacks the capacity to bear fruit.

Upon this "dew," which Little-face[46] receives from the Holy Distant One, the Shechinah must subsist in lieu of "rain" and seed, and go to the *Tehiru* to receive female juices. And thus *to Benjamin he said: Blessed of YHVH is his earth—from the delicacies of heaven, from the dew, from the crouching abyss*, and so forth[47]—from which we learn that she enters the *Tehiru*-waters equipped only with this "dew." No sex is involved; she is consequently without any heat from that northern fire that manifests itself during intercourse as *his left hand under my head*,[48] and which is the very essence of sexual coupling.

Lacking that fiery heat—the fire upon the altar, so to speak, having gone out[49]—she has no way to purge and purify the *Tehiru*-waters. The only heat at her disposal comes through her fasting, since she does not receive any male juices. Yet fasting does generate heat, as is well known, and one can employ that heat to perform purgations. This is the significance of fasting; understand it.[50]

---

44. Above, chapter 5, section 7.

45. Talmud, b. Ta'an. 3a-b.

46. *Ze'ir Anpin*, the Kabbalistic "shape" that for our author is the "Enclothement" of the God of Israel. He here recapitulates what he has already said in chapter 5, section 7.

47. Deut 33:13; where, however, the blessing is addressed not to Benjamin but to Joseph. The author's error—found in all mss.—is all the stranger since Joseph would better suit his argument: he is *Yesod* in the traditional Kabbalah, as well as the Shechinah in the author's own system. "Earth" is of course understood as the Shechinah.

48. Song 2:6, understood following the Zohar (e.g., I, 133a): the stimulus for sexual passion comes from the left side of the sefirotic system. On the symbolism of left = north = fire, see above, chapter 7, section 2.

49. For the context of this image, see chapter 4, section 3.

50. The language is awkward, the author's thought unclear. What does he mean by the Shechinah's "fasting"? Her sexual deprivation?

[p. 157] At such a time, the vessels[51] receive "dew" from the Distant One, as we have said, while the God of Israel effuses no seed or "rain" into the Female. Quite the contrary—he is in the role of recipient, inasmuch as Little-face (who is his Enclothement) must receive everything from the Holy Distant One and from the Father-and-Mother of Enclothement, and must enter the womb of Infancy and Nursing.[52] For no "rain" falls upon the earth, and all life has come to an end.

So it is that Job, speaking in the person of the God of Israel, says that *those who are younger than I now do play upon me*;[53] for the recipient of effluence takes on the female role, while "playing" is prelude to sex, as we know from *let the lads rise up and play before us*.[54] When he says, *Those younger than I now do play upon me*, he refers to the upper worlds,[55] which are "younger" than he, in that he is ADAM, THE FIRST OF THEM ALL;[56] and these *do play upon me*, having sex with me, I serving them as female.

4. Passage of Effluence—The Danger and the Problem

[So the theory of prayer laid out in section 1 is doomed to remain just that: a theory, without any practical application. Far from being a fused unit, the God of Israel and his Shechinah are hopelessly alienated from one another; praying to him is just as hazardous as to the permanently Shechinah-less Distant One.

---

51. That is, the sefirotic entities.

52. As he did after the Shattering: above, chapter 5, section 3 (cf. chapter 3, section 1). It is no doubt under the influence of this womb imagery that the author diverges from chapter 5, section 7, where Little-face receives the "dew" from the "Shape" of Long-face (= Distant One; the *sefirah Keter* in the classical Kabbalah), transferring this function to the slightly lower "Shapes" of Father and Mother (*Hokhmah* and *Binah* in the classical Kabbalah).

53. Job 30:1. On Job as representation of the God of Israel, see above, chapter 6, note 213.

54. 2 Sam 2:14. It is unclear why the author sees the "play" as sexual; the Biblical context points instead to mass bloodshed, and so the midrash understands it (e.g., Exodus Rabbah 42:1). The reading "prelude to sex" (*mevo tashmish*) is found only in ms. Oxford 955. The other mss. all read מצאת השמש. ("From the going forth of the sun," cf. Judg 5:31? "From the withdrawal of the penis," cf. Talmud, b. Nid. 12a? Neither makes much sense.)

55. The "shapes" of Long-face, Father, and Mother, all of which are higher than *Tif'eret* in the sefirotic hierarchy.

56. Slightly altered quotation of Zohar, II, 55a; cf. *Tiqqunei Zohar* 70, 120a. On "Adam" as representation of the God of Israel, see above, chapter 6, sections 6–7.

Our prayers must operate not through the essences of divinity but through its external shells, the entities of Enclothement; and it is truly said of us that we have no true God, that we cry aloud to the God to whom we are covenanted and we get no answer.]

It follows that, in time of exile, we must *not* dedicate our intention and prayer when we say *blessed are you, O Lord*, to the God of Israel and his Shechinah with the aim of attaching them to the Root, in the manner set forth previously.[57] He spills no effluence into the Shechinah, *a heaven's distance lying between them*;[58] consequently, when we set our intention to bring down the effluence, it all comes in the form of uncontained ejaculate, no Female receiving it. It thus brings about devastation, Shattering of the Vessels in all the worlds. For inasmuch as he has no sexual connection with the Female, he is precisely like the Distant One to whom we must not pray.

Accordingly, *all the pious must pray above This-One*—pray, that is, to the entity that is above the Shechinah (who is called This-One), namely the God of Israel—but specifically *at a time when he may be found*, a time when he is present and unhidden here, not when he is in a state of concealment.[59] And the text goes on to give the reason we must not pray to him at a time when he is not coupling with the Shechinah, nor to the Distant One Holiest of All the Holy, Most Hidden of All the Hidden:[60] *that the mighty waters*, it says, *not reach him with their flooding*. Never again, in other words, must he undergo the Flood, the Shattering of vessels that is *the flooding of the mighty waters*; for when [the effluence] takes the form of uncontained ejaculate, then it is that *flooding of mighty waters*. Understand.

[p. 158] All this is the evident lesson of the Shattering of the Vessels: they received effluence in the form of uncontained ejaculate, and therefore were shattered. So says the *Idra*: THESE ARE THE KINGS, and so forth: THIS IS THE SECRET OF THE TESTIMONY CONCERNING THE SECRET OF THE

---

57. In section 1, above. The words "in time of exile" are found only in ms. Oxford 955 but are necessary to understand the thrust of this passage, and its apparent contradiction to section 1.

58. A rabbinic expression for the sexual alienation of wife and husband: Mishnah, m. Ned. 11:12.

59. Ps 32:6, its beginning more normally understood as "for this let all the pious pray"; but the author follows the exegesis of the verse in Zohar, III, 79b. The identification of *zot*, "this one," with the *sefirah Malkhut* and hence with the Shechinah is a staple of the classical Kabbalah.

60. The full title of the Distant One of Interiority; above, chapter 4, note 174.

PRAYER OF FAITH—which at first sight seems unintelligible.[61] But in accordance with what we have said it makes perfect sense. We learn from it that, inasmuch as they were Shattered on account of their receiving uncontained ejaculate, we must not pray to the Distant One or even to the God of Israel when he is not coupling with the Shechinah. For the consequence will be uncontained ejaculate, laying waste to the worlds.

Our prayer, rather, must be to join the Shechinah to Little-face, from there to Father and Mother, and from there to Long-face, all of it via the path of Enclothement—multiple paths, elaborated by [fol. 35a] Luria and in the Zohar[62]—for such is the path of effluence.

This is why the Bible says that *Israel shall pass many days without a true God*,[63] meaning that for the bulk of the exile—the self-concealment, the hiddenness—they cannot direct their prayers and intentions toward the God of Israel, who is the *true God*.[64] Indeed, when things are as they should be and effluence goes down from the God of Israel into the Shechinah, he is the one to whom prayer and intention ought to be directed. For he is our God and we his servants,[65] and it is written, *They shall cry aloud and no one saves, to YHVH, and he does not answer them*,[66] meaning that one is to pray only to YHVH. Yet, in a time of [divine] self-concealment, even though *they cry aloud to YHVH, he does not answer them*.

---

61. Free quotation of Zohar, III, 128a, expounding Gen 36:31 on the "kings of Edom" (see above, chapter 4, section 5; and chapter 5, section 8; cf. Hellner-Eshed, *Seekers of the Face*, 174–84). The author apparently read the Zohar text as "it is a testimony concerning the faith of all prayer," taking the word *tzelota*, "prayer" as going with what comes before rather than what comes after. (He transposes the Zohar's preceding reference to "the supreme secrets of the Torah" into this passage, in the form of the twice-repeated "secret.") The passage at first sight seems unintelligible, he says—for what could the Shattering (represented by the death of the "Edomite kings") come to teach us about any "prayer of faith" (or "faith of prayer")?

62. The language is awkward and the reading uncertain: in place of the "multiple paths" of the majority of the mss., Oxford 955 reads "in the *Idra Zuta*," qualifying and refining the citation of the Zohar. The reference would presumably be to the final section of the *Idra Zuta* (Zohar, III, 296a–b), a breathless description of the descent of the effluence through the divine potentialities and its ejaculation by the Male into the Female—at the climax of which Rabbi Shimon, embodiment of the divine phallus, dies in orgasm.

63. 2 Chr 15:3, a standard Sabbatian motto (see above, chapter 8, note 191).

64. But must restrict themselves to bringing down the effluence along the "path of Enclothement," not invoking or even recognizing the Interiorities within.

65. Following Ps 100:3.

66. Ps 18:42, ignoring the Biblical context, in which "they" are the psalmist's enemies.

5. The Solution: The Distant One and the Messiah

[There is a way out of the dilemma. The Messiah may provide the Distant One with a Shechinah substitute in the form of his own feminized body. This is what he does when, as "David," he "seeks to engage in alien worship" (i.e., converts to Islam), offering his buttocks for the divinity's sexual penetration. (Section 7, with which this passage must be read in conjunction; cf. also the Torah scroll brought into the latrine, at the end of chapter 6.) In the process he ascends to a realm superior to the God of Israel's—a realm where Torah and commandments are irrelevant, where no one is judged or cast away, where every distinction between Jew and Gentile is dissolved in the all-encompassing divine love.

We must understand: *the Messiah's breakthrough is our breakthrough*, "we" no longer being the Jews but all the people of the world. And we must understand; *the Christian God, the heretofore "Distant One," is now our God*, present unto us through the sacrifice, not of Jesus Christ, but of Sabbatai Zevi.]

But know this: the true Messiah copulates with the Distant One in the Shechinah's role,[67] such that with him as well [as with the Shechinah] the ejaculate is not uncontained; and he prays in [the Distant One's] presence. This is the *prayer of Poor-Man*—for he is called *Poor-Man, the donkey's rider*[68]—*when he enwraps himself*,[69] which is to say, he enwraps himself in prayers unto the very highest heights—as the Zohar says, that the poor man's prayer rises to the highest heights[70]—he being in the role

---

67. Reading, conjecturally, *she-hu be-sod ha-shekhinah*, omitting the word *rosh* from the reading shared by all the mss. (*she-hu be-sod rosh ha-shekhinah*), which would have to be translated "who is the head of the Shechinah" and referred back to the Distant One instead of the Messiah. The Distant One has been identified throughout the treatise as the "head" (*rosh*) of the divine Shape (beginning with chapter 2, section 1), and this identification will be reprised in the crucial passage that ends it. But nowhere else is he called "head of the Shechinah," and it is hard to see even what this designation would mean. (The Messiah, by contrast, is said to be *be-sod ha-shekhinah* a few lines below.) Most likely, the familiar Distant One = *rosh* equation influenced some early copyist to insert the word here, even though it does not fit the context.

68. Zech 9:9, universally understood to refer to the Messiah (e.g., Talmud, b. Sanh. 98a).

69. Ps 102:1.

70. Probably referring to the exposition of Ps 102:1 in Zohar, II, 86b: "Every prayer of Israel is genuine, but the prayer of a poor person transcends them all. Why? Because this one rises to the King's Throne of Glory, crowning His head, and the blessed Holy One is glorified by that prayer" (Matt, trans., *Zohar*, 4:487). For the Zohar, unlike for our author, there is no specific allusion to the Messiah.

of the Shechinah. Thereupon does he *pour out his speech before YHVH,* praying to the Distant One, [p. 159] who is called *before-YHVH*.[71]

Accordingly, *he remains fixed in Supernal Grace*;[72] and accordingly Rav Hamnuna Saba, who stands for the Messiah, says that IT IS TO THE POSSESSOR OF THE NOSE, referring to the Distant One, who has a single nose, THAT I PRAY.[73] The Distant One, you must realize, consists of pure Mercy, without any bit of Judgment even for those who violate the Torah; and thus *af,* "nose," designates the Holy Distant One, who has a single *af,* in contrast to the God of Israel, who is called *appayim,* "double-nosed."[74] *Af loves the peoples,*[75] even the Gentiles, inasmuch as he is without any Judgment.

This is why on Purim *one must drink until he cannot tell the difference between "Cursed be Haman"* and so forth;[76] for the Distant One, who is Mercy, then holds sway. He is alluded to in Hannah's prayer: *Do not speak*

71. Taking the Bible's *lifnei,* "before," as temporal: "prior to"—the Distant One is "prior to" the God of Israel (= the Biblical YHVH). Cf. the beginning of chapter 8, section 8, where it is the Root that is "prior to" the God of Israel (= the Talmudic "Blessed Holy One").

72. Ps 21:8, speaking of "the king"—understood as the Messiah, who remains permanently in the realm of the Distant One who is *hesed 'elyon,* "Supernal Grace."

73. Zohar, III, 130b (*Idra Rabbah*). The context of this passage, which represents 'Attiqa's "nose" as emblematic of his unalloyed grace and mercy, is discussed in Hellner-Eshed, *Seekers of the Face,* 203–5. Rav Hamnuna Saba ("Hamnuna the Elder") appears in the Talmud as a rabbinic authority, along with several other Hamnunas with whom he may or may not be identical. The Zohar elevates him to a numinous, quasi-divine being, whose appearance as a donkey-driver in I, 5a–7a links him to the donkey-riding Messiah of Zech 9:9. (He is said in that passage to dwell in "a certain tower soaring in the air," occupied by "the blessed Holy One and a certain poor person"; our author may have seen this as one more link to the "Poor-Man's prayer" of Ps 102:1.) See Matt's note to *Zohar,* 1:37–38.

74. As in the phrase *erekh appayim,* literally "long of [dual] nose" but meaning "slow to anger," which the Bible regularly applies to God (e.g., Exod 34:6). In the Bible, singular *af* and dual *appayim* both mean "nose," the latter emphasizing the two nostrils; but our author takes *appayim* hyperliterally as conveying the presence within the God of Israel of both Mercy and Judgment. There is no such duality, he says, within the "single-nosed" Distant One, who is pure Mercy and Grace.

75. Deut 33:3. In the Biblical context, *af* is a particle meaning "even" or "indeed"— "he indeed loves the peoples"—but the author chooses to take it as a noun, the single "nose" that is the Distant One.

76. ". . . and 'Blessed be Mordecai'"; Talmud, b. Meg. 7b. This is the sinister, destructive aspect of the Distant One's undiluted Mercy: essential moral distinctions, such as that between the noble Jew Mordecai and the genocidal anti-Semite Haman collapse as though in the alcoholic haze of the Purim festival. Hence Hannah's warning, which reiterates what we have seen earlier: the Distant One is not to be invoked in prayer—except, as we shall see shortly, by or through the mediator/sex object Sabbatai Zevi.

profusely toward the Lofty One or let Distance emerge from your mouth, i.e., do not speak or pray to the Distant One and the Root.⁷⁷ And in reply:⁷⁸ *Because he is the God of YHVH's knowledge*, referring to the Distant One, who is the God of Israel's knowledge and thought, as we have said,⁷⁹ *and deeds are not measured*, meaning that the Distant One's *deeds are not measured* because destruction and Shattering are inherent to him.⁸⁰ (The God of Israel, by contrast, is able to couple with the Shechinah.) The text therefore goes on to speak of the Shattering of the Vessels—*while the barren woman has borne seven, the one who had many sons is wretched*, as Luria explains, applying these words to the Shattering.⁸¹

6. Shechinah: Virgin No More

> [In this new dispensation, what role remains for the God of Israel? Although his Torah has become irrelevant—permanently profaned, perhaps, by having been thrust into the latrine that is the Messiah's anus?—he and his Shechinah are neither discarded nor diminished. Like the world itself, they are redeemed. *Va-avo ha-Yom* climaxes in a glowing rhapsody of their ceaseless lovemaking, performed not primarily as a vehicle for the transmission of effluence (though we may assume it has that effect), but in the sheer joy of being she-God and he-God, together forever.]

77. 1 Sam 2:3, slightly altering the text so that Hannah's "do not profusely speak lofty things" can be made to mean "do not profusely speak toward the Lofty One." The word I have translated "Distance," *'ataq*, is usually taken to mean "arrogance," "impudence," or the like. But it is from the same root as *'attiqa*, "the Distant One" (see above, chapter 2, note 15), and our author understands it accordingly.

78. To the implied question: why should one not pray to the Distant One? But the text is uncertain, and these words possibly should be deleted as a scribal error.

79. See above, chapter 8, note 141. The explicit reference to the God of Israel is found only in ms. Oxford 976, but is implied in the other mss.

80. That is, the Distant One's activity is confined to the realm of thought, since whatever "deeds" he is able to generate are rendered unstable through the destructive power of his uncontained ejaculate, and therefore cannot be "measured." The author rests his argument on the Ketiv of 1 Sam 2:3, which gives the first word of *ve-lo nitkenu 'alilot* as ולא, "not" (vs. the Qeri ולו, "by him," followed by most translations). He goes on to draw the contrast with the God of Israel, who has the Shechinah—as the Distant One will presently have Sabbatai Zevi—as safe receptacle for his ejaculate.

81. 1 Sam 2:5. I do not know what passage in the Lurianic literature the author has in mind. The Biblical verse's link to the Shattering may lie in the rabbinic tradition, reported by Rashi *ad loc.*, that the ten sons of Hannah's rival wife Peninnah (= ten primordial *sefirot*) all died, except for two who were spared by Hannah's intercession.

Know this: in future time the Shechinah will be sexually opened. So it is written, *Fallen, no more to rise is the virgin of Israel*,[82] meaning that she will no longer stand as a virgin. For then there will be no fear of the Insolent Waters since they will all have been mended, and she will engage in sex—*spread wide the place of your "tent."*[83]

So *the moon will be "dug"*—the language of "digging" used as in *the well that the princes dug* and so forth,[84] to mean that she will be sexually penetrated—*and the sun will linger*.[85] At present their coupling is intermittent; in future time it will be continual, "lingering" as in *Moses lingered*, meaning that he will remain perpetually.[86] [p. 160] The verse goes on to explain: *For YHVH*, namely the God of Israel, *rules in Zion, and in the presence of his elders*, namely the Root, *he is a Glory*—i.e., it is he who is called his Female's "Glory."

In future time the Higher Shechinah will be above the God of Israel, *the worthy woman her husband's crown*.[87] *Then Moses shall sing*.[88] At present, whenever the Shechinah wants to make love, she must serenade, as in *I am the singing rose*.[89] But in future time the God of Israel will do the serenading—*then Moses*, who is the God of Israel, *shall sing*.

This is the meaning of *the moon's light shall be like the light of the sun*,[90] conveying that the Shechinah will be in a lofty rank like the God of Israel, who is represented by the sun. The sun's light will take the place of the moon: *the sun's light shall be like the light of Seven-days*, that is, like the light of the Shechinah, who is called "Seven-days."[91] Not meaning,

82. Amos 5:2.

83. Isa 54:2.

84. Num 21:18, which continues: " . . . which the nobles of the people hewed out, with a rod and with their staffs."

85. Isa 24:23, normally translated "the moon will be confounded and the sun will be ashamed." The author, for whom "moon" and "sun" are the Shechinah and the God of Israel, offers his own lexical treatment of the two verbs.

86. With the Shechinah. The author explains the sun's *boshah* in Isaiah by reference to Moses's *boshesh* ("lingered") in Exod 32:1. Like the sun, Moses is a symbolic representation of the God of Israel, a function he will exercise again in the next paragraph.

87. Prov 12:4; see the end of chapter 5, section 6.

88. Exod 15:1. The Hebrew verb "sing" is in the future tense, although all modern translators, following the context, treat it as past.

89. Song 2:1, as interpreted in Zohar, I, 221a (= III, 107a), which derives "Sharon" from *sharah*, "she sings," and says that the Shechinah is called "rose" (*havatzelet*) "at the time when she wants to make love with the King."

90. Isa 30:26.

91. As proposed at the end of chapter 8, section 10. The author quietly omits from

of course, that his light will be diminished; rather, that the Shechinah's rank will be elevated until the God of Israel is in comparison to her as the Shechinah is now in comparison to him. At that time *YHVH will be One and his name One.*[92] Blessed be he forever! Amen!

7. Why Sabbatai Zevi Became a Muslim

This is why David, when *he came to the Head*[93] *which is the Distant One, where he was to prostrate himself for God*—the language of copulation—*David sought to engage in alien worship,*[94] in accordance with *Af loves the peoples.*[95] Understand.

---

the text of Isaiah the word "sevenfold" (*shiv'atayim*), which would not suit his argument.

92. Zech 14:9, regularly used by the Kabbalists to describe the ultimate harmonious synthesis of all the Divinity's diverse aspects.

93. Ms. Jerusalem 2491 inserts at this point the word *qibbalti*, "I have received as a tradition"—marking it, however, with an overline, which may mean it is to be excised. The equation of "Head" with the Distant One is made in chapter 2, section 1, and remains a staple of the author's argument throughout.

94. 2 Sam 15:32, quoted in Talmud, b. Sanh. 107a: "David sought to engage in alien worship, as it is written: 'David came to the head [in the Biblical context, the "summit" of the Mount of Olives] where he was to prostrate himself to God' [or, 'the gods']; and the word 'head' must refer to alien worship, as in 'that image had a head of fine gold' [Dan 2:32]." The Talmud goes on to explain David's motivation: so that people will not speak ill of God's justice, he must commit a crime worthy of the punishment that his son Absalom is trying to kill him. The author ignores this, however, and represents the Talmud's opening assertion as referring to the apostasy of Sabbatai Zevi (= David, "the true Messiah"), which he interprets as a transition from—or transcendence of—the domain of the "God of Israel," in favor of the loftier, judgment- and distinction-free realm of the higher divinity who "loves the peoples." In performing this transition, Sabbatai/David symbolically offers his back parts for the Distant One's penetration ("prostrate himself for God"), thus stepping into the role of the Distant One's missing female. See the beginning of section 5, above; and, on the feminization of David implied here, chapter 8, section 12.

95. Deut 33:3; see above, note 75. In place of *be-sod af hovev 'ammim* ("in accord with 'Af loves the peoples' "), ms. Oxford 955 has only the two words *av* [in place of *af*] *hovev*, "loving father." Whether the replacement of *af* with *av* is simply a scribal error, or whether it is significant, I am unable to say.

Appendix

Zoharic Passages Quoted and Interpreted in *Va-avo ha-Yom*

(Translated by Daniel C. Matt, *The Pritzker Zohar*)

1. Zohar II, 9a (to the Torah portion *Shemot*):

He too [Rabbi Shimon ben Yohai] rose and said, "*O YHVH our God! Lords other than You possessed us, but only by You will we utter Your name* (Isaiah 26:13). This verse has been established, but this verse contains a supernal mystery within faith. יהוה אלהינו (*YHVH Eloheinu*), *YHVH our God*—beginning of supernal mysteries, source of all radiance of lamps, all kindling. Upon there depends the whole mystery of faith; this name reigns over all.

"*Lords other than You possessed us.* For no one but this supernal name rules over the people of Israel, yet now in exile another[1] rules over them."

2. Zohar I, 245a (to the Torah portion *Va-yehi*):

"Come and see: There are three souls, ascending by certain rungs, and as for their being three, they are four. One: transcendent soul that cannot be grasped. The supreme royal treasurer is unaware of it, let alone the lower one. This is soul of all souls, concealed, eternally unrevealed, unknowable—and all of them depend upon it.

---

1. The text translated by Matt reads *ahra*, "another." The Mantua edition gives *sitra ahra*, "the Other Side," and this is the text followed by our author.

311

APPENDIX: ZOHARIC PASSAGES IN *VA-AVO HA-YOM*

"This envelops itself in a wrapping of crystal radiance within radiancy, and drips pearls, drop by drop, all linking as one, like the joints of the limbs of one body—one. It enters into them, displaying through them its activity; this and they are one, inseparable. This supernal soul is hidden to all.

"Another soul: female concealing herself within her forces. She is their soul, and out of them a body is woven, to display activity through them to the whole world—like the body, which is an instrument for the soul to convey action."

Bibliography

Alleson-Gerberg, Shai. "The Way of a Man with a Maiden: The Way of a Serpent upon a Rock—R. Jonathan Eibeschütz's View of Christianity in *And I Came this Day unto the Fountain*" (Hebrew). In *R. Jonathan Eibeschütz: And I Came this Day unto the Fountain*, edited by Paweł Maciejko, 278–300. Los Angeles: Cherub, 2014.

Ashlag, Yehuda. *Sefer ha-Zohar . . . 'im Perush ha-Sullam*. 19 vols. Jerusalem: Yeshivat Me'orot, 1975.

Atwood, Craig D. *Community of the Cross: Moravian Piety in Colonial Bethlehem*. Max Kade German-American Research Institute Series. University Park: Pennsylvania State University Press, 2004.

———. *The Theology of the Czech Brethren from Hus to Comenius*. University Park: Pennsylvania State University Press, 2009.

Avivi, Joseph. *Binyan Ariel: Introduction to the Homilies of R. Isaac Luria* (Hebrew). Jerusalem: Misgav Yerushalayim, 1987.

Benarroch, Jonatan. "'Piercing What Has Been Closed Up'—The Story of the One Who Blasphemies [sic] by Envoking the Name (Lev. 24: 10–16) and *Toledot Yeshu*: From the Homilies of the Zohar to *And I Came this Day unto the Fountain*" (Hebrew). In *R. Jonathan Eibeschütz: And I Came this Day unto the Fountain*, edited by Paweł Maciejko, 243–77. Los Angeles: Cherub, 2014.

Ben-Shlomo, Joseph. *The Mystical Theology of Moses Cordovero* (Hebrew). Jerusalem: Bialik Institute, 1986.

Berger, Abraham. "Ayalta: From the Doe in the Field to the Mother of the Messiahs." In *Salo Wittmayer Baron Jubilee Volume*, edited by Saul Lieberman and Arthur Hyman, 1:209–17. 3 vols. Jerusalem: American Academy for Jewish Research, 1974.

Birnbaum, Philip. *Daily Prayer Book: Ha-Siddur ha-Shalem*. New York: Hebrew, 1949.

Brown, Jeremy. "Niddah 17b—The Chatam Sofer, Rationalism, and Anatomy That Isn't There." *Talmudology* (blog), November 7, 2019, https://www.talmudology.com/jeremybrownmdgmailcom/2017/2/8/bava-basra-24a-anatomy-that-isnt-there-ddbns.

Carlebach, Elisheva. *The Pursuit of Heresy: Rabbi Moses Hagiz and the Sabbatian Controversies*. New York: Columbia University Press, 1990.

Cordovero, Moses ben Jacob. "Sha'ar 'Erkhei ha-Kinnuyim." In *Sefer Pardes Rimmonim*. Munkacz: n.p. 1906. Reprint, Jerusalem: n.p. 1962.

BIBLIOGRAPHY

Daley, Brian E. "The 'Closed Garden' and the 'Sealed Fountain': Song of Songs 4:12 in the Late Medieval Iconography of Mary." In *Medieval Gardens*, edited by Elisabeth B. MacDougall, 255–78. Washington, DC: Dumbarton Oaks Research Library and Collection, 1986.

Eibeschuetz, Jonathan. *Shem 'Olam: Igrot u-Teshuvot . . . be-Haqirah Elohit u-ve-Hokhmat ha-Qabbalah*. Edited by Arthur S. Weissmann. Vienna: n.p., 1891.

Evans, R. J. W. *The Making of the Habsburg Monarchy, 1550–1700: An Interpretation*. Oxford: Clarendon, 1979.

Finkelstein, Louis, ed. *Sifre on Deuteronomy* (Hebrew), by Saul Horovitz and Louis Finkelstein. *Corpus Tannaiticum*, 3:3:2. New York: Jewish Theological Seminary of America, 1969.

Freud, Sigmund. *The Interpretation of Dreams*. Edited and translated by James Strachey. 8th rev. ed. A Discus Book. New York: Avon, 1965.

Gikatilla, Joseph. *Sha'are Orah: Gates of Light*. Translated by Avi Weinstein. New York: HarperCollins, 1994.

Giller, Pinchas. *The Enlightened Will Shine: Symbolization and Theurgy in the Later Strata of the Zohar*. SUNY Series in Judaica. Albany: State University of New York Press, 1993.

Ginzberg, Louis. *The Legends of the Jews*. Translated from the German manuscript by Henrietta Szold. 7 vols. Philadelphia: Jewish Publication Society of America, 1968.

Greenblatt, Rachel L. *To Tell Their Children: Jewish Communal Memory in Early Modern Prague*. Stanford Studies in Jewish History and Culture. Stanford: Stanford University Press, 2014.

Hacohen, Malachi Haim. *Jacob & Esau: Jewish European History Between Nation and Empire*. Cambridge: Cambridge University Press, 2019.

Hallamish, Moshe. *Kabbalah in Liturgy, Halakhah and Customs* (Hebrew). Ramat-Gan: Bar-Ilan University, 2000.

Halperin, David J., trans. *Abraham Miguel Cardozo: Selected Writings*. Classics of Western Spirituality. Mahwah, NJ: Paulist, 2001.

———. *The Faces of the Chariot: Early Jewish Responses to Ezekiel's Vision*. Texte und Studien zum antiken Judentum 16. Tübingen: Mohr Siebeck, 1988.

———. "The Hidden Made Manifest: Muslim Traditions and the 'Latent Content' of Biblical and Rabbinic Stories." In *Pomegranates and Golden Bells: Studies in Biblical, Jewish, and Near Eastern Ritual Law and Literature in Honor of Jacob Milgrom*, edited by David P. Wright et al., 581–94. Winona Lake, IN: Eisenbrauns, 1995.

———, trans. *Sabbatai Zevi: Testimonies to a Fallen Messiah*. Oxford: Littman Library of Jewish Civilization, 2007.

———. "The Son of the Messiah: Ishmael Zevi and the Sabbatian Aqedah." *Hebrew Union College Annual* 67 (1996) 143–219.

Hellner-Eshed, Melila. *Seekers of the Face: Secrets of the Idra Rabba (The Great Assembly) of the Zohar*. Translated by Raphael Dascalu. Stanford: Stanford University Press, 2021.

Horowitz, Isaiah. *Shnei Luhot ha-Berit ha-Shalem*. 5 vols. Jerusalem: Oz Vehodor, 1993.

Jastrow, Marcus, comp. *A Dictionary of the Targumim, the Talmud Babli and Yerushalmi, and the Midrashic Literature*. 2 vols. New York: Pardes, 1950.

Klatzkin, Jacob. *Thesaurus Philosophicus Linguae Hebraicae et Veteris et Recentioris* (Hebrew). 4 vols. Berlin: Eschkol, 1928.

BIBLIOGRAPHY

Kohut, Alexander. *Aruch Completum, sive Lexicon vocabula et res, quae in libris Targumicis, Talmudicis et Midraschicis continentur* (Hebrew). 5 vols. Vienna: Brög, 1878–1892.

Koren, Sharon Faye. "Kabbalistic Physiology: Isaac the Blind, Nahmanides, and Moses de Leon on Menstruation." *AJS Review* 28 (2004) 317–39.

Lefler, Noam. "'When They Came to Take Her from the Clouds She was Already Adorned': The Homily of the Generation of the Flood in *And I Came This Day Unto the Fountain*" (Hebrew). In *R. Jonathan Eibeschütz: And I Came this Day unto the Fountain*, edited by Paweł Maciejko, 211–42. Los Angeles: Cherub, 2014.

Leiman, Sid Z. "Mrs. Jonathan Eibeschuetz' Epitaph: A Grave Matter Indeed." In *Scholars and Scholarship*, edited by Leo Landman, 133–43. New York: Yeshiva University Press, 1990.

———. "When a Rabbi Is Accused of Heresy: The Stance of Rabbi Jacob Joshua Falk in the Emden-Eibeschuetz Controversy." In *Rabbinic Culture and Its Critics*, edited by Daniel Frank and Matt Goldish, 435–56. Detroit: Wayne State University Press, 2008.

Liebes, Yehuda. "Ketavim Hadashim be-Qabbalah Shabbeta'it mi-Hugo shel Rabbi Yehonatan Eibeschuetz." *Mehqerei Yerushalayim be-Mahshevet Yisra'el* 5 (1986) 191–348.

———. *On Sabbateaism and Its Kabbalah: Collected Essays* (Hebrew). Jerusalem: Bialik Institute, 1995.

———. *Studies in the Zohar*. SUNY Series in Judaica. Albany: State University of New York Press, 1993.

Lipiner, Elias. *The Metaphysics of the Hebrew Alphabet* (Hebrew). Jerusalem: Magnes, 1989.

Louthan, Howard. *Converting Bohemia: Force and Persuasion in the Catholic Reformation*. Cambridge: Cambridge University Press, 2009.

Maciejko, Paweł. "Controverse sur la crypto-chrétienté de Rabbi Jonathan Eibeschütz." *Les cahiers du judaïsme* 29 (2010) 130–34.

———. "The Jews' Entry into the Public Sphere—The Emden-Eibeschütz Controversy Reconsidered." *Jahrbuch des Simon-Dubnow-Instituts* 6 (2007) 135–54.

———. *The Mixed Multitude: Jacob Frank and the Frankist Movement, 1755–1816*. Jewish Culture and Contexts. Philadelphia: University of Pennsylvania Press, 2011.

———. *R. Jonathan Eibeschütz: And I Came This Day unto the Fountain*. Los Angeles: Cherub, 2014.

———. "The Rabbi and the Jesuit: On Rabbi Jonathan Eibeschütz and Father Franciscus Haselbauer Editing the Talmud." *Jewish Social Studies* 20 (2014) 147–84.

Magid, Shaul. *From Metaphysics to Midrash: Myth, History, and the Interpretation of Scripture in Lurianic Kabbala*. Indiana Studies in Biblical Literature. Bloomington: Indiana University Press, 2008.

Matt, Daniel C. *The Zohar: Pritzker Edition*. 9 vols. Stanford: Stanford University Press, 2004–2016.

Meacham, Tirzah. "Legal-Religious Status of the Female According to Age." In *The Shalvi/Hyman Encyclopedia of Jewish Women*. https://jwa.org/encyclopedia/article/legal-religious-status-of-female-according-to-age#pid-18960.

Meroz, Ronit. "The Archaeology of the Zohar—*Sifra Ditseni'uta* as a Sample Text." *Da'at: A Journal of Jewish Philosophy and Kabbalah* 82 (2016) 10–85.

Mikkelson, Barbara. "Do Orthodox Jews Have Marital Relations Through a Hole in a Sheet?" Snopes. https://www.snopes.com/fact-check/sheet-dreams-are-made-of-these.

Molho, Isaac R., and Rivka Shatz. "A Sabbatian Commentary on *Lekh-Lekha*" (Hebrew). *Sefunot* 3–4 (1960) 433–521.

Paine, Thomas. *The Age of Reason, Being an Investigation of True and Fabulous Theology.* New York: Thomas Paine Foundation, n.d.

Perlmuter, Moshe Arie. *Rabbi Jonathan Eibeschuetz and His Attitude Towards Sabbatianism* (Hebrew). Jerusalem: Schocken, 1947.

Poppers, Meir ben Judah Loeb. *Meʾorot Natan: Gimaṭriya.* Frankfurt: n.p., 1709.

Preuss, Julius. *Biblisch-talmudische Medizin: Beiträge zur Geschichte der Heilkunde und der Kultur überhaupt.* 1911. Reprint, New York: Ktav, 1971.

Scholem, Gershom. *Kabbalah.* Library of Jewish Knowledge. Jerusalem: Keter, 1974.

———. *Major Trends in Jewish Mysticism.* 3rd rev. ed. New York: Schocken, 1954.

———. *Sabbatai Ṣevi: The Mystical Messiah, 1626–1676.* Princeton: Princeton University Press, 1973.

Schuchard, Marsha Keith. *William Blake's Sexual Path to Spiritual Vision.* Rochester, VT: Inner Traditions, 2006.

Sefer Tiqqunei ha-Zohar. Zhitomir: Shapira, 1863.

Sefer Zohar Hadash. 2 vols. 1911. Reprint, Brooklyn: Kelilat Yofi, 1981.

Shatz-Uffenheimer, Rivka. "Portrait of a Sabbatian Sect" (Hebrew). *Sefunot* 3–4 (1960) 395–431.

Singer, Isaac Bashevis. *The Spinoza of Market Street.* New York: Farrar, Straus & Giroux, 1958.

Strack, Hermann L. *Introduction to the Talmud and Midrash.* Philadelphia: Jewish Publication Society of America, 1931.

Tishby, Isaiah. *The Doctrine of Evil and the 'Kelippah' in Lurianic Kabbalism* (Hebrew). Jerusalem: Magnes, 1942.

———. *The Wisdom of the Zohar: An Anthology of Texts.* 3 vols. Translated by David Goldstein. London: Littman Library of Jewish Civilization, 1989.

Trachtenberg, Joshua. *Jewish Magic and Superstition.* New York: Behrman's, 1939.

Van Praagh, Richard, and Stella Van Praagh. "Aristotle's 'Triventricular' Heart and the Relevant Early History of the Cardiovascular System." *Chest* 84 (1983) 462–68.

Verman, Mark. "The Development of *Yihudim* in Spanish Kabbalah." In *The Age of the Zohar: Proceedings of the Third International Conference on the History of Jewish Mysticism* (Jerusalem Studies in Jewish Thought 8), edited by J. Dan, English section, 25*–41*. Jerusalem: Hebrew University, 1989.

Vital, Hayyim. *Sefer ʿEtz Hayyim.* Edited by Yehuda Brandwein. 3 vols. Jerusalem, 1988.

———. *Sefer Mevo Sheʾarim.* Edited by Yehuda Brandwein. Jerusalem, 1988.

———. *Sefer Shaʿar ha-Gilgulim.* Edited by Yehuda Brandwein. Jerusalem, 1988.

———. *Sefer Shaʿar ha-Haqdamot.* Edited by Yehuda Brandwein. Jerusalem, 1988.

———. *Sefer Shaʿar ha-Kavvanot.* Edited by Yehuda Brandwein. 2 vols. Jerusalem, 1988.

Weiner, Herbert. *9½ Mystics: The Kabbala Today.* 2nd ed. New York: Collier, 1992.

Weiss, Zeev. "Matai Hehelu Moridin Sheliah Tzibbor Lifnei ha-Tevah?" *Cathedra* 55 (1990) 8–21.

BIBLIOGRAPHY

Wirszubski, Chaim. "Ha-Teʾologiyah ha-Shabbetaʾit shel Natan ha-Azati." *Keneset* 8 (1944) 210–46. Reprinted in *Between the Lines* (Hebrew). Jerusalem: Magnes, 1990.

Wolfson, Elliot R. *Language, Eros, Being: Kabbalistic Hermeneutics and Poetic Imagination*. New York: Fordham University Press, 2004.

———. "*Malkhut Ein Sof* and *Ṣimṣum*: Gender Construction in the Kabbalistic Speculation of Jonathan Eibeschütz with Special Reference to *Wa-Avo ha-Yom el ha-Ayin*." *Kabbalah: Journal for the Study of Jewish Mystical Texts* 50 (2021) 9–79.

———. *Through a Speculum That Shines: Vision and Imagination in Medieval Jewish Mysticism*. Princeton: Princeton University Press, 1994.

Yosha, Nissim. "Ha-beriʾah ve-ha-zeman: vikkuah teʾologi-filosofi shel Qardozo ʿim Natan he-ʿAzati." *Mehqerei Yerushalayim be-mahshevet Yisraʾel* 12 (1996) 275–84.

Zinz, David. *Gedullat Yehonatan*. Piotrkow: Kopelmann, 1930.

www.ingramcontent.com/pod-product-compliance
Lightning Source LLC
Chambersburg PA
CBHW021648230426
43668CB00008B/550